MODERN
TEXTILES

MODERN TEXTILES

DOROTHY SIEGERT LYLE

JOHN WILEY & SONS, INC.

NEW YORK   LONDON   SYDNEY   TORONTO

Cover design and chapter opening illustrations: Kiffi Diamond.
Text design: Eileen Thaxton.

Library of Congress Cataloging in Publication Data:

Lyle, Dorothy Siegert.
  Modern textiles.

  Bibliography: p.
  Includes index.
  1. Textile industry.   2. Textile fabrics.
3. Textile fibers.   I. Title.
TS1445.L9   677   75-38558
ISBN 0-471-55726-9

Printed in the United States of America

10 9 8 7 6 5 4 3

*To my family and to the
professional and business friends
who helped and encouraged me to
develop my unique career*

FOREWORD

During the past few decades, the textile industry has gone through a period of unprecedented changes. The production of man-made fibers and their use for apparel and for decorative and industrial fabrics in the United States has greatly surpassed that of natural fibers. These developments would not have been possible without fundamental research on the structure and morphology of fibers and on how these concepts affect the end-use properties of textiles.

Today, the textile industry applies scientific parameters to optimize production processes and, in doing so, develops textile products tailored to meet specific consumer needs and demands. Fiber scientists predict that only a few, if any, new revolutionary fibers will enter the textile market in the future. This does not mean that the development of textiles has reached its peak. Future research efforts will concentrate on textile performance during consumer use and how their performance can be optimized to meet our societal needs better. This is a challenging task for textile experts, since textiles can be evaluated not only on the basis of controlled laboratory measurements; psychological, physiological, and economic factors also must be considered, since they significantly influence consumer choices and acceptance of textile products.

Educators, students, and consumers will be confronted more often with new developments and information directly related to all aspects of wear and care of fabrics. Introductory textile courses at the college level undoubtedly will be adjusted to include more material on fabric properties and performance under end-use conditions.

The Flammability Act and the Permanent Care Labeling Rule enacted by Congress underline the need for this information. In this context, it must be understood that regulations on textiles intended to protect the consumer are only useful if they are technically and economically feasible. Otherwise, they may very well achieve the opposite effect: denying the consumer a desired product. A constructive input on behalf of the consumer is essential to prevent expensive and unreasonable textile legislation. This can be achieved only if consumers understand the functioning of the product and marketplace and the interrelation between business and government.

This book satisfies a definite need for beginning textile students at the college level because it discusses the current issues and trends outlined above. When Dr. Lyle first told me about her intention to write an introductory textbook on textiles, I was enthusiastic and strongly encouraged her to go ahead.

Her professional career in the field of textiles is unique. Because of her educational and business background, she has been able to gain insight into the complexity of a fascinating field and, in writing this book, she is sharing her rich and valuable experience with us. Educators, career-bound students, and consumers will certainly join me in thanking Dr. Lyle for her contribution to the study of textiles.

Manfred Wentz
Associate Professor in Textile Science
University of Wisconsin, Madison

PREFACE

Textile manufacture comprises one of America's greatest industries. The fabrics and fashions created by it play a very important role in our personal, business, and industrial life.

The scope of our economic system of production and distribution is such that frequently we fail to recognize that some of the problems experienced with textiles in use and care may never be solved.

Today's student wants to learn what is relevant. There are many approaches to the study of textiles. Curriculums have been developed in historic textiles, the mechanical production or engineering of fibers and fabrics, the chemistry and physics involved in the producing and testing of textiles, the marketing and merchandising of fabrics and fashions, and the economic, sociological, and psychological aspects of textiles.

There is an apparent shift in curriculums to give the student relevant information needed to become a better consumer of textile products and to teach others how they may select and purchase wisely.

Unfortunately, most texts on textiles consider only fibers and fabrics and fail to recognize the end product. They do not define the principles that are a guide to selection in relation to wear and care performance. This is not an easy task because of the complex technology involved and the lack of understanding of the variables that affect textile performance.

There is also a lack of understanding of the interrelationship of business, industry, and government to produce fabrics to meet consumer demands. The career-bound student of textiles needs practical information that can be applied or drawn on for a more satisfactory professional performance, whether it be in teaching, business, industry, or government.

It is not unusual for a student to grope for help in career shaping. Once students are introduced to the practical application of textiles, they are inspired to develop their course of study to achieve their desired goals in the more technical areas.

This book is not a complete treatise on textiles. It is written in an unorthodox manner to bring together current, relevant information to the beginning student to help him understand textiles.

From 1971 to 1973, I taught seminars at the University of Rhode Island, Oregon State University, and the University of

North Carolina. Based on this experience, I learned that we are creatures of habit. Sometimes a logical approach to a subject becomes illogical. For example: Why should every textbook on textiles begin with the natural fibers when man-made fibers account for 70 percent used; cotton 29 percent; wool 1 percent; and silk and linen together account for less than 1 percent? Based on this, I first discuss the basic concepts of producing man-made fibers and the major and minor man-made fibers, followed by the natural fibers.

This book differs from other texts in that:

- The subject matter is adapted to meet the needs of schools with textile laboratories as well as schools that do not have laboratory facilities.
- Emphasis is given to the consumer aspect of the selection and care of fabrics.
- The seven basic concepts of textile performance are presented early in the text: once understood, they can be applied to any new textile development or any consumer performance problem. Chapter arrangement and presentation are based on these concepts.
- Some of the surface finishes are discussed as applied surface designs to make it easier for the student to understand and identify them in relation to selection, performance, and care.
- The finished item or the component parts of an item that results in either satisfaction or dissatisfaction for the consumer are discussed. When fabrics are studied, the end use must be considered. It cannot be ignored.
- Fashion, aesthetics, and economics are interrelated and discussed early in the text so that they will be applied throughout the study of the text.
- Psychological values are presented so that the student may experiment with fabrics and thus be made aware of the subconscious and conscious psychological stimuli that affect people's lives.
- The physical and chemical properties of the textile fibers are reduced to a simple and uniform format for easy comparison of fiber properties and for easy reference.
- Fabric performance and textile labeling are interrelated, so they are presented in a single chapter.
- Learning experiences are suggested at the end of each chapter for independent study and experimentation by the student. They provide an opportunity to go beyond the subject matter presented in the text.

The Appendix is the most valuable part of the text for the student with a scientific bent. It contains information on how textile fibers react to heat and flame; how fibers may be identified by use of the microscope; and how fibers may be identified by solubility tests, staining tests, and specific gravity measurements. The convenient metric and conversion charts eliminate calculations when such information is needed. All students will find helpful the list of publications for reference and study, the fiber trademark names, and the list of fiber producers and associations.

There is so much to learn about the selection, use, and care of fabrics. It has been a frustrating experience to eliminate necessary information to meet the demands of a beginning course in textiles because of time limitations. I hope that my efforts in this text may stimulate students to pursue advanced textile courses.

Dorothy S. Lyle

ACKNOWLEDGMENTS

An individual is a product of the lives of people that touch him. In my professional career, I have had the encouragement of many people — too many to list here. However, I do want to acknowledge the generous support of the people at the International Fabricare Institute, Karl M. F. Wilke, Executive Vice-President and General Manager, and Charles R. Riggott, Assistant General Manager and Secretary; Dr. Manfred Wentz, former research director and now professor at the University of Wisconsin; my professional friends in secondary schools, colleges, and universities and extension but, in particular, Dean Dorretta Hoffman and Dr. Wayne A. St. John, Kansas State University; Dr. Virginia Carpenter, University of Rhode Island; Dean Betty Hawthorn, Dr. Florence Petzel and Mrs. Janet L. Bubl of Oregon State University; Dean Naomi Albanese and Dr. Pauline Keeney, Universty of North Carolina; Dr. Betty Smith, Dr. Steven Spivak, and Dr. Ira Block of the University of Maryland; and the reviewers for their helpful and constructive criticism. I am indebted to Dr. Block for his guidance in the preparation of the final manuscript.

Many of the photographs and charts in this text were made available for use by the International Fabricare Institute and by firms and people in the textile industry who believe in and support the educational process. I am indebted to Bill Fisher, IFI Research Department for the photographs made by him especially for this text and to Professor Arthur Price and Allen Cohen for the illustrations on forming knit stitches.

I am grateful for the hours of effort spent by my brother, John Siegert and his wife Anne, in the typing, retyping, and proofing of the manuscript, and to my husband, Ernest Tyrrell, for his patience, helpfulness, and understanding during the long hours I spent in preparing this manuscript. And last, but by no means least, I thank Deborah Wiley and her staff for guidance and support given me in the final preparation of the manuscript in order that it might reach its printed form.

I would also like to thank the following people without whose efforts this book would not have been possible: Penny Doskow, Production Supervisor; Malcolm Easterlin, Manager, College Editing Department; Vivian Kahane, Senior Editor; Arnold Carolus, Assistant Manager, Illustration Department; Eileen Thaxton, Text Designer; and Kiffi Diamond, Chapter Opening and Cover Designer.

D. S. L.

CONTENTS

MODERN TEXTILES

INTRODUCTION
AN OVERVIEW

For most of recorded history, mankind has relied on the natural fibers, particularly cotton, linen, wool, and silk, for its textile products. In addition, the technology of fabric manufacture and care were relatively simple. Since there were only a few fibers and even fewer methods of fabric care, it was possible for the consumer to learn at an early age how to choose fabrics, from the relatively few available, that would satisfy her requirements. This simple world no longer exists. The twentieth-century consumer can now choose among cotton, linen, wool, silk, rayon, acetate, triacetate, nylon, aramid, acrylic, modacrylic, polyester, novoloid, vinyon, saran, vinal, olefin, azlon, spandex, rubber, and glass. The difficulty of choosing is compounded because many of these fibers can be blended with each other (e.g., polyester/cotton or nylon/wool). In addition to the different fibers, the consumer is also faced with different yarn constructions, fabric constructions, and a variety of applied finishes.

What new textile developments will be seen in the years ahead? According to an American Chemical Society Study and predictions made in the textile trade press, there will be:

- A new generic fiber that will combine the best properties of both the naturals and man-mades; the comfort of cotton, the loft and warmth of wool, the dye brilliance of silk, the performance and ease of care of polyester. It will be antistatic, lightweight, and soil and flame retardant.
- A "swell" fiber, with variable geometry, that can dilate or contract, achieving a breathing cloth.
- An ultradry fiber, a fiber or yarn construction that achieves superdry moisture evaporation.
- Direct fabric formation (nonwovens) will achieve parity with knit/woven fabrications and create a new level of production economics and style aesthetics.
- Automated custom clothes ordered at retail counters. The size will be electronically recorded and stored, and the product will be computer produced to deliver full fashioned/contour molded/custom fit products on the spot.

1

- Clothes will be cleaned at home in a microwave closet, where a high-frequency wave or electrical charge will polarize and reject dirt, not unlike NASA's decontamination process for spacesuits.

The development of these materials and processes is not undertaken in a vacuum. The industry cannot last if it does not satisfy the needs of its most important customer — you.

CONSUMER WANTS AND NEEDS

Many studies have been undertaken to determine the wants and needs of the consumer. Some of the questions raised are: What is really wanted? Is the price quoted for a particular item satisfactory? What is the consumer's life-style; its affect on the value system? Who shops where for goods and services?

When the broad area of clothing and household fabrics is considered, it has been found that the consumer wants a multitude of textile product benefits — durability, convenience, price, performance, and fashion. However, all consumers do not want the same benefits.

For example: Consumer A may feel that fashion appeal, color, and design are most important in relation to the price quoted; Consumer B may feel that durability or serviceability at a fair price is most important.

The complexity of consumer demands places a great burden on the manufacturer, since the particular benefits that a consumer wants from textile purchases often constitute the value of the product. Research surveys and actual buying trends indicate that beauty and fashion more and more are considered to be of "value" by consumers. This is in addition to the requirements for high quality and good performance in wear and care.

There is that elusive word "quality." Is the consumer willing to pay more for higher quality? That depends on the individual's definition of quality. Some people are more concerned with price and fashion than they are with quality. For example, some would rather pay less for a fashionable, less durable garment than pay more for a quality garment that will "go out of style before it wears out."

Economic cycles often influence the price we are willing to pay for clothing. Apparel manufacturers and retailers are aware that consumers are showing an increased interest in prices. In 1974 manufacturers of ladies' apparel considered themselves fortunate to make a 3 percent profit after taxes as against 4 to 4½ percent several years ago. Yet seldom do we understand what

Manufacturer's Cost

Shirt	
1¼ yards	$ 1.72
Skirt	
2½ yards	$ 3.44
Labor wages	
(operator, finisher, presser)	$17.06
Labor, fringe benefits	
(health and welfare, Social	
security, vacation, pension)	$ 5.46
Overhead	
(rent, insurance, utilities,	
salaries, costs of samples,	
trade discounts, etc.)	$16.12
Total cost	$43.80
Taxes	2.60
Profit	2.00
Wholesale cost	$48.40

Retailer's Cost

$48.40 less discount for	
prompt payment	$44.53
Markdowns	
(averaged over all	
sportswear in stock)	$ 8.25
Shortages, pilferage, etc.	$ 1.50
Alterations	
(cost of maintaining	
department averaged out)	$ 1.50
Salaries Sales staff	$ 3.75
Merchandising and	
buying staff (including	
expenses)	$ 2.25
Clerical and stockroom	
(receiving, marking,	
deliveries, etc.,	
including expenses)	$ 2.25
Advertising, display,	
sales promotion	$ 3.00
Administrative	
(executives, credit and	
accounting offices,	
including expenses)	$ 6.00
Employee fringe benefits	$ 1.50
Overhead	
(rent, insurance, utilities,	
cleaning, security)	$ 6.75
Miscellaneous	$ 1.50
Total	$82.78
Taxes	2.61
Profit	2.61
Selling price	$88.00

Figure I-1

Behind the Price Tag of an $88 Ensemble
Cotton Madras Shirt and Skirt
Wholesale — $48.40   Retail — $88.00

(*From* the *New York Times,*
April 23, 1974, by permission. Adapted.)

enters into the price we pay for a garment. Figure I-1 shows the costs associated with a moderately priced dress.

GOVERNMENT INPUT

The "free market" economy is not completely free. Some consumer choices are limited and regulated by government. This regulation is meant to protect the consumer, physically and economically. Many consumers want and welcome protection. However, the cost of the government regulation is seldom considered by the consumer (e.g., business bears the investment costs of research and development for technology such as flame retardant fabrics and flame resistant fibers). The cost of adding a flame retardant finish to a fabric or using a flame resistant fiber and performing the required testing must be covered in the price the consumer pays for an item. The taxpayers, who are consumers too, must also pay for enforcement of regulations.

Some consumers may not want protection. Some buy flame retardant sleepwear for children but, after reading the care requirements, return it to the store. When confronted with two fabrics, similar in appearance, one of which contains a flame resistant fiber, the consumer may settle for the regular fiber product because it is cheaper. Research indicates that the consumers would like to have flame retardant products available but with a choice of either fiber, as needed.

There is a need for some government regulation in business. However, there is a concern that increasing government regulation may occur in every area until the consumer eventually will have virtually no choice in products.

BUSINESS-INDUSTRY INPUT

Industry, at times, seems to be slow in responding to consumer and government demands. The technology and investments required for research and development are often not able to keep up with the rapid development of needs. Constant research goes on in textiles to meet government regulations and consumer demands.

The textile industry, like other businesses, is improving its techniques for learning more about the American consumer. The industry wants to be able to meet the changing needs and desires of the consumer almost as quickly as these needs and desires are discovered and expressed. The industry recognizes and accepts the challenge to improve two-way communications between industry and consumers. How can the industry do this?

Market research has become more important in the textile industry. Most companies are attempting to meet consumer demands. Textile companies are advertising and using other marketing communications to inform consumers about products and their availability. However, this role is limited by budget considerations. Packaging is another way that business communicates with the consumer. Packages and inserts may have fiber content, washing or cleaning instructions, size, and color.

The greatest consumer communication problems seems to be at the point of sale. Consumers rely on the salesperson for information. Although many retailers have developed educational programs to educate sales personnel as to the products they are selling, many times the salesperson is uninformed or misinformed. To reduce customer reliance on sales personnel, some companies have created consumer education departments that prepare and distribute educational and informational materials.

One might ask who represents the consumer. There is a concern that a vocal minority of so-called consumer extremists is regarded by government as the spokesman for all consumers.

WHAT ARE THE BASIC ISSUES?

Consumerism has become an important word in today's system of communications.

What is consumerism? It is a vague term meaning different things to different people. Webster says: "A consumer is one who consumes; one who purchases economic goods; one who uses goods and so diminishes or destroys their utility (as opposed to a producer)."

The American economy did not grow to a trillion-dollar gross national product by disregarding the consumer or creating shoddy merchandise and selling it through dishonest channels. Yet consumer problems do exist in the area of satisfaction of textile performance in use and care.

A wonderful world of fabrics and fashion exists. Ninety percent of all the fabrics made in this country or imported from abroad give good satisfaction in wear and care. Consumer problems may occur in 10 percent of total production, because this is where:

1. The new is developed.
2. A period of experimentation transpires when the manufacturer develops and market tests new products.
3. There is a lack of understanding on the part of the manufacturer as to what is involved in the wear, care, and storage of fabrics.
4. There is a lack of knowledge and understanding on the part of the consumer as to what is involved in textile production or manufacture in relation to its use and care.

The consumer should consider the following when purchasing textiles: budgeting for upkeep, life expectancy of garment or household textile, and subsequent performances in wear and care.

There is nothing more exciting than the world of fabrics and fashion, which is always in a state of evolution. Nothing is static; therefore a student of fabrics and fashion cannot remain static. The constant challenge of keeping abreast with new developments may not be easily accomplished — not a strange fact with the realization that the apparel industry is the second largest manufacturing industry, the third largest consumer industry, and the fourth largest employer.

This text will help you to develop an understanding of basic concepts and principles of fabric selection, care, and performance with the hope that you will become a better consumer and a better employee.

LEARNING EXPERIENCES

1. What predictions on new textile developments are being made in the textile trade or public press? Do you believe the predictions will come true? Support your point of view.
2. Read the trade press and advertisements to discover what new fibers and fabrics have been introduced this past year. What is your assessment of them?
3. Explain the consumer's role in fashion. How are their buying habits studied and analyzed?

TEXTILE PERFORMANCE

Fabric is the backbone of fashion, and quality is the backbone of fabrics and fashions.

What is quality? It is difficult to define. It might be compared to electricity; what it is, is unknown, yet the result is evident. Quality is intangible, meaning different things to different people. Sometimes quality is tied to an emotional feeling.

what is quality?

Quality is determined largely through materials, design, and workmanship. It is defined by its fitness for purpose as measured by performance characteristics. In addition, there is the aesthetic pleasure that comes from the use of a quality fabric. The appreciation for quality must be coupled with a feeling for fashion.

The textile and apparel industries are constantly striving to improve their products by enhancing performance and fashion appeal. Major technical developments of the 1950s and 1960s such as wash and wear, durable press, soil release, improved dyestuffs and prints and, more recently, flame retardancy are but a few of the advances. Fashion changes required considerable use of color and prints with better resistance to crocking, light fading, and laundering.

Most products and services are manufactured at more than one quality level. For example, a manufacturer may indicate quality levels with such terms as "Good," "Better," "Best." For the most part, manufacturers make every effort to follow through on promised product performance. It is recognized, however, that the industry must develop minimum standards of performance for all items. Only in this way can the consumer have some reference point from which to judge the quality of a product.

It is becoming more difficult to keep up with all the new developments in fiber production, technological changes, fabric styling, proper techniques for sewing or fabrication and caring for new fabrics. Consumers have taken these changes in their stride; they have had to learn new care techniques and, for the most part, have gone along with increased costs.

new developments technological changes

9

There are seven basic keys or concepts for guidance in the purchase of a textile product. They are:

Fiber content.   What is the fiber content of the fabric? Does the fiber (or fibers) have certain characteristics that require special instructions in the use and care to derive satisfactory performance?

Yarn construction.   Does the yarn construction of the fabric limit its serviceability?

Fabric construction.   How is the fabric constructed or made? Is it woven, knitted, laminated, or bonded? Does the special construction dictate special handling for the fabric?

Color.   Is the dye or print colorfast? Do the labels provide any assurance of good colorfastness to light, perspiration, washing or dry cleaning, and crocking (rubbing off of color)?

Applied surface design.   Does the fabric have a surface design that may limit its serviceability in wear or care?

Finish.   Does a special finish really contribute to the functional or aesthetic property of the fabric? Is it a durable or nondurable finish? For example, will the durable press finish give protection against wrinkling for the wear life of the item?

Component parts.   Are all the individual component parts of the product such as lining, interlining, shoulder pads, belts, and buttons as washable or dry cleanable as the fabric used to make the item?

For a better understanding of the analytical approach to textile performance, let us analyze the mundane fabric, burlap. It is a fabric that is used for wearing apparel, home furnishings, accessories, and decorations. It is readily available.

USING THE SEVEN KEYS TO ANALYZE BURLAP

Fashion headlines read, "Don't Burn That Old Potato Sack!" Stories go on to say that both manufacturers and consumers know that burlap has none of the virtues of a wearable fabric, but this does not seem to restrain anyone from buying and selling burlap fashions.

Burlap is being used for a variety of clothing and household items. Clothing items range from coats, suits, jackets, skirts, slacks, and shorts to shoes, bags, and hats.

Let us analyze burlap in relation to the seven keys of quality for performance. (See Table 1-1.)

Table 1-1   The Analytical Approach to Textile Performance According to the Seven Basic Concepts

1. Performance of fabrics in wear and care is affected by the fiber's properties.	List the fiber characteristics that determine performance in wear and care.
2. Yarn construction of fabrics may affect fabric performance.	List the characteristics of yarn construction that determines performance in wear and care.
3. Fabric construction may vary and affect performance in wear and care.	List the basic construction. How may the construction be varied?
4. Fabrics may be dyed or printed to give them color.	List the basic principles that determine the colorfastness properties of a dyed or printed fabric that might be desired for a given end use.
5. Finishes may be added to a fabric to give it aesthetic or performance properties.	List the finish and method used to give the fabric its aesthetic or performance characteristics. Does it require renewal after wear and care? Will it give satisfactory performance in wear and care?
6. Fabrics may be given surface decorative treatments to make them eye appealing.	List the ways and means by which a decorative design may be applied to the surface of the fabric to give it more eye appeal. Will the design limit serviceability?
7. A variety of fabrics and trim may be used to make wearing apparel or household items. All component parts of an item must be compatible.	Examine the item carefully to determine if all parts are compatible. Even look for the hidden component parts in making your decision.

Fiber Content

Burlap is made of a naturally grown fiber called jute. Its natural color varies from light beige to brown. It has a natural odor that

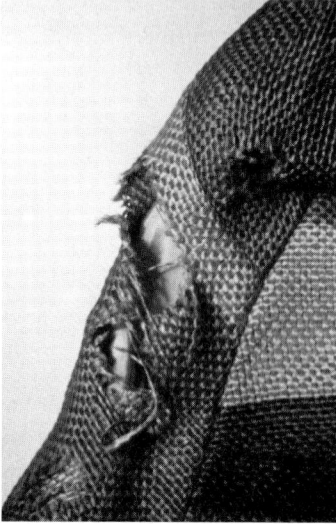

Figure 1-1 The coarse, stiff, but low-strength yarn of this burlap fabric broke from strain across the shoulder and arm area of the garment during wear.

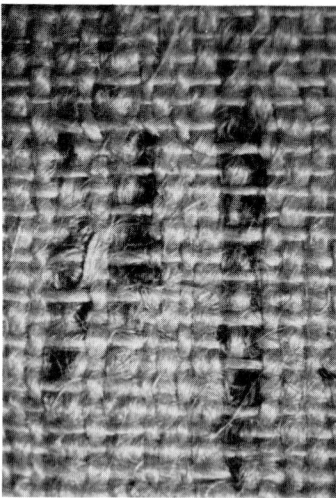

Figure 1-2 Wood and bark slubs indicate that the burlap fabric is of low quality.

can be objectionable. Because the fiber is coarse and stiff, fabric made of jute wrinkles easily. If the fabric is creased or pleated, it may split or break along folds or where strain occurs in wear (see Figure 1-1). The fiber contains bark or slubs that cause the fabric to lint (see Figure 1-2). Jute has a very low resistance to water. It is, therefore, usually recommended that burlap fabrics be dry-cleaned. However, some manufacturers state that their burlap fabrics are washable. Jute is easily affected by light, and it is therefore not the best fabric for curtains or draperies.

Yarn Construction

Yarn construction depends on the type of jute used, yarn fineness, and the yarn count, which determines the looseness of the weave.

Tossa jute is a high-grade fiber; hence it is used for high-quality jute fabrics. The better quality jute fabrics are made with finer yarn, characterized by evenness of yarn and lack of slubs and bark. A slub is an irregularity that makes the yarn at a particular place larger than the regular diameter. Some burlap has what is called a "natural slub," such as that present in silk shantung. However, these slubs are different from the wood and bark slubs found in lower-quality burlap fabrics.

Fabric Construction

Burlap is a plain-weave fabric. The plain weave may be varied to form a basket weave. If the fabric is loosely woven, a garment made of it will not retain its shape. It will bag, sag, and snag. The higher-quality fabric has a higher thread count (more yarns per inch) and a tighter and more closely woven construction.

Burlap may be laminated to urethane foam or it may be bonded to a woven or knitted tricot lining fabric.

Some fabrics are called burlap when they are not made of jute; an example is an import from Spain made of rayon, which is sold as burlap (see Figure 1-3). This may be compared with the practice of calling a 100 percent linen fabric "linen" and a 100 percent rayon fabric "Butcher Linen."

Color

Burlap is available in a range of colors from off-white natural and champagne to yellow, chartreuse, light and dark green, navy and

Figure 1-3 The fabric on the left
was labeled Super Burlap; on the
right, Super Burlap Stripe. Both
labels stated, "100 per cent rayon,
imported from Spain."

medium blue, pink, red, wine, terra cotta, orange, gray, charcoal, brown, and black.

Because of the natural characteristics of burlap, it is difficult to get good penetration of dye (see Figure 1-4 in color section). Some burlap shows poor colorfastness to light and to crocking. Some manufacturers say their burlap is dyed with commercial-fast colors, while others state that since vat dyes cannot be used to dye burlap, no guarantees can be given for colorfastness of dyed burlap fabrics.

Applied Surface Design

Burlap may be printed in a variety of decorative designs such as stripes, needlepoint, and floral. Applique and embroidered designs may be applied to burlap fabrics (see Figures 1-5 and 1-6). Burlap may also be overprinted or coated with gold or silver metallic particles. Hand-painted designs also may be applied to burlap.

Finish

Various finishing processes may be used in the manufacture of burlap. Bleaching removes the original tan-to-brown coloring matter and makes the fabric white.

Figure 1-5 Burlap may be given applied surface design by conventional printing processes.

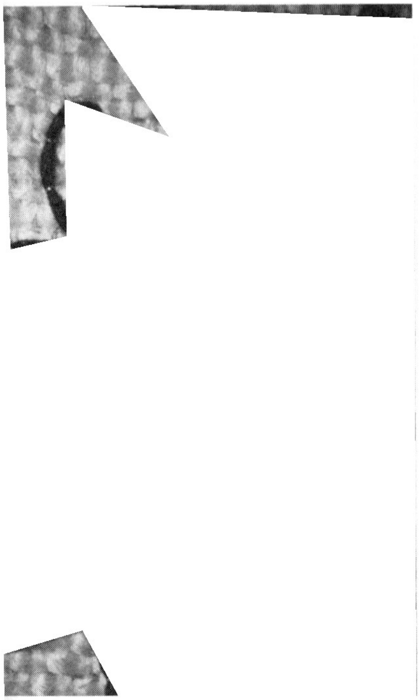

Chemical treatments may be applied to remove some or all of the characteristic pungent odor of jute (see Figure 1-7).

Chemical treatments may also be applied to make burlap fabrics softer and more supple.

Component Parts

Because burlap is scratchy, most items are lined and trimmed with contrasting fabrics ranging from gingham to taffeta.

Care should be taken in combining dark-colored fabrics with burlap. The dark-colored fabric will pick up lint from the burlap.

When making draperies, the heading should be selected in relation to the care method to be used for cleaning them. A heading that will not lose its finish in dry cleaning or in laundering is important if satisfaction in use and care is desired.

ANALYZING AESTHETIC VALUES

Clothes that convey a good feeling, comfort, poise, and confidence are the clothes that tell others about the best of the wearer. If these positive feelings are missing, the wrong choice has been made. These same values influence the purchase of

Figure 1-6 Applied surface designs may be embroidered with a Schiffli embroidery machine.

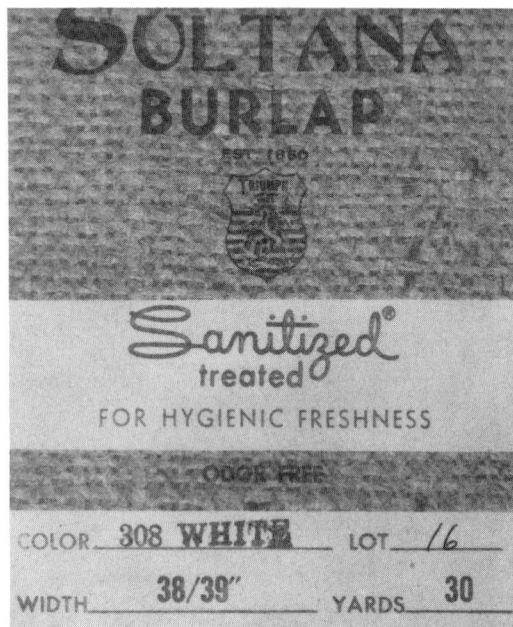

Figure 1-7 Some finishes cannot be seen or felt. The label or hangtag reveals that the fabric has been given a special finish. The "Sanitize" finish helps to deter germ or bacteria formation in the fabric.

household textiles such as the draperies and bedspread for a bedroom.

Clothing is very personal. People identify with their clothes; it is sometimes called a second skin. Clothes are not worn just for protection. Aesthetic values are involved because they become an extension of one's self. Fabrics and fashion cannot be studied without considering aesthetic values.

What creates the feeling that something seen or heard is beautiful? Philosophers have long pondered the true nature of aesthetics. Whether it is a song, a poem, a picture, or clothing, a feeling about something depends on many complex stimuli.

At one time it was thought that scientists could not measure the way people felt about their clothes. Today, however, the scientists use psychology, mathematics, the electronic computer, and old-fashioned ingenuity to determine aesthetic values. This study is called the science of psychometrics. Hoffman* has developed a system for rating aesthetic value (Figure 1-8). An object appears to have high or low aesthetic value according to reactions to its stimuli.

The pairs of stimuli are arranged opposite each other, good and bad: order-disorder, completeness-incompleteness, variety-monotony. For example, raw silk fabric has many slubs and nubs that may be called defects, but it is not monotonous. The charm and natural richness of raw silk depend on its variety, the irregularities or imperfections present in the fiber.

Fabrics with good aesthetic value are pleasing to both the hand and the eye.

*R. M. Hoffman, "Measuring the Aesthetic Appeal of Textiles," *Textile Research Journal*, 35 (5), May 1965.

Figure 1-8

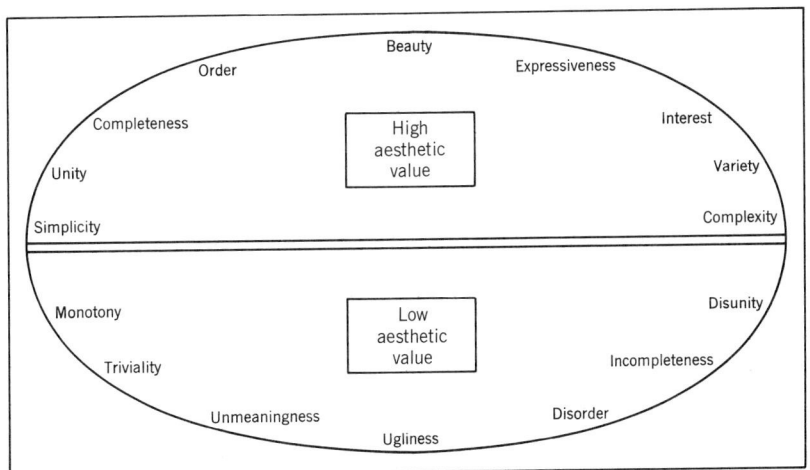

Figure 1-9

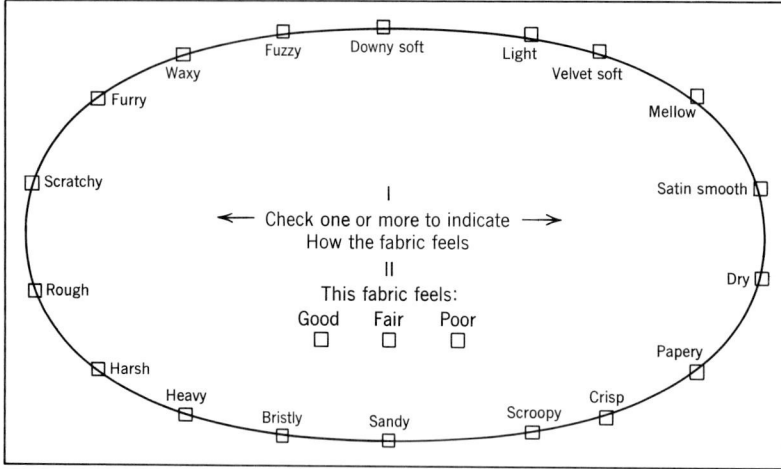

Check one or more to indicate →
How the fabric feels

II
This fabric feels:

Good	Fair	Poor
☐	☐	☐

Figure 1-9 shows how feelings can be described about the sensation to the hand or feel of the fabric.

Figure 1-10 will assist in describing the way a fabric looks.

Emotional reactions to garments also influence their desirability. Figure 1-11 illustrates how one may react to an article of clothing under consideration for purchase.

For garments with "good" aesthetic value, the five most frequently checked terms are attractive, smart, pleasing, well-dressed, and good taste. The five terms most frequently as-

Figure 1-10

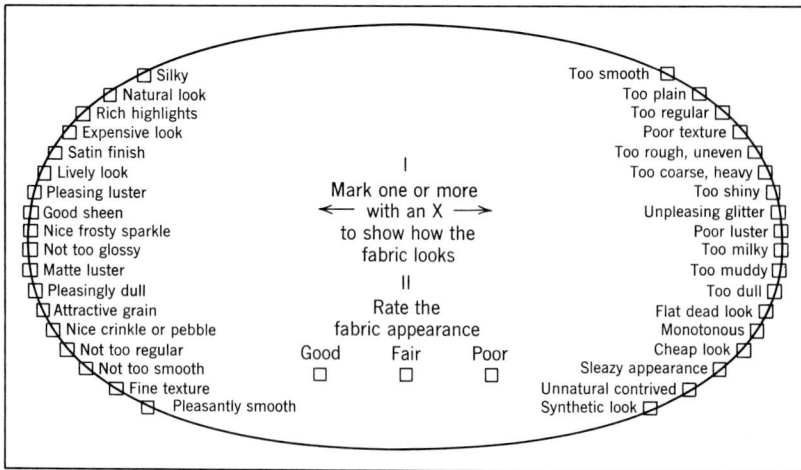

Mark one or more
← with an X →
to show how the
fabric looks

II
Rate the
fabric appearance

Good	Fair	Poor
☐	☐	☐

Figure 1-11

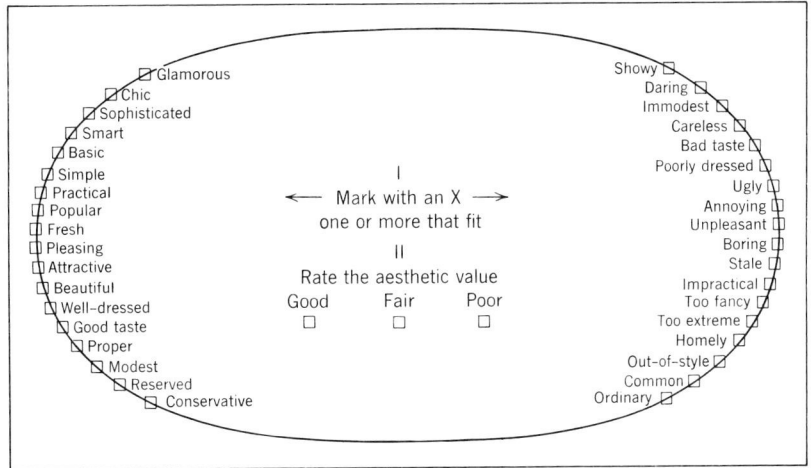

sociated with garments rated "poor" in aesthetic value are un-
pleasant, ordinary, annoying, common, and boring.

THE PSYCHOLOGY OF COLOR

There is an aesthetic logic that provides a scientific base for
coordinating colors, whether it be in fabric, garment design, or
household decorating. One color is not an isolated phenomena.
It is seen in relation to other colors. This is the science of color
interaction. For example, the identical color may look entirely
different under incandescent, fluorescent, daylight, sunlight,
black, or ultraviolet light.

Fashion is dependent on color. People engaged in fashion are
usually trained in the arts; they travel and learn to know world
cultures. Through long training and experience, they become
"leaders of good taste." They develop an aesthetic taste that
gives them the ability to sense which colors work well together
for a particular situation. In a particular season a color or several
colors may be selected for womenswear, menswear, and home
furnishings. This may require coordinating different shades of
color in accessories. Taste — the ability to give color its proper
weight in a given application — comes into play once agreement
is reached on the basic color or colors. This is where sensitivity is
important in the selection of a given or appropriate shade, and

Dark pure red—love and amiability
Medium red—health and vitality
Bright red—passion
Dark, greyed red—evil
Strong light pink—femininity, festivity
Pure medium pink—delicacy, innocence
Greyed light pink—daintiness
Greyed medium pink—frivolity
Strong dark orange—ambition
Strong medium orange—enthusiasm, zeal
Strong light orange—intensity
Dark medium brown—utility
Light medium brown—maturity
Medium yellow—prudence, goodness
Light medium yellow—wisdom, attention
Strong light yellow—gaiety, stimulation
Dark medium yellow—love of humanity
Strong light gold—glamour, distinction
Medium gold—luxury, glory

Dark medium gold—riches
Light strong yellow-green—freshness
Light medium yellow-green—youth
Light strong yellow-green—vitality
Strong medium green—sociability
Medium green—frankness, practicality
Greyed medium green—naïveté, innocence
Strong light blue-green—restlessness
Strong dark blue-green—longing, nostalgia
Medium light blue-green—calm, repose
Greyed light blue-green—placidity
Strong medium blue—idealism
Dark medium blue—sincerity
Greyed medium blue—kindness
Light medium blue—calmness
Strong light blue-purple—sternness
Strong light purple—magnificence
Light medium purple—fragility, softness
Dark greyed purple—royalty

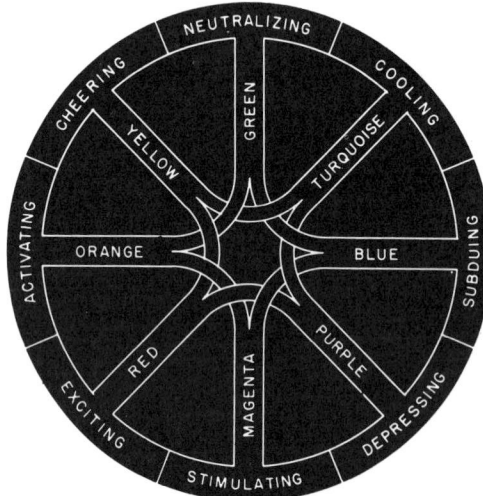

Color "barometer" shows the relation of color to mood
in planning the decorative scheme for a home.

Figure 1-12   Some psychological connotations of color. (Courtesy: American Fabrics and Fashions)

why there is a psychological connotation to color (see Figure 1-12).

The source of color is light. A prism held in the sunlight will produce a range of colors from violet to red. How is this spectrum created? Light consists of electromagnetic waves, similar to radio or television waves. The ripples of water in a pond are a visual representation of these waves. The human eye is sensitive to wavelengths from 400 to 700 millimicrons,* which are perceived as color from violet to red.

The color of an object depends on the light that is reflected from its surface. That is, if the full spectrum is reflected more or less equally, the object appears white. If the full spectrum is absorbed, the object appears black. This is why the theory has been developed that one should wear white clothes in the summer: they reflect back the rays of light, thereby reducing heat. Black clothes absorb rays of light and are warm to wear in the summer. What if only some of the light is absorbed? The object will appear as the complement of the color that is absorbed. An object appears green if the red sector of the spectrum is absorbed. If the blue sector is absorbed the object will appear orange. This is the manner in which fabrics are colored by the application of dyes. The dye absorbs light so as to give color to the fabric. By carefully mixing and applying dyes, an infinite number of colors can be achieved.

Colors are defined in three dimensions: hue, value, and intensity.

Hue

Hue is the name of the color family. Hues are described as reds, oranges, yellows, greens, blues, and purples.

Value

The lightness or darkness of a color is called value, sometimes called tone. Any color can be lightened with white to make a tint or darkened with black to make a shade.

Intensity

Intensity is the strength or sharpness of color due especially to the degree of freedom from admixture with its complementary color. Colors with similar intensities can make pleasing combinations. Colors of different intensities can be combined for contrast (see Figure 1-13 in color section).

Each color can have a range of colors, for example, shades of red from a very weak or light red to a very strong or bright red. There is a great latitude or range of color within one family.

The color stylist or designer must know the effect of one color

*A millimicron is one-billionth of a meter, about 25 millionths of an inch.

on another and the art of combining color to achieve the desired result. There was a day when colorists would not use pink with red or blue with green. Color taste is ever changing. That is why industry employs color stylists who study and record color trends over the years. These records serve as a guide to color forecasting. Companies like Celanese, DuPont, Hoechst Fibers employ specialists who keep records on sales based on color appeal.

Color is one of the most important tools in design and marketing. In the past, the matching of color to create pleasing color combinations was done with the eye and the hand. Today, this is accomplished by scientific instruments and computer techniques. This has resulted in great economic savings to the producer. However, there is still a need for the human emotions and sensitivity that create good taste in the selecting and combining of colors.

LEARNING EXPERIENCES

1. What is your definition of quality? Visit retail stores, shops, and boutiques and study your concept of quality in relationship to the price of items. Report on your reactions.
2. Study a mail-order catalog to determine if there is a distinction made between quality levels for wearing apparel, over-the-counter fabrics, and home furnishings. Report on your findings.
3. Collect samples and photos of burlap, denim, or any other fabric and prepare a visual display of how the seven basic concepts of fabric performance can guide one in selection of a textile product.
4. Collect samples of fabric that show high aesthetic values and low aesthetic values. Rate them for aesthetic value, appearance, and feel.

2
TEXTILE FIBERS

PART I
IDENTIFICATION — STRUCTURE — PROPERTIES

Fiber is the basic unit of fabric. Until the twentieth century, selection and care of fabrics was relatively simple, because all fabrics used came from natural fibers. The situation changed with the introduction of the man-made fibers.

Never before in history has the consumer been offered such a wide choice of wearing apparel and household fabrics. But the proliferation of fibers has also brought consumer problems. Each manufacturer gives a new trademark or name to each of the new fibers he produces, and the trademark names are highly promoted in advertising.

In addition, imported fabrics from all over the world have contributed further to consumer confusion. How is it possible for an individual to become acquainted with over 1875 trademark fabric names? What does the trademark name mean in relation to selection, performance, and care?

In the United States, Congress has attempted to bring order out of chaos through the Textile Fiber Product Identification Act

23

(see page 348), which became a law in 1958. This law established generic or family names for the different fibers. This provides a framework whereby man-made fibers may be grouped under generic names, and the law provides for addition of new generic names. The Federal Trade Commission has outlined criteria for establishing new generic names as follows.

- The fiber for which a generic name is requested must have a chemical composition radically different from other fibers, and this distinctive chemical composition must result in distinctive physical properties or significance to the general public.
- The fiber must be in active commercial use or such must be immediately foreseen.
- The grant of the generic name must be of importance to the consuming public at large, instead of to a small group of knowledgeable professionals such as purchasing officers for large government agencies.

In our discussion we will use generic names (see Table 2-1). By learning the properties and characteristics of a class of fibers,

Table 2-1   Modern Textile Fibers

Man-Made Fibers			
Petroleum Based		Cellulosic	Mineral and Metal
Acrylic	Nytril*	Acetate	Glass
Anidex*	Olefin	Rayon	Metallic
Aramid	Polyester	Triacetate	
Azlon*	Rubber		
Lastrile*	Saran		
Modacrylic	Spandex		
Nylon	Vinal*		
Novoloid	Vinyon		

Natural Fibers			
Cellulosic	Protein	Mineral	Rubber
Cotton	Wool	Asbestos	Rubber
Linen	Silk		
Jute	Specialty hair		
Ramie			
Hemp			

*Not currently produced in United States.

we will be able to make reasonably accurate estimates of the properties of uncounted number of combination of trademarked fibers, yarns, and finishes. Fiber trademark names for various generic names are given in Appendix A, page 363. Members of the Fiber Producers and Associations are listed in Appendix B, page 373.

FIBER STRUCTURE

A fiber is a material that has a length at least 100 times its diameter or width. This high length-to-width ratio gives a fiber its peculiar properties, such as flexibility. For example, a glass rod cannot be bent without breaking, whereas a glass filament can be tied into a knot. The major characteristics that give fibers their different properties are physical structure, chemical structure, and morphology.

The physical structure is that which you can see with a microscope. For example, a cotton fiber is made of single-celled seed hairs; wool is made of an elongated, multicellular structure; linen or flax is a mass of elongated cells; rayon, acetate, and other man-made fibers are a continuous filament of long-chain molecules. The physical structure affects spinnability, luster, felting, physical and thermal properties, loftiness, and appearance of the final fabric.

The chemical structure has to do with the makeup of the fiber's molecules. For example, cotton is made of cellulose, the chemical constituents of which are hydrogen, carbon, and oxygen. The way in which these elements are arranged is what makes cotton different from polyester, which also contains hydrogen, carbon, and oxygen (see pages 93 and 95). The chemical structure affects many of the fiber properties such as strength, elongation, resiliency, density, moisture content, sunlight and weathering resistance, dye absorption, and electrical behavior.

The fiber morphology is the manner in which the molecules of the fiber arrange themselves. To understand this, it is necessary to understand the concept of the polymer. The word is derived from Greek; polymeres of many parts. Unlike most materials that are made of many small molecules (e.g., water), polymeric materials are made of a few large molecules. These molecules are composed of a long chain of short molecules (monomers) joined end to end as shown below. Their chains may be thousands of units long.

$$-----A-A-A-A-A-A-A-A-A-A-A-----$$

The more units in a chain, the higher the degree of polymerization.

Figure 2-1 *(a)* High-oriented molecules within a fiber (crystalline). *(b)* Low-oriented molecules within a fiber (amorphus).

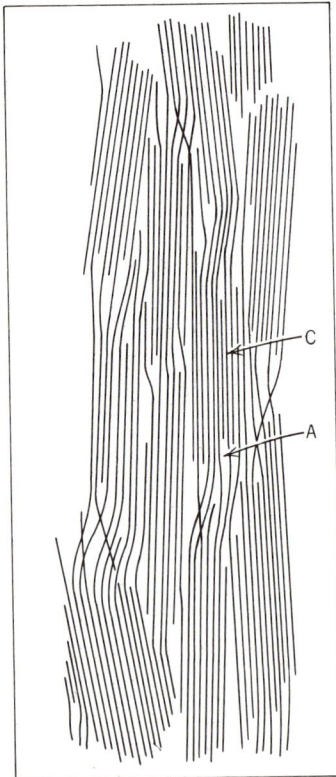

Figure 2-2 Two-phase structure of fibers: C = crystalline region and A = amorphus region.

The fiber morphology may be described in terms of molecular orientation and amorphous regions. In a *high-oriented fiber*, the molecules are parallel to each other and the longitudinal axis of the fiber. In a *low-oriented fiber*, the molecules may be arranged at random — they may be criss-crossed, irregular, far apart (see Figure 2-1). A *crystalline structure* occurs when fiber molecules are parallel to each other but not necessarily parallel to the longitudinal fiber axis. An *amorphous structure* results when the molecules are arranged at random (see Figure 2-2). Many factors may contribute to imperfect alignment. Therefore amorphous and crystalline regions usually coexist in a fiber structure.

Fiber morphology may be affected by the chemical nature of the polymer. For example, where hydrogen bonding (attraction between atoms at different molecules) exists, a higher degree of crystallinity may be found. Hydrogen bonding makes a strong contribution to the high crystallinity of nylon, especially the high wet strength of cotton. In addition, cross-linking, the chemical bonding of one long-chain molecule with another, can greatly affect the fiber morphology. The cross-links in wool give it its high resiliency.

The fiber morphology affects the fiber physical properties such as strength and elongation; the higher the orientation in a fiber, the higher the strength and the lower the stretch. It also affects the melting temperature. The more crystalline the material, the higher the melting temperature. Fiber morphology can also affect moisture absorption, dyeing, and fiber density.

FIBER PROPERTIES

What properties are necessary to make a material qualify for a textile fiber? It is generally agreed that the essential qualities are: adequate length, strength, flexibility, and spinnability.

FIBER LENGTH

Staple fibers, natural or man-made, are short lengths measured in inches or a fraction of an inch. All the natural fibers except silk are staple fibers. Staple fibers may be made from man-made fibers.

Filaments are long continuous strands of fibers; they are measured in yards or meters. Yarns made from filaments may be classed as *mono*filament or *multi*filaments.

FIBER STRENGTH

A fiber must possess strength adequate for processing to be acceptable for spinning into a yarn and making into a fabric.

Strength may vary from one fiber to another, and it may vary within one fiber. The strength of a fiber is defined as its ability to resist stress and is usually expressed in gram-force per denier (referred to as tenacity). Denier is equal to the weight in grams of 9000 meters of filament. Fiber tenacity varies from about 1 gram per denier for acetate to 8 grams per denier for glass. One should not confuse the strength of a fiber with the strength of a yarn or fabric, because relatively weak fibers can be made into strong fabrics.

FLEXIBILITY

Flexibility may be defined as the property of a fiber that permits it to bend without breaking, not only once, but repeatedly. This quality affects the durability of a fabric; it determines if a fabric can or should be creased or pleated. It also affects the aesthetic qualities of a fabric such as drapability and comfort. For example, a wool fiber is very flexible; it can be made into a durable, drapable, comfortable fabric that can be pleated. Mohair, a stiffer fiber, makes a fabric that is stiff and may split along the creases of a trouser leg because the fiber lacks sufficient flexibility to withstand repeated creasing and flexing during wear.

SPINNABILITY

A fiber must have good spinnable qualities if it is to have commercial value. This term may be defined as the ability of the fibers to cling together (cohesion) so that they can be made into a yarn. This property is dependent on the surface structure and the internal structure of a fiber. For example, the twist in the cotton fiber, the crimp in the wool fiber, and the induced crimp of a man-made fiber give each of these fibers cohesiveness, thereby making them spinnable.

OTHER DESIRABLE PROPERTIES

Not all fibers possess identical properties. In addition to the essential qualities, fibers may possess additional qualities that are distinct to each particular fiber. These properties include: natural or induced physical shape; uniformity; density; luster; moisture absorbency; elasticity; resiliency; and resistance to chemicals, environmental conditions, and biological organisms.

NATURAL OR INDUCED SHAPE

The importance of the external and internal structure of fibers has already been mentioned. Physical shape includes the surface contour (smooth, rough, serrated), the shape of the cross section, and the width and length of the fiber. The shape of the cross section, for example, influences the luster, body, and hand of the final fabric. Hand is the way a fiber (yarn or fabric) feels when handled. The surface contour influences cohesiveness, resiliency, loft, and thickness. It contributes to resistance to abrasion and pilling and comfort factors such as warmth and absorbency.

UNIFORMITY

Natural fibers vary in uniformity. Yet one of the most important qualities that determines their spinnability and commercial utility is their length. The textile manufacturer may use techniques to bring about the uniformity needed for a particular end use. For example, the U.S. Department of Agriculture has set up a system for grading cotton not only on the fiber but bundles of fiber. Uniformity is also obtained through mechanical processes such as carding, which separates the longer from the shorter fibers. Man-made fibers can be made uniform by controlling the diameter, shape, and length.

DENSITY

Density is the mass of a unit volume of material. It is usually expressed as grams per cubic centimeter (g/cc) or pounds per cubic foot. All textile fibers are heavier than water except olefin. Olefin fibers float on water. Glass and asbestos have high density; nylon and silk have low density. How does this relate to fabrics? The lower the density, the greater the covering power. A pound of wool and a pound of olefin fibers weigh the same, but there would be more fibers in the pound of olefin because of its low density (less than one — or lighter than water). This also explains why there is more covering power with the olefin fibers in comparison with wool fibers. Heavy fabrics result from fibers of high density; lightweight fabrics result from fibers of low density.

A lightweight fiber helps a fabric to be warm without being heavy. A fabric can be made thick and lofty and still be relatively lightweight. The acrylic fiber is an excellent example. Because of its woollike properties, although it is much lighter in weight than wool, it is used extensively to make lightweight yet warm blankets and sweaters.

LUSTER

Luster is the amount of light reflected from the surface of the fiber. It is measured by its degree of brightness or dullness. The natural fibers silk and mohair have high luster; cotton and wool have low luster. Luster can be controlled in man-made fibers by adding pigments to make it dull or by changing the shape of the fiber to reflect more light from the surface of the fiber. The luster of any natural or man-made fiber or filament can also be altered by different finishing processes, such as mercerization of cotton. The dulling of a fiber can also be induced by the use of chemicals and by varying the twist in a yarn. There are times when high luster is a desirable feature; other times it may be a drawback.

MOISTURE AND MOISTURE REGAIN

Textiles are naturally hygroscopic (i.e., they pick up moisture from the air). However, this moisture also evaporates back into the air. Since relative humidity affects the rate of evaporation of water, the natural moisture content of textiles varies with relative humidity. The equilibrium moisture content measured at 65 percent relative humidity and 70°F is known as the moisture regain. Moisture regain varies from 15 percent for wool to 0 percent for glass. At ambient temperature the moisture content of the fiber increases as the relative humidity increases.

Absorbency is the ability to take in moisture. Fibers that absorb water easily are called hydrophilic fibers. Examples are the natural animal and vegetable fibers, rayon and acetate. Fibers that have difficulty absorbing water are hydrophobic. Examples are the man-made fibers except rayon and acetate. Glass absorbs no water at all.

Absorbency is related to many fabric factors. They are:

1. *Skin comfort.* Little absorption of perspiration results in a clammy feeling.
2. *Static buildup.* Problems such as sparks and clinging clothing occur with hydrophobic fibers because there is little moisture content to help dissipate the built-up charge on the fiber surface. Dirt is also drawn to the fiber and will cling to it because of this.
3. *Dimensional stability in water.* Hydrophobic fibers shrink less when washed than hydrophilic fibers.

4. *Dyeability.*   It is easier to dye hydrophilic fibers, since the dye is usually dissolved in water that is then absorbed into the fiber.
5. *Stain removal.*   It is easier to remove waterborne stains from hydrophilic fibers because water and detergent can be used.
6. *Water repellent fabric.*   A more repellent fabric usually occurs with hydrophilic fibers such as cotton because the chemicals used to achieve the repellency react better with these fibers.

ELASTICITY, ELASTIC RECOVERY, ELONGATION

Elasticity is defined as that property of a fiber that causes it to return to its original size, shape, or length when the stress that causes the deformation is removed. The elasticity of textile fibers varies greatly. Spandex is highly elastic and recovers almost immediately on the release of the stress. Wool and silk are relatively elastic, whereas linen and jute possess only a small degree of elasticity. The elasticity of a fiber is measured as the recovery at 2 percent elongation.

Elongation is the deformation in the direction of the load caused by a tensile force. The deformation strain may be measured at any specific load or when the specimen breaks. It is expressed as a percentage of the original length of the fiber, yarn, or fabric. The elastic modulus is a measure of the fiber's resistance to elongation. It is measured as the load at 1 percent elongation. The higher the modulus, the more force required to stretch a fiber. Glass has a very high modulus, while spandex has a very low modulus. Elasticity and elongation are very basic to the designing of stretch fabrics for active sportswear, lingerie, and panty hose. They are necessary for comfort, fabric strength, seam strength, and to prevent bagging and sagging at the elbows, knees, and seats of garments. In practical application, a cotton knit undershirt may change size with laundering; however, because of its elasticity, it still can be extended to fit. As with elasticity, elongation in textile fibers varies greatly. Wool, silk, and rayon have high elongations; linen and jute have little elongation. It is apparent that elasticity and elongation must be considered together in evaluating fibers, yarns, or fabrics.

RESILIENCE AND COMPRESSIBILITY

When a person puts his head on a pillow and then removes it, the pillow springs back. The degree it springs back depends on the resiliency of the stuffing fiber. Resilience may be defined as the springing back of a fiber mass when it is released from compression. Wool and silk fabrics are considered resilient. They can be deformed, crushed, or wrinkled during wear; upon hanging, the deformations disappear. Compressibility is a measure of the ease with which a fiber mass can be crushed. Very soft fibers usually have high compressibility. Some fibers may have high compressibility but low resilience. A rigid fiber may have low compressibility but high resilience.

> like a pillow springs back

CHEMICAL, ENVIRONMENTAL, AND OTHER PROPERTIES

Fibers have other properties that help in determining their performance in use and care. Some of these are: flammability characteristics; behavior to high, medium, and low temperatures; reaction to chemicals, environmental conditions, and microorganisms. These properties will be discussed in relation to the basic concepts of fabric performance in the following chapters.

FIBER IDENTIFICATION

It is not possible for the average consumer to identify fabrics by look or feel, yet the fiber content is of great importance to the consumer. If you buy silk you want silk, not acetate. Fiber identification is not a simple matter. Knowledge and skill are important. Even the simple burning tests are not always reliable. In some cases laboratory facilities and expensive equipment are required.

There are five relatively simple methods that may be used to identify fibers. They are:

1. A burning test.
2. Microscopic examination (longitudinal and cross section).
3. Solubility tests in various reagents.
4. Staining tests (fibers are dyed or stained with specific dyes).
5. Fiber density.

Burning tests may give a clue to fiber type (i.e., natural or man-made). Microscopic examination and staining tests may help confirm identification by burning. Solubility and fiber density tests are particularly necessary when one must separate the individual fibers used in a blend. However, in some instances, the use of the burning test, microscopic, staining, solubility, and fiber density tests are of little value for fiber identification purposes. The use of an infrared spectrophotometer or gas chromatograph is the most accurate method of identification (see Figure 2-3 and 2-4).

BURNING TESTS

When making a burning test, look for three things.

1. *How it burns.*   Does it burn rapidly; does it go out quickly; does it smolder?
2. *How it smells.*   When the flame goes out, smell the smoke.
3. *The ash.*   Its color; its shape; can you crush it, or is it hard?

Test procedures for the reaction of textile fibers to heat and flame are given in Appendix C, page 379.

MICROSCOPIC EXAMINATION

The textile fiber is first examined at low magnification (10 to 40X). The results of this examination are to verify or modify the conclusions reached during preliminary inspection.

Selected groups of fibers from the fabric are then mounted and examined at a higher magnification. The longitudinal appear-

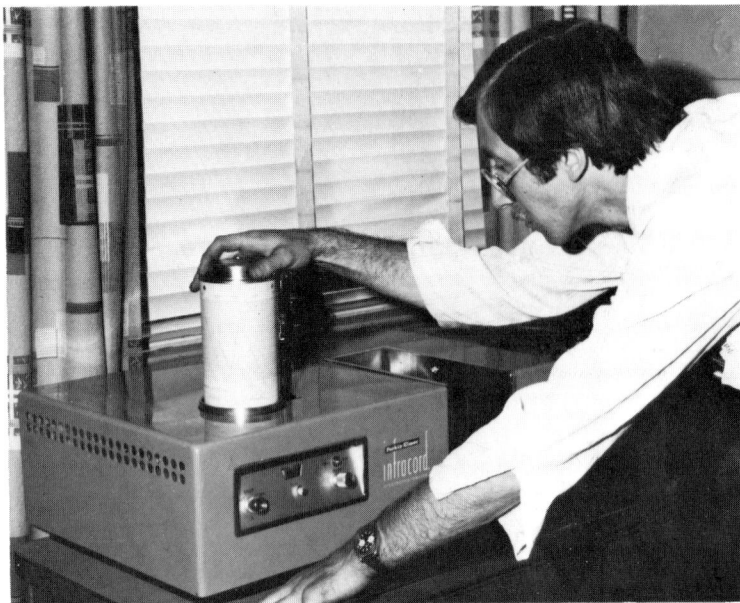

Figure 2-3   Infrared spectrophotometry is being used an increasing extent for the recognition and quantitative analysis of structural units in unknown compounds. Each textile fiber has its own identifying infrared absorption band. (Courtesy: International Fabricare Institute)

Figure 2-4 Gas chromotography is an instrumental method of analysis for the separation, identification, and quantitification of volatile mixtures. The series of peaks and valleys on the strip chart may identify not only the generic classification of a fiber but the tradename fiber and manufacturer within a generic classification. (Courtesy: International Fabricare Institute)

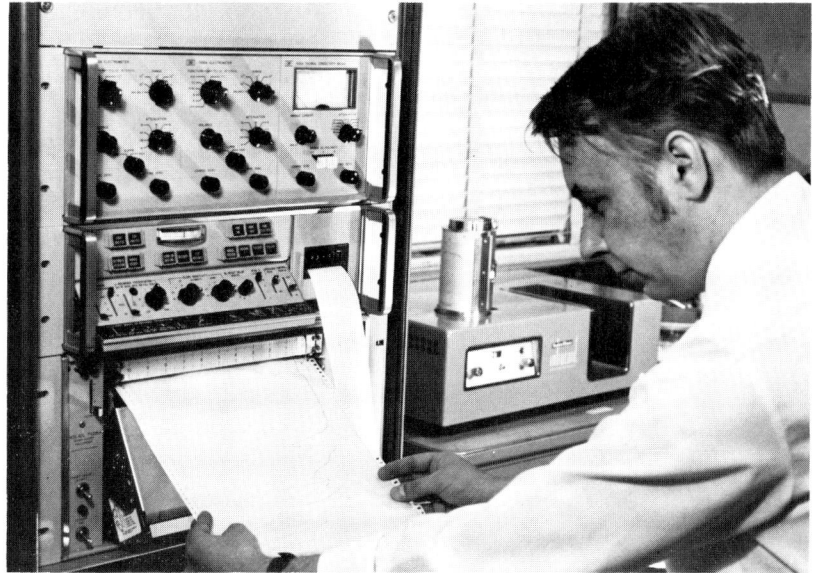

[handwritten notes in margin: good for natural fibre combination not for man-made]

ance of individual fibers is noted and compared with that of known fibers. The cross sectional appearance may also be determined.

Examination of the fibers by microscope can provide positive identification of the principal natural fibers. The appearance of the man-made fibers, however, may be changed radically by variations in their manufacturing processes; hence this test is of limited value for positive identification of man-made fibers. Even if these variations are not known, the microscope can still be a very useful tool in extending the information obtained in a preliminary inspection and in selecting fibers for subsequent testing.

For the student who wishes to study the microscopic appearance of fibers, the test procedure and the descriptions of the longitudinal and cross sections of the fiber, along with photomicrographs, may be found in Appendix D, page 381.

SOLUBILITY TESTS

Solubility tests are valuable to: (1) determine the fiber content of an unknown fabric, and (2) verify other tests used to identify fibers.

There are many solvents that may be used to distinguish one fiber from another. The principle of solubility of the natural fibers is based on their reactions to common acid and alkaline solutions. Solubility becomes more complex when dealing with the man-made fibers. Many of the tests must be carried out under carefully controlled conditions. Some of the liquids are hazardous and must be handled with care. Exhaust hoods, gloves, aprons, and goggles should be used for fiber solubility work.

Solubility tests are necessary to distinguish between the various plastic fibers. For example, acetone dissolves acetate rapidly; modacrylics slowly. Clip a small piece from an unexposed seam or use a fabric sample if available. Put a drop of acetone on it and press between your fingers. If it dissolves immediately, it is acetate; if, after a few seconds, it becomes tacky, it is modacrylic. Glacial acetic or mixture of 80 parts (by volume) of acetone and 20 parts of water dissolves acetate, but not modacrylics. See Appendix E (Solubility of Fibers) for procedural details and solubility interpretations.

DYE AND STAIN TESTS

Dyes and stains may be used to confirm the identity of fibers and to study the various fibers' structure.

A number of different stain tests are used to identify man-made textile fibers. Various dye manufacturers prepare dyes and stains for this purpose. These tests are applicable only to white or light-colored fibers. In order to identify a colored fabric or fiber, it is first necessary to strip the dye. Most dye manufacturers provide instructions on staining procedures as well as cards showing the typical color of each fiber after staining. It is sometimes difficult to distinguish one fiber from another in blended yarns or fabrics because they are stained approximately the same color. In such a case, examine the stained material under a microscope and compare it with a standard colored specimen. It is advisable not to rely on one staining solution; if several different identification stains give the answer you will be certain it is right.

Methods of staining may vary slightly but, in all cases, the fiber should be wet out thoroughly in hot water before dyeing. Place the fiber in the dye solution recommended by the manufacturer. Remove the material, rinse lightly, and dry before evaluation is made. Follow the procedure outlined in Appendix E, page 395.

SPECIFIC GRAVITY TEST

The specific gravity test provides another method of differentiating between fibers or of confirming identifications made by other methods. In this test, a specimen of the unknown fiber is placed in a liquid of known specific gravity, and it is observed to determine whether the fiber sinks or floats.

The test procedure for determining specific gravity of textile fibers is given in Appendix F, page 399.

PART II
BASIC CONCEPTS OF PRODUCING MAN-MADE FIBERS

In the 1974 energy crisis, most of the nation's attention was focused on the use of crude oil or natural gas as fuel. Will there be enough gasoline? How about fuel oil for heating? Will electric utilities be able to generate power? About 94 percent of these natural resources are consumed in energy products for power or heat.

We tend to forget that the small remainder of our oil and gas is used to make a variety and quantity of man-made materials essential to modern life. About 5 percent of the oil and 10 percent of the gas goes into the manufacture of petrochemicals unknown to most consumers. Key petrochemicals include ethylene, propylene, benzene and naphthalene, methanol, and acetylene. Today man-made materials encompass petrochemicals and thousands of products based on them including synthetic rubber, plastics, synthetic fibers, and agricultural chemicals.

Like the initial plastic, the first man-made fiber was based on cellulose — a natural material. But, beginning in 1939, a variety of fibers made from petrochemicals was introduced. Today petrochemical-based fibers account for 70 percent of the fibers we need. Cotton accounts for 29 percent and wool for 1 percent.

Man-made fibers first became popular with the introduction of nylon. Consumers had a fiber that was stronger, more durable, and easier to clean than the natural fibers. Then along came acrylic with its woollike warmth and great resistance to sunlight. Next, polyester fibers, with superior wrinkle resistance, created a whole new world of "permanent press" clothing.

Today 70 percent of the fibers that go into clothing for women and children are man-made — as are 40 percent of the fibers in men's and boys' clothing. Man-mades are used to make 93 percent of our carpets and 81 percent of our blankets.

Without these fibers, clothing and carpets would have a much shorter life. The nation's consumers would also lose many conveniences such as permanent press and stain resistance.

There is serious doubt that we could ever return completely to natural materials. To do this would require at least another 16 million acres of cotton — an increase of 100 percent, and it would consume a tremendous amount of agricultural products also based on petrochemicals.

36

Natural fibers are already in fiber form as harvested and are ready for the start of yarn spinning operations. However, man-made fibers start out as a plastic that must first be converted into fiber form. Therefore we will discuss the conversion process before proceeding with the discussion of individual fibers.

THE SPINNERET

Most man-made fibers are formed by forcing a syrupy or viscous substance, of about the consistency of molasses, through tiny holes. The streams emerging from the holes are then hardened or solidified to form filaments. The device through which the material is forced is called a spinneret. The process of extrusion and hardening is called spinning, not to be confused with the yarn forming operation of the same name.

THE CHEMICAL BASE

The fiber-forming substances ordinarily exist as solids. In order to extrude them through the spinneret, they must be converted to a fluid state — dissolved in a solvent or melted by the application of heat. Fiber-forming materials that cannot be melted or dissolved directly must be converted chemically into soluble derivatives.

The thick, syrupy material forced through the spinneret may be (1) a solution derived from a fibrous material found in nature, such as cellulose, the fibrous material of plants, or (2) a solution or a melt of a fiber-forming substance that has been produced by chemical processes called polymerization.

THE METHOD OF SPINNING

In some cases the fibers may be hardened by extruding the filaments into chemical baths that convert or "regenerate" the soluble compound into the insoluble substance that will constitute the fiber. This is called wet spinning.

When a derivative to be spun is dissolved in a solvent that can be evaporated, leaving the desired filament to be hardened by drying in warm air, the process is called dry spinning.

When the fiber-forming substance is melted for extrusion and hardened by cooling, the process is called melt spinning.

The three spinning methods are illustrated in Figure 2-5.

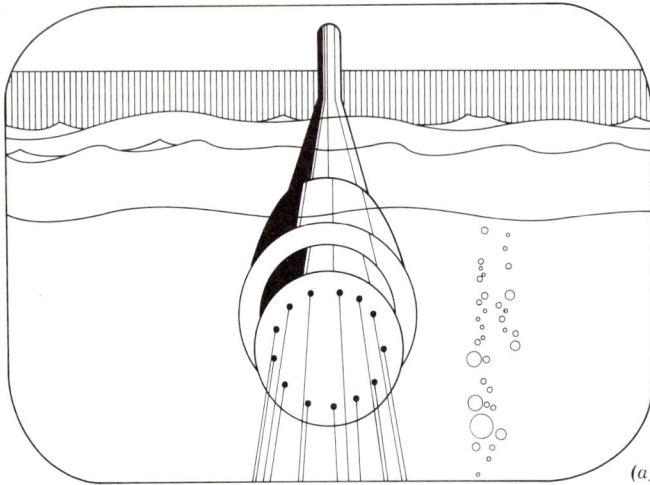

Figure 2-5a   Wet spinning. Rayon, spandex, and acrylic fibers (Acrilan, Creslan, Zefran) are made by the wet spinning process. (Courtesy: Man-Made Fiber Products Association, Inc.)

(a)

Figure 2-5b   Dry spinning. Acetate, acrylic (Orlon), modacrylic, spandex, triacetate, and vinyon are made by the dry or solvent spinning process. (Courtesy: Man-Made Fiber Products Association, Inc.)

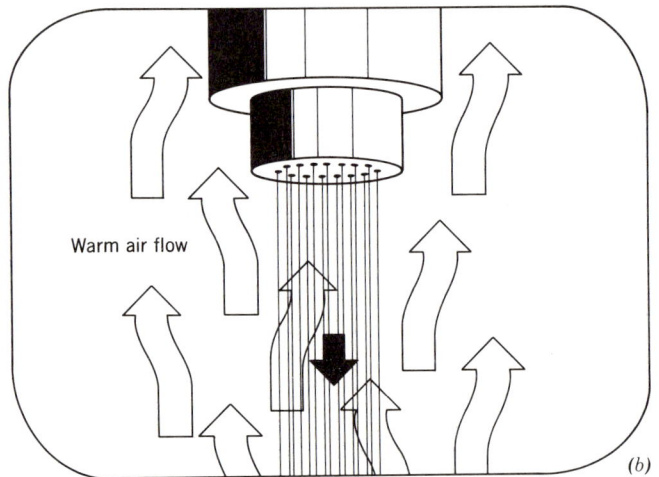

Warm air flow

(b)

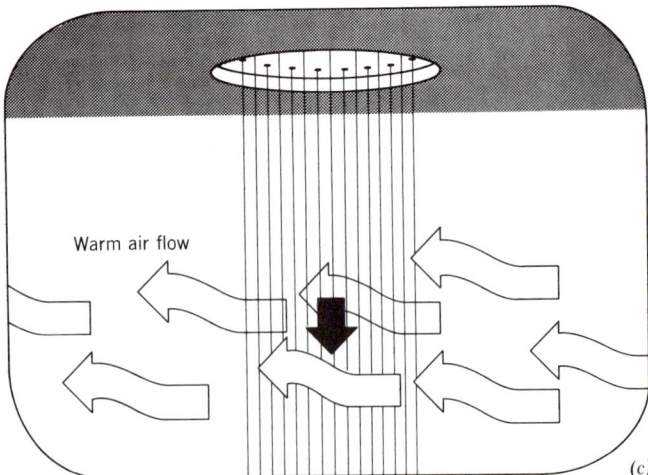

Warm air flow

(c)

Figure 2-5c   Melt spinning. Nylon, polyester, olefin, and saran are made by the melt spinning process. (Courtesy: Man-Made Fiber Products Association, Inc.)

STRETCHING AND ORIENTATION

While the fibers are hardening, or afterward, they are stretched in a process called drawing. This reduces the fiber diameter and causes the molecules in the fiber to arrange themselves into a more orderly (oriented) pattern. In a given fiber type, drawing increases the fiber's strength and decreases its ability to stretch without breaking.

MONOFILAMENTS, FILAMENT YARNS, TOW, AND STAPLE

Man-made fibers are made in a variety of forms, each of which is adapted for a particular use. Single filaments (monofilaments) may be woven into items such as sheer curtains or knitted into items such as hosiery. Continuous strands of two or more filaments may be twisted or otherwise held together to form filament yarns. Large groups of continuous filaments assembled without twist are referred to as "tow." Tow can be cut or broken into any desired length and, after such cutting or breaking, the fibers are called "staple" — a form suitable for textile spinning (see Figure 2-6).

MODIFICATION OF MAN-MADE FIBERS

There are many methods and techniques whereby a fiber producer may change man-made fibers to achieve the end use he desires. To change luster, he may modify cross sections, roughen the fiber surface, or add pigments. To change hand or scroop,* he may modify the cross section, roughen the fiber surface, induce bulk, or permanently crimp the fiber.

Fiber producers have learned to provide loft by physical treatments, chemical treatments, additives, or by using bicomponent fibers, blended fibers, or mixed polymer fibers. To improve whiteness and moisture absorbency, to eliminate static buildup, and to improve wrinkle resistance and washing and cleaning performance, the fiber producer gives the fiber a chemical treatment or puts in additives.

To improve aesthetics, fibers may be modified by physical and chemical treatments. Smooth surfaced filaments can be modified physically to give spunlike aesthetics.

Fibers can be made with improved flame retardancy through chemical modifications. Additives or treatments can be used to produce temperature control by using conductive polymers.

*Scroop is the rustling sound noted when some fabrics are handled or worn.

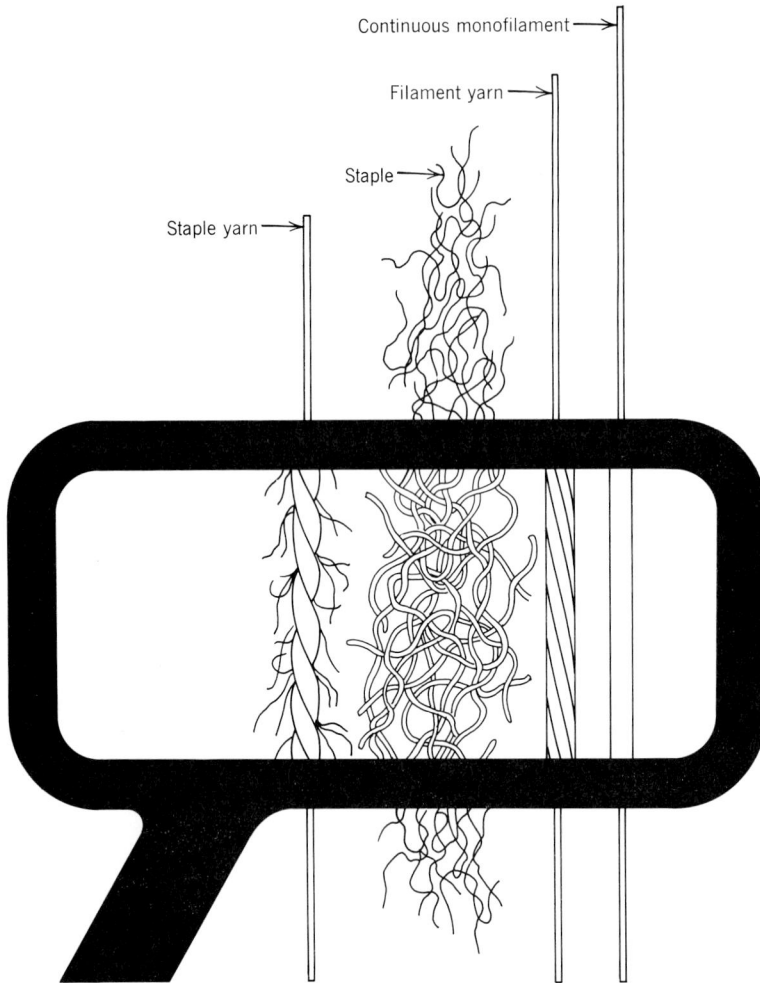

Figure 2-6 Forms of man-made yarns. (Courtesy: Man-Made Fiber Products Association, Inc.)

Fibers can be made moldable by chemical modifications in order to produce low-cost garment manufacture.

Each of these methods will be referred to throughout the text as they relate to consumer goods.

HOMOGENEOUS AND HETEROGENEOUS FIBERS

With the evolution of fibers, producers have learned to put components of two or more fibers together to create entirely new fiber properties. In fact, no fiber is completely pure. If the fiber is essentially a single polymer type, it is homogeneous. If it is

Figure 2-7 Principles of bi-component and matrix spinning. Cross sections of fibers showing arrangement of components. (Courtesy: American Fabrics and Fashions)

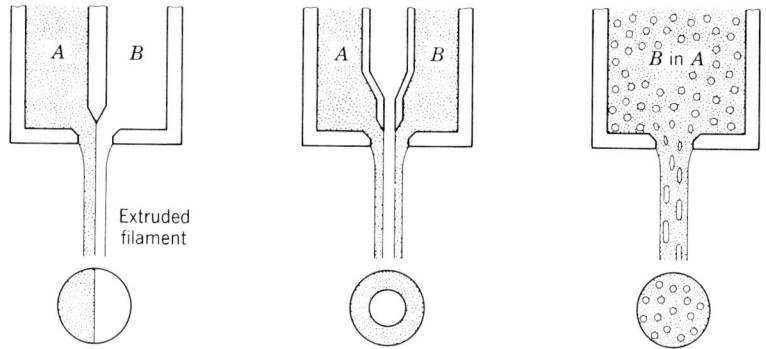

composed of a combination of two or more polymers, it is heterogeneous. The most common heterogeneous fiber types are "bicomponent" and "biconstituent" fibers (see Figure 2-7).

A bicomponent or multicomponent fiber is defined as: "A fiber or filament composed of two physically and chemically distinct polymeric components in continuous longitudinal contact within the fiber."*

For example, the fiber may be made of two different types of nylon or two different types of acrylic fibers (see Figure 2-8).

Various effects may be obtained such as self-crimping and cross-dyeing effects.

A *biconstituent fiber* or *multiconstituent fiber* is defined [ASTM (D123)] as: "A fiber or filament consisting of a continuous matrix of one polymer in which a different fiber-forming polymer is dispersed as a second distinct, discontinuous phase."

Biconstituents can be produced in three major ways: (1) mixing polymers to produce an entirely different fiber; (2) introducing additives to change functional or aesthetic characteristics such as soil release properties or dyeability; and (3) adding components that are later removed to modify optical properties or change specific gravity.

Monvelle®, a biconstituent fiber made by Monsanto, is made of 50 percent spandex and 50 percent nylon. At present it is used in panty hose. The spandex provides stretch properties, while nylon offers durability.

A *matrix* or *matrix-fibril* fiber is composed of two or more chemically distinct components in a matrix-fibril configuration. In fiber form very short filaments (fibril) are embedded in the

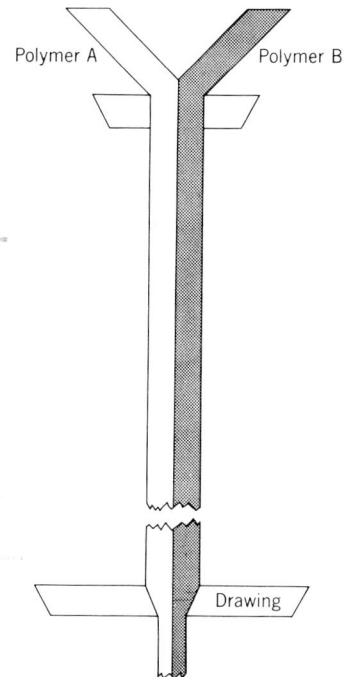

Figure 2-8 Bicomponent. (Courtesy: American Fabrics and Fashions)

*The American Society For Testing And Materials, Definition of Textile Terms (D123).

rest of the fiber (matrix). The fibril and matrix are made of differ-ent generic material.

Source®, a matrix fiber made by Allied Chemical Company, is made of 70 percent nylon (matrix) and 30 percent polyester (fibril). Cordelan®, a matrix fiber made by Kohjin International Corporation, is made of 50 percent vinal and 50 percent vinyon.

CHANGE IN FIBER SHAPES

The cross-sectional shape of a fiber may be changed to produce greater luster, brighter colors, or the dullness one desires.

The typical reflectance pattern from a smooth surface with a round cross section looks like this.

Trilobal

A man-made fiber whose cross section has been modified from circular to three-sided reflects more light than a round fiber; hence it gives more luster to a yarn and a fabric (Antron nylon).

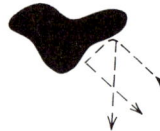

Pentalobal

A man-made fiber whose cross section has been modified from circular to a five-surfaced, star-shaped fiber reflects more light; hence it gives more luster to the yarn and the fabric (Trevira Star polyester).

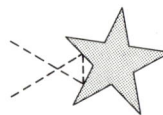

The reflectance pattern of a pentalobal fiber looks like this.

Light rays bounce about the five lobes of each filament, trap-ping and reflecting beams again and again and making the fabric glow with a very subdued sheen.

Octolobal

Fiber producers created an octolobal fiber to reduce the objectionable glitter seen from normal round cross-sectional polyester used in men's apparel. When processed through a falsetwist machine, the round cross section is compressed into flat-sided hexagons, and these flat sides reflect considerable light. By spinning the eight-sided polyester, the surfaces are quite irregular after texturing and more light is scattered away from the observer, causing a more subdued fabric luster.

Flat Filaments

A flat filament reflects light to a greater degree than a round filament. To make a flat filament, the holes in the spinneret are shaped like a rectangle.

Texturizing

Fibers can be texturized to produce bulk, hand, and stretch (see Chapter 3, page 129).

Fiber Variants

There is a developing interest in fiber variants instead of in the development of new generic fibers. Fiber producers are broadening their range of fiber variants to include finer deniers, uncommon filament counts, modified cross sections, and luster variations. It is predicted that production of fiber variants will grow because of the trend toward lightweight, supple fabrics to satisfy the demand of fashion.

PART III
MAJOR MAN-MADE FIBERS: PETROLEUM-BASED, CELLULOSE-BASED, GLASS

PETROLUEM-BASED FIBERS

ACRYLIC

As defined by the Federal Trade Commission, acrylic is a manufactured fiber in which the fiber-forming substance is any long-chain synthetic polymer composed of at least 85 percent by weight of acrylonitrile units $(-CH_2-CH-)$.
$$\begin{array}{c} | \\ CN \end{array}$$

MANUFACTURE

Acrylic fibers are formed by dry spinning. Polymerization of acrylonitrile and small amounts of other monomers is followed by dissolving in dimethyl formamide. The solution is filtered and extruded through spinnerets into a heated spinning container where the solvent is evaporated, the filaments solidify, and the solvent is recovered. The hot fiber is stretched to increase molecular orientation and fiber fineness and then dried (see Figure 2-9).

ACRYLICS IN CONSUMER USE

Acrylics are unique among man-made fabrics for their aesthetic properties. Many fabrics made from acrylic fibers are of a soft, light, fluffy construction. They have a soft, warm hand, similar to wool, good drape, and a soft luster, and they can be dyed with bright colors or muted hues. However, since acrylic fibers are thermoplastic, they can be damaged by the application of heat. This is why it is important to check the label for proper care instructions. The most common trademark names are Acrilan, Creslan, Orlon, and Zefran (see Appendix A).

Acrylic fibers are relatively strong. They have good elasticity and high bulking power. These factors are used to advantage in making a great variety of fabric constructions. They can be heat-set for dimensional stability, and they have good crease and pleat retention when properly heat-set. Acrylics have good resistance to sun and weather. They blend well with other fibers, particu-

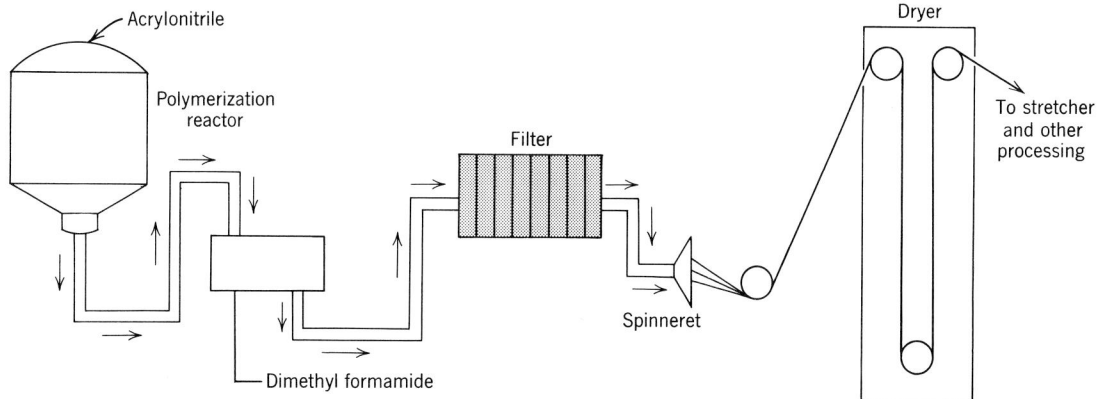

Figure 2-9 Flow diagram for production of acrylic Orlon. Other acrylic fibers are produced similarly with variation of the basic polymer, the dissolving solvent, and spinning method.

larly wool and rayon. When blended with at least 50 percent wool, fabrics can be given a durable crease or pleat. Some acrylic items pill readily; this is related to yarn and fabric construction. They have very low moisture absorption in some fabric constructions. Some acrylic fabrics do have a tendency to accumulate static electricity. They also have a tendency to hold oily stains, but not to the degree of polyester fabrics. Acrylics dye easily, offering a large selection of colors.

Acrylic fabrics may be laundered, wet-cleaned,* or dry-cleaned, depending on hue, finish, design application, and garment construction. They dry rapidly. Wrinkles can become hard set during extraction and drying, washing, or dry cleaning. Some finishes are removed in dry cleaning and wet cleaning, resulting in a harsh hand or feel. Acrylic fabrics may be bleached with a chlorine-type bleach. Bulked acrylic knit fabrics are readily affected by high temperatures, causing them to stretch. Acrylics should be pressed at 250°F; if the temperature goes above 275°F, they will glaze and become yellow. They will stick to the sole of the iron at 480 to 490°F and melt above this temperature. Acrylics are very heat-sensitive. In some fabric constructions, acrylics will distort in finishing. Excessive stretching can occur.

Some uses of acrylic fabrics are: knits and wovens for sweaters; skirts; simulated fur fabrics; dresses, suits, and pantsuits; ski, snow, and snowmobile outfits; slacks; blankets; carpets; rugs; and draperies and upholstery fabrics for household items.

*Wet cleaning is an essential part of cleaning plant procedure. Sometimes it is the only method of restoring garments and household textiles when conditions of wear or use, fiber content, or garment construction make dry cleaning alone insufficient or unsuitable. It is a water-detergent process using precautions to prevent shrinkage, loss of color, and fabric distortion.

Physical and chemical properties of acrylic fibers are given in Table 2-2.

Table 2-2   Acrylic Fibers

Fiber Composition
Acrylonitrile and small amounts of other monomers.

Physical Properties
1. *Microscopic appearance:* A uniform rod with smooth surface and one or more irregularly spaced striations. (See Appendix D.)
2. *Length:* Mainly a staple fiber but some filament.
3. *Color:* White; off-white.
4. *Luster:* Bright, semidull, or dull, depending on pigment added to fiber.
5. *Strength:* Fair to good strength.
6. *Elasticity:* Good elasticity.
7. *Resilience:* Good. Resists wrinkling.
8. *Water absorption:* Low, ranges between 1 and 3 percent at 70°F and 65 percent relative humidity. Not normally affected by water. Only slight swelling when immersed in water.
9. *Heat:* Yellowing may occur above 300°F. Softening or sticking can occur about 450°F. An ironing temperature up to 275°F is safe for acrylic fibers.
10. *Flammability:* Burns with yellow flame and produces hot residue.
11. *Electrical conductivity:* Fair to good.
12. *Specific gravity:* 1.14 to 1.19. Good bulk and covering power.

Chemical Properties
1. *Acids:* Not affected by acids used in spot and stain removal. Good resistance to mineral and organic acids, but strong concentrated acids cause damage.
2. *Alkalies:* Not affected by alkalies used in spot and stain removal. Fair resistance to other alkalies that may cause degradation.
3. *Organic solvents:* Resistant to dry-cleaning solvents.
4. *Bleaches:* Not affected by oxidizing or reducing bleaches used in spot and stain removal.
5. *Mildew:* Wholly resistant to mildew. Other fibers with which acrylics are blended may not be.
6. *Moths and insects:* Wholly resistant to moths.
7. *Light, atmospheric conditions:* Very resistant to ultraviolet light. Orlon acrylic fiber is particularly resistant to sunlight.
8. *Dyeing:* Acid and basic dyes can be used to dye acrylics. Staple fibers can be dyed at temperatures near the boiling point using basic and acetate dyes. Some acrylics can be dyed with dispersed dyes; chrome; neutral; naphthol; or premetalized and cationic dyes.

MODACRYLIC

As defined by the Federal Trade Commission, modacrylic is a manufactured fiber in which the fiber-forming substance is any long-chain synthetic polymer composed of less than 85 percent but at least 35 percent by weight of acrylonitrile units ($-CH_2-CH-$).
$\quad\quad\quad\quad$ |
$\quad\quad\quad\quad$ CN

MANUFACTURE*

Let us consider Verel, an example of a modacrylic fiber. Trademark names of other modacrylics are given in Appendix A. Verel is composed of less than 85 percent but at least 35 percent of acrylonitrile and vinylidine chloride. The two chemicals are polymerized in an autoclave to form a white powder. The copolymer is dissolved in a suitable solvent; it then flows through a spinneret and heated air where the fibers are formed and the solvent is recovered. The fiber is dried and stretched while hot to impart the desired crimp. It may be cut to any desired length (see Figure 2-10).

There are two classes of Verel fibers — regular and Verel R. These fibers are available in several different deniers and crimp

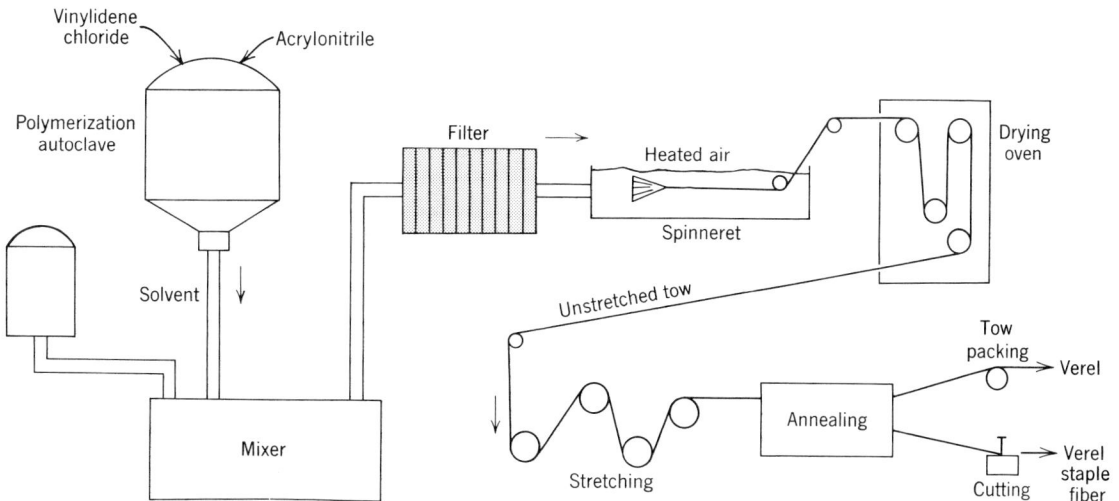

Figure 2-10 Flow diagram of the production of modacrylic Verel.

*Dynel modacrylic entered the fiber market in 1949. Union Carbide ended production in 1975.

levels developed for specific applications. The following is a regular fiber.

Verel A is the general-purpose Verel fiber for normal textile processing. Having a high level of crimp with good crimp retention, it is used in scatter rugs, draperies, and other applications where spun yarns are required. Verel A is also used in pile fabrics when high crimp is desirable.

Verel B has the same number of crimps per inch as Verel A but a lower degree of crimp permanence. Thus it can be electropolished more readily than Verel A. It is used in pile fabrics where good crimp at the base of the pile is desired along with ease of electropolishing of the fiber tips.

Verel D is the basic "guard hair" type of fiber for pile fabric use. It has low crimp with low crimp permanence and is very easily electropolished. Verel D is not completely stabilized in manufacture and, as a result, has 5 to 10 percent hot water shrinkage.

Verel F combines the properties of Verel D and Verel A. This fiber has a crimp level similar to Verel A, with low crimp permanence and ease of crimp removal, resembling Verel D. Also like Verel D, this fiber has 5 to 10 percent hot water shrinkage. Verel F is generally used for guard hair and in rugs where electropolishing is employed.

Verel R has a ribbon cross section and was developed chiefly for pile fabrics where increased luster and sparkle in the finished fabric is desired. Verel R is available with the crimps of Verel D and F.

MODACRYLICS IN CONSUMER USE

The modacrylic fibers have many general characteristics similar to those of the acrylic fibers, yet they are different. Fabrics made from modacrylic fibers have a warm, pleasant hand, good drape, resiliency, and wrinkle resistance.

Heat shrinkage of the fibers can be controlled. Fibers of different shrinkage can be mixed in the surface of pile fabrics, resulting in different heights to resemble the guard hair and undercoat fibers of natural fur. Modacrylic pile fabrics can be varied in construction, printed, embossed, and sheared to resemble a wide variety of living animals. Some of the simulated fur fabrics are dry-cleanable; others should be cleaned by the furrier method. Check for labels giving special cleaning instructions (see Table 2-3).

The modacrylic fibers have a soft, warm feel and are fairly resilient. The fibers are strong (about 3 grams per denier); hence they can be used to make durable fabrics. They are resistant to moths, mildew, and insect damage, and they have good weather resistance.

Modacrylic fibers have good bulking power, blend well with other fibers, and can be made into fabrics that have fairly good crease retention and good wrinkle recovery. They have moderate abrasion resistance. The modacrylic fibers have excellent affinity for dyes. Fabrics made of modacrylic fibers absorb very little moisture or water and they dry quickly.

Table 2-3   Important Care Instruction Terms

Dry-clean — no steam	Restricts use of steam where shrinkage or damage may occur.
Dry-clean (or clean) pile fabric method. No tumble.	Professionally dry-clean only, but do not tumble dry. Use short running cycle and minimum extraction.
Dry-clean (or clean) pile fabric method. Tumble cold.	Professionally dry-clean only, but tumble dry at room temperature only and use short running cycle and minimum extraction.

Fur clean only.
  Clean by furrier method.
  Clean by fur coat method.
	Clean in a drum with a special compound moistened with solvent; cage to remove compound; finish by electrifying fabric.

The modacrylics are fire-resistant. They will not support combustion; instead, they char and melt. Verel has gained in importance in the drapery field because it is inherently fire-resistant, has excellent resistance to sunlight degradation, is nonyellowing, and has good weathering qualities. Modacrylics are used widely to make fabrics that possess excellent protection where flammability is a consideration but, at the same time, the fabrics are susceptible to burn holes by careless dropping of cigarette embers.

Monsanto has announced a new process for imparting increased durable fire retardancy to modacrylic. The first to be marketed is SEF® (self-extinguishing flame) modacrylic in children's sleepwear. The company states that the fiber has excellent flame resistance and an acryliclike hand. The durable fire retardant system developed by Monsanto can be applied to carpets, flannelette of cellulosic fibers, cotton knits, drapery, and upholstery fabrics.

Modacrylic fabrics may be laundered, wet-cleaned, or dry-cleaned, depending on dyes, finishes, design application, and garment design. Verel can be bleached with 30 percent hydrogen peroxide and 5 percent chlorine bleach without any ill effect. Modacrylics are fairly resistant to alkaline solution. Verel is relatively heat-resistant and can be ironed up to 300°F. Above this temperature, glazing and softening occurs. It is recommended that Verel be dryer dried.

Modacrylics are used widely in draperies, slipcovers, bedspreads, pillows, upholstery, rugs, carpeting, and bathroom accessories. Some other uses of modacrylic fabrics are: sweaters; dress and suiting fabrics; nonwoven lining fabrics; simulated fur coats, jackets; and linings in coats, jackets, and trim.

Physical and chemical properties of modacrylic fibers are given in Table 2-4.

Table 2-4 Modacrylic Fibers

Chemical Composition
Less than 85 percent but at least 35 percent by weight of acrylonitrile.

Physical Properties
1. *Microscopic appearance:* Clear, transparent tube with longitudinal striations (see Appendix D). Cross-sectional peanut shape.
2. *Length:* Spun as a filament and cut into staple lengths.
3. *Color:* White.
4. *Luster:* Depends on pigmentation.
5. *Strength:* Good.

Table 2-4   Modacrylic Fibers *(Cont'd)*

6. *Elasticity:* Good.
7. *Resiliency:* Fair to good.
8. *Moisture absorption:* Verel absorbs up to 4 percent moisture. Water has no appreciable effect on the modacrylic fibers.
9. *Heat:* The modacrylics are rather heat sensitive. Verel will glaze, stiffen, and discolor at temperatures over 300°C. Modacrylics melt and char only while in flame. When flame is removed, modacrylics do not continue to char or to melt.
10. *Flammability:* Self-extinguishing. Will not support combustion.
11. *Electrical conductivity:* High. Fibers can be charged to restore upright position in pile fabrics.
12. *Specific gravity:* 1.33 to 1.37.

Chemical Properties

1. *Acids:* Excellent resistance to acids. No effects from acids used for stain and spot removal.
2. *Alkalies:* High resistance to alkalies. No effects from alkalies used for stain and spot removal.
3. *Organic solvents:* Resistant to dry-cleaning solvents. Acetone will damage modacrylic fibers.
4. *Bleaches:* No effect from bleaches in the concentrations used for spot and stain removal.
5. *Mildew:* Resistant to mildew.
6. *Moths, insects:* Resistant to moth and insect damage.
7. *Light, atmospheric conditions:* Resistant to sunlight.
8. *Dyeing:* Acetate, acid, basic, and some vat dyes are used.

NYLON

In 1973 the Federal Trade Commission redefined nylon as a manufactured fiber in which the fiber-forming substance is a long-chain synthetic polyamide in which less than 85 percent of the amide ($-\underset{\underset{O}{\|}}{C}-NH-$) linkages are attached directly to two aromatic rings. (Effective date: January 11, 1974.)

The most common and heavily produced polyamides are nylon 66 and nylon 6, which are nearly identical. The chemical formula of nylon 66 is as follows:

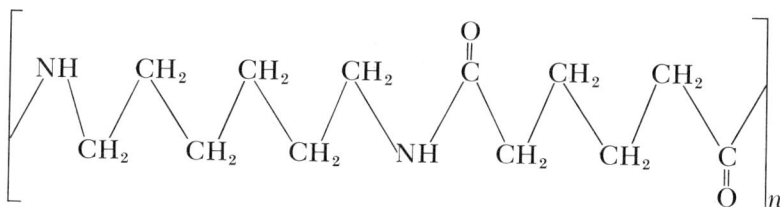

$$\left[NH-CH_2-CH_2-CH_2-CH_2-CH_2-CH_2-\underset{\underset{O}{\|}}{C}-NH-CH_2-CH_2-CH_2-CH_2-\underset{\underset{O}{\|}}{C} \right]_n$$

This formula is typical of those of most present commercial polyamides. They differ mainly in the number of CH_2 groups that lie between the amide groups.

MANUFACTURE

The fiber's size, strength, weight, elasticity, and luster can be controlled in the preparation of nylon. The raw materials used to make nylon 66 are an organic acid (adipic acid) and an organic base (hexamethylene diamine). They are chemically combined to form a substance called nylon salt. The salt is polymerized at high temperature in the absence of air (nitrogen atmosphere), and water is continually removed. The polymer is poured out as a ribbon and cut into small chips, flakes, or pellets. These are blended, remelted, and pumped through spinnerets. The filaments solidify as they cool on exposure to air and are gathered together to form a yarn. The yarn is stretched between rollers and twisted. During the twisting operation, sizing or oils may be applied. Finally, the yarn is wound on bobbins and packaged (see Figure 2-11).

NYLON IN CONSUMER USE

Nylon is used widely in hosiery, lingerie, outerwear, and household furnishings in 100 percent fabrics, blends, and combinations. Fabric types cover a wide range of woven and knit goods including suiting blends, washable fleeces, and novelties. Many

Figure 2-11 Flow diagram of the production of Nylon.

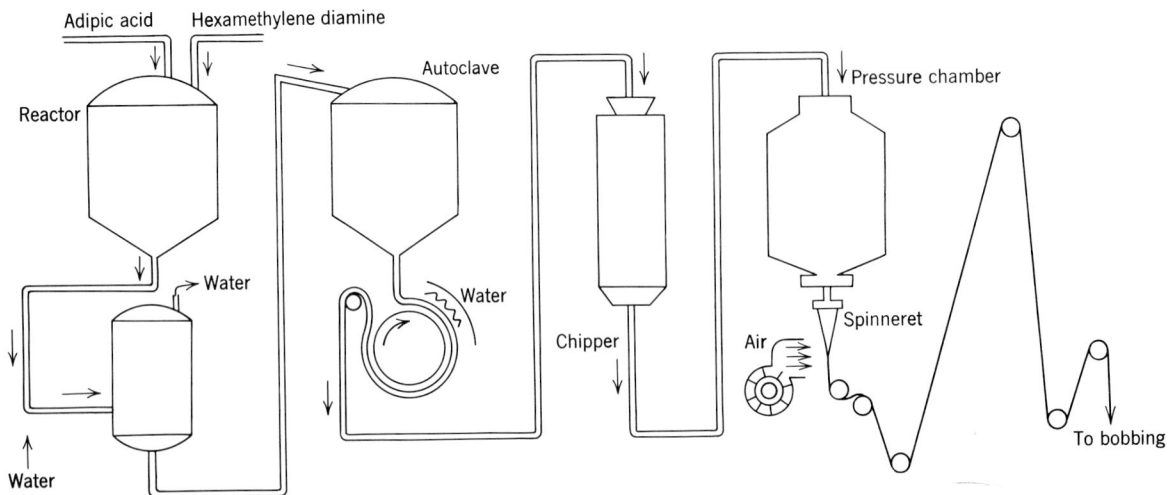

companies produce nylon. For trademark names, descriptions, and manufacturers of nylon, see Appendix A.

Nylon is a very strong, quick-drying fiber with high wet strength, which is important in outerwear and swimwear fabrics. It resists nonoily stains. Nylon is a resilient and heat-sensitive fiber. It can be heat set to be dimensionably stable. Durable crease pleat retention can be obtained by heat setting the fabric. Nylon blends well with other fibers and adds strength to such blends (15 to 20 percent nylon is needed to give additional strength to most fabrics). It is resistant to mildew and insect damage; it also resists alkaline substances. However, some fabrics made of spun nylon yarns have a tendency to pill.

In some fabric constructions nylon has low moisture absorption, making the wearer hot in warm surroundings and cold in cold surroundings. Nylon has poor resistance to sunlight when compared with cotton, rayon, and acrylics. "Bright-" type nylon has better resistance to sunlight than dull type. Nylon fabrics, unless treated, have a tendency to accumulate static and cling to the wearer. Special finishes can minimize this. Nylon is affected by strong acidic substances. Some nylon fabrics have the ability to absorb and hold body oils and perspiration.

Nylon fabrics may be laundered, wet-cleaned, or dry-cleaned, depending on dyes, finishes, design application, and garment construction. They have a tendency to gray and yellow with age. Some nylon fabrics seem to have the power to attract and hold soil and dye in laundering and dry-cleaning. This can be avoided by cleaning and washing separately. White nylon should be bleached with hydrogen peroxide or sodium perborate bleach. Nylon is discolored and its strength is affected by chlorine-type bleaches.

Nylon is a heat-sensitive fiber. Ironing temperature should not exceed 250°F. It will glaze and turn yellow at temperatures above 275°F. It sticks to the iron at 480 to 490°F. It will melt above this temperature. Physical and chemical properties of nylon fibers are given in Table 2-5.

Table 2-5   Nylon (Polyamide) Fibers

Fiber Composition

Nylon 66 — polyamide (polyhexamethylene adipamide); Nylon 6 — polyamide (caprolactum).

Physical Properties

1. *Microscopic appearance:* Very smooth and even, like a glass rod (see Appendix D).

Table 2-5   Nylon (Polyamide) Fibers *(Cont'd)*

2. *Length:* Filaments may be any length desired. Also manufactured as a staple fiber.
3. *Color:* Off white.
4. *Luster:* High natural luster. Luster can be controlled to any degree desired.
5. *Strength:* Exceptionally high, 60,000 to 108,000 pounds per square inch.
6. *Elasticity:* Exceptionally high.
7. *Resiliency:* Very good recovery from wrinkling or creasing.
8. *Moisture absorption:* 3.8 percent at 65 percent relative humidity and 70°F. A slight loss of strength when wet. Dries very quickly.
9. *Heat:* High resistance. Melts at 482°F. Slight yellowing at 300°F after five hours. An ironing temperature of 275°F is satisfactory for nylon fabrics.
10. *Flammability:* Melts slowly. Does not support combustion. Hot residue can cause severe burns.
11. *Electrical conductivity:* Low. Generates static electricity during wear.
12. *Specific gravity:* 1.14. Low density.

Chemical Properties

1. *Acids:* Weakened by concentrated strong acids. Boiling in 5 percent hydrochloric acid causes it to disintegrate. Resistant to acids used in spot and stain removal.
2. *Alkalies:* High resistance to alkalies.
3. *Organic acids:* Resistant to dry-cleaning solvents and reagents used in spot and stain removal. Nylon is insoluble in acetone, but soluble in concentrated formic acid.
4. *Bleaches:* Not affected by oxidizing or reducing bleaches used to remove spots and stains. May be affected by chlorine bleach. Strong oxidizing bleaches damage nylon.
5. *Mildew:* Wholly resistant to mildew, but finishes on nylon may be attacked.
6. *Moths, insects:* Wholly resistant to moth and insect damage under normal conditions of use.
7. *Light, atmospheric conditions:* Loses strength on prolonged exposure. Bright yarn is more resistant than dull yarn.
8. *Dyeing:* Acid, direct, vat, dispersed, and basic dyes can be used.

POLYESTER

As defined by the Federal Trade Commission, polyester is a manufactured fiber in which the fiber-forming substance is any long-chain synthetic polymer composed of at least 85 percent by weight of an ester of a substituted aromatic carboxylic acid, including but not restricted to substituted therephthalate units

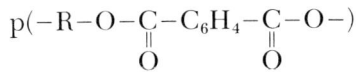

$$p(-R-O-\underset{O}{\overset{\|}{C}}-C_6H_4-\underset{O}{\overset{\|}{C}}-O-)$$

and parasubstituted hydroxybenzoate units.

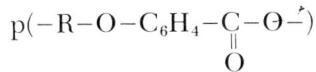

$$p(-R-O-C_6H_4-\underset{O}{\overset{\|}{C}}-O-)$$

MANUFACTURER

To make poly (ethylene terephthalate), terephthalic acid or dimethyl terephthalate and ethylene glycol are combined, polymerized, and made into chips. The blended chips are fed to the melt spinning tank. The molten material is forced through a spinneret and solidifies into fiber form on contact with air. The fiber is stretched while hot. The higher the stretch, the stronger the fiber, and the lower the elongation. Polyester is made in both filament and staple form (see Figure 2-12).

BENZOATE (A-TELL)

A new generic name was proposed to the Federal Trade Commission by Unitika Ltd., Japan, to describe their polymer compound of at least 85 percent by weight of paraethyleneoxy-

Figure 2-12 Flow diagram of the production of poly (ethylene terephthalate).

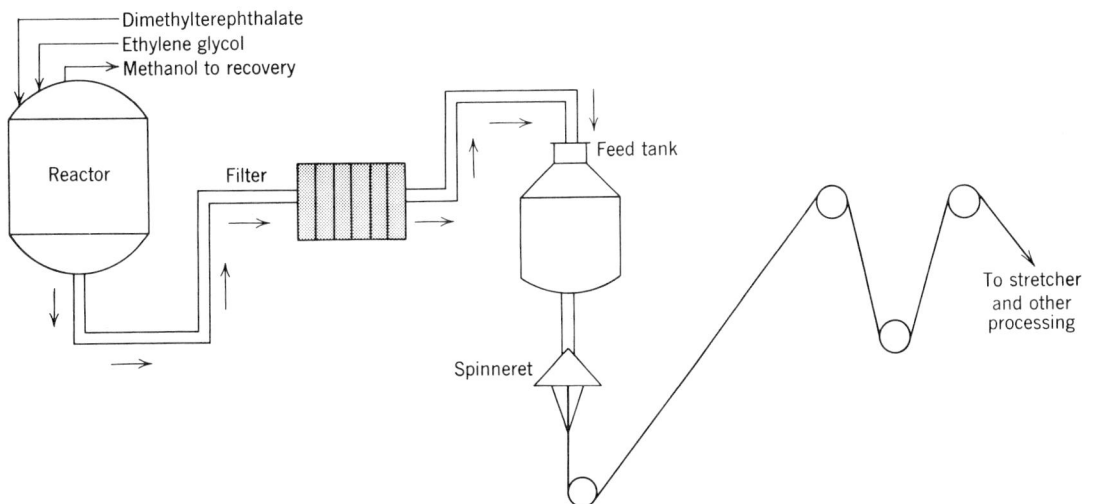

benzoate units. "A-Tell" benzoic acid is described as a "linear polymer having alternating ether and ester linkages, based on hydroxyl benzoic acid and ethylene oxide." The company claims that A-Tell has some very distinctive properties: a dry feel like the natural fibers, excellent dyeability, a soft hand, minimum static electricity (quick discharge of static electricity), and good elastic recovery (good crease resistance and fit). However, with the amendment of the definition of the generic name polyester, the FTC rejected the proposal stating that the A-Tell benzoate fiber falls within the definition of polyester.

POLYESTER IN CONSUMER USE

No other man-made fiber quite matches the performance qualities of polyester, yet gives us so many fashion fabrics, both woven and knitted. The outstanding characteristics of polyester is its ability to resist wrinkling and to spring back to shape when creased with wear. Polyesters have good dimensional stability and possess minimum care characteristics. Polyesters absorb and tenaciously hold oily stains and soil. They can be laundered and dry-cleaned, but laundering does not remove the oily soil and stains unless fabrics are pretreated.

Common trademark names are Avlin, Dacron, Fortrel, Kodel, Quintess, Spectran, and Trevira.

Polyester is seen in a wide range of end uses such as dresses, uniforms, suits and pantsuits, slacks, blouses, coats in womenswear, ties, men's suits, slacks, jackets, dress shirts, sport shirts in menswear, and curtains, draperies, bedspreads, slipcovers, upholstery, rugs, and carpets in household items.

The polyesters are very strong fibers; therefore strong fabrics can be made from them. Polyester fabrics may be heat-set for dimensional stability, so some fabrics have good pleat and crease retention. Polyesters blend well with other fibers, contributing to wrinkle resistance. In wool blends, at least 40 to 70 percent polyester must be present to impart this quality; at least 25 percent polyester must be present in rayon blends. The most popular blend with cotton is 65 percent polyester.

Polyester can be finished to make flame-resistant fabrics and blended with fibers that can be finished with flame-retardant finishes, and textile fiber producers are experimenting with building flame retardancy into the fiber itself.

Polyester fibers are relatively insensitive to water. They resist weathering. Because they have low absorption in 100 percent applications, garments may feel hot and uncomfortable. Some polyester outerwear fabrics seem to have a wicking action, so moisture seems to be pulled through the fabric, which may feel cool to the wearer. White fabrics tend to discolor from static-attracted airborne soil, but this may be controlled with special finishes. Polyesters have been improved to take many dyes. Some resin-bonded pigment colors possess poor colorfastness. Fabrics made of polyester are resistant to moths and mildew. Some knitted 100 percent polyester fabrics and polyester and cotton fabrics have a tendency to pill.

Polyester fabrics can be laundered, wet-cleaned, or dry-cleaned, depending on dyes, finishes, design application, and garment construction. White polyester fabrics may be bleached with a chlorine-type bleach. Polyester fabrics must be ironed at low temperature (250°F). They will start to glaze at 275°F, stick to the sole of the iron at 400 to 450°F, and melt above this temperature. If blended with fibers that are heat-sensitive, a temperature setting safe for the other fiber must be used.

The physical and chemical properties of polyester fibers are given in Table 2-6.

Table 2-6   Polyester Fibers

Fiber Composition

Poly (Ethylene Terephthalate).

Physical Properties

1. *Microscopic appearance.* Smooth and even. Rodlike (see Appendix D).
2. *Length.* Both filament and staple lengths.
3. *Color.* White.
4. *Luster.* Can be either bright or dull.
5. *Strength.* Good to excellent.
6. *Elasticity.* Fair to good. Less than nylon; greater than cotton and rayon.
7. *Resiliency.* Excellent. Good recovery from wrinkling.
8. *Moisture absorption.* Very low. Less than 1 percent.
9. *Heat.* Softening or sticking temperature is above 400°F. Irons and other finishing equipment adjusted for finishing acetate are satisfactory for finishing polyester fibers. Polyester fibers have good stability when heat set.
10. *Flammability.* Burns slowly. Drops off residue when hanging free.
11. *Electrical properties.* Low moisture absorption encourages the accumulation of static charges.
12. *Specific gravity.* Dacron 1.38; Kodel 1.22; Vycron 1.37.

Table 2-6   Polyester Fibers *(Cont'd)*

Chemical Properties

1. *Acids.* Not affected by acids used in spot and stain removal. Good resistance to most acids.
2. *Alkalies.* Not affected by alkalies used in spot and stain removal. Good resistance to most alkalies at low ph level.
3. *Organic solvents.* Resistant to dry-cleaning solvents.
4. *Bleaches.* Not affected by oxidizing or reducing bleaches used in spot and stain removal.
5. *Mildew.* Completely resistant to mildew which, however, may attack finishes used on polyester.
6. *Moths, insects.* Completely resistant to moth damage under normal conditions of use.
7. *Light, atmospheric conditions.* Good sunlight resistance.
8. *Dyeing.* Dispersed (acetate) dyes; azoic (developed). Some pigments are also used.

OLEFIN (POLYPROPYLENE; POLYETHYLENE)

As defined by the Federal Trade Commission, olefin is a manufactured fiber in which the fiber-forming substance is any long-chain synthetic polymer composed of at least 85 percent by weight of ethylene, propylene, or other olefin units.

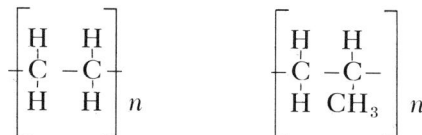

$$\begin{bmatrix} \text{H} & \text{H} \\ -\text{C} & -\text{C}- \\ \text{H} & \text{H} \end{bmatrix}_n \qquad \begin{bmatrix} \text{H} & \text{H} \\ -\text{C} & -\text{C}- \\ \text{H} & \text{CH}_3 \end{bmatrix}_n$$

MANUFACTURE

The major olefin fiber is polypropylene. Some common trademark names are Herculon, Marvess, and Vectra (see Appendix A).

Olefins are unsaturated hydrocarbons derived from petroleum as by-products of the "cracking" process. Chemists have learned to join olefin molecules together into long chains called polymers. The first of these olefin polymers was polyethylene. It was first made from ethylene gas about 20 years ago, and it is now quite familiar to all because of its fine properties as a transparent film material.

The success of polyethylene encouraged the chemical industry to develop a similar polymer from propylene. Polypropylene has some very superior properties compared with most thermo-plastic resins, and its success as a plastic was immediate and widespread. This new plastic material, in 10-years' time, has found thousands of commercial applications, and the production figures quickly reached the 100 million-pound level as company after company rushed into production. The pioneer producer was Montecatini in Italy, and the first American producer was Hercules Powder Company.

Naturally, the potential of this superb plastic was investigated early as a base for textile fibers. In 1957, Montecatini exhibited polypropylene fabrics at the Milan Fair. Some were staple fiber fabrics almost indistinguishable from wool; others were silklike fabrics made from filament yarns.

It looked then as though polypropylene was destined to sweep through the textile industry like a hurricane. The fibers had so many superb properties that the negative ones were brushed aside by the optimists. However, these negatives would not go away, and soon they blunted and finally stalled the triumphant march of polypropylene fiber in the textile apparel field.

FIBER CHARACTERISTICS

The major negative that has limited use of polypropylene is heat sensitivity. Its melting point is 325 to 340°F, but it has a softening point at 220 to 230°F. For this reason, polypropylene is very vulnerable to hot irons and steam presses, and great care is needed in finishing.

Polypropylene is also sensitive to oxidation and to ultraviolet light. Even more of a handicap is its characteristic "waxy" hand that many people find objectionable in clothing textiles. In addition, polypropylene, because of its low moisture absorption, tends to have a clammy feel when used in apparel. Another thing that has retarded polypropylene's conquest of the textile market is the difficulty encountered in dyeing it. Polypropylene is not readily dyeable by commercial dyeing processes; however, suitable color pigments are available that will give a wide variety of colors and shades. The resin can be used in its natural form or color, or it may be precolored prior to use. Most coloring or pigmentation is done by using a color concentrate that is added to the natural resin. In this way, only a portion of the resin is precolored. This offers the advantage of inventorying only natural resin and relatively small quantities of colored resin. These raw materials can be packaged in 50-pound bags, 1000-pound boxes, or large railroad hopper cars for the convenience of the processor.

Recently, however, several solutions to the above problems have been offered. They should not be regarded as permanent handicaps to the use of polypropylene.

Despite the problems that have stopped polypropylene in apparel textiles, its good properties have enabled it to find ready acceptance in at least two other big textile markets: carpets and cordage fibers. One of the useful properties of polypropylene is its very low density. In fact, the fiber floats on water. This means the buyer gets more fiber per pound at a given cost, and, therefore, greater yardage and covering power, which is very important in carpets.

Polypropylene has excellent resistance to chemicals and abrasion, good wet strength, controlled shrinkage in hot water, good resilience, and resistance to wrinkling.

POLYPROPYLENE IN CONSUMER USE

The first commercial use for polypropylene was in carpeting. The carpets are made of either staple or bulked textured yarns. Manufacturers of carpeting state that carpets made of polypropylene are outstanding in the following performance factors: soil resistance and durability; ease of cleaning; greater bulk and coverage; and locked-in color and freedom from static.

As far back as 1964, samples of carpeting were dry-cleaned for the National Institute of Rug Cleaning, Inc. (now known as AID's International). At that time, two bulletins were issued: Spotting of Herculon and Cleaning of Herculon.* NIRC studies show that professional spotting chemicals can safely be used on polypropylene carpeting. There are no immediate or delayed effects. It was also determined that polypropylene carpeting can be satisfactorily cleaned by in-plant or on-location professional procedures. Exceptions may be noted where finishing agents used in manufacture remain on the fibers. The NIRC recommends that the amount of moisture used on location should be kept to a minimum to prevent browning.

In addition to carpets, polypropylene is finding uses in other home furnishings such as woven and nonwoven upholstery fabrics and woven and needle-punched blankets. Also, later generation polypropylene fibers are finding an increasing use in apparel.

*Bulletin T-173, Spotting of Herculon; Bulletin T-174, Cleaning of Herculon. National Institute of Rug Cleaning, Arlington, Virginia.

Dry-cleanable fabrics made of olefin fibers should be dry-cleaned in petroleum solvent. The fiber swells in perchlorethylene and shrinkage results. Unfortunately, many of the fabrics are not labeled for specific cleaning instructions. The fabric should be dried at temperatures below 120°F, since shrinkage results at higher temperatures. Washable fabrics of olefin fibers should be laundered at the low temperature setting and air dried. To iron, place a press cloth between the fabric and the iron, set at the lowest possible setting. Before pressing, test an unexposed seam of the garment.

POLYETHYLENE

Polyethylene was the first olefin fiber to reach commercial importance. Since the early 1950s, a new technique of polymerizing ethylene or the joining of molecules into long-chain polymers was discovered. This improved fiber properties and brought wider use of polyethylene in textiles.

POLYETHYLENE IN CONSUMER USE

Fabrics containing polyethylene have been used quite widely as slipcover and upholstery fabrics by the airplane and car industries. As far back as 1956, commercial upholstery fabrics that contained polyethylene were tested. Since the upholstery fabric was permanently attached to the furniture, it was not anticipated that they would be dry-cleaned.

Manufacturers of furniture are now making frames with foam pillows and then slipcovering them. This is an advantage over heavily upholstered furniture, because the consumer can easily remove the soiled cushion covers and send them to a professional dry cleaner. Many of these items dry-clean satisfactorily. Trouble occurs when the manufacturer uses a fabric that contains a heat-sensitive fiber. Neither the consumer nor the dry cleaner is aware of its presence. After dry cleaning and drying, the heat-sensitive covers shrink, so they no longer fit the foam cushion. Home sewers are now selecting slipcover and drapery fabrics to create their own favorite clothing design. They should consider performance of the fabric in wear and cleaning. The standards for shrinkage tolerances in drapery and upholstery fabrics are higher than those for wearing apparel fabrics. The physical and chemical properties of olefin fibers are given in Table 2-7.

Table 2-7   Olefin Fibers

Fiber Composition

Polypropylene; polyethylene

Physical Properties
1. *Microscopic appearance.* Smooth and rodlike. See Appendix D.
2. *Length.* Produced in both filament and staple lengths.
3. *Color.* Translucent.
4. *Luster.* Dull, semidull, bright.
5. *Strength.* Polyethylene fibers have fair to good strength. Polypropylene fibers have excellent strength. Strength is dependent on the degree of polymerization.
6. *Elasticity.* Good.
7. *Resiliency.* Good resistance to crushing.
8. *Moisture absorption.* None at 70°F and 65 percent relative humidity. Not appreciably affected by water.
9. *Heat.* Polyethylene fibers are quite heat-sensitive. They will melt at about 260°F. Polypropylene fibers are more heat-resistant. They melt at about 330°F. Progressive shrinkage can occur from heat at 140 to 212°F.
10. *Flammability.* Slow burning.
11. *Electrical conductivity.* Excellent.
12. *Specific gravity.* 0.90 to 0.91.

Chemical Properties
1. *Acids.* Very resistant, with the exception of nitric acid at elevated temperatures.
2. *Alkalies.* Very resistant.
3. *Organic solvents.* Resistant to petroleum and fluorocarbon dry-cleaning solvents. Perchlorethylene causes some swelling of the fiber that results in shrinkage.
4. *Bleaches.* Resistant.
5. *Mildew.* Not attacked.
6. *Moths, insects.* Not attacked.
7. *Light, atmospheric conditions.* Loses strength; degrades on long exposure.
8. *Dyeing.* Pigments are added to the liquid before the fibers are extruded. Recent developments, such as adding a dye-receptive compound to solution before spinning and by grafting dye-receptive molecular units to the filament, enables dyeing to produce a large range of colors.

CELLULOSE-BASED FIBERS

RAYON

As defined by the Federal Trade Commission, rayon is a manufactured fiber composed of regenerated cellulose, as well as manufactured fibers composed of regenerated cellulose in which substituents have replaced not more than 15 percent of the hydrogens of the hydroxyl groups.

There are two methods of producing rayon: (1) viscose rayon — wood pulp dissolved in an alkali, aged, and chemically treated before spinning; and (2) cuprammonium — cotton linters dissolved in cuprammonium hydroxide solution, aged before spinning. Since only a small amount of cuprammonium rayon is made today, we will omit it from our discussion.

MANUFACTURE

Rayon is made from cellulose. The major source of cellulose is wood pulp. Wood pulp is treated with caustic soda (sodium hydroxide), causing the wood pulp fibers to swell, forming a substance called alkali cellulose. The alkali cellulose is treated with carbon disulfide, changing it to a new compound called cellulose xanthate. The cellulose xanthate is dissolved in diluted caustic soda solution, forming a thick solution similar to molasses in appearance. This solution is the viscose spinning solution. The viscose is then filtered to remove any remaining solid matter that could clog the spinnerets. Any air present is removed to prevent air bubbles in the subsequent fibers. The viscose solution is pumped through tiny holes in spinnerets into an acid bath at a steady rate (see Figure 2-13). From the spinning bath, it passes over a series of reels to a bobbin. When it reaches the last reel, it is dry. It is wound on bobbins and given a certain amount of twist at the same time. The continuous spinning process produces a high-quality yarn. Rayon can be cut into staple fibers and spun into a yarn (see Figure 2-13).

FIBER MODIFICATIONS

Technology permits the fiber manufacturer to vary the basic viscose rayon production methods to produce rayon fibers (hence yarns and fabrics) that have regular, high, and medium strength and elongation properties. The fiber can be modified to produce

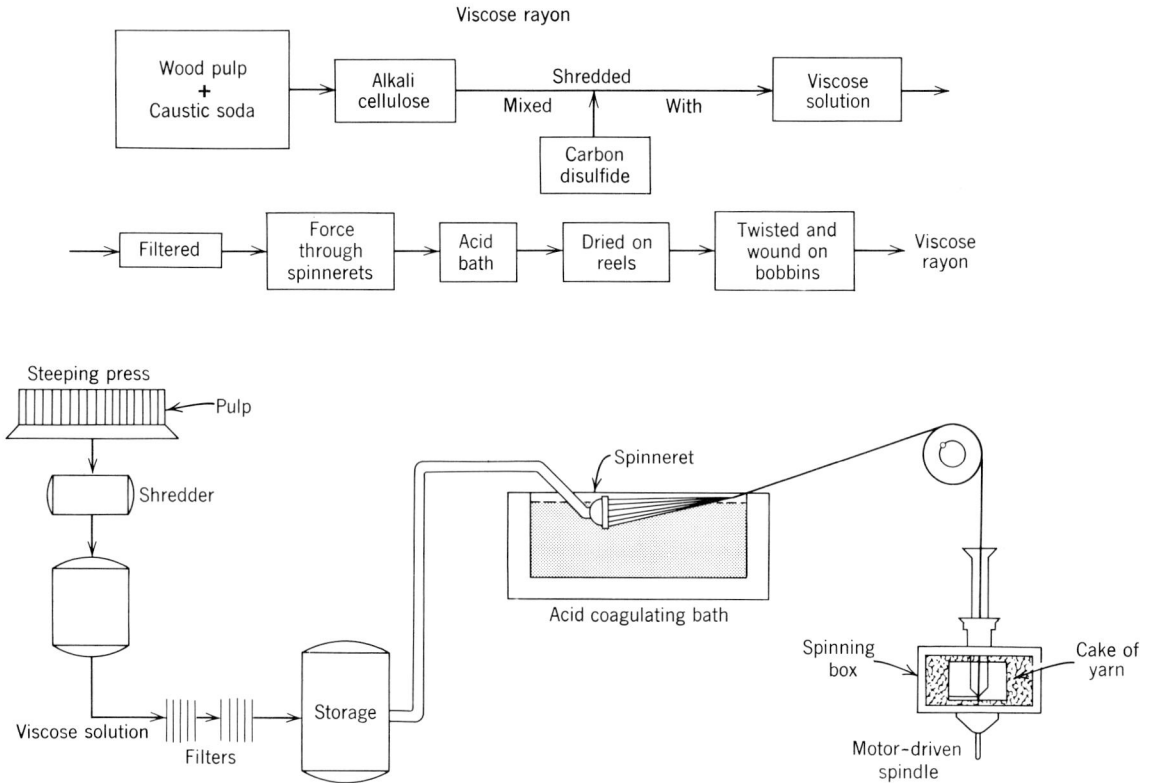

Figure 2-13 Steps in the production of rayon.

the desired properties for end-use requirements. Some of these are high wet strength for washability, wrinkle resistance, crimp for aesthetic appearance, and flame resistance.

High-Strength Viscose Rayon

High-strength rayon is the result of modifications of the regular viscose rayon process of manufacture: decreasing the spinning speed; the addition of zinc sulfate to the coagulating bath; increasing the temperature of the spinning bath; and then stretching the filaments while passing through a hot water bath.

High-strength rayons contribute good properties to fabrics: improved washability, abrasion resistance, and crease resistance.

High Wet-Strength Rayon

To produce a high wet-strength rayon, the fiber producer modifies the regular viscose rayon procedure by omitting or reducing the aging or ripening steps; using a weaker solution of sodium hydroxide in mixing; and using a weaker sulfuric acid coagulation bath. The resultant fiber is more like cotton in its chemical, physical, and mechanical properties. The fibers have higher wet and dry strength than regular rayon: 50 percent stronger dry; 100 percent stronger wet. They absorb less water than conventional rayons and swell less. Fabrics made of the high wet-strength rayon can be given shrinkage treatments to make them dimensionally stable; crease resistant finishes without loss of strength. Finishing treatments used on cotton fabrics can also be applied to fabrics made of high wet-strength rayon fibers.

Self-Crimping Viscose Rayon

Self-crimping viscose may be made in two ways. First, the acidity of the coagulating bath is lowered and the salt content is raised. The second method includes spinning a solution that is fresh and one that has been aged side by side through a spinneret. (See bicomponent fiber, page 41.)

In each method a fiber is produced with two sides that react differently in water. One side of the fiber will swell more than the other and cause the fiber to curl or produce crimp. This property is important to manufacturers of yarns and fabrics. It permits them to create interesting aesthetic effects in wearing apparel and household fabrics.

Viscose Rayon — Built-In Flame Resistance

More than one manufacturer has developed a rayon fiber that is made fire-resistant during the spinning process. Rayon fibers with excellent flame retardancy are produced by mixing a liquid flame retardant with viscose dope before spinning. The flame retardant is described as an organophosphorous compound, 20 to 30 percent by weight. Dispersion of the flame retardant in the fiber does not seriously change or degrade the properties of rayon as do flame-retardant finishes. Fabrics made of this fiber are designed for both wearing apparel and household fabrics. There is no decrease in flame retardancy of fabrics after many launderings and dry cleanings.

RAYON IN CONSUMER USE

There are more than 300 trademark names for rayon fibers. The names most commonly used are given in Appendix A, page 363.

Rayon has many advantages. It is comparatively low in cost. It can be used to make a wide range of fabrics, from very lightweight luxury types to heavy, strong, durable fabrics for both wearing apparel and household use. It dyes and prints easily, offering a wide selection of colors and designs. Rayon can be made to look like cotton, linen, silk, or wool and can be given many different finishes, including a finish that reduces the risk of shrinkage. Rayon is absorbent and, therefore, comfortable to wear; it is resistant to alkalies. It is also resistant to moths.

Rayon can be laundered, wet cleaned, or dry cleaned, depending on dye, finish, design application, and garment design. Rayon fabrics can be bleached with chlorine-type bleaches. It should be ironed at 250°F. Rayon is weakened if ironed at temperatures over 300°F.

Rayon also has some disadvantages. Regular rayon loses nearly 50 percent of its strength when wet, but high wet-strength rayon has good wet strength. Rayon fabrics shrink considerably unless they are stabilized. It has low resiliency and, therefore, wrinkles badly unless given a finish to make it wrinkle-resistant. Lengthy exposure to light weakens rayon, especially when the yarns have been highly pigmented to create a dull yarn appearance. Rayon is susceptible to mildew unless treated to resist it. Rayon is easily damaged by strong acids.

The physical and chemical properties of rayon fibers are given in Table 2-8.

Table 2-8   Rayon Fibers

Fiber Composition

Regenerated cellulose

Physical Properties

1. *Microscopic appearance.* Viscose and high-strength rayon have a number of striations (lines) running the same way as the fiber. If delustered, scattered specks of delustering pigment can be seen. Cuprammonium is smooth in appearance (see Appendix D).
2. *Length.* Any length desired.
3. *Color.* Transparent unless dulled by pigments.
4. *Luster.* High luster unless delustering pigments are added.
5. *Strength.* Fair to excellent. Regular rayon has fair strength. High-tenacity types have good to excellent strength.

Table 2-8   Rayon Fibers *(Cont'd)*

6. *Elasticity.* Varies according to method of manufacture. Regular rayon is low; high-strength rayon, good.
7. *Resiliency.* Regular rayon: low; high wet-strength rayon; medium.
8. *Moisture absorption.* Higher than natural cellulose. Fibers swell in water. Weaker when wet. Unlike cotton, which is stronger when wet. The original dry strength is regained on drying.
9. *Heat.* Loses strength above 300°F. It will decompose between 350 and 400°F. Ironing temperatures of 275°F are satisfactory.
10. *Flammability.* Burns rapidly unless treated.
11. *Electrical conductivity.* Fair. Static charge can be reduced with special finishes.
12. *Specific gravity.* 1.52 (similar to cotton).

Chemical Properties (Similar to Cotton)

1. *Acids.* Like cotton, easily damaged by strong acids. Hot dilute mineral acids or cold concentrated acids will disintegrate the fibers.
2. *Alkalies.* Resistant to alkalies. Concentrated alkalies will cause swelling and reduce strength.
3. *Organic solvents.* Good resistance to dry-cleaning solvents.
4. *Bleaches.* Both oxidizing and reducing bleaches, in the concentrations used in spot and stain removal, may be used on rayon. Temperatures should never be above 120°F. Attacked by strong oxidizing bleaches such as sodium hypochlorite.
5. *Mildew.* Depends on humidity and temperature. Mildew discolors and weakens the fabric. Resists mildew if clean and dry.
6. *Moths, insects.* Resistant to moths. Many fibers, although resistant to moths, may be damaged by insects cutting the fibers to get to a food stain on a fabric.
7. *Light, atmospheric conditions.* Lengthy exposure weakens the fabric.
8. *Dyeing.* Rayon has a greater affinity (attraction) for dyes than cotton. Direct, vat, and sulfur dyes are usually used. Acid dyes are used for modified rayon.

ACETATE

As defined by the Federal Trade Commission, acetate is a manufactured fiber in which the fiber-forming substance is cellulose acetate. Where not less than 92 percent of the hydroxyl groups are acetylated, the term triacetate may be used as a generic description of the fiber.

METHODS OF MANUFACTURE

Two manufacturing processes will be discussed, one for regular or secondary acetate and one for triacetate.

Regular Acetate

Cellulose for the production of acetate is obtained from wood pulp. The cellulose pulp is dissolved by first adding acetic acid and later acetic anhydride. Further treatment produces solid flakes of acetate. These flakes are water washed until free of acid. Acetate fibers are produced by first dissolving the solid cellulose acetate particles in acetone. The spinning solution formed is filtered and pumped through spinnerets against a current of warm air that evaporates the acetone, leaving solid filaments. All the filaments from one spinneret are twisted together and wound onto a bobbin, forming a finished yarn. The acetate yarn is lubri-

Figure 2-14   Production of acetate.

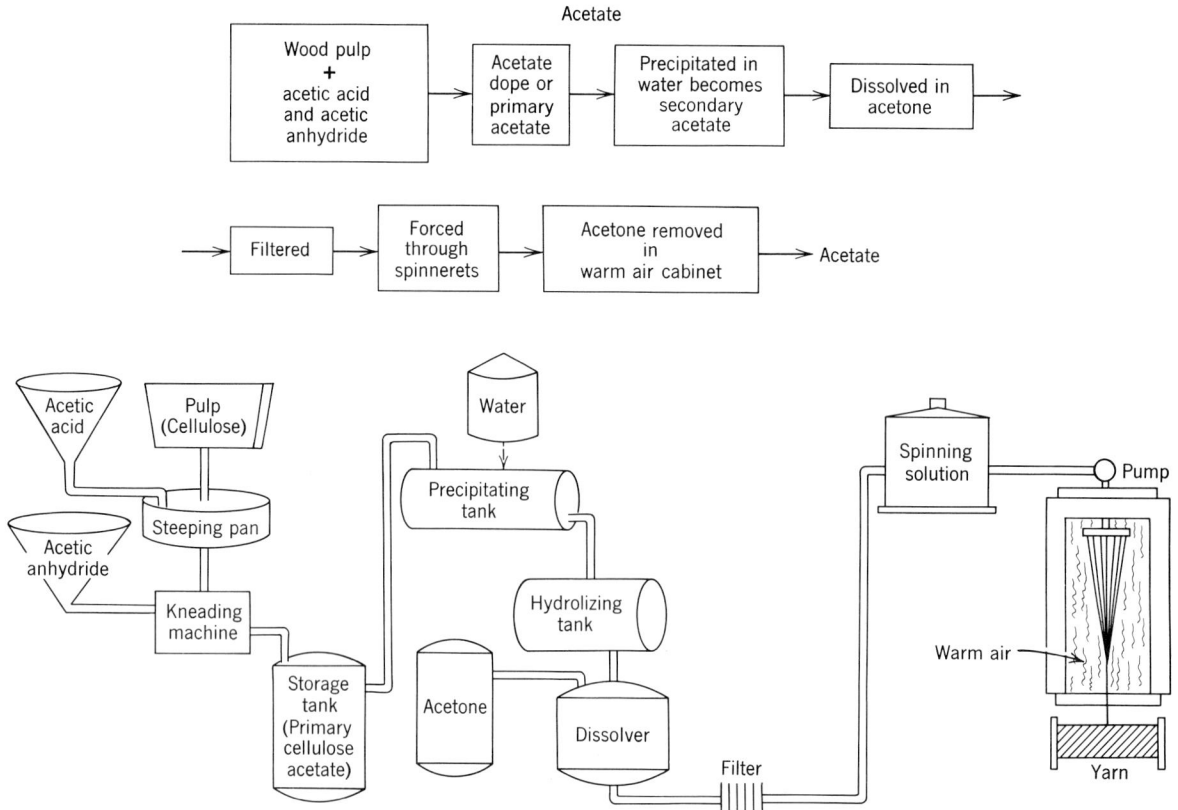

cated to protect it in textile manufacture and to reduce the possibility of static electricity. Acetate filament fibers can be cut to staple lengths and spun into a yarn.

Triacetate

Arnel is the only triacetate fiber and is manufactured only by the Celanese Corporation. It is spun from a solution of cellulose triacetate. The procedure is similar to that for secondary acetate, but the spinning solution of dried triacetate flakes dissolved in methylene chloride is dry spun into a warm air chamber. The ripening stage is omitted in making triacetate.

FIBER MODIFICATIONS

Delustering

Titanium dioxide is added to the spinning solution. Regular acetate is bright and lustrous. The amount of titanium dioxide added controls the final effect from dull to semidull to bright. Dull acetate is damaged readily by sunlight; bright acetate is very resistant. For aesthetics, people prefer the dull to the bright lustrous acetate fabrics. Light and moisture in the atmosphere react with the titanium dioxide to produce hydrogen peroxide. The hydrogen peroxide reacts with the cellulose acetate ether linkage and degradation results. (See Sunlight Resistant Acetate.)

Solution Dyeing

Solution dyeing* was developed to overcome a deficiency of acetate fibers to sunlight and ozone in the atmosphere. The dispersed dyes used to give color to acetate yarns and fabrics changed color because of the nitrogen oxide in the atmosphere. The dye industry, along with the fiber industry, introduced a method of dyeing called solution or dope-dyed fabrics. Pigments in a limited color range were introduced into the viscous solution before it was spun into a filament.

The solution-dyed yarns and fabrics show good colorfastness to sunlight and chlorine.

*Celanese Fiber Company phased out its production of solution-dyed acetate and triacetate in 1975, terminating the use of Celera and Celaperm trademark names.

Crimping

Technological developments also brought about methods and techniques whereby the acetate filament and staple would give a crimp through spinning (self-crimping) and two-faced fibers with the property of water crimping. These fibers are used for batts and interlinings.

Sunlight Resistant Acetate

Presently one company produces a fiber having resistance to ultraviolet degradation not known before in an acetate fiber: Estron SLR — a trademark name of Eastman. Fabrics can be made with dull acetate yarns having resistance to sunlight tenderization because Estron SLR has higher resistance to sunlight than bright acetate yarns. Bright acetate yarns have higher resistance to sunlight degradation than the regular dull acetate yarns.

Although the sunlight resistance of Estron SLR is greater than standard dull acetate, the luster, tensile strength, and atmospheric discoloration are essentially the same as in standard dull acetate.

Flame Resistant Acetate

Several fiber producers have developed acetate fibers with built-in flame resistance. These fibers are expected to find intial use in home furnishings and institutional applications where flame resistance is of prime importance. Because flame resistance is an integral part of the fiber, fabrics properly constructed and processed from FR Acetate are said to withstand washing and dry cleaning without loss of flame resistance.

ACETATE IN CONSUMER USE

There are many trademark names for acetate fibers. The names most commonly used are given in Appendix A, page 363.

Acetate has many advantages. It can be made into a large range of fabrics, sheer to heavy weight, that have a luxurious soft feel, silky appearance, and excellent draping qualities. Acetate is resilient and resists wrinkling. It retains creases and pleats fairly well because of its thermoplastic property. Acetate is faster drying than rayon. It is absorbent; therefore it can be warm or cool, depending on fabric construction. Dilute acidic and alkaline substances have little effect on acetate. It is resistant to mildew and moths.

Acetate requires a special class of dyes for dyeing and printing. Because of its different dyeing characteristics from other fibers, many interesting effects can be created by cross-dyeing and in blends (see page 302). Acetate can be solution-dyed, giving excellent colorfastness properties to wear agencies such as light, atmospheric gas fading, crocking, perspiration, washing, and dry cleaning. Some piece-dyed fabrics, unless treated with an inhibitor or antifume finish, are subject to atmospheric gas fading. Solution-dyed yarns have overcome this problem.

Acetate fabrics may be laundered, wet cleaned, or dry cleaned, depending on dyes, finishes, decorative design, and garment design. To bleach white acetate fabrics, use hydrogen peroxide or sodium perborate-type bleaches or a chlorine-type bleach. Temperature of bath should not exceed 90°F. Acetate loses strength when wet, but not to the degree of rayon.

Acetate has some disadvantages. It is somewhat heat-sensitive. Ironing temperature should not exceed 275°F. It will glaze at 300°F, stick to the iron at 350°F, and melt at 400°F. Acetate is soluble in acetone, acetic acid, alcohol, and other chemicals in this family; some nail polishes and removers contain acetone. Some acetate fabrics generate static electricity and cling to the body; special finishes may be applied to overcome this disadvantage. Lengthy exposure to light weakens acetate fabrics, especially when they have been highly pigmented to make them dull.

CELLULOSE TRIACETATE (ARNEL)

Arnel is made in a large range of fabrics from very sheer lightweight to heavyweight fabrics. It has better resistance to abrasion than acetate and has good stability because it can be heat-set. It takes dye readily, offering a wide selection of colors. Arnel is quick drying and resistant to glazing. It possesses good wrinkle resistance and is resistant to moths and mildew. Arnel fabrics may be made to have durable crease and pleat retention.

Arnel is not affected by weak acidic or alkaline substances. It can be laundered, wet cleaned, or dry cleaned, depending on dyes, finishes, decorative design, and garment design. White Arnel fabrics can be bleached with a chlorine-type bleach. It can be ironed at high ironing temperatures (400 to 425°F). It will discolor at 440°F and melt at 572°F. Unless properly heatset or treated with an antifume finish, the ozone in the air may change the color of some dyes used on Arnel.

The physical and chemical properties of acetate and triacetate fibers are given in Table 2-9.

Table 2-9   Acetate, Triacetate Fibers

Fiber Composition

Acetate, acetate ester of cellulose (secondary acetate), triacetate, triacetate ester of cellulose (ternary acetate).

Physical Properties

1. *Microscopic appearance.* Acetate is uniform in width with longitudinal striations farther apart than viscose rayon. Cross-section is lobed. No sharp serrations like those found in viscose rayon. Triacetate has clearer striations and cross-section may be lobed and serrated (see Appendix D, page 381).
2. *Length.* Both are unlimited, unless cut into staple fibers.
3. *Color.* Both are transparent, unless dulled by pigments.
4. *Luster.* Available either bright, semibright, or dull.
5. *Strength.* Moderate strength. Less than rayon when wet.
6. *Elasticity.* About the same as rayon. Not very high. Triacetate slightly higher than secondary acetate.
7. *Resiliency.* Acetate, poor; triacetate, good.
8. *Moisture absorption.* Acetate, 6.0 percent; triacetate 3.5 percent. Does not lose much strength when wet.
9. *Heat.* Ironing temperatures of 275°F are satisfactory for regular acetate. Triacetate has high heat resistance. Ironing temperatures up to 400°F may be used.
10. *Flammability.* Cellulose acetate and triacetate are slowly combustible but produce a molten material that can cause severe burns.
11. *Electrical conductivity.* Cellulose acetate, good; triacetate, high. High electrical resistance, poor conductor, hence develops static especially when dry.
12. *Specific gravity.* Acetate and triacetate, 1.32.

Chemical Properties

1. *Acids.* Unaffected by solutions of acids used as spotting agents. Concentrated strong acids will decompose it. Acetic acid cannot be used over 33 percent concentration.
2. *Alkalies.* Diluted solution of alkalies have little effect. Strong alkalies will damage it.
3. *Organic solvents.* Dry-cleaning solvents do not damage acetate fibers. Regular acetate is soluble in acetone, over 33 percent acetic acid, chloroform, formic acid 88 percent, over 10 percent pyridine, and a mixture of alcohol (methyl) and benzene. Trichlorethylene causes some swelling of acetate fibers and will bleed many acetate dyes, especially when warm. Triacetate is also damaged by the chemicals mentioned.
4. *Bleaches.* In recommended concentrations oxidizing and reducing bleaches are safe. Strong oxidizing agents will damage acetate.
5. *Mildew.* Resistant to mildew; may cause discoloration.
6. *Moths, insects.* Resistant to moths and insects.

Table 2-9   Acetate, Triacetate Fibers *(Cont'd)*

7. *Light, atmospheric conditions.* Long exposures to sunlight produce a weakening effect on acetate. Triacetate more resistant.
8. *Dyeing.* Special dyes called acetate dyes are used to dye acetate. These dyes bleed to alcohol if dry-cleaned while wet with water. Acetate can also be dyed while in solution. Solution-dyed acetate fibers have excellent colorfastness properties.

GLASS

Glass is classed as an inorganic fiber made from borosilicate glasses. As defined by the Federal Trade Commission, glass is a manufactured fiber in which the fiber-forming substance is glass.

MANUFACTURE

The basic raw materials of glass are silica, sand, and limestone. Other ingredients are aluminum hydroxide, soda ash, and borax. The raw materials are mixed according to formulas and prepared in precisely controlled furnaces. The molten glass flows to marble-forming machines that turn out small glass marbles. One reason for forming these marbles is to permit visual inspection for impurities. The marbles are remelted in small electric furnaces. The melted glass is forced through small holes at the base of the furnace, forming filaments of glass fibers. The filaments are drawn out and twisted to form yarns (see Figure 2-15). It is predicted that a new process may replace the present forming process for a number of products. The process uses a pressurized system instead of gravity to form the fiber.

Figure 2-15 Flow diagram of the production of glass fiber.

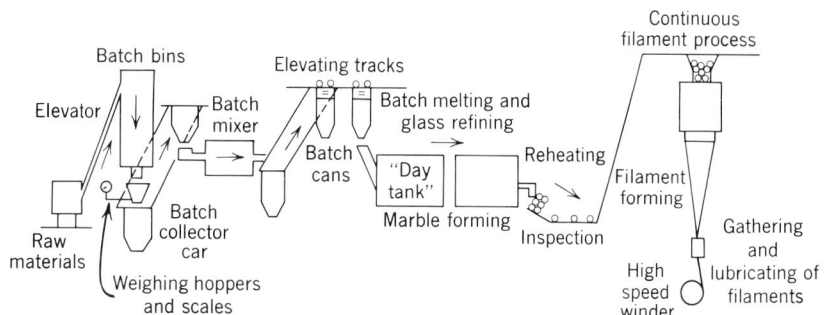

GLASS IN CONSUMER USE

It is truly a miracle when you think that man can take a glass marble, melt it, and draw it to very fine filaments that can be made into yarns and then fabric. Glass filaments can also be cut in short lengths, spun into yarns, and made into fabrics. Because this is possible, glass fabrics can range from shiny, smooth-surfaced fabrics to dull, textured-looking surfaces that are hardly recognizable as glass fabrics.

Glass fiber is used to make fabrics for curtains, draperies, bedspreads, and tablecloths, and it is predicted that glass will be used in carpeting soon. At present, manufacturers are experimenting, trying to make glass fabrics suitable for wearing apparel, but so far this has not been possible because of glass irritant characters when it penetrates the skin pores.

Glass fibers are also used in the manufacture of electrical insulation, flame-resistant fabrics and decorations (where safety is a factor), and filter cloths. Some of the common trademark names are Beta, Fiberglas, Fiberfrax Ceramic Fiber, PPF Fiber Glass, Unifab, Uniformat, and Unirove.

Glass is very strong and is weather- and sun-resistant, which is why it is in demand in homes for draperies where the fabrics are exposed to large window areas. In hospitals and homes for the aging where precautions must be taken against fire hazards, glass is used almost exclusively, since it will not burn. Another advantage is that soil is easily removed, unless it is allowed to become ground or embedded in the interstices of the fabric. It does not absorb moisture — an important quality in curtain and drapery fabrics. It is not damaged by moths, mildew, and many chemical substances it comes in contact with during use and cleaning.

Glass fibers have very low abrasion resistance. For example, curtains and draperies may show wear if they are drawn across a window sill or floor or across the edge of the top of the rod in drawn draperies. This can be accommodated by making double headers and hems so that if this condition occurs in use, the hem and header can be changed to hide this damage. In some constructions, seams and yarn slippage may occur because of the smoothness of the yarns.

Because of its low absorption ability, dyeing and printing of glass is limited. A process called "Coronizing" enables colors and prints to be applied more readily. The process involves the padding or saturation of the fabric with a colloidal suspension, followed by heat-setting. After this, the pigment is applied with a resin, dried, and treated with a compound to give good colorfastness. The fabric is dried and this process softens and flattens the yarn to prevent yarn and seam slippage.

I have learned from research that many glass fabrics can be dry-cleaned satisfactorily. In fact, many glass draperies must be dry-cleaned to remove the oily, sooty materials they encounter in use. The majority of manufacturers have chosen to go the laundering or wet-cleaning route only because of costs involved to produce a dry-cleanable fabric. For this reason, it is recommended that glass curtains and draperies be wet-cleaned or laundered. Although manufacturers recommend washing at home, many home installations are so large that it is impossible to handle the item in the bathtub, washtubs, or the home washing equipment. Therefore there is a need for professional wet-cleaning service.

Glass fibers are easily damaged by excessive mechanical action in use and in cleaning. White glass may be bleached with chlorine-type bleaches. It is attacked by weak alkaline solutions and hydrofluoric acid that is sometimes needed to remove spots and stains. Glass fabric should be finished with steam. Temperature should not exceed 500 to 550°F.

BETA FIBERGLAS

Bedspreads, throws, coverlets, decorative pillows, and flounces of Fiberglas Beta yarn are being made in a variety of colors, prints, textures, and weaves. It is a superfine glass yarn created and manufactured by Owens-Corning Fiberglas Corporation. The filaments of the new yarn are approximately one third the diameter of any fiber being used in glass textiles. These filaments are less than one half the thickness of silk, one third that of cotton, one fourth that of the finest wool, and one fifth the thickness of rayon, nylon, and other synthetics. Fabrics woven of the new yarn have a look and hand never before attained with glass. It is difficult to distinguish them from fabrics made from rayon, acetate, and other synthetic yarns.

The manufacturers cite several definite plus factors of fabrics made with the Beta yarn. They state that the unusual fineness of the yarn imparts a softness of hand, a draping quality, and an ease in sewing that has never been attainable before with glass. Fabrics made of this yarn are easy to sew without any special equipment.

Some of the special performance qualities claimed for fabrics made of Fiberglas Beta are that they cannot burn, shrink, sag or stretch, rot or mildew; they resist wrinkles, soil, and spots; they can be washed or wet-cleaned with minimum effort; and they do not need to be ironed. The manufacturer also states that because of its very fine filament, the new yarn has improved wear and flex strength. Abrasion resistance is improved. This allows the use of draperies woven from this yarn in areas where glass fiber materials may have been considered impractical because of excessive wear.

The physical and chemical properties of glass fibers are given in Table 2-10.

Table 2-10   Glass Fibers

Chemical Composition

Borosilicate

Physical Properties

1. *Microscopic appearance.* Smooth, rodlike appearance (see Appendix D).
2. *Length.* Either filament or staple fibers.
3. *Color.* Colorless or white.
4. *Luster.* Good.
5. *Strength.* Strongest of all fibers; 204,000 to 220,000 pounds per square inch. Stronger than a steel wire of the same diameter.
6. *Elasticity.* Good.
7. *Resiliency.* In fiber form for industrial batts, excellent.
8. *Moisture absorption.* No moisture absorption. Not affected by water. No shrinkage. Good wrinkle resistance.
9. *Heat.* Fireproof. Strength begins to decrease at 600°F. Melts at 900°F.
10. *Flammability.* Nonflammable, melts with decomposition. Excellent for cubicle curtains in hospitals and homes for the aging.
11. *Electrical conductivity.* Excellent.
12. *Specific gravity.* 2.5 (dense but modern technology has produced fine fibers.)

Chemical Properties

1. *Acids.* Resistant. Not affected by acids used for spot and stain removal, except hydrofluoric acid in rust removers. To remove rust on glass fibers, use oxalic acid.
2. *Alkalies.* Not affected by alkalies in concentrations used in spot and stain removal. Attacked by hot solutions of weak alkalies and cold solutions of strong alkalies.
3. *Organic solvents.* Resistant to all dry-cleaning solvents. Colors affected to a greater extent in perchlorethylene than petroleum solvents.
4. *Bleaches.* Not affected by oxidizing and reducing bleaches in the concentration used for spot and stain removal.
5. *Mildew.* Wholly resistant to mildew.
6. *Insects, moths.* Wholly resistant.
7. *Light, atmospheric conditions.* No strength loss from sunlight and conditions of weathering. Some colors may be affected.
8. *Dyeing.* Resin-bonded pigments are primarily used. Solution dyeing has been used, but limited color range has restricted its use.

PART IV
MINOR MAN-MADE FIBERS

RUBBER (RUBBER, POLYISOPRENE)

The Federal Trade Commission amended the definition of rubber in February 1966. They redefined rubber as a fiber in which the fiber-forming substance is comprised of natural and/or synthetic rubber, including Lastocarb, Lastride, and Lastrochlor.

MANUFACTURE

Synthetic rubber is classed as a man-made elastomer that has many of the properties of natural rubber without some of natural rubber's limitations. Fiber may be made by the same method as for cultural rubber: by cutting and by extrusion through a spinneret. Synthetic rubber may be used alone or covered with a textile yarn (see discussion on core yarns, pages 129 and 146).

SYNTHETIC RUBBER IN CONSUMER USE

Synthetic rubber compares favorably with natural rubber in strength and holding power. The end uses of synthetic rubber are generally the same as for natural rubber.

Synthetic rubber may be dry-cleaned, wet-cleaned, or laundered. If not properly cured, synthetic rubber may become tacky from perspiration and dry cleaning. Strains from stretching may cause the yarns to break, resulting in loss of elasticity.

SPANDEX

As defined by the Federal Trade Commission, spandex is a manufactured fiber in which the fiber-forming substance is a long-chain synthetic polymer comprised of at least 85 percent of a segmented polyurethane.

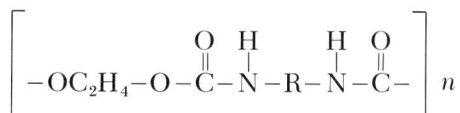

$$\left[-OC_2H_4-O-\overset{\overset{\displaystyle O}{\|}}{C}-\overset{\overset{\displaystyle H}{|}}{N}-R-\overset{\overset{\displaystyle H}{|}}{N}-\overset{\overset{\displaystyle O}{\|}}{C}- \right]_n$$

MANUFACTURE

The spandex fibers are elastic fibers used for many of the same uses as are the rubber fibers. However, these synthetic elastomers are quite different from rubber chemically. Like the other synthetic fibers, the spandex fibers are formed by forcing a liquid through spinnerets.

Many methods can be utilized for the production of spandex: (1) from polyurethane through normal rubber processing procedures; (2) by dry-spinning from a solvent solution of a polyurethane into a heated chamber; (3) by wet-spinning a urethane polymer into a coagulating bath; and (4) by melt-spinning a solid urethane polymer.

SPANDEX IN CONSUMER USE

Spandex can be used uncovered or covered with other textile yarns to make both woven and knitted fabrics used for delicate laces, shirtings, suitings, slacks, jackets, ski pants, bathing suits, intimate apparel, and household and other items where stretch is desired.

Common trademark names are Glospun, Lycra, Numa, Unel, and Vyrene. Monvelle is a new heterogeneous hosiery yarn of spandex and nylon (see Appendix A).

Spandex is superior to rubber in resistance to sunlight, weather, abrasion, oils, and flexing. Spandex has the ability to spring back to its original shape. After repeated stretching, it shows only a small increase in length. Even though it possesses a low tensile strength compared to most other synthetic fibers, fabrics made of it have good holding power. Spandex may be used to make a wide range of fabrics, from light, sheer fabrics with good strength to heavier-weight fabrics with good control. It resists deterioration caused by oxidation, perspiration, cosmetic oils, and lotions.

Fabrics made of spandex may be dry-cleaned, wet-cleaned, or laundered, depending on garment construction. Avoid high temperatures in laundering or wet cleaning. Repeated machine laundering and tumble drying can result in loss of strength and elasticity and gray discoloration. Avoid the use of chlorine bleaches as chlorine causes degradation. Over a period of long use and storage from one season to another, chlorine from the water in swimming pools can cause degradation of spandex in swimsuits. Some consumers have complained of dermatitis from intimate apparel containing spandex but, spandex producers have refuted these complaints.

Early fabrics had a tendency to discolor quickly with wear. Some improvement has been made with this problem. New finishes have been developed to check yellowing of either the bare or covered spandex fabrics. Physical and chemical properties of spandex fibers are given in Table 2-11.

Table 2-11 Spandex Fibers

Fiber Composition
Synthetic polymer with a minimum 85 percent of segmented poly-urethane.

Physical Properties
1. *Microscopic appearance.* Relatively smooth even appearance. See Appendix D.
2. *Length.* Can be any length. May be used as filament or staple fiber.
3. *Color.* White or nearly white.
4. *Luster.* Usually dull luster.
5. *Strength.* Low strength compared to most other synthetic fibers.
6. *Elasticity.* Elastic properties are excellent. This is the outstanding characteristic of the fiber.
7. *Resiliency.* Very good.
8. *Moisture Absorption.* Very low, less than 1 percent at 65 percent relative humidity and 70°F. Not appreciably affected by water.
9. *Heat.* The heat resistance varies considerably among the different types. Some spandex fibers are damaged at 250°F. Yellows and degrades over 300°F. Ironing temperature should not exceed 250°F.
10. *Flammability.* Burns slowly.
11. *Electrical conductivity.* Low.
12. *Specific gravity.* 1.21 to 1.35. Low. See Appendix F.

Chemical Properties
1. *Acids.* Good resistance to most acids, unless exposure is over 24 hours.
2. *Alkalies.* Good resistance to most alkalies. Hot alkalies will damage some types more than others.
3. *Organic solvents.* Resistant to dry-cleaning solvents.
4. *Bleaches.* Can be degraded by sodium hypochlorite (chlorine bleach). Chlorine bleach should not be used.
5. *Mildew.* Not affected.
6. *Moths, insects.* Not attacked.
7. *Light, atmospheric conditions.* Resistant.
8. *Dyeing.* A full range of color is available. Some types are more difficult to dye than others. Can be dyed with acid, dispersed dyes, and some other dyes.

ANIDEX

The Federal Trade Commission, in September 1969, established and defined Anidex as a manufactured fiber in which the fiber-forming substance is any long chain of synthetic polymer composed of at least 50 percent of weight of one or more esters of a monohydric alcohol and acrylic acid. It is not currently used in the United States.

$$\begin{bmatrix} \begin{array}{c} \text{H} \quad \text{H} \\ -\text{C}-\text{C}- \\ \text{H} \quad | \\ \quad \text{C}=\text{O} \\ \quad | \\ \quad \text{O} \\ \quad \text{R} \end{array} \end{bmatrix}_n$$

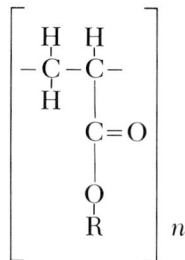

Chemical unit of Anidex

SARAN

As defined by the Federal Trade Commission, saran is a manufactured fiber in which the fiber-forming substance is any long-chain synthetic polymer composed of at least 80 percent by weight of vinylidene chloride units (CH_2-CCl_2-).

MANUFACTURE

Vinylidene chloride is the basic fiber substance. Sometimes this is polymerized with vinyl chloride or vinyl cyanide in the presence of heat and a catalyst. The hot liquid is forced through spinnerets to form fibers. The fibers are drawn and stretched to impart desirable fiber characteristics. See Fig. 2-16.

SARAN IN CONSUMER USE

The saran fibers have limited uses in clothing. They are especially suited to weather-resistant furniture and household applications, including carpeting. They are used generally in monofilament form, but some staple fiber is used for "diffusion-" type drapery clothes. The fabrics are stiff and heavy compared with dress goods.

Saran is extremely resistant to acidic and alkaline substances. It has a natural resistance to staining and is weather-resistant. Saran is flame-resistant; it does not support combustion. Saran fibers are solution-dyed; therefore they possess good colorfastness to light. However, this also limits the range in colors. Saran fabrics have good abrasion resistance and are resistant to moths and mildew. Saran is resistant to moisture, a desirable property for curtain, drapery, and upholstery fabrics. In some constructions, saran fabrics provide sound control, heat control, and sun glare control. However, ultraviolet light turns saran brown. Saran fabrics may be wet-cleaned or dry-cleaned, depending on the construction of the item. Temperature should not exceed 100°F. However, it should be dry-cleaned in petroleum solvent. Saran yarns shrink when dry-cleaned in perchlorethylene.

Figure 2-16 Saran curled staple is unique in the field of man-made fibers in that the curl is inherent and closely simulates that of natural wool. Only under microscopic examination is this curl distinguishable from wool. Saran curled staple lends itself perfectly to processing on conventional woolen or worsted systems.

In wet cleaning or laundering, chlorine-type bleach may be used on white fabrics, but bath temperature should not exceed 100°F. Saran should not be dried at temperatures above 140°F. Wrinkles from use and cleaning are difficult to remove. Fabrics cannot be pressed, because the steam required for finishing causes excessive shrinkage of the fabric. Temperatures over 160°F cause shrinkage and sticking; higher temperatures cause fabric damage.

Physical and chemical properties of saran fibers are given in Table 2-12.

Table 2-12   Saran Fibers

Fiber Composition
Eighty percent by weight of vinylidene.

Physical Properties
1. *Microscopic appearance.* Smooth uniform outer surface (see Appendix D).
2. *Length.* Made in both filament and staple form.
3. *Color.* Depends on pigmentation of fiber.
4. *Luster.* High luster unless dulled by pigments.
5. *Strength.* Good.
6. *Elasticity.* Good.
7. *Resiliency.* Good.
8. *Moisture absorption.* None at 70°F and 65 percent relative humidity. Low moisture regain.
9. *Heat.* Low resistance. Softens at 240 to 280°F.
10. *Flammability.* Self-extinguishing.
11. *Electrical conductivity.* Good.
12. *Specific gravity.* 1.7 High.

Chemical Properties
1. *Acids.* Resistant to acids at room temperature. Some effect from concentrated sulfuric acid over extended period of time.
2. *Alkalies.* Resistant to most alkalies, except concentrated ammonium hydroxide.
3. *Organic solvents.* Synthetic solvents (perchlorethylene) causes softening and swelling of saran. Unaffected by petroleum solvents.
4. *Bleaches.* Not harmed by oxidizing and reducing bleaches in concentrations used.
5. *Mildew.* Not attacked by mildew.
6. *Moths, insects.* Not attacked by moths.
7. *Light, atmospheric conditions.* Darkens on exposure. Does not cause strength loss.
8. *Dyeing.* Usually pigment dyed in spinning solution before spun. Can also be dyed with acetate dyes.

VINYON

As defined by the Federal Trade Commission, vinyon is a manufactured fiber in which the fiber-forming substance is any long-chain synthetic polymer composed of at least 85 percent by weight of vinyl chloride units (CH_2-CH-).

$$CL$$

MANUFACTURE

Vinyon fibers are either polymers of vinyl chloride or copolymers of vinyl chloride and vinyl acetate. The chemicals are polymerized under pressure or by use of catalyst. The polymer is dissolved in a solvent. The viscous solution is filtered and then forced through spinnerets into water or warm air. The fibers are stretched to impart the desired characteristics.

VINYON IN CONSUMER USE

Vinyon is no longer manufactured in the United States for wearing apparel fabrics. Rhovyl is manufactured and imported from France, Movil from Italy, and Kurchalon from Japan. These are tradenames that appear on labels. Vinyon fibers are nonflammable as well as being sunlight-, mildew-, and weather-resistant. The fiber may be solution-dyed for good colorfastness. It can be blended with other fibers. Fabrics possess good insulating properties.

Since the fiber is thermoplastic at temperatures above 212°F, fabrics made from it can be heat stamped, embossed, and permanently pleated. The thermoplastic property permits bonding, sealing, fusing, shaping, and molding.

Rhovyl is made in two basic forms — Rhovyl T, a non-shrink fiber that is dimensionally stable, and Rhovyl 55. The latter can shrink up to 55 percent at 212°F. It will melt at 365°F. Because of its heat-shrinking ability, it is used to an advantage in producing three-dimensional effects, two-height pile fabrics, sculptured suede, and bulk-type fabrics. Rhovyl fabrics made of yarns that are not relaxed by heat when manufactured may shrink when the fabric is finished or pressed. Regardless of tradenames, if the heat-sensitive vinyon fiber is not labeled, items that are tumble dried and steam finished shrink excessively.

The physical and chemical properties of vinyon fibers are given in Table 2-13.

Table 2-13   Vinyon Fibers

Fiber Composition
Copolymer, vinyl chloride and vinyl acetate.

Physical Properties
1. *Microscopic appearance.* Round, smooth, regular, and clear. Dog bone cross section.
2. *Length.* Staple length as desired; also filament.
3. *Color.* White.
4. *Luster.* Translucent.
5. *Strength.* Controlled, low to high.
6. *Elasticity.* Low for strong fibers; high for weak fibers.
7. *Resiliency.* Low to medium.
8. *Moisture absorption.* Low.
9. *Heat.* Very heat sensitive. Softening temperature 150°F.
10. *Flammability.* Does not support combustion.
11. *Electrical conductivity.* Poor, and generates an electric charge through friction.
12. *Specific gravity.* 1.53 to 1.35.

Chemical Properties
1. *Acids.* Resistant to weak acids; generally resistant to strong acids.
2. *Alkalies.* Resistant to weak and strong alkalies.
3. *Organic solvents.* Unaffected by petroleum dry-cleaning solvents. Slight swelling in perchlorethylene. Can be damaged by acetone in spot and stain removal.
4. *Bleaches.* Resistant to bleaches.
5. *Mildew.* Resistant.
6. *Moths, insects.* Resistant.
7. *Light, atmospheric conditions.* Resistant.
8. *Dyeing.* Dispersed dyes with swelling agents; acetate and naphthol dyes with swelling agents.

VINAL

As defined by the Federal Trade Commission, vinal is a manufactured fiber in which the fiber-forming substance is any long-chain synthetic polymer composed of at least 50 percent by weight of vinyl alcohol units $(CH_2-CHOH-)$ and in which the total of the vinyl alcohol units and any one or more of the various acetal units is at least 85 percent by weight of the fiber. Vinylon is the common international designation for fibers of polyvinyl alcohol.

MANUFACTURE

The polymer from which the fiber is spun is made from the hydrolysis of poly (vinyl acetate). Poly (vinyl alcohol) is water-soluble. The fiber is treated with formaldehyde to make it insoluble. This cross linking makes a stable fiber.

VINAL IN CONSUMER USE

Vinal is not manufactured in the United States. Air Reduction Company is the United States licensee on the process of Kurashiki Rayon of Japan for making polyvinyl alcohol resin and Vinylon fiber. Air Reduction has the right to license other companies here. The firm was given the generic term Vinal to identify Vinylon. The yarn and fabric are imported from Japan.

Vinal may be combined with both natural and synthetic fibers. It has high tensile and tear strength. Vinal is a good compromise between hydrophobic and hydrophilic fibers. This contributes a comfort factor in wearing apparel fabrics. It contributes a pleasing hand to knit constructions. Vinal is resistant to abrasion, chemicals at moderate temperatures, and microbiological attack. It is sun- and weather-resistant. It can be dyed readily with dyes that are resistant to sunlight.

Vinal is softened to some extent by water at high temperatures. It should not be put under any strain while wet. It can be bleached with hypochlorite or chlorite bleaches or with hydrogen peroxide under controlled conditions. Vinal fabrics should not be pressed while damp or wet. This may cause stiffness and glazing.

The physical and chemical properties of vinal fibers are given in Table 2-14.

Table 2-14   Vinal Fibers

Fiber Composition

Polyvinyl alcohol.

Physical Appearance

1. *Microscopic appearance.* Smooth, faint striations; cross section, bean shaped.
2. *Length.* Available in both filament and staple length.
3. *Color.* White.
4. *Luster.* Can be made bright, semidull, dull.
5. *Strength.* Good. Approximately 25 percent weaker when wet then when dry.

Table 2-14   Vinal Fibers *(Cont'd)*

6. *Elasticity.* Good. The higher the molecular orientation, the lower the elasticity.
7. *Resiliency.* Low.
8. *Moisture absorption.* Low.
9. *Heat.* Shrinks 1 percent at 212 to 230°F in dry heat, 1.5 to 10 percent in moist heat at 122 to 212°F. Melts at 425°F.
10. *Flammability.* Burns with difficulty.
11. *Electrical conductivity.* Moderate.
12. *Specific gravity.* 1.30.

Chemical Properties

1. *Acids.* Resistant to weak acids; attacked by strong acids.
2. *Alkalies.* Resistant to weak and strong alkalies.
3. *Organic solvents.* Resistant. Attacked by phenol.
4. *Bleaches.* Use chlorine bleaches. Dissolved by oxygen bleaches such as hydrogen perioxide unless controlled.
5. *Mildew.* Resistant.
6. *Moths, insects.* Resistant.
7. *Light, atmospheric conditions.* Weakening occurs on prolonged exposure to sunlight.
8. *Dyeing.* Acid, basic, and dispersed dyestuffs.

AZLON (MAN-MADE PROTEIN)

The Federal Trade Commission defines azlon as a manufactured fiber in which the fiber-forming substance is composed of any regenerated, naturally occurring protein.

Azlon fibers are not currently in production in the United States. Some azlon fibers are produced in Europe: *Fibrolane* (England) and *Merinova* (Italy). Chinon is imported from Japan.

CHINON

The Federal Trade Commission has been asked to give a special generic designation for Chinon. Until this is accepted or rejected, Toyobo will use the designation of azlon.

According to the application to FTC, the fiber is composed of about 30 percent by weight of casein, which has been chemically modified by the grafting thereon of vinyl monomers, including acrylonitrile. It is the first man-made fiber that is a copolymer of natural protein combined with acrylic resins.

Toyobo Co., Ltd. of Japan has been commercially producing Chinon for more than two years. In Japan about 60 percent of the production goes into the manufacture of the native Japanese kimonos and 40 percent into Western clothes. Some of the fiber and fabrics have been exported to France, West Germany, and Britain.

Beaunit Corporation has an agreement with Toyobo whereby it will market Chinon fiber and fabric in the United States. At the present time, the company is only importing limited quantities.

The manufacturer of this fiber states that Chinon fabrics have aesthetic properties closest to silk. They are: warm texture, excellent drapability, and silky rustling; elegant deep luster; excellent affinity with any type of dyes and clear, beautiful dye acceptance (better than that of silk); no waxiness; little static electricity charge; excellent colorfastness to sunlight and little yellowing; and lightweight, crease-free, and easy care.

Chinon can be dyed or printed. Acid dyestuffs mainly are used for dyeing Chinon. When bright or fluorescent hues are required, cationic dyestuffs are used. Other dyestuffs, such as anionic dispersed, are chosen according to the expected end use of the dyed fabric.

Chinon fabrics are delicate and should be handled like any fine silk fabric. The manufacturer lists these instructions on use and care: Drycleaning is recommended. Some Chinon fabrics are washable. Iron at a low temperature (dry heat or below 120°C.), using an ironing cloth. Avoid steam ironing.

Unlike silk, Chinon is mothproof and mildew-proof.

NYTRIL

Nytril is a manufactured fiber containing at least 85 percent of a long-chain polymer of vinylidene dinitrile ($-CH_2-C(CN)_2-$) where the vinylidene dinitrile content is no less than every other unit in the polymer chain.

The United States production of nytril fibers was discontinued in mid-1961. It was sold under the trademark name of DARVAN. The B. F. Goodrich Chemical Company was the original producer. They sold patent rights to the Celanese Fiber Company.

METALLIC

As defined by the Federal Trade Commission, metallic is a manufactured fiber composed of metal, plastic-coated metal, metal-coated plastic, or a core completely covered by metal.

MANUFACTURE

There are several manufacturing methods. In one, a thin sheet of aluminum foil is sandwiched between two layers of plastic. An adhesive bonds together the plastic and metal. The plastic film may be an acetate or polyester type film. To obtain colors other than silver (the color of aluminum), metallic pigments are added to the adhesive bonding agent.

In another method, metallic pigments are deposited on a plastic film that is then covered by clear plastic film. Sometimes plain metal may be used. However, the plastic-coated types are the most popular. The metallic fibers may be combined with other textile fibers to give a stronger yarn. Plastic-coated metallic yarns are discussed in more detail in Chapter 3, page 134.

METAL IN CONSUMER USE

During the past few years, the variety of metallic fibers commercially available has increased rapidly. These now include: stainless steel, chromium nickel alloys, platinum, titanium, copper, aluminum, beryllium, and tungsten.

The concept of using metallic copper, zircon, and stainless fibers in carpet yarn for permanent static control represents a new development that has proven valid and is now becoming widely accepted.

Metallic fabrics can be manufactured in an unlimited range of weights and densities from flimsy fabrics of tungsten as sheer as the sheerest nylon stockings to heavy industrial fabrics. In precious metals, the finest goes to 0.0045 inch for pure silver and to 0.0025 inch for gold-plated copper. Knit fabrics can be made on standard circular knitting machines with modified heads.

PART V
NEW FIBER CLASSIFICATIONS

ARAMID

As defined by the Federal Trade Commission, aramid is a manufactured fiber in which the fiber-forming substance is a long-chain synthetic polyamide in which at least 85 percent of the amide linkages are attached directly to two aromatic rings.

E. I. DuPont de Nemours and Company manufactures aramid. Up to the time of the FTC's decision of a new generic classification, the fiber was described as nylon. Since aramid fell within the definition of nylon, the commission has redefined nylon to exclude Nomex and Kevlar (trademark names of the DuPont Company). The FTC explains that aramid and the conventional type nylon differ significantly in chemical structure and properties. The unique qualities of aramid fibers includes high tensile strength, heat resistance, and toughness.

Nomex is a high temperature resistant product used in space suits, military fabrics, and protective clothing. There are two types of Kevlar, one for tires and the other for reinforcing plastics.

Nomex has a future in consumer goods, since the fiber is inherently flame-retardant. Developed for the space program, it is now being used in consumer goods — pajamas, cubical curtains, pillows, pillow cases, sheets, robes, ironing board covers, protective clothing, career apparel, upholstery, drapery fabrics, and carpeting. A big breakthrough occurred when it was discovered that a pigment dye system that is flameproof can be used to give Nomex color and design. Up to this time it was necessary to rely on expensive solution dyeing or yarn dyeing.

Kevlar has been recently commercialized for use in tire cords. It is stronger than steel fibers, bonds well to the rubber of the tire, has high flex and temperature resistance, and does not flat spot as readily as nylon.

The physical and chemical properties of aramid fibers are given in Table 2-15.

Table 2-15   Aramid Fibers

Fiber Composition

Polyamide

Physical Properties
1. *Microscopic appearance.* Very similar to other nylon fibers.
2. *Length.* Filament, staple and tow.
3. *Color.* Off white.

Table 2-15   Aramid Fibers *(Cont'd)*

4. *Luster.* Varies.
5. *Strength.* High. Wet strength is 75 percent of dry strength.
6. *Elasticity.* High.
7. *Resiliency.* Good.
8. *Moisture absorption.* Low.
9. *Heat.* Not affected by dry heat.
10. *Flammability.* Very resistant. Does not melt or drip. Above 700°F degrades.
11. *Electrical conductivity.* Good.
12. *Specific gravity.* 1.38.

Chemical Properties

1. *Acids.* Better than nylon 6.6; not as good as polyester or acrylic.
2. *Alkalies.* Good resistance. Degraded by strong alkalies at elevated temperatures.
3. *Organic solvents.* Resistant.
4. *Bleaches.* Resistant to chlorine and oxygen bleaches.
5. *Mildew.* Resistant.
6. *Moths, insects.* Resistant.
7. *Light, atmospheric conditions.* Protect from the direct rays of light of the sun and other sources of ultraviolet light.
8. *Dyeing.* Cationic dyes. Other classes of dye exhibit no affinity for aramid fibers.

NOVOLOID

The Federal Trade Commission recently established a new generic name, "novoloid," for a fiber manufactured by Carborundum Company, Niagara Falls, New York. The new generic classification became effective on February 15, 1974.

By definition, the FTC describes novoloid as a manufactured fiber containing at least 85 percent by weight of cross-linked novolac.

Carborundum has been marketing the fiber under the tradename Kynol. The manufacturer states that Kynol is more flame-resistant than any other man-made organic fiber. It is superior to high-temperature polyamides such as aramid, glass fibers, and other recently developed fibrous materials in withstanding high-temperature flames. The phenomenon of charring without melting is due to the nature of Kynol's structure, which consists of aromatic molecules cross-linked in a novel manner.

Fabrics are available in a variety of weights, weave styles, and widths. Fabrics made from 100 percent Kynol fiber or from blends with other natural or synthetic fibers can be made. Engineered fabrics incorporating Kynol fiber are being used for protective clothing, curtains, upholstery, and many other applications where flame resistance is the prime requirement.

A quilted structure may be made by using 100 percent Kynol batting of various weights as the filler material and Kynol fabrics or other synthetic or natural fabrics as the face materials. A large variety of stitch patterns and batting-fabric combinations can be designed to produce quilted yard goods for use in garments, gloves, and similar products. Again, flame resistance and good insulating properties are the prime factors for selecting this material.

The physical and chemical properties of novoloid fibers are given in Table 2-16.

Table 2-16 Novoloid Fibers

Fiber Composition
Novolac

Physical Properties
1. *Microscopic appearance.* Longitudinal, smooth, uniform diameter, translucent; cross section, round or oval, translucent.
2. *Length.* Staple and filament.
3. *Color.* Golden-hued.
4. *Luster.* Semibright.
5. *Strength.* Good because of cross-linked amorphous structure.
6. *Elasticity.* Good.
7. *Resiliency.* Good.
8. *Moisture absorption.* Similar to polyamide fiber.
9. *Heat.* High resistance.
10. *Flammability.* Very resistant. Chars without melting due to aromatic molecules cross-linked in novel manner.
11. *Electrical conductivity.* None. Good dielectric insulator.
12. *Specific gravity.* 1.25.

Chemical Properties
1. *Acid.* Resistant to all nonoxidizing acids.
2. *Alkalies.* Resistant except concentrated alkalies at high temperatures.
3. *Organic solvents.* Resistant.
4. *Bleaches.* Can be affected by too high concentration of both chlorine and oxygen-type bleaches.
5. *Mildew.* Resistant.
6. *Moths, insects.* Resistant.
7. *Light, atmospheric conditions.* Good.
8. *Dyeing.* Can be dyed in a variety of colors — but limited because of natural gold fiber color.

CORDELAN® (POLYVINYL ALCOHOL GRAFTED TO POLYVINYL CHLORIDE)

Cordelan is the tradename of a new synthetic fiber produced by an emulsion spinning process of Kohjin Co., Ltd., in Japan. It is classified as a biconstituent matrix fiber. A 50-50 vinyl alcohol and vinyon composition, the fiber has been patented in the United States and is distributed by Amerimex, a yarn brokerage firm. In 1975 the rumor was that the Kohjin Co. was in financial stress. However, this was denied. It was stated the fiber would always be in demand because of its flame-resistant properties.

Amerimex claims the fiber is inherently flame-retardant, about one third more so than flame-retardant fibers in the modacrylic category and, unlike most synthetic fibers, Kohjin Cordelan does not release highly toxic fumes when ignited and forced to burn. Therefore the danger of side effects from inhalation is significantly reduced. The fiber can be dyed at temperatures up to 250°F, is easily dyeable with basic, disperse, and cationic dyes, and has excellent light and colorfastness. In a blend of 75 percent Coredelan and 25 percent cotton, it is claimed that they can get 100 percent compliance on FTC fire-retardancy standards. This is especially important in children's sleepwear, blankets, bedding, curtains, upholstery fabrics, and carpeting. It is also used in nonwoven fabrics.

The physical and chemical properties of Kohjin Cordelan are given in Table 2-17.

Table 2-17   Kohjin Cordelan® Fibers

Fiber Composition
Polyvinylalcohol and grafted polyvinyl chloride.

Physical Properties
1. *Microscopic appearance.* Similar to Vinylon and Orlon, but in cross section consists of only a single uniform layer instead of a skin and core.
2. *Length.* Filament and staple.
3. *Luster.* Bright, dull.
4. *Strength.* Fair. In range of silk and wool.
5. *Elasticity.* Good.
6. *Resiliency.* Fair to good.
7. *Moisture absorption.* Moderate (higher than polyester, acrylics, modacrylics).
8. *Heat.* Begins to yellow at 150°C (302°F). Begins to shrink at 110°C (230°F).

Table 2-17   Kohjin Cordelan® Fibers *(Cont'd)*

9. *Flammability.* No spontaneous combustibility. Begins to shrink at 140°C (284°F).
10. *Electrical conductivity.* Poor. Generates static electricity at low relative humidity.
11. *Specific gravity.* 1.32 (approximates wool, lighter than cotton, rayon, polyester).

Chemical Properties
1. *Acids.* Resistant to weak acid solutions; affected by strong acid solutions.
2. *Alkalies.* Resistant to weak alkalies.
3. *Organic solvents.* Resistant generally; attacked by phenol.
4. *Bleach.* Sodium hypochlorite will degrade. Should be avoided.
5. *Mildew.* Resistant.
6. *Moth, insects.* Resistant.
7. *Light, atmospheric conditions.* Resistant.
8. *Dyeing.* Cationic, basic, dispersed dyes.

PART VI
NATURAL FIBERS: CELLULOSE; PROTEIN; MINERAL; RUBBER

CELLULOSE

Vegetable fibers consist mainly of cellulose, and cellulose is also basic to the man-made cellulosic fibers, rayon, and acetate. Cellulose is classified chemically as a carbohydrate and has the formula $(C_6H_{10}O_5)_x$. The cellulose molecule is made up of a number of units linked together, as shown in Figure 2-17. This structural formula shows how two of many units are joined together in cellulose. Each individual cellulose unit is chemically similar to a simple sugar (glucose), but linking many such units together makes the entire molecule insoluble in water.

The chemical structure of cellulose is very important in determining the properties of cellulosic fibers. The hydroxyl ($-OH$) units attract water and contribute to the high moisture regain of cotton. They are also the sites for combination with acetic acid in the manufacture of acetate. The regular repeat structure of cellulose leads to ordered, crystalline regions that give cotton its high strength. Finally, oxidation, by weathering or other processes, destroys the $-C-O-C-$ linkages by converting cellulose into sugar that provides food for plant and animal life.

COTTON

Cotton is the most important and widely used vegetable fiber. It is also one of the most versatile of all fibers. It has an endless number of uses in 100 percent cotton fabrics and in blends and combinations with most of the man-made fibers. It may be used in simple constructions that are inexpensive or designed into fabrics that are very expensive.

Cotton is classed as a seed fiber. It is grown and harvested as shown in Figure 2-18. The fibers are removed from the seeds and spun into yarns. The cotton seed is processed to give oil that is used in making soap and cooking oil and to provide cattle feed.

Figure 2-17 Chemical structure of a cellulose chain. (Courtesy: Mathew's Textile Fibers)

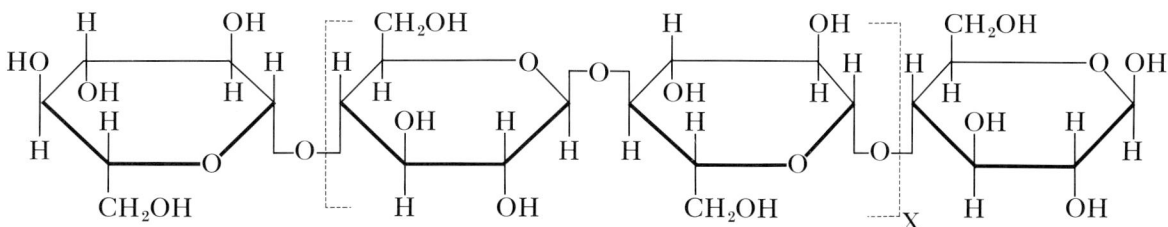

93

Figure 2-18 Cotton fibers grow in the boll or seed pod on cotton plants. Different species of cotton plants produce fibers of different lengths. Long fibers are spun into fine, smooth, lustrous, comparatively strong yarns. Short fibers produce coarser yarns that can be made into durable fabrics, but they are not as fine, smooth, or lustrous. (Courtesy: U.S. Dept of Agriculture)

MERCERIZATION

Mercerization is a process whereby cotton is treated under tension to reduce shrinkage and increase strength. Yarns or woven fabrics are treated with a 20 percent solution of sodium hydroxide (caustic soda) for two minutes at room temperature. The fibers swell; while in the swollen condition, the material is stretched. This increases the tensile strength between 15 and 20 percent. Fibers of mercerized cotton viewed under a microscope no longer appear flat and twisted, but round and smooth. As a result, mercerized cotton offers a smoother surface for light reflection and is more lustrous than ordinary cotton. Durene is a tradename for a highly mercerized cotton yarn.

COTTON IN CONSUMER USE

Cotton has many advantages. Strong, durable, and serviceable fabrics and sheer, lightweight, luxury-type fashions may be made from cotton. For example, denin work pants or percale sheets can be made of 100 percent cotton. Cotton can be spun and woven into a variety of constructions that are comfortable to wear. It absorbs moisture readily and dries fairly quickly. Cotton garments can be laundered, wet-cleaned or dry-cleaned, depending on the dye, finish, design of the fabric, and construction of the garment. White cotton fabrics can be bleached with the chlorine-type bleaches if there is no resin treatment or if the resin is of the type that resists chlorine-type bleaches. Cotton is resistant to alkalies. It withstands high ironing temperatures. A temperature up to 400 to 425°F is safe for cottons. Starch may cause scorching at 450 to 475°F.

Cotton dyes and prints readily, offering a wide selection of colors and designs. Many of the dyes give good colorfastness to light, perspiration, crocking, washing, wet cleaning, and dry cleaning. It is adaptable to many special finishes such as mercerizing, glazing, Sanforizing®, sanitizing, wrinkle resistance, chlorine resistance, flame resistance, and water repellency. It is adaptable to many surface treatments to create beautiful designs such as moiré, embossed, flocked, and lacquer stencil prints.

Cotton is extensively used with man-made fibers to achieve new combinations of properties that are not available in the fibers separately. However, pressing temperatures recommended for cotton may damage heat sensitive thermoplastic fibers in blends. Use of these combinations provide wrinkle resistance and shape and crease retentive qualities.

Cotton has some disadvantages, too. Untreated cotton lacks elasticity; it creases and wrinkles easily. Cotton is easily weakened by mildew and silverfish unless treated to resist them. It is readily attacked by acid reagents or substances, and it is slowly affected by sunlight, causing yellowing and fiber degradation.

The physical and chemical properties of cotton fibers are given in Table 2-18.

Table 2-18   Cotton Fibers

Fiber Composition

Composed of 87 to 90 percent cellulose, 5 to 8 percent water, and the rest is natural impurities.

Physical Properties

1. *Microscopic appearance.* Cotton looks like a flat, twisted ribbon. There may be from 150 to 400 twists per inch. The twists give the fiber an uneven surface. It has a central canal called a lumen (see Appendix D).
2. *Length.* Individual fibers range from 1/8 to 2½ inches. The longer cotton fibers are Egyptian and Sea Island cotton. Most American cottons range from 3/4 to 1⅜ inches in length. Long staple length in cotton is desirable because the fibers can be spun into yarns of higher tensile strength.

Table 2-18　Cotton Fibers *(Cont'd)*

3. *Color.* Ordinarily white. Sometimes it is cream colored or brown.
4. *Luster.* Cotton has very little luster. A process called "mercerization" increases the luster.
5. *Strength.* Nonmercerized cotton is moderately strong. Mercerized cotton is stronger with a tensile strength of 80,000 to 120,000 pounds per square inch. Cotton is 10 to 20 percent stronger when wet. (Fiber strength is 3.0 to 5.0 grams per denier.)
6. *Elasticity.* It is more elastic than linen but less elastic than silk and wool. The natural twist in cotton increases the elasticity and makes it easier to spin the fiber into yarn. (Elastic recovery 70 to 74 at two percent. Elongation 3 to 7 percent.)
7. *Resiliency.* Low.
8. *Moisture absorption.* Seven to 10 percent at 65 percent relative humidity and 70°F. Water has little effect on cotton other than swelling of the fiber, which may cause shrinkage. Even boiling water has no action on cotton. Cotton is stronger when wet.
9. *Heat.* Withstands high temperatures well. Ironing temperatures up to 400 to 425°F may be used for a short period of time. Cotton will start to scorch and turn brown at 475°F; disintegrates above this temperature. Can withstand hot water up to 212°F; can be dried at 160 to 200°F.
10. *Specific gravity.* 1.5 (dense).

Chemical Properties

1. *Acids.* Cotton is easily damaged by strong acids such as concentrated hydrochloric and sulfuric. Hot sulfuric acid changes cotton into a gummy substance. Nitric acid and cotton form guncotton, an explosive. Weak acids like acetic or citric, even concentrated, do not damage cotton. Oxalic acid, if allowed to crystallize in the fiber, weakens it.
2. *Alkalies.* Has a high resistance to alkalies. Cotton can be washed in strong alkaline solutions without damage to the fiber.
3. *Organic solvents.* Highly resistant to most organic solvents.
4. *Bleaches.* Cotton will stand bleaching very well, but strong oxidizing bleaches such as potassium permanganate and sodium hypochlorite can gradually convert cotton to an oxycellulose condition. It is much weaker in this condition. Overbleached cotton tears easily when wet.
5. *Mildew.* Susceptible to mildew unless treated to resist it. Sizings and starches, in the presence of moisture, promote mildew growth.
6. *Moths, insects.* Resistant. However, silverfish will attack starched cottons.
7. *Light, atmospheric conditions.* The ultraviolet rays of sunlight in time change cotton to oxycellulose. After two weeks in the sun, for example, a sample of cotton lost 50 percent of its tensile strength.
8. *Dyeing.* Usually dyed with direct, vat, and basic dyes. Vat dyeing gives excellent fastness to light and washing on cotton.

FLAX

Flax is a bast (stem) fiber that is secured by splitting the stalk of a plant. In the flax stalk, the fibers are bound together with resinous or gluelike substances. These must be loosened by a process called "retting" (Dutch for rotting), so the fibers can be separated. Retting is often done by soaking the flax stalks in stagnant water for several weeks. Modern methods using specially built tanks and carefully controlled conditions have speeded up the reaction. Overretting of flax makes the fibers weak.

Flax is made into linen. It is used for draperies, slip covers, and ready-to-wear clothes. Sometimes it is blended with cotton and rayon.

According to the Trade Practice Rules issued by the Federal Trade Commission:

1. No fabric may be labeled "linen," "pure linen," or "pure flax" or carry a name implying that it is linen unless the fabric is made of 100 percent linen.
2. If a fabric contains linen and another fiber or other fibers, the percentage of each fiber must be stated or the contents disclosed in the order or predominance by weight.
3. Fibers other than linen, but treated or woven into fabrics that resemble linen in appearance, may be labeled "rayon linen," "silk linen," and so forth.
4. A fabric is mislabeled if the fabric name contains "-lin," "-lyn," or similar terms.

LINEN IN CONSUMER USE

Linen has many advantages. Strong, durable fabrics, stronger than cotton, can be made from linen. It can also be made into sheer, lightweight fabrics. Linen absorbs moisture more readily and dries more quickly than cotton. Because of this property linen fabrics are cool and comfortable to wear. Linen does not lint and rarely frays or slips at the seams. Linen dyes well, but it does not take dyes as readily as cotton. Some of the dark colors crock readily. Linen is naturally moth-resistant.

Linen can be laundered, wet-cleaned, or dry-cleaned, depending on the dye, finish, design application, and garment construction. It is resistant to alkaline substances and reagents. White linen fabrics can be bleached with chlorine-type bleaches. Linen withstands high ironing temperatures (450 to 500°F).

Linen also has some disadvantages. Linen fabrics are generally more expensive than cotton fabrics. It is not very resilient and wrinkles readily unless it is treated with a wrinkle-resistant finish. Some crush-resistant finishes decrease the comfort in wear; such finishes make some fabrics lose strength more readily and scorch more easily. Linen is easily damaged by acidic substances or reagents. It is susceptible to mildew and rot unless treated with a mildew-resistant finish. Pressing along creases and folds weakens linen fabrics. Linen is apt to be weakened by bleaches, too.

The physical and chemical properties of linen fibers are given in Table 2-19.

Table 2-19   Flax-Linen Fibers

Fiber Composition
About 70 to 85 percent cellulose. The remainder is natural impurities.

Physical Properties
1. *Microscopic appearance.* Flax appears to be composed of a number of small fibers cemented together. It looks much like a bamboo pole. Flax has a large central canal.
2. *Length.* It will range from 6 to 40 inches. Good flax should average 20 inches. It should not be less than 12 inches.
3. *Color.* A yellowish-buff to grey.
4. *Luster.* It has greater luster than cotton. Flax is almost silky in appearance.
5. *Strength.* Flax fiber is much stronger than cotton and it gets stronger when wet (5.5 to 6.5 grams per denier).
6. *Elasticity.* Linen is not very elastic (2.5 to 3.3 percent elastic recovery; 2.0 percent elongation).
7. *Resiliency.* Little resilience. Creases and wrinkles badly. Finishes can be applied to improve this property.
8. *Moisture absorption.* Good. Higher than cotton, about 10 to 12 percent at 65 percent relative humidity and 70°F. Water causes the fiber to swell slightly. This can cause shrinkage. Fabrics can be stabilized in the finishing process.
9. *Heat.* Will withstand high temperatures, similar to cotton (400 to 450°F). Finishing can cause scorching or discoloration. Degrades at higher temperature.
10. *Flammability.* Burns rapidly.
11. *Electrical conductivity.* Low.
12. *Specific gravity.* 1.50. Comparable to other cellulosic fibers.

Chemical Properties
1. *Acids.* Flax is easily damaged by strong acids. Being essentially cellulose, it is affected much like cotton.
2. *Alkalies.* Has a high resistance to alkalies, like cotton. It can be washed in strong alkaline solutions without damage to the fiber.
3. *Organic solvents.* Flax is resistant to organic solvents.

Table 2-19   Flax Linen Fibers *(Cont'd)*

4. *Bleaches.* More difficult to bleach than cotton because of more natural impurities. More sensitive to hypochlorite bleaches than cotton.
5. *Mildew.* Like cotton, linen is attacked by mildew.
6. *Moths, insects.* Like cotton, linen is resistant to moths and insects.
7. *Light, atmospheric conditions.* Like cotton, extended exposure to sunlight will produce oxycellulose. Slightly more resistant than cotton.
8. *Dyeing.* Like cotton, usually dyes with direct and vat dyes. It does not dye as well as cotton.

JUTE

Jute is a fiber obtained from the bast of a species of plants.

The principal producers of jute are India and Pakistan. A hot, moist climate is necessary for proper growth. Jute is inexpensive but has only moderate strength. It is difficult to bleach, and it softens and weakens in water. It is used for gunny sacks, bags, cordage, and binding threads for rugs and carpets.

JUTE IN CONSUMER USE

Burlap, a popular wearing apparel and household decorative fabric, is made of jute. The coarseness of jute yarns is an advantage in creating fabrics of rough texture. Jute can be bleached, but bleaching is accompanied by loss of fabric strength. Surface applied or printed designs on burlap result in many varieties of decorative and wearing apparel fabrics. It can be laminated to urethane foam for outerwear fabrics. Chemical finishing can improve the drape and hand of jute. Chemical finishes may also be applied to overcome the natural odor of jute. Burlap may also be bonded to acetate tricot.

Jute fabric should be dry-cleaned unless labeled washable, because it has a low wet tensile strength.

Jute has very low resistance to light; therefore is easily damaged by light, resulting in fabric deterioration. Unless lined, garments made of it are scratchy and stiff. Jute is brittle and breaks or splits easily on folds. It wrinkles easily, snags readily, and lints badly. It is difficult to dye and bleach jute. Some dyes have poor penetration and, therefore, poor colorfastness. Jute sometimes develops a natural objectionable odor that cannot be removed in dry cleaning, wet cleaning, or laundering.

The physical and chemical properties of jute fibers are given in Table 2-20.

Table 2-20   Jute Fibers

Composition

Jute is different from cotton and linen. It is composed of a modified form of cellulose called lignin cellulose. This is a compound of cellulose and lignin. The lignin acts as a cement and is a weak link. The fibers are weak chemically, since lignin is easily attacked by chemicals.

Physical Properties

1. *Microscopic appearance.* Similar to flax, but the cross markings are usually missing.
2. *Length.* Four to 7 feet.
3. *Color.* White to brown. Air changes the fiber's color and quality.
4. *Luster.* Good luster.
5. *Strength.* Not very strong. Weaker than linen.
6. *Elasticity.* Fair.
7. *Water.* Weakened by dampness.
8. *Heat.* Susceptible to damage by heat.

Chemical Properties

1. *Acids.* Easily damaged. Iodine and sulfuric acid cause jute to turn yellow. Pure cellulose turns blue from iodine and sulfuric acid.
2. *Alkalies.* Easily damaged.
3. *Bleaches.* Seldom bleached. Never with chlorine bleach. Weakened by bleaching.
4. *Mildew.* Easily attacked.
5. *Light.* Like cotton, affected by sunlight.
6. *Dyeing.* Very readily dyed by basic, direct, and vat dyes. Jute contains some tannin, which aids in the dyeing.

RAMIE

Ramie or China grass is grown in most tropical and semitropical countries. The fiber is obtained from the stalks of the ramie plant. These stalks are 5 to 8 feet high. This is why it is classified as a bast fiber.

Ramie is used in twine, fishing nets, canvas, fire hoses. Some ramie is also used in upholstery fabrics and fine doilies and scarves.

RAMIE IN CONSUMER USE

Ramie is more expensive than linen and cotton. Supply or availability is limited. Ramie is more resistant to light than linen and cotton. Strong, durable fabrics can be made of ramie because of the natural strength of the fiber. It has a natural luster, comparable to silk and linen. Ramie dyes fairly easily. It is available in a variety of colors. Ramie reacts very much like cotton: it is resistant to alkalies and mildew.

Ramie fabrics can be laundered, wet-cleaned, or dry-cleaned, depending on the dyes, finish, design application, and garment design. White ramie fabrics may be bleached with chlorine-type bleaches, but precaution should be taken. Ramie fabrics withstand ironing temperatures up to 400 to 450°F.

The physical and chemical properties of ramie fibers are given in Table 2-21.

Table 2-21   Ramie Fibers

Composition

Mainly cellulose with about the same percentage of impurities as cotton

Physical Properties

1. *Microscopic appearance.* A broad and flat ribbon. May be confused with other cellulose fibers.
2. *Length.* Four to 16 inches.
3. *Color.* Usually white.
4. *Luster.* Silklike luster that surpasses linen. Excelled only by silk among the natural fibers.
5. *Strength.* Strongest of the natural fibers. Stronger when wet than dry.
6. *Elasticity.* Not very elastic.
7. *Water absorption.* Above 12 percent at 65 percent relative humidity and 70°F. It absorbs more moisture than linen.
8. *Water.* Has very little effect on ramie. Like cotton, boiling water has very little effect.
9. *Heat.* Withstands high temperatures well, similar to cotton.

Chemical Properties

1. *Acids.* Easily damaged by strong acids.
2. *Alkalies.* High resistance to alkalies.
3. *Bleaches.* Similar to cotton, strong oxidizing bleaches such as potassium permanganate and heated sodium hypochlorite will cause an oxycellulose condition.
4. *Mildew.* Very resistant to mildew.
5. *Moths, insects.* Resistant to moths and insects.
6. *Light.* More resistant than linen. Prolonged exposure in sunlight changes it to oxycellulose.
7. *Dyeing.* Easy to dye. Use same dyes as cotton. These are direct and vat dyes.

HEMP

Hemp is grown in Europe, Asia, South America, and the United States. It is used chiefly in making rope, twine, and baggage. It is also used as a backing for rugs. Italy has developed hemp that is used for producing a soft, lustrous fabric.

The physical and chemical properties of hemp fibers are given in Table 2-22.

Table 2-22   Hemp Fibers

Composition

Mostly cellulose with a small amount of lignin.

Physical Properties

1. *Microscopic appearance.* Like linen, appears to be composed of a number of small fibers cemented together. Looks very much like a bamboo pole.
2. *Length.* Four to 6½ feet.
3. *Color.* Yellowish-gray to dark brown.
4. *Luster.* High luster, like linen.
5. *Strength.* Very strong, next to ramie.
6. *Elasticity.* Less elastic than linen. Not elastic enough to use as a textile fiber.
7. *Water absorption.* Twelve percent at 65 percent relative humidity and 70°F, about 30 percent at 95 percent relative humidity; more than cotton or linen.
8. *Water.* Like cotton, very little effect.
9. *Heat.* Little effect, withstands high temperatures.

Chemical Properties

1. *Acids.* Easily damaged by strong acids, like cotton.
2. *Alkalies.* High resistance to alkalies, like cotton.
3. *Bleaches.* Difficult to bleach; loses its strength.
4. *Mildew.* Highly resistant.
5. *Moths, insects.* Highly resistant.
6. *Light.* Highly resistant.

PROTEIN

All animal fibers are composed of protein. Protein, one of the basic substances of animal tissues, is made up of amino acids. The amino acids are joined together into polymeric chains by amide (peptide) links. Protein, like nylon, is a polyamide. It has the same organization of monomeric units as nylon 6. However, instead of using just one monomeric unit repeatedly, protein is made up of several monomeric units (amino acids) in a precise order that differs from one protein to another.

The long peptide chains are also joined at intervals by cystine ($-S-S-$) and salt ($NH_2^{+=}-$) links. These cross-links contribute to the curl characteristics of wool and its high resiliency. When the cystine linkage is broken, damage will result. The cystine linkage may be broken by overoxidation (bleaching), overreduction (bleaching), alkalies, excessive heat, and overdigestion with enzyme products.

WOOL

Sheep's wool is the most important of the animal fibers. Wool is the hairy covering (fleece) of sheep. The fleece from the shoulders and sides of a sheep are the best quality (see Figure 2-19). Wool is commonly graded by the diameter of the fibers. The large diameters are the coarser grades. The smaller diameters are the finer grades.

Technically, wool also includes the so-called specialty fibers such as cashmere, camel's hair, mohair, llama, vicuna, and rabbit's hair. The Wool Products Labeling Law is discussed in Chapter 9, page 347.

SHRINKAGE OF WOOL

There are two types of wool shrinkage.

1. *Relaxation.* Shrinkage caused by steaming or immersion in water. The amount of shrinkage is not very great. It can be restored by stretching if the garment is made of preshrunk wool. This is referred to as temporary shrinkage.
2. *Felting.* Very drastic shrinkage. Felted wool garments cannot be stretched back to their original size. The factors that may cause wool to felt are: mechanical action, moisture, temperature, soap, alkalies, sudden changes in temperature, and many oxidizing and reducing agents. Mechanical action is the most important single factor. When one or two of these factors are present, relaxation will occur, if mechanical action is small. Three or more of the listed factors can cause felting (permanent shrinkage), but one of them must be mechanical action. Fine grades of wool shrink and felt more easily than coarser grades. Woolen yarns shrink and felt more easily than worsted yarns.

$$
\begin{array}{c}
CO \\
-CH \\
NH \\
CO \\
CH-CH_2-S-S-CH_2-CH \quad \text{Cystine linkage} \\
NH \\
CO \\
-CH \\
NH
\end{array}
\qquad
\begin{array}{c}
CO \\
CH- \\
NH \\
CO \\
NH \\
CO \\
CH- \\
NH
\end{array}
$$

$$
\begin{array}{c}
CO \\
-CH \\
NH \\
CO \\
CH-CH_2-CH_2-COO^- \quad \text{Glutamic acid} \\
NH \\
CO \\
-CH \\
NH \\
CO \\
CH-CH_2-COO^- \quad \text{Aspartic Acid} \\
NH
\end{array}
\qquad
\begin{array}{c}
CO \\
CH- \\
NH \\
CO \\
\overset{+}{N}H_3-CH_2-CH_2-CH_2-CH_2-CH \quad \text{Lysine} \\
NH \\
CO \\
CH- \\
NH \\
CO \\
\overset{+}{N}H_3-C-NH-CH_2-CH_2-CH_2-CH \quad \text{Arginine} \\
\underset{NH}{\|} \\
NH
\end{array}
$$

Salt Linkages

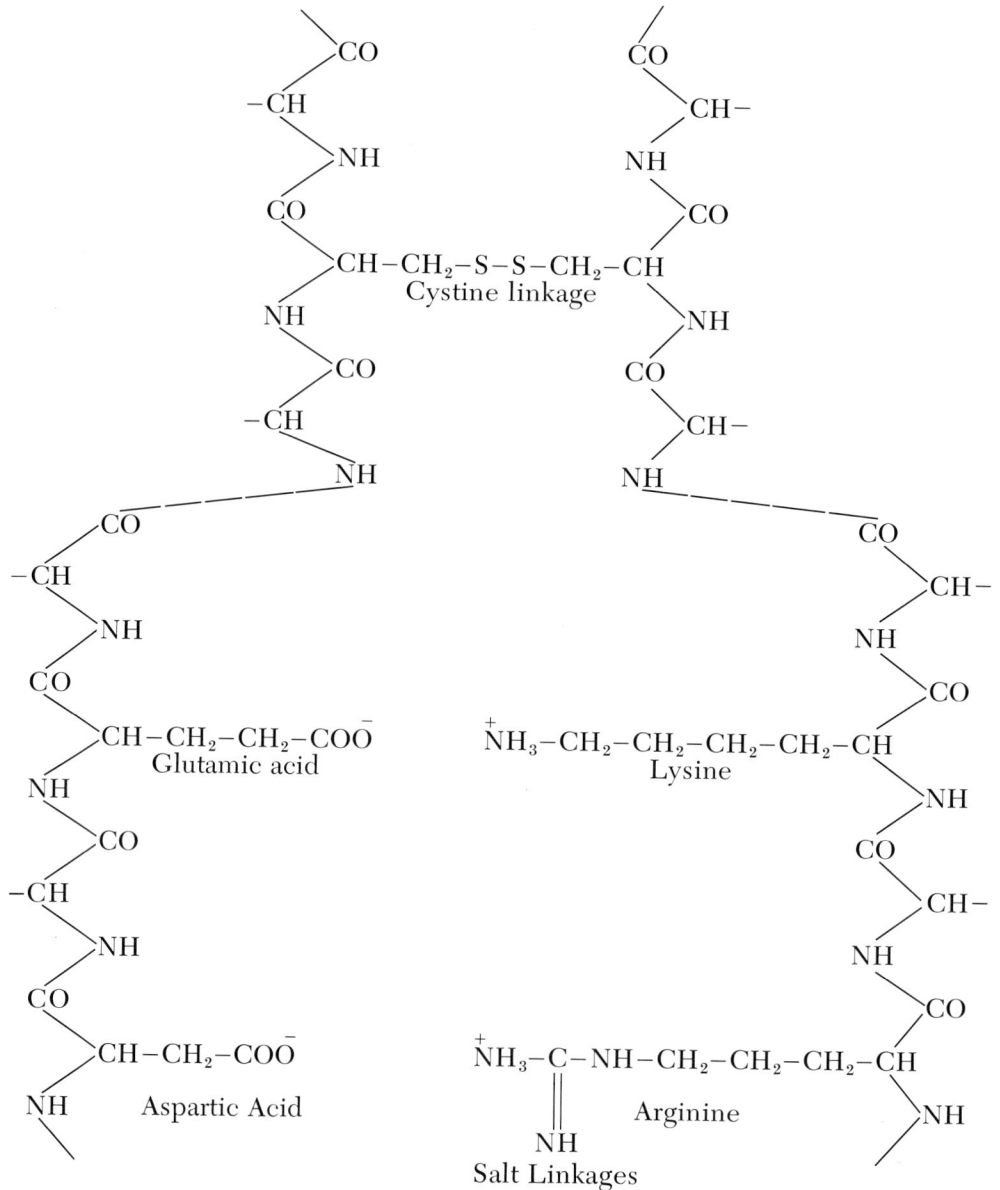

Figure 2-19 Structural formula for wool. (Courtesy: Astburry and Speakman, American Wool Handbook)

WASHABLE WOOL

Washable wool is a wool fabric that has been treated to decrease the tendency of the wool to felt. This is done by coating the fibers so as to prevent them from binding together under heat, moisture, and mechanical action.

At present two fabric finishes are being used in some volume. (1) the first is a thin coating of nylon in which the nylon polymer is formed directly on the fabric. A disadvantage of this treatment is a tendency for increased slippage of yarns. As a result, this finish is limited to plain weaves. (2) The fabric is treated with polyolefin. This finish allows the use of twill and hopsack weaves but is said to be somewhat less effective in controlling shrinkage than the nylon process.

Washable wools may also be achieved by blending 85 percent wool with 15 percent nylon. The blend is less expensive than the other processes and is used extensively by the children's wear market, popular-priced volume apparel producers, and retail chains.

Because of the present scarcity and high price of wool, it is being used more and more in blends with man-made fibers to improve dimensional stability, crease retentive qualities when wet and, in some uses, for washability without ironing or steam finishing.

REPROCESSED WOOL, REUSED WOOL

There is an increased use of reused and reprocessed wool in the clothing and trousers market, particularly in fabrics imported from Italy. (Recycled Wool, see Chapter 9, page 347.) Many of the fabrics are pleasing to the eye, and some may be quite good in quality. Consumers naturally feel that any product made of reprocessed wool or reused wool is inferior in quality when, in fact, reprocessed wool today is one of the best bargains, provided it is spun and woven by a reputable mill that is capable of constructing a fine and durable piece of goods. It is wiser to purchase a well-constructed wool-and-polyester blend with recycled wool than a poorly constructed new wool blend.

SEAL OF QUALITY

To provide consumers a means of identification of virgin or pure wool or wool blend products, the Wool Bureau licenses certain manufacturers to use the Woolmark and Woolblend Mark (see Figure 2-20). To be allowed use of these marks, manufacturer's products must pass the Wool Bureau's demanding battery of tests, including colorfastness, fiber content, and inspection for quality of workmanship.

WOOL IN CONSUMER USE

Wool is used for many apparel fabrics, both woven and knitted, and decorative and utility household items such as rugs, carpets,

(a)

(b)

Figure 2-20a   Pure WOOLMARK. The WOOLMARK is awarded by the Wool Bureau, Inc., to apparel products of pure virgin wool and carpets of pure wool pile that meet internationally enforced standards of quality. (Courtesy: The Wool Bureau)

Figure 2-20b   The WOOLBLEND mark. The WOOLBLEND mark is awarded by the Wool Bureau, Inc., for the promotion of products containing wool combined with other fibers, synthetic or natural, based on a minimum of 60 percent wool as a blend level or the requirements of the product. (Courtesy: The Wool Bureau)

blankets, and upholstery. Wool has the ability to hold a deep nap without matting and, therefore without making the wearer feel cold. It is very resilient and resists wrinkling. Wool fabrics hold creases and shape very well. Many wool fabrics are naturally water-repellent and flame-resistant. Wool tailors very well because of its ability to be shaped. It dyes easily, permitting a wide range of colors, and it is fairly resistant to acidic substances.

Wool may be laundered, wet-cleaned or dry-cleaned, depending on the dyes, finish, and garment design. Some wool fabrics require special handling in laundering, wet cleaning, and dry cleaning to prevent felting shrinkage. Some special finishes help to reduce this hazard. White wool fabrics may be bleached with hydrogen peroxide or sodium perborate bleaches. Chlorine-type bleaches should not be used, since they cause wool to yellow and may even dissolve it. Wool becomes harsh at 212°F and scorches at 400°F.

Wool has several disadvantages: it is very sensitive to alkaline substances; it is readily attacked by moths and carpet beetles unless treated to resist them; it is difficult to bleach; and it felts easily.

Current demand for washable wool is: children's wear, men's shirts and robes, and women's casual sportswear. The knitwear market is interested in shrink-control worsted yarns for sweaters.

The physical and chemical properties of wool fibers are given in Table 2-23.

Table 2-23   Wool Fibers

Fiber Composition
Largely protein with both peptide and cystine linkage.

Physical Properties
1. *Microscopic appearance.* Wool has a layer of scales on the outer surface. This layer is called the external covering or horny layer. The scales are very tough and transparent. They resemble the scales of a fish or reptile. These scales give wool a rigidity it would not otherwise have. The layer under the scales is very soft and spongy. This is the portion that absorbs water and dyes (See Appendix D).
2. *Length.* One to 20 inches. Most fibers are from 1 to 8 inches. One- to 3-inch fibers are used in woolen yarns; 4- to 8-inch fibers are used in worsted yarns.
3. *Color.* Usually white, but degree of whiteness may vary. Some gray, brown, and black wool.

Table 2-23   Wool Fibers *(Cont'd)*

4. *Luster.* Varies considerably. Luster varies with origin and breed of animal and with climate. Many wools have excellent luster. Finest grades of wool do not have as high a luster as the poorer grades.
5. *Strength.* Much less than cotton. Loses 10 to 20 percent of its strength when wet.
6. *Elasticity.* Very elastic. Can be stretched 30 percent without weakening.
7. *Resiliency.* Very good. Springs back if creased or crushed.
8. *Moisture absorption.* Sixteen percent at 65 percent relative humidity and 70°F. More hygroscopic (water absorbing) than any of the vegetable fibers. Slightly more than silk.
9. *Water.* Boiling water breaks down the cystine linkage if wool is boiled for a long time. It reduces the luster and strength.
10. *Heat.* When wool is heated in dry air at 212 to 230°F over a period of time, it loses its moisture. The fiber becomes harsh and loses strength. In moist air at a temperature of 212°F, wool becomes plastic. It may be worked or bent in any shape. When cooled, this shape is retained. This property is of great value in wool finishing or pressing.
11. *Flammability.* Moderate. Burns slowly and is self-extinguishing when the flame is removed.
12. *Electrical conductivity.* Poor conductor. It is easily charged by friction, forming static electricity. Especially noticeable on dry, cold days with low humidity.
13. *Specific gravity.* 1.34 (comparatively light).

Chemical Properties

1. *Acids.* Not easily damaged by acids, but concentrated solutions of strong acids such as nitric acid or sulfuric acid will destroy wool.
2. *Alkalies.* Very easily attacked by alkalies. Very rapid effect except with very weak solutions.
3. *Organic solvents.* Not affected by dry-cleaning solvents.
4. *Bleaches.* Sodium hypochlorite will cause the wool fiber to turn yellow and dissolve. Reducing bleaches are not as damaging to wool as the oxidizing bleaches. Reducing bleaches will make the wool more easily attacked by oxidizing bleaches.
5. *Mildew.* Least damaged of the natural fibers, but it is attacked if left in a damp condition for a period of time. If the cystine link has been damaged, mildew can more easily occur.
6. *Moths, insects.* Easily damaged by the larvae of clothes moth, and carpet beetle. They attack the cystine linkage. They will attack stained wool more quickly than clean woolen or worsted fabrics.
7. *Light.* Sunlight breaks down the cystine linkage. The wool fiber is then weakened.
8. *Dyeing.* Acid and basic dyes can be used. Some direct cotton dyes will also dye wool. Sunlight will damage the cystine link; this damaged wool will take a deeper shade of dyeing.

SILK

Next to wool, silk is the most important animal fiber. It is mostly protein and has only peptide linkages, while wool has peptide and cystine linkages (see Figure 2-21).

The silk fiber is a continuous filament produced by a caterpillar (silkworm) in forming its cocoon, which will yield 1300 to 2000 feet of fiber. The raw silk that comes from the cocoon consists of two fibroin (fiber) filaments and sericin (silk glue) to hold the filaments together. The sericin (20 to 30 percent) is left on the fiber as sizing until after weaving and then removed by hot, soapy water to reveal the soft, glossy character silk is known for.

SILK IN CONSUMER USE

Silk has many advantages. Silk fabrics are luxurious in appearance and feel. It is a very strong fiber in relation to its filament fineness. It is very elastic and very wrinkle-resistant. Silk is comfortable to wear because it is so absorbent. It dries quickly and gives up soil readily. Silk dyes and prints readily to beautiful, brilliant shades. It is adaptable to a variety of fabric constructions, from the very sheer drapable fabrics to the heavy, stiff, bouffant fabrics.

Silk can be laundered, wet-cleaned, or dry-cleaned, depending on dye, finish, design, and garment construction. White silk

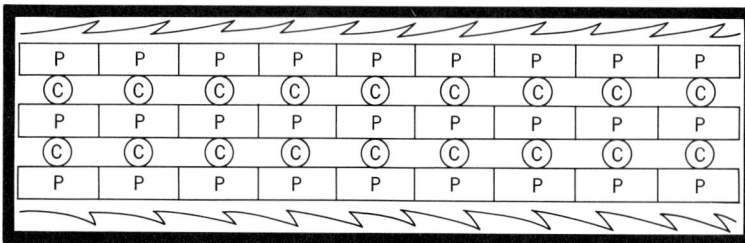

(a)

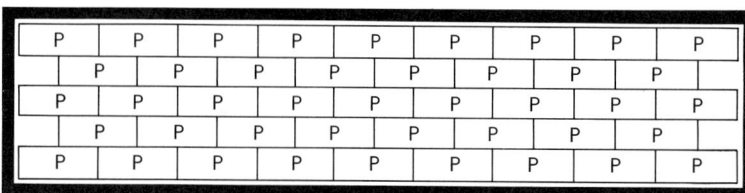

(b)

Figure 2-21 (a) Wool fiber (peptide and cystine linkage). (b) Silk fiber (peptide linkage).

fabrics may be bleached with hydrogen peroxide or sodium perborate-type bleaches.

Silk also has some disadvantages. Alkaline soaps and high ironing temperatures over 340°F tend to weaken and yellow silk fabrics, and some silks may yellow with age. Sunlight and perspiration weakens silk fabrics. Many dyes that are used are affected by sunlight and perspiration. Silk may be damaged by acidic and alkaline substances and reagents. In some constructions, silk is very susceptible to abrasion. In other constructions, silk yarns have low strength and have a tendency to split or break. Silk can be attacked by insects.

Comparatively little silk is seen in this country. A small amount is imported, such as raw silk, China silk, and Thailand silk.

The physical and chemical properties of silk fibers are given in Table 2-24.

Table 2-24   Silk Fibers

Fiber Composition

Composed mostly of protein. The fiber has only peptide linkages; no cystine linkages.

Physical Properties

1. *Microscopic appearance.* Raw silk appears as a double fiber with an irregular surface structure. After degumming, silk appears as a single fiber, smooth, regular and transparent. (See Appendix D.)
2. *Length.* 1300 to 2000 feet. May be as long as 4000 feet.
3. *Color.* Yellow to gray.
4. *Luster.* Very high luster after the sericin has been removed.
5. *Strength.* Strongest of the animal fibers. Loses 15 to 25 percent of its strength when wet.
6. *Elasticity.* Very elastic. Will stretch 20 percent of original length.
7. *Resiliency.* Silk ranks next to wool in resiliency. Wrinkles hang out fairly readily but not as quickly as wool.
8. *Moisture absorption.* High, absorbs 11 percent at 65 percent relative humidity and 70°F. Water does not affect silk. Silk is more resistant to water than wool.
9. *Heat.* Can withstand finishing temperatures up to 340°F for short periods of time. More resistant to heat than wool.
10. *Specific gravity.* 1.25. Less dense than cotton, linen, and wool.

Chemical Properties

1. *Acids.* Similar to wool. It is not damaged by most acid solutions. Concentrated strong acids will destroy silk; nitric acid causes silk to become yellow.

Table 2-24   Silk Fibers *(Cont'd)*

2. *Alkalies.* More resistant to alkalies than wool. Alkalies may affect some dyes used on silk. Silk can be dissolved by hot 5 percent sodium hydroxide (caustic soda).
3. *Chloride salts.* Silk fibers are damaged by substances containing chloride salts, which are found in perspiration, deodorants, and plain salt water.
4. *Organic solvents.* Not affected by dry-cleaning solvents.
5. *Bleaches.* Damaged by oxidizing bleaches. Three percent hydrogen peroxide is safe at room temperature. Very similar to wool.
6. *Mildew.* High resistance. Attacked only under extreme conditions.
7. *Moths, insects.* Do not attack clean silk fabrics. Finishes and soil may attract moths and insects.
8. *Light.* Not very resistant to strong light. Repeated exposure to sunlight destroys silk faster than cotton or wool.
9. *Dyeing.* Much like wool, but takes a deeper shade. Silk will absorb dyestuff at lower temperature than wool. Acid, direct, basic, and vat dyes can be used.

SPECIALTY HAIR FIBERS

Specialty hair fibers such as vicuna and mohair are obtained from several families or species of animals. Fabrics made of the specialty hair fibers are soft and luxurious. Fabrics may be made of 100 percent specialty hair fibers or blends of specialty hair fiber with wool or other natural or man-made fibers. The fabrics are usually very soft, lustrous, and natural in color or dyed from pastel to dark hues.

The Federal Trade Commission ruling states that when a fabric is made of one of the specialty fibers classed as wool, or a blend of the fibers and wool, the name of the fiber may be used on the label, providing the percentage of each fiber is given. If the specialty fibers fall within the classification of reprocessed or reused wool, such information must also be stated on the label.

CLASSIFICATION

Specialty hair fibers are classified into three generic groups: the camel family; the goat family; the fur-bearing animals (see Figure 2-22).

Generic names

The Camel Family	Fur-Bearing Animals	The goat Family
Alpaca	Beaver	Mohair (Angora goat)
Camel's hair	Mink	
Guanaco	Seal	Cashmere
Llama	Angora (rabbit)	Kashmir
Vicuña		

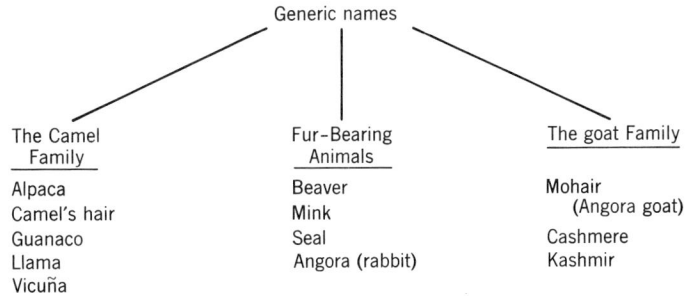

Figure 2-22 Specialty hair fibers.

SPECIALITY HAIR FIBERS IN CONSUMER USE

Cashmere garments must be considered as "luxury" garments. It does have some limitations in wear and cleaning.

1. *Abrasion in wear.* Cashmere fabrics are very susceptible to abrasion in wear. This usually occurs at the neckline, cuffline, along the front opening, and at the edge of pockets. The seat of the garment may show abrasion, too.
2. *Pilling.* Pilling is a term used to describe the bunching together of surface fibers into a ball. This is usually more noticeable in knit goods than in woven goods. It occurs most frequently in the underarm area where the sleeve rubs against the body.
3. *Small dark hairs.* You may wonder about the small, dark hairs that many times appear throughout pastel-colored cashmere fabrics. This is sometimes very noticeable because of the color contrast, the darker color against the lighter pastel shade. These are the guard hairs that were not removed or separated from the fine down fibers before the fibers were spun into a yarn.

The use of the work "Kashmir" generally refers to a lower grade of cashmere. Over the years, however, the words "Kashmir" and "cashmere" have been used interchangeably.

Many beautiful and luxurious fabrics are made by introducing a small percentage of fur fibers from beaver, chinchilla, fox, mink, muskrat, nutria, and rabbit into fabrics made of wool or man-made fibers.

Rabbit hair is often called Angora wool in error. True Angora wool is mohair. Angora rabbit hair is expensive — too expensive for general textile use — and it is usually blended with various fibers (e.g., wool).

The fabrics containing these fibers must be classed as "luxury" items because their cost is relatively high and performance properties low. They excel in aesthetic value. They require special handling in dry cleaning.

MINERAL; RUBBER

ASBESTOS

This fiber is found in veins of rock formation. Asbestos is found chiefly in Quebec, Russia, South Africa, and Italy, and in New York, Vermont, and Arizona. Asbestos will not burn. It is a poor conductor of heat. It may be blended with cotton, rayon, or wool, depending on the fabric's end use, such as draperies, towels, ironing board covers, and protective clothing.

In 1972, the Food and Drug Administration proposed a ban on the use of asbestos in clothing, claiming that it may cause cancer. They claimed approximately 200,000 women's coats to be the main offender. According to FDA's bureau of hazardous substances, asbestos fibers can become airborne and then be inhaled into the respiratory system, where they permanently line the lung.

RUBBER

The Federal Trade Commission amended the definition of rubber in February 1966. They have redefined rubber as a fiber in which the fiber-forming substance is comprised of natural and synthetic rubber, including Lastocarb, Lastride, and Lastrochlor.

MANUFACTURE

Natural rubber comes from the thick, gummy liquid obtained from a specific species of trees. Natural rubber is classed as an elastomer. Rubber fiber is made by two methods: by cutting and by extrusion through a spinneret.

RUBBER IN CONSUMER USE

Rubber has low strength but exceptional holding power so that it can be adapted to a variety of uses such as waistbands, webbing, and stretch fabrics. It may also be used for decorative effects. It can be made in very light to medium and heavyweight fabrics.

Fabrics containing rubber should be wet-cleaned or laundered and dried at low temperatures but should not be dry-cleaned unless labeled dry-cleanable by the manufacturer. Most rubber is affected by dry-cleaning solvents, but several manufacturers are making elastic yarns that are dry-cleanable. Rubber may discolor from perspiration, wet cleaning, or laundering or by exposure to light, and it may degrade on long exposure.

Swelling and flexing of the rubber yarn covered with a textile yarn can result in the segmenting of the rubber core yarn. This causes the loss of elasticity and elongation.

LEARNING EXPERIENCES

1. Explore if another department on campus might have an infrared spectrophotometer or a gas chromatograph. Arrange for an explanation and demonstration of the use of the instruments in identifying textile fibers.
2. Make a chart to show when the burning test is effective to identify or distinguish fiber content of a fabric. When is it ineffective?
3. Use a swatch of composite test cloth. Immerse in a staining solution used to distinguish different fibers. Dry and mount. Illustrate how one dye can be used to distinguish different fibers. Explain conditions when this test is ineffective.
4. Assemble samples of fabric that you can use to demonstrate that certain fibers can be damaged because of their solubility in various reagents.
5. Dissect yarns and illustrate the following: staple length; filament length; monofilament; multifilament; a flexible fiber; a rigid fiber; a nonspinnable fiber.
6. Make a survey of your local retail stores and shops. Observe and analyze fiber content labels. Report on your findings.
7. Collect and analyze advertisements that feature fiber content. Why do you think the fiber or fibers were used in each textile product?
8. Cut a 2″ × 5″ swatch of wool, cotton, acetate, nylon, polyester, and spandex woven fabric. Fold 1 inch and hang on a stretched line with a given weight at the free end of the swatch. Allow to hang one hour. Measure and record. What conclusions do you make from the results?
9. Explain how an oil tariff can raise fiber prices.
10. Make a chart showing the end-use consumption of textile fibers in the United States this year.
11. Make a visual display to show the difference between dry, wet, and melt spinning. Mount samples of fibers or fabrics made by each process.

12. Assemble swatches of fabrics. Dissect them and illustrate if they are made of a continuous monofilament, continuous multifilament, or staple yarn.

13. Gather fabric swatches to illustrate various modifications of man-made fibers. Mount them. Describe the properties the modification contributes to the fabric.

14. Read the textile trade journals and papers and report on the United States imports of textile fibers and products. How does this compare with United States exports?

15. Explain how social and economic events in United States history influenced the development of the textile industry. What current events are affecting it now?

16. Devise an experiment to illustrate that modacrylic fibers and fabrics are fire-resistant. List the end uses where this property is desirable.

17. Make a chart to show the similarities and differences of regular nylon, Qiana nylon, and Antron nylon.

18. Place paper toweling under a swatch of acrylic, nylon and polyester fabric. Drop machine oil on the fabric. Be certain the amount of oil applied to each swatch is the same volume. Allow the samples to stand for a week. Wash each sample in lukewarm water and detergent solution. Rinse and dry samples. Record your observations. What conclusions can you make?

19. Survey your local stores and determine the amount and cost of polyester or polyester blends being sold as flame retardant. Record, study, and report on the special care instructions you find on labels and hangtags.

20. Explain why the olefin fibers have been used successfully in rugs and carpeting but have limitations in wearing apparel and upholstery uses.

21. Devise an experiment to illustrate that glass fibers and fabrics are fire-resistant and that they have low abrasion resistance. List the end uses of glass fibers. What performance facts make them desirable or limit their use in each case? Why is laundering or wet cleaning recommended as the desired care method for glass fabrics?

22. Gather samples of fabric made from wool, glass, Verel modacrylic, Nomex aramid, Kynol novolid, and Kohjin Cordelan. Devise an experiment to demonstrate their flame resistance. Mount samples and record results.

23. Cut three sets of samples measuring 2″ × 2″ of representative fabrics. Maintain sample 1 for comparative purposes. Place lukewarm water into a container and immerse the second set of samples for one-half hour. Remove samples and dry. Place

perchlorethylene dry-cleaning solvent in a container and immerse the third set of samples for one-half hour. Remove samples and dry. Mount and compare the original sample with those immersed in water and dry-cleaning solvent. Record observations. What conclusions do you draw?

24. Cut and assemble representative acetate and triacetate fabrics. Use a hand iron at its various settings to determine at what temperature the iron resists sliding, glazes, sticks, and damages the fabric. Record your results. What conclusions do you draw?

25. Assemble a 100 percent white cotton, linen, silk, and wool fabric. Cut three sets of samples measuring $2'' \times 3''$ of each fabric. Maintain sample 1 for comparative purposes. Using manufacturers' directions, make a solution of a chlorine bleach and a perborate bleach. Immerse the second set of samples in the chlorine bleach and the third set in perborate bleach. Allow the samples to soak one hour. Remove samples, rinse in clear water, and dry. Mount and compare the original sample with those immersed in the chlorine bleach solution and the perborate bleach solution. Record observations. What conclusions do you draw?

3

YARN CONSTRUCTION

Yarn bridges the gap between fiber and fabric. Yarn manufacture is an essential step that enables fibers to be made into fabric by weaving, knitting, or other fabric-forming methods.

YARN CONSTRUCTION

A yarn is the basic component of a woven, knitted, braided, net, or lace fabric. The characteristics of the fibers and the way they are assembled determine the characteristics of the yarn. The characteristics of the yarns and the way they are assembled determine the characteristics of the fabric. The way a yarn is made also determines the type of finish or the kind of applied design that is given a fabric. The type of yarn used to make a fabric determines how a fabric may perform when you wear, launder, or dry-clean the fabric. Study Figure 3-1, which shows modern yarn technology.

Some fabric characteristics that are determined by yarns include the surface texture (rough, smooth, crinkled); its weight (light, heavy, medium); its comfort (cool, warm, clammy, comfortable); its texture (harsh, smooth, soft); and its performance (abrasion, strength, pilling).

The process used to make yarns is called spinning. This term applies to two processes: (1) the twisting together of natural or man-made staple fibers, and (2) the extrusion of a polymer solution or melt through a spinneret to form a continuous filament.

"Staple" is a term used to describe discontinuous lengths of fibers that have been cut or broken into desired lengths from large bundles of untwisted continuous monofilaments (tow).

117

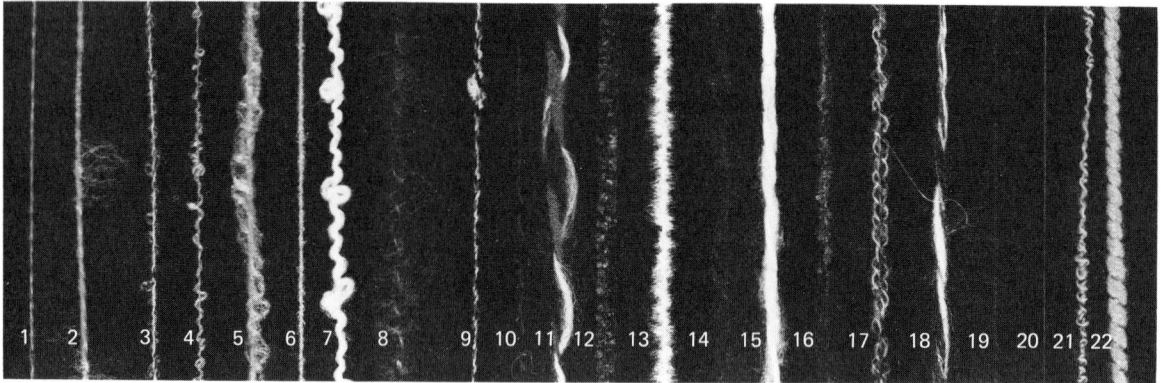

Figure 3-1 Behind the vast panorama of today's fabrics are the fiber and yarn producers stimulating new ideas and concepts of fiber combinations and variations in yarn construction. This illustration shows modern yarn technology. (Courtesy: The DuPont Company)

NUMBER	DESCRIPTION
1	95% ''Orlon'' acrylic T-42/5% Nub silk
2	100% ''Orlon'' T-28-brushed
3	65/35 ''Orlon'' T-28/T-42 with 100% ''Orlon'' T-28-loop effect and 100% ''Orlon'' T-42 core and binder
4	''Orlon'' T-28 loop effect/nylon core and binder
5	''Orlon'' T-29/''Orlon'' T-44
6	''Orlon'' 16 with 20-denier monofilament nylon
7	100% ''Orlon''
8	100% ''Orlon'' T-28
9	46% ''Orlon'' T-42/34% ''Orlon'' T-44/20% C.S. Black ''Orlon''
10	50% ''Orlon'' T-42/45% ''Orlon'' T-44/5% Trital Viscose
11	68% ''Orlon'' Sayelle/32% ''Orlon'' Colorsealed Black and T-44
12	Pile: ''Antron'' nylon core with ''Orlon'' T-42
13	100% 200-denier nylon — Bright Luster
14	60% ''Orlon'' T-29/40% ''Orlon'' T-44
15	''Orlon'' T-21 — ''Orlon'' T-28 Slubs
16	1 end Bright Nylon with 1 end Bright ''Antron''
17	40% ''Orlon'' T-42/40% ''Orlon T-44/20% C.S. Black ''Orlon''
18	70% ''Orlon''/30% Flax Slub Mail
19	70% ''Dacron'' polyester/30% wool
20	''Taslan'' textured ''Dacron''
21	''Orlon'' T-42/''Lycra'' spandex
22	''Orlon'' T-42/''Orlon'' T-21/''Lycra''

SPUN YARNS

The principal spinning systems used are: (1) the cotton system, (2) the wool system, and (3) the worsted system. Regardless of the system, the object of spinning is to produce a strong, uniform yarn. This is done by aligning the individual fibers to form an untwisted rope called a sliver; blending a set of slivers and drawing them out to form a roving; drafting or drawing down the roving to the desired count or weight per unit length; inserting twist, the amount of which is determined by fiber length and end use (strength, aesthetics); and winding the yarn on bobbins. Terms used to describe the steps in the spinning systems are given in Table 3-1.

Table 3-1   Terms Used To Describe The Steps in Draft or Ring Spinning

Staple fiber	Natural staple fibers or man-made fibers cut to a definite length from continuous filaments.
Opening	Staple fibers are loosened, blended, and cleaned to form a web of fibers called a lap.
Scouring	Applied to wool fibers only. Washing with warm, soapy water to remove natural grease, dirt, and grime.
Carding	The parallelization of an entangled mass of fibers by working the fibers between two closely spaced moving surfaces clothed with sharp points — result, sliver.
Combing	Several slivers are combined and drawn onto a comb machine where they are cleaned, straightened, and short fibers are removed. The long staple is further combed to produce long, uniform fibers — result, comber sliver.
Drawing	Operation by which slivers are blended (or doubled), leveled and, by drafting, reduced to the size of roving.
Roving	A strand of fibers in a high state of parallelization with just enough twist to provide cohesion. An intermediate stage between sliver and yarn.
Spinning frame	A machine by means of which roving is drawn out to the required fineness twist inserted, and the finished yarn wound onto bobbins.
Winding	A process of transferring yarn from one type of package to another (e.g., from cakes or bobbins to cones or tubes).
Twisting	Process of combining two or more single yarns by twisting them together to produce a ply yarn. Twisting is employed to obtain greater strength, smoothness, and increased uniformity.

Table 3-1   Terms Used To Describe The Steps in Draft or Ring Spinning *(continued)*

Turns per inch	The number of turns of twist inserted into 1 inch of roving or yarn. Usually expressed as t.p.i.
Ply	Yarns twisted together are said to be plied. Such yarns are referred to as two-ply, three-ply, and so on.
Bobbin	A cylindrical or slightly tapered barrel, with or without flanges, for holding roving or yarn. The term is usually qualified to indicate the purpose or process for which it is used (e.g., Roving Bobbin, Spinning Bobbin).
Cone	Yarn wound on a package of conical form.
Skein	A continous strand of yarn of any desired length in the form of a collapsible coil, obtained by winding a definite number of turns on a reel.
Greige	Descriptive of yarns as spun or textured, or fabric as knitted or woven, before bleaching or dyeing.
Yarn count (worsted)	A method of expressing the thickness or length per unit weight of a roving or yarn based on the number of 560 yard hanks in 1 pound of yarn. Thus 1 pound of 1/1's yarn measures 560 yards; 1 pound of 1/5's yarn 2800 yards, and so on. The higher the yarn count, the finer the yarn. Yarn count is usually written as: 2/12's. The first numeral indicates the ply, the second the count of the individual yarns comprising the plied structure.
Yarn count (woolen)	Yarn is measured by the number of 300-yard hanks per pound.
Yarn count (cotton)	Cotton yarns are numberd by measuring the weight in pounds of one 840-yard hank. The count is reported as the number of 840-yard hanks weighing 1 pound (1's; 40's; 150's).
Denier	The weight in grams of 9000 meters of a filament or yarn is the standard count system used to express the thickness of nylon, polyester, or other continuous filament yarns. Yarns spun from man-made staple fibers are usually designated by the count system appropriate to their method of spinning (e.g., worsted, cotton), although the thickness of individual fibers comprising the yarn is denoted by denier per filament (d.p.f.).

Each of the three processes is similar in its methods, but the machinery has been adapted to the characteristics of the fibers being processed. The cotton system is suitable to short, smooth, stiff fibers such as cotton. The wool system is suited to long, weak, coarse, elastic fibers such as wool. The worsted system is similar to the wool system, but the final product is finer and smoother. The cotton and wool systems can be used with any fiber that has the required characteristics.

Yarns spun from staple are more irregular than filament yarns. The short ends of fibers, projecting from the yarn surface, produce a fuzzy effect. Spun yarns are also more bulky than filament yarns of the same weight. They are, therefore, more often used for porous, warm fabrics and for the creation of nonsmooth surfaces for fabrics. They may pill, lint, or become fuzzy with wear. The forms of manmade fibers are shown in Figure 3-2.

Cotton yarns may be made from fibers of various lengths. A cotton yarn made from the shorter irregular fibers is called a *carded* yarn (see Figure 3-2). Fabrics made from carded yarns are muslin, crash, and cretonne. After the shorter cotton fibers have been removed, the yarn is called combed cotton (see Figure 3-3). Fabrics made from combed yarns are organdy, lawn, and Indian Head. Fabrics made of combed yarns have a finer, more luxurious hand than those made of carded yarns. *Pima* is a term used to describe a long, fine staple Peruvian cotton. *Supima* is a term used to describe an American-grown long staple cotton. Cotton yarns can be given chemical treatments to make the yarns more lustrous, absorbent, and stronger. They are called *mercerized* cotton yarns or fabric.

Wool yarns may also be made from long or short fibers. Shorter wool fibers twisted together make a soft yarn called a *woolen* yarn. Examples of woolen fabrics are flannel, tweed, and cheviot. Long wool fibers are laid parallel to make a smooth, highly

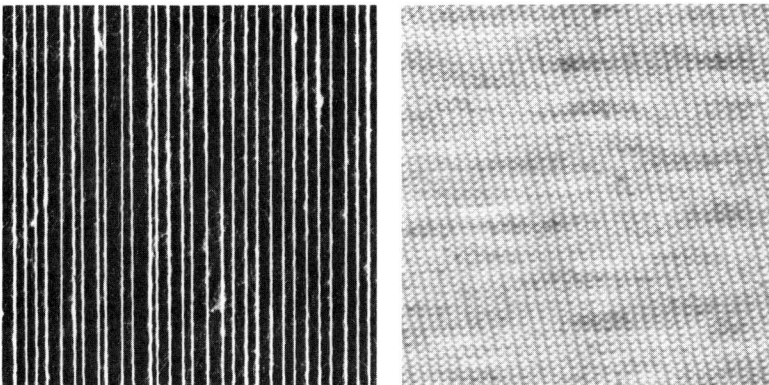

Figure 3-2   22/1 carded cotton yarn and 22 cut single knit fabric made from 22/1 carded yarn. (Courtesy: Cotton Incorporated)

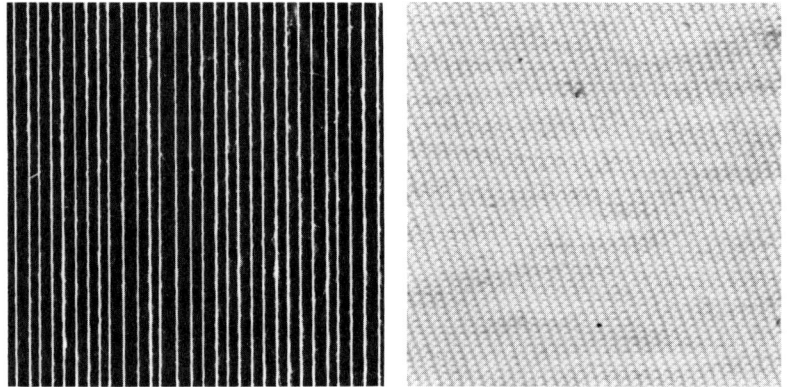

Figure 3-3 22/1 combed cotton yarn and 22 cut single knit fabric made from 22/1 combed yarn. (Courtesy: Cotton Incorporated)

twisted yarn called a *worsted* yarn. Examples of worsted fabrics are gabardine, cavalry twill, and serge (see Figures 3-4 and 3-5).

FILAMENT YARNS

Filament yarns may be a single continuous fiber (monofilament) or a bundle of many continuous fibers (multifilament). Most yarns are multifilament and may be made from silk or any of the man-made fibers. Filament yarns, because of the length of their

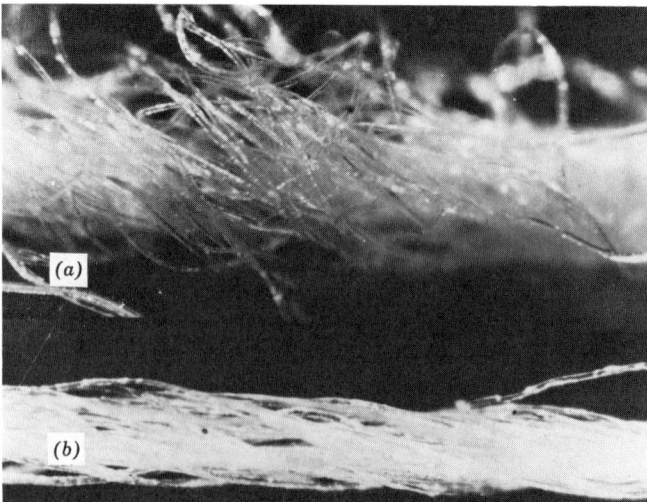

Figure 3-4 Photomicrographs. *(a)* A woolen yarn. *(b)* A worsted yarn. (Courtesy: The Wool Bureau, Inc.)

Figure 3-5 Woolen and worsted fabrics. (Courtesy: The Wool Bureau, Inc.)

fibers, need not be twisted to hold together. The smooth nature of filament yarns results in fabrics that are lustrous. In some applications the fabrics may appear too brassy or bright, so that the fibers must be delustered in the spinning process. Examples of fabrics made from filament yarns are chiffon, satin, and taffeta.

Fabrics made from filament yarns have a smooth, almost slick hand, tend to shed soil and lint, are usually quite strong, and tend to resist pilling. However, they tend to snag easily, especially when made from untwisted yarns.

Twist

Twist in yarns brings the fibers closer together and makes them more compact for the weaving and knitting of fabrics. Twist is usually described as low, medium, or high. The twist is measured in turns per inch, and the amount of twist is related to yarn diameter. For example, a larger yarn requires less twist; a finer one requires more twist.

The strength of a yarn is relative to the amount of twist in a yarn. Low twist is associated with low strength, high twist with high strength. However, too much twist can cause a yarn to kink and have poorer strength.

Yarn manufacturers refer to "balanced yarns" and "unbalanced yarns." Balanced yarns are defined as yarns where the twist is such that the yarn hangs in a loop without doubling, kinking, or twisting. An unbalanced yarn will untwist and retwist. In fabrics, a smooth fabric such as satin is made of balanced yarns; textured and crepe fabrics are made of unbalanced yarns.

The degree of twist in a yarn determines the performance and appearance of the finished fabric. Usually, the higher the twist, the stronger the yarn. High-twist yarns are used to make crepes and hard-surface fabrics. Low-twist yarns are used to make smooth, lustrous or soft, dull fabrics.

Twist in a yarn also may be classified as to its direction, either "S" or "Z." Yarn has an S twist if, when the yarn is held in a vertical position, the spirals around its central axis conform in direction of slope to the central position of the letter S. In a Z-twist yarn, the visible spirals conform in direction of slope with the central portion of the letter Z. Fabric designers can combine S- and Z-twist yarns into ply yarns of a variety of constructions to enhance aesthetic and performance properties of a fabric (see Figure 3-6).

SIMPLE YARNS

Simple yarns are those that are relatively uniform in size, smoothness, and turns per inch from one part to another. A simple single yarn is the first product of spinning; examples are crepe and sewing thread. A simple-ply yarn is made of two or more simple single yarns twisted or plied together. Fabrics may

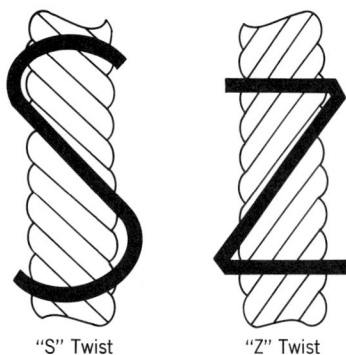

"S" Twist   "Z" Twist

Figure 3-6 Twist can be inserted in the yarn in either direction. When held in a vertical position, right-hand or regular twist will have the spirals running upward toward the right, conforming to the slope of the central portion of the letter Z, which lends itself to the designation "Z twist." Left-hand twist yarn has the spirals running upward conforming to the central portion of the letter S, and it is called "S twist," or reverse twist. (Courtesy: Cotton Incorporated)

be described as made of two-ply yarns, four-ply yarns, and so forth. Two or more ply yarns twisted together can be made into a simple cable yarn.

Crepe yarns are a highly twisted variation of a simple yarn. The yarns are evenly twisted and are even in size. A combination of simple yarns of different size, a different amount of twist, and even a different fiber content can produce many unusual and interesting effects.

Usually, simple yarns produce smooth surfaces and durable fabrics. Yet a variety of interesting fabrics can be made by varying the size, number, and ply of the yarns used.

Crepe yarns can cause consumer disappointment because of shrinking and stretching of the fabric. Uneven balance of simple yarns, although creating aesthetic appearance, can result in consumer disappointment in wear and use because of splitting and holes that develop in wear and care.

COMPLEX OR NOVELTY YARNS

There is no limit to the way irregularities or "novelty" are built into yarns to produce an unusual appearance and texture to a fabric (see Table 3-2).

The structure of complex or novelty yarns is characterized by the irregularities in size, twist, and effect. Complex yarns may be single or plied (see Table 3.3).

Three-ply complex yarns are composed of (1) a base yarn, (2) an effect yarn, and (3) a binder or tie yarn. The base yarn controls the length and stability, while the effect yarn gives the aesthetic value to the finished fabric, and the binder or tie yarn is used to bind the effect yarn to the base yarn.

The performance of novelty yarns in wear and care depends on the type and size of the yarn used, the degree of twist for the novelty effect, the firmness and composition with which the core and effect yarns are held together, and the firmness of the woven or knitted fabric. In general, novelty yarns have less strength, reduced abrasion resistance, and are more subject to pilling and snagging than the simple yarns (see Figure 3-7).

ANALYZING FABRICS MADE OF COMPLEX YARNS

A beautiful woolen fabric is pictured in Figure 3-8. Study the yarn formations in relation to the fabric's appearance and performance.

Table 3-2   Examples of Complex Single Yarns

Slub

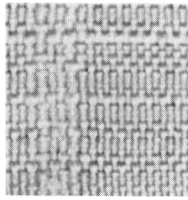

Tension of twist varied at regular intervals, incorporating soft, thick areas at intervals. May be single or two-ply.

Nubs

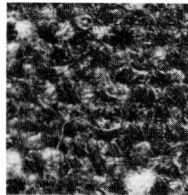

Sometimes called Spot. One yarn is twisted around another many times within a short space, causing enlarged places on the surface of the base yarn. When brightly colored yarns are introduced, the yarn is called a *knot* yarn.

Seed or splash

Similar to nub except nub is very small. When elongated and twisted tightly, the yarn is called a *splash* yarn.

Brushed or clipped

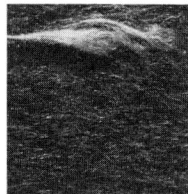

Fibers are brushed to the surface to form a design.

Table 3-3   Examples of Complex Ply Yarns (Descriptions of Some Core and Effect Yarns)

Bouclé

Tight loops project from the body of the yarn at regular intervals. A three-ply yarn.

Table 3-3 *continued)*

Chenille

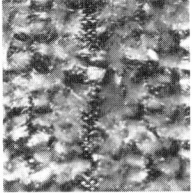

A velvet effect achieved by fibers held between plied core yarns woven in a double-cloth construction and then cut to resemble velvet. Pile fibers are perpendicular to the base yarn.

Loop or curl

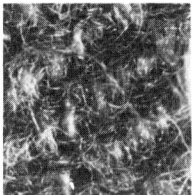

Closed loops of a two-ply yarn are spaced at regular intervals along the body of the core yarn.

Ratiné or gimp

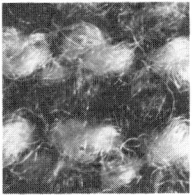

Similar to bouclé except loops are twisted continuously and then are closely spaced.

Snarl

Two or more yarns are twisted at one time under different tension, forming enclosed loops along the body of yarn.

Spiral or
corkscrew

Two yarns of different thickness and twist, one soft and heavy, the other fine. The heavy yarn is twisted around the fine yarn.

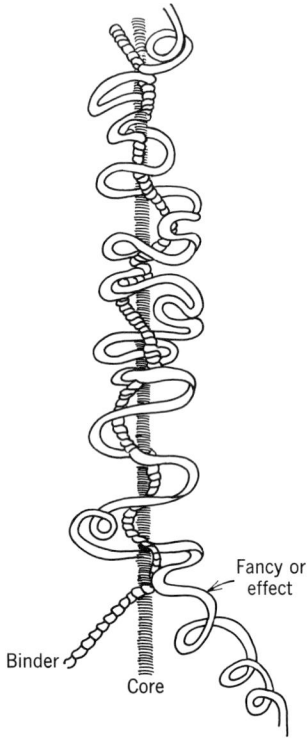

Figure 3-7 Diagram of a complex yarn.

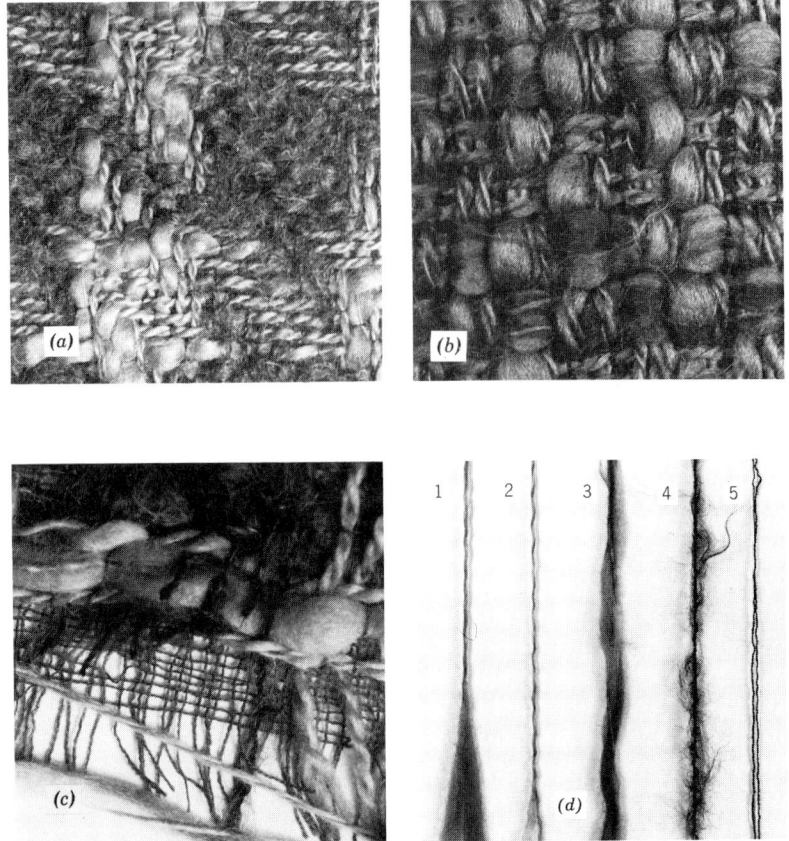

Figure 3-8 Analyzing yarn construction in relation to fabric construction can be interesting. *(a)* and *(b)* show the face and underside of a complex woolen fabric. Some of the face yarns have been removed in *(c)* to show the underside more clearly. The surface of the fabric varies in color and in the way the yarns are interwoven. In *(a)* the surface design looks like broken herringbone, but it is not a true herringbone construction. The fabric is made by interweaving light-ply roving yarns and light-ply fiber-spun yarns in both the warp and filling directions. A roving is a strand of only slightly twisted textile fibers. The plied roving yarns (see *d*-1) are made as follows. Pink and orange rovings are spun into a "thick and thin" yarn. This is a yarn that is alternately thick and thin, and there is no twist in the thick sections of the yarn. A second two-ply yarn is made by loosely twisting a green yarn together with a gold one (see *d*-2). Then this two-ply green and gold yarn is twisted around the "thick and thin" plied roving yarn (see *d*-3). The picture shows how loose the twist becomes in the thick sections. A second set of face yarns is made by spinning dark green and bronze fibers into a two-ply tightly twisted black yarn (see *d*-4). The fuzzy fibers held between the tight twists extend away from the yarn, creating an irregularly hairy effect. The underside fabric construction, as shown in *(b)*, is made of fine highly twisted yarns (see *d*-5) in a loosely spaced plain weave construction to hold in place the surface yarns described above.

STRETCH YARNS

The term "stretch" is used to describe any knitted or woven fabric that acquires its elastic properties directly from the yarns of which it is made. The yarns are in themselves elastic. Knitted fabrics possess a degree of elasticity because of the loop arrangement of the yarns. They are not called stretch fabrics unless the yarns themselves are elastic.

What Is Core-Spun Stretch Yarn?

The art of covering an elastic fiber is not new. However, the process of enclosing a spandex yarn in such a way as to be buried in a sheath of fibers is new. Core spinning hides the core, gives additional insurance against snagging and looks like a normal yarn.

Even a small amount of spandex in a yarn (two to three percent) can improve the stretch of knitted fabrics and maintain almost complete recovery. In some fabric constructions, core-spun yarns can provide extremely easy stretch and thereby improve form fitting without restriction. Suitable application of core-spun yarns can give added resistance to distortion during washing and drying knitted cuffs, collars, and waistbands, but they may also result in consumer problems such as loss of elasticity or the breaking of the stretch yarn and working to the surface of the fabric.

TEXTURED FILAMENT YARNS

The textile industry made a unique contribution to the consumer through the technology that results in textured yarns. Textured yarns are made by some man-made fiber producers and by yarn throwsters. Filament yarns are treated physically and thermally so that they are no longer straight and uniform and so certain properties are added. The added properties (bulk or stretch) are achieved through the use of special processing machinery, and advantage is taken of the capacity of man-made fibers to "remember" twists and turns imparted to the filaments and "locked in" by heat-setting.

Fabrics and garments made with textured yarns have many advantages.

1. They simulate some of the characteristics of fabrics made from spun yarns and have improved resistance to pilling and creasing, better shape retention and durability, and uniform appearance.

2. They combine the high abrasion resistance, strength and toughness of nylon or polyester with bulk, thermal insulation comfort, and moisture absorption.
3. They are easy to wash and dry rapidly.
4. They give greater covering power.
5. They feel warmer than fabrics constructed from untextured yarn, which removes body heat faster than textured yarn because of its greater area of surface contact with the skin. Both laboratory and wear tests have shown that fabrics woven and knitted from textured yarns have surface characteristics similar to that of fabrics constructed from spun yarns.
6. Their texture can be varied from crispness to softness, depending on the method and conditions under which the yarn is textured.
7. In many cases their use enables garment manufacturers to produce stretch-to-fit items in a smaller number of sizes that span the complete size requirements.
8. Fabrics have improved dyeing properties.

Textured yarns have really brought us to a new dimension to both woven and knitted fabrics. Textile technologists have developed at least 12 ways to texturize yarn. The most common methods are shown in Figure 3-9. Examples of yarns made by each of these methods are shown in Figure 3-10. The basic steps in making textured yarns are shown in Figure 3-10a.

Three of the most widely used are False Twist, Knit deKnit, and Stuffer Box. Each of these methods is a way to put a different shape into the slim, straight filament extruded from spinnerets in

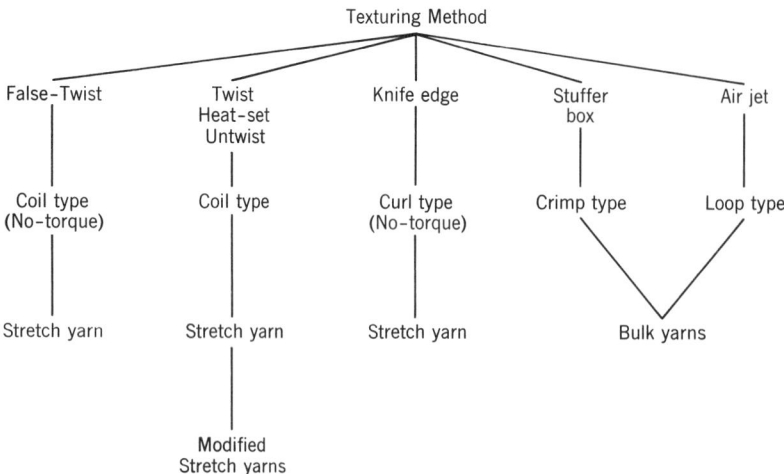

Figure 3-9 New filament yarns are created by processes such as twisting and untwisting, false twisting, crimping, and knitting and deknitting. The bulk or stretch properties that are added to filament yarns add an important new dimension to textile fibers.

Saaba

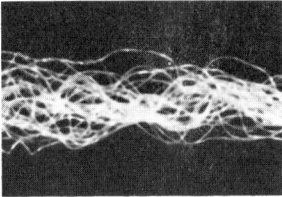

| nylon, *Dacron* | False-twist type stretch yarn modified to remove some of the stretch, retain maximum bulk, and controlled surface texture
Stretch yarn, modified type | Leesona |

Helanca

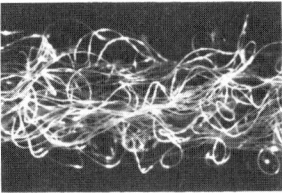

| nylon, *Dacron* | Twist, heat-set, untwist
Several types: stretch yarn, conventional type; no-torque and modified type | Heberlein |

Agilon

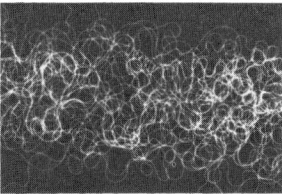

| nylon, *Dacron* polyester | Edge crimping process
Stretch; no-torque type | Deering
Milliken |

Spunized

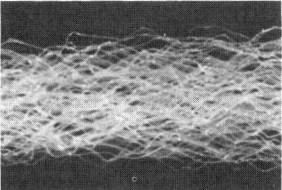

| nylon, *Dacron* | Stuffing box followed by heat-setting
Bulk yarn, crimp-type filament | Spunize |

Taslan

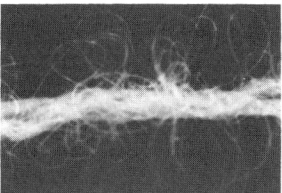

| all fibers, including glass | Air jet; yarn structure is opened, loops formed, and structure closed again
Bulk yarn, loop type | du Pont |

Figure 3.10

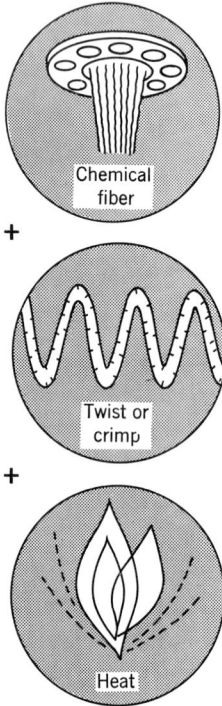

the manufacturing process and stabilize that change in shape so it is permanently impressed.

False Twist

In this method, the thermoplastic yarn is twisted, heat-set, and untwisted, giving a stretch quality. False twist textured yarns are used where bulk is desired, and nylon and polyester yarns textured by this method are found in many knit garments (seeFigures 3-11 and 3-12).

Knit de-Knit

This process is also known as knit, heat-set, unravel. The wavelike yarn produced by this method is achieved by first knitting the yarn into a small tubular fabric, heat-setting the knit tube, and unraveling the yarn. Polyester, triacetate, nylon, and acetate filament yarns are textured through this method (see Figure 3-11).

Stuffer Box Crimping

This method produces a heat-set, saw-tooth yarn that is used primarily on nylon and polyester filament yarns because of their superior strength (see Figures 3-11 and 3-15).

Other methods include processes known as the three stage; the false twist; the duo, edge crimp, air jet, gear crimp, Stevetex, compacting, chemical, and spun textured processes. Of these the edge crimp method and the air jet method are most widely used (see Figures 3-12 to 3-15).

Figure 3-10a Steps in making a textured yarn.

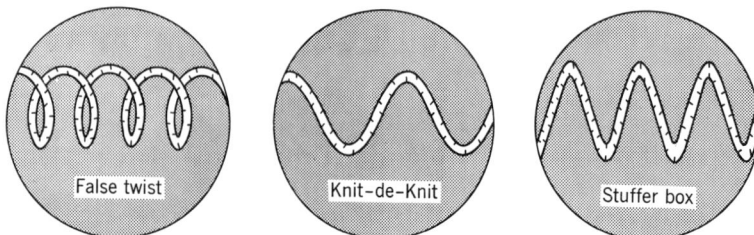

Figure 3-11 False twist, knit-deknit, stuffer box.

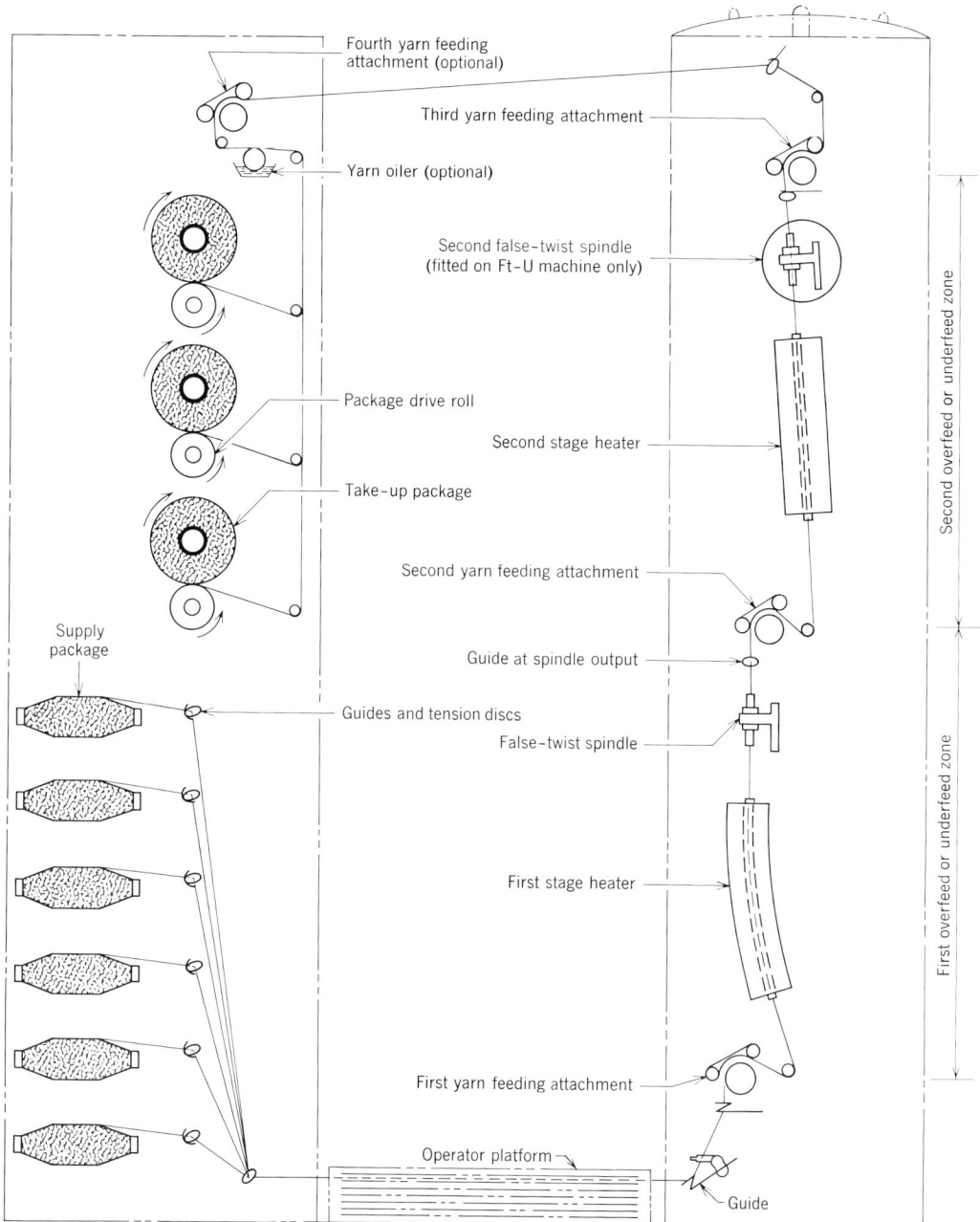

Figure 3-12 False-twist texturing. Textured yarns are produced on high-speed stretch yarn machines. Phase one of the two-stage continuous operation consists of twisting, heat-setting, and untwisting — steps that impart great stretch and bulk to the yarn. In phase two, the yarn is fed through a heat zone. Stabilizing in this manner develops the crimp, sets the yarn in a partially extended condition, and imparts to it: (1) stitch clarity in knit structures (a characteristic lacking in regular nonstabilized stretch yarns), (2) smoothness and softness of hand, and (3) increased bulk per unit weight with less stretch and lower relaxation shrinkage. (Courtesy: ARCT, Inc.)

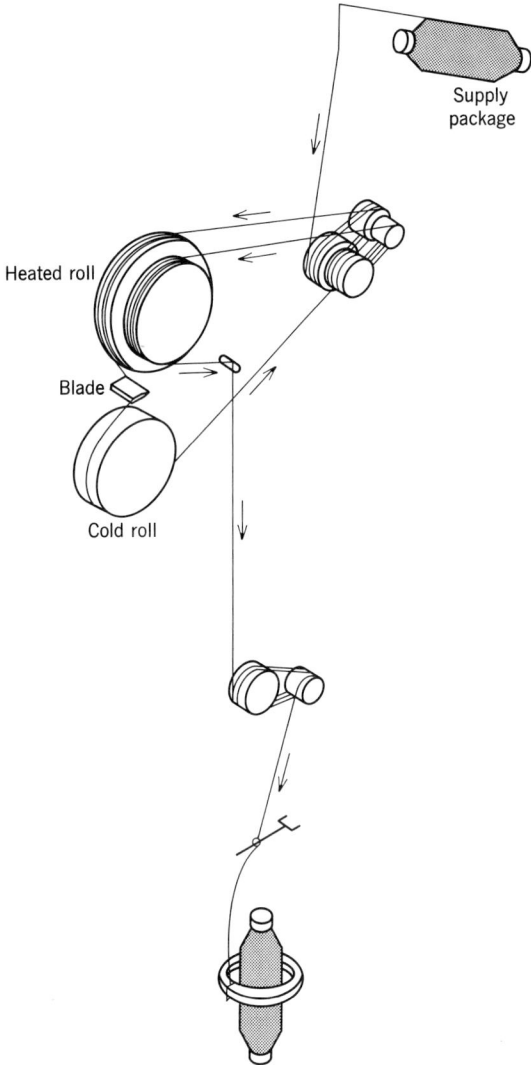

Figure 3-13 Textured yarns made from the knife-edge crimping method possess a spirallike coil or curl. Yarns are passed over a heated knife edge or heated and passed over a hot knife edge. The edge of the yarn in contact with the heat and knife changes the bicomponent yarn to have a quality similar to wool.

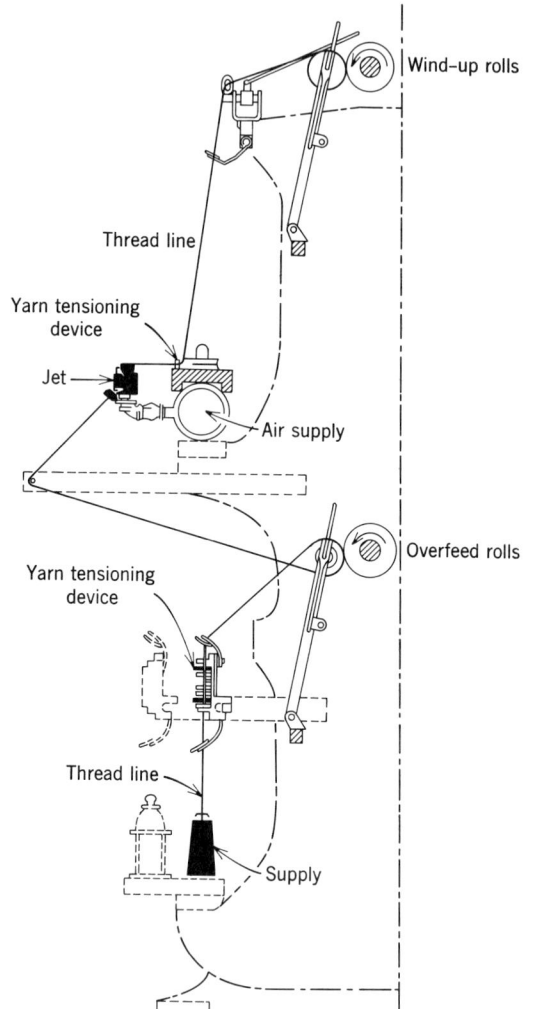

Figure 3-14 Loop-type crimping or air jet machine. This process is dependent on a rewinding operation that provides the exposure of a multifilament yarn to a stream of compressed air that blows the filaments apart to form loops in the individual fibers. This produces a bulked yarn without stretch.

Weighted tube

Heated stuffur tube

Crimped yarn column

Crimping point

Feed rolls

Nylon yarn from supply package

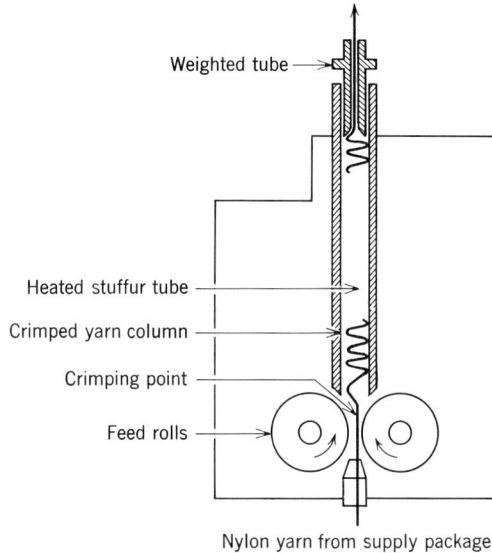

Figure 3-15 Schematic showing crimping unit used in textured nylon yarn production by stuffer box method. In stuffer-box crimping, nylon yarn is positively fed by two rolls into a heated tube (stuffer box). A smaller, weighted tube or slug in the top portion of the stuffer box restricts the progress of the crimped yarn going up the tube, thereby causing the yarn to back up inside the tube. The action of the feed rolls pushing additional yarn against the backed up mass of yarn in the tube causes the filaments of the yarns being fed to bend, or crimp, in a three-dimensional saw-tooth configuration at the nip of the feed rolls. As additional yarn is fed into the stuffer box and processed yarn is taken up onto the take-up package, the yarn continues to move up the tube at a predetermined speed and is heat-set inside the stuffer box by the heaters surrounding the chamber. On emerging from the top of the tube, the crimped yarn is oiled and coned. (Courtesy: National Spinning Co., Inc.)

METALLIC YARNS

Metallic yarns are not new. As far back as 3000 years ago, gold and silver were hammered into extremely thin sheets, then cut into ribbons and worked into fabrics.

Later, gold- and silver-plated copper yarns were made. These are still used today in some metallic fabrics. This type of yarn has several disadvantages: (1) the yarns are not very flexible; hence, they are difficult to weave into fabrics; (2) the fabrics are harsh to the touch; and (3) the yarns tarnish readily; perspiration may discolor them.

It has been very difficult to develop fine, flexible metallic yarns for knitting. However, several American firms and a French firm have developed a nontarnishing metallic yarn for knitting.

The American-made yarns can best be described as a ham sandwich. The metal foil, metallized pigment, and coloring matter might be considered the meat. The meat is placed between two layers of transparent plastic film. The adhesive used between layers to bind all the layers into one film might be compared to the butter or mayonnaise that holds the bread and meat together. These yarns resist tarnishing to atmospheric conditions and perspiration.

Type of Film

There are various types of films used to make metallic yarns. They are (1) cellophane, (2) acetate, (3) cellulose acetate butyrate, and (4) "Mylar," a transparent polyester film.

The cellophane, acetate, and cellulose acetate butyrate films are affected by some spotting reagents such as acetone, methyl, ethyl, ketone, or other members of the ketone family.

Mylar is a tough film of very high tensile strength and high resistance to attack by the chemicals used in cleaning and spotting. The chemical resistance of "Mylar" permits manufacturers to produce metallic yarns that are machine-washable. It has high temperature resistance, resulting in yarns that can withstand tumbler temperatures and can be ironed safely with either a steam or dry iron.

Method of Metallic Construction

Wide webs of aluminum film are placed between the two other films and laminated. Silver-colored foil is made by using a clear adhesive. A yellow-orange pigment in the adhesive produces a gold yarn. A wide variety of colors may be achieved by using different color pigments.

Metallizing is a second way of producing color. It might be compared to electroplating metals. A clear plastic film is exposed to aluminum vapor under high vacuum. This results in an aluminized sheet. Clear adhesives are used to produce silver yarns, while pigments are introduced for color. This method of production results in brighter, more lustrous yarns. Metallized films may be used also to make the foil-type yarn construction (see Figure 3-16).

YARNS CLASSIFIED BY MODIFICATION OF FIBERS

Yarns may be varied by physical or chemical changes that result in aesthetic or better performance characteristics.

BULK YARNS; HIGH-BULK YARNS

Bulked yarns are defined as the ratio of volume to weight; the individual filaments of a yarn are fluffed up causing air spaces that result in a lofty yarn or fabric. Bulked yarns contribute aesthetic properties to the fabric.

A large part of knitting yarn spun from acrylic fibers today is made to take advantage of the important high-bulk technique (see Figure 3-17). High-bulk yarn is a combination of two kinds

There are two types of metallic yarns made in the United States: the foil type and the metallized type.

I. Foil type

Transparent film
Aluminum foil
Transparent film

Metallic yarn

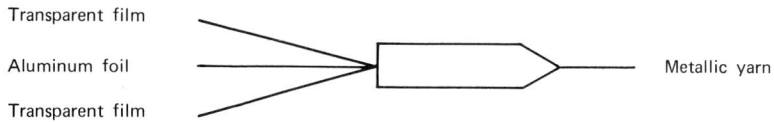

When a silver color is desired, the adhesive that holds the film and foil together is clear. If a gold color or other colors are desired, pigments are added to the adhesive or printed on the film before the film and foil are joined together.

II. Metallized type

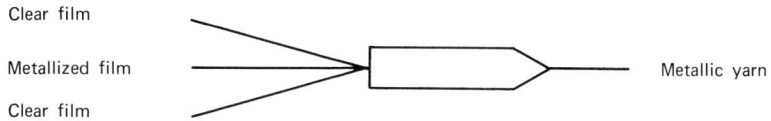

Clear film
Metallized film
Clear film

Metallic yarn

This is a sandwich construction as described above except that the inside layer is a clear film that has been coated with metal in a vacuum–plated process.

Figure 3-16 Types of metallic yarns.

Figure 3-17 High-bulk yarn — the bulking mechanism. (Left) Before bulking: a blend of high and non-shrinking acrylic fibers. (Right) After dyeing, the high-shrinkage fibers have shrunk, causing the nonshrinking (relaxed) fibers to buckle and increase the diameter of the yarn. The high-bulk blend made in the drawing generally consists of a combination of unrelaxed high-shrinkage fibers, and relaxed nonshrinkage is induced in the unrelaxed fibers, which contract to form the core of the yarn while the relaxed fibers loop, bloom, and are forced to the surface of the yarn. The net result is an increase in yarn bulk that imparts high loft, superior cover, and softness — without increasing fabric weight. (Courtesy: National Spinning Co. Inc.)

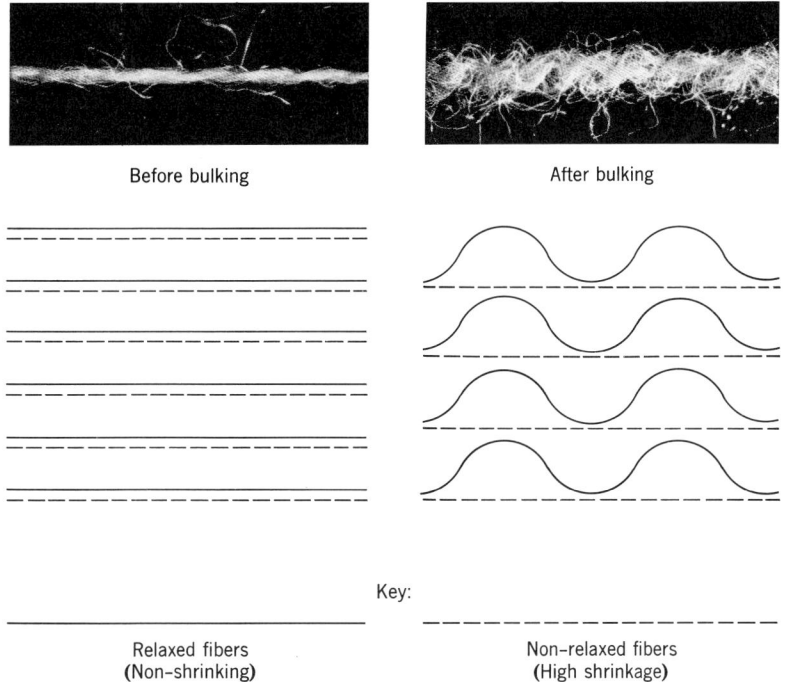

Before bulking

After bulking

Key:

Relaxed fibers
(Non-shrinking)

Non-relaxed fibers
(High shrinkage)

137

of acrylic fiber. One kind is called a "high-shrinkage" fiber. When immersed in boiling water, it shrinks about 20 percent of its length. The other fiber is called a "low-shrinkage" fiber, which means that it hardly shrinks at all. The "high-shrinkage" fiber becomes the center of the yarn because it is shorter, and the "low-shrinkage" fiber, because of its extra length, is forced to buckle and loft or fluff up. This fluffing makes the yarn look thicker, yet no extra fiber has been added. Only the bulk has been increased. Because the yarns have been preshrunk, high-bulk sweaters resist further shrinkage when they are washed.

Trademark names for high-bulk yarn are contained in Table 3-4.

Table 3-4 Definition of Terms and Trademark Names of High-bulk Yarns

Bulked yarns	The ratio of volume to weight; the individual filaments of a yarn are fluffed up causing air spaces that result in a loft yarn or fabric. Bulked yarns contribute aesthetic properties to the fabric (bulky knits).
High-bulk yarns	Yarns that are blended of high-shrinkage fibers and low-shrinkage fibers to give increased bulk or volume-to-weight ratio.
Bicomponent	A man-made filament fiber in which two chemical components have been combined. Often the two components have different shrinkage characteristics.
Wintuck	(DuPont) bicomponent acrylic Orlon combined with homoacrylic Orlon (usually 60/40 composition), *formerly called Orlon Sayelle.*
Sayelle	A bicomponent acrylic fiber. See Wintuk. Trademark name for hand knitting yarns in the United States.
Nomelle	(DuPont) Acrylic Orlon that has a soft, luxurious, cashmere hand. The yarns have high loft, good resiliency, and dye readily.
Bi-Loft	Yarns of Acrilan bicomponent acrylic.
Spun Pak	High-twist acrylic yarns spun from 100 percent relaxed sliver.
Spun Gee	High-bulk acrylic yarns spun from variable denier blends.

NEW DEVELOPMENTS IN YARN SPINNING PROCESSES

Recent methods of yarn spinning were developed to bypass some or all of the conventional systems. They are (1) fiber to sliver; (2) sliver or tow to yarn; and (3) fiber to yarn (see Figure 3-18).

FIBER TO SLIVER

An automatic machine moves the fiber directly from the bale to sliver. The fiber moves from the bale to the blender. It then goes through a carder or comber. This method produces a strong, uniform yarn at greater speed and reduced labor cost.

SLIVER OR TOW TO YARN

This method is used widely. The tow is fed into a machine where rollers operating at different speeds breaks up the fibers, but they still remain parallel. The fibers are fed to regular drawing and spinning equipment and converted into yarns that are uniform, soft, and strong. They can also have high bulk if desired.

Figure 3-18 *(a)* Position of fiber in a ring spun yarn. *(b)* Position of fibers in an open-end spun yarn.

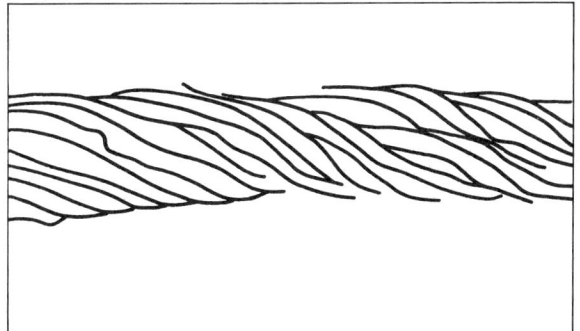

(a)

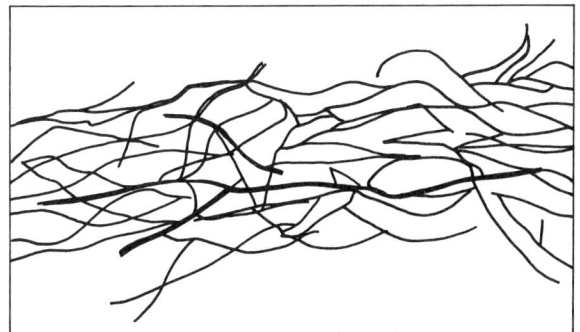

(b)

The advantage of this production is flexibility, economy, and a reduction of waste.

FIBER TO YARN

This method is called open-end spinning. It differs from conventional ring spinning in that fibers are thrown loose in a rotating chamber where turbulence forms them into a yarn structure. The advantages of this method are: (1) it produces bulkier and loftier yarns for better coverage; (2) the yarns dye better, particularly brighter shades and prints; (3) it produces a more uniform, strong yarn; and (4) it produces a yarn that resists pilling. The disadvantages of the method are: (1) it is less versatile, and (2) it results in a harsher hand, crisper feel and stiffer fabric.

An open-end yarn-producing procedure that uses a "linear" system instead of a turbine system has been developed. The new method is said to produce yarn to compete directly in many areas with the turbine open-end and twistless spinning systems with a much greater efficiency of organizing staple fibers into a useable yarn construction for fabric forming.

SPLIT FIBER PROCESS

Split fiber is produced by a continuous in-line process that involves essentially three steps: film production, film preparation for fibrillation, and fibrillation or splitting. These steps are varied, depending on whether the end product is staple or continuous yarn (see Figure 3-19).

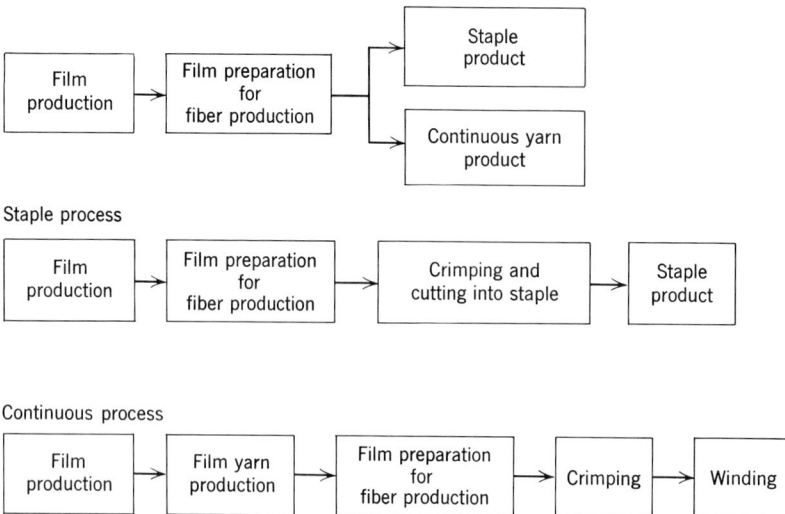

Figure 3-19 Flow diagram of the production of split fibers. (Courtesy: Phillips Petroleum Company)

The film is produced by an extrusion process in such a way to make possible the formation of fibers. This fiber formation is primarily due to differences in strength between the machine and transverse directions of the film. After formation, the fiber can be crimped and cut into staple or crimped and used as continuous yarn. The diagrams illustrate the differences in process between staple and continuous yarn.

Virtually any thermoplastic material exhibiting crystalline properties may be adapted to this process. Materials that potentially can be processed into split fiber for various applications include polyethylene, polypropylene, nylon, polyesters, polyvinyl alcohols, polyvinyl chloride and acrylics. Both high-density polyethylene and polypropylene were employed in the development of the process, with major emphasis on polypropylene because of its overall advantages in physical properties related to textile applications.

Once the raw material has been converted into fibers by this process, it is handled as any other textile fiber. There are antistat and spin finish chemicals that can be added at one or several points during the process.

BLENDS

Frequently, the characteristics of two or more staple fiber types may be combined by blending the fibers together before the fibers are spun into yarn. Fabrics manufactured from such blended spun yarns are called "blends."

When are Fibers Blended?

Blending is done before the spinning operation, that is, from the opening and picking operation through the making of the roving. Blending during the first operation usually results in a better blend.

Why are Fibers Blended?

No one is perfect! That is also true of fibers. Each has its good and limited qualities. By blending, textile technologists can select the qualities for a given end product.

Fibers are blended to (1) produce better performance; (2) achieve aesthetic qualitites; (3) obtain cross-dyed effects; (4) obtain unusual or desired texture, hand or feel, and appearance; (5) improve properties for spinning, weaving, dyeing or printing, and finishing; and (6) achieve economic savings.

BLEND LEVELS

Because of the number of reasons for blending, there is little agreement among fiber, yarn, and fabric producers as to the desired blend levels for a variety of fabrics produced today. The percentages of fibers in blends do not always predict what the consumer may expect in wear and care.

A fabric must have sufficient amount of man-made fiber in a blend to give the performance that the consumer expects. Some manufacturers use a lower percentage of man-made fibers in blends because of the price advantage. Such a practice results in fabrics of lower strength, poor hand, and poor performance properties. One of the important developments in blended fabrics is the polyester-wool blends that give lightweight fabrics with good strength, wrinkle resistance, and crease resistance.

FILAMENT BLEND YARNS

This is a recent development to provide different aesthetic and performance characteristics than were available in filament yarns of a single fiber. The filaments can be combined after the spinnerett, during drawing, or during texturizing (see Figure 3-20). The following blends are being sold currently; no doubt more will be added as developed or there is demand.

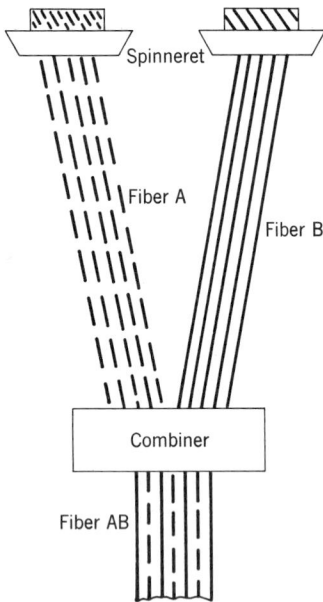

Figure 3-20 Blended filament. (Courtesy: American Fabrics and Fashions)

Fibers in Filament Blend	Tradename
Polyester (core) + acetate (exterior bulked)	Lanese
Triacetate + nylon	Arnel Plus
Triacetate + polyester	Arnel 100
Polyester + nylon	Bytrece

The intent, as with blending staple fibers, is to get the best qualities of each fiber (e.g., the aesthetic qualities of triacetate and the strength of nylon). For this reason, these yarns are finding uses in a variety of textile end products from apparel to home furnishings.

A blend of polyester and wool results in a good combination of hand, strength, comfort, durability, draping, and wrinkle resistance. Both 55 percent polyester/45 percent wool and 70 percent polyester/30 percent wool in yarn counts ranging from 20's to 30's are used for knits and sweaters.

YARN COMBINATIONS OR FABRIC COMBINATIONS

A yarn combination may be achieved in two ways: (1) monofilaments or filament yarns of different fibers may be twisted together to form a "combination" filament yarn; and (2) a combination spun yarn is made by plying together "single spun yarns of different fibers."

Fabrics manufactured from such yarns are called "combinations." A fabric made with the warp or lengthwise yarn of a spun or filament yarn made of one fiber and the filling or crosswise yarn made of a spun or filament fiber made of another fiber is called a "fabric" combination. For example: silk — warp; wool — filling. It is important to recognize these two structures, since they frequently explain the way a fabric performs in wear and care.

COMBO YARNS OR COMBINATION YARNS

"Combo" or the combination of filament and spun yarns in knit constructions is a relatively new concept. In knitting spun yarns are thrown to the surface or face of the fabric and filament yarns to the underside of the fabric. This technique provides better covering power in knitting and gives fabrics that have great adaptability to design by piece dyeing greater comfort in wear and a fuller, crisper hand and feel.

YARNS IN CONSUMER USE

Many times the performance of a fabric in use and care is very dependent on yarn structure. More commonly, performance is a combination of yarn and fabric construction, so it is difficult to separate the effect of yarn construction from fabric construction. Some fabrics used in today's wearing apparel and household textiles are prone to yarn and seam slippage during wear or when laundered or dry-cleaned. Satins, crepes, jacquard weaves with prominent surface designs, and novelty rib and twill weaves are among the fabrics that are affected by abrasion and rubbing during wear.

SLIPPAGE

Yarn slippage is a sliding or shifting of smooth yarns relative to one another that alters the surface appearance of the fabric (see Fig. 3-21).

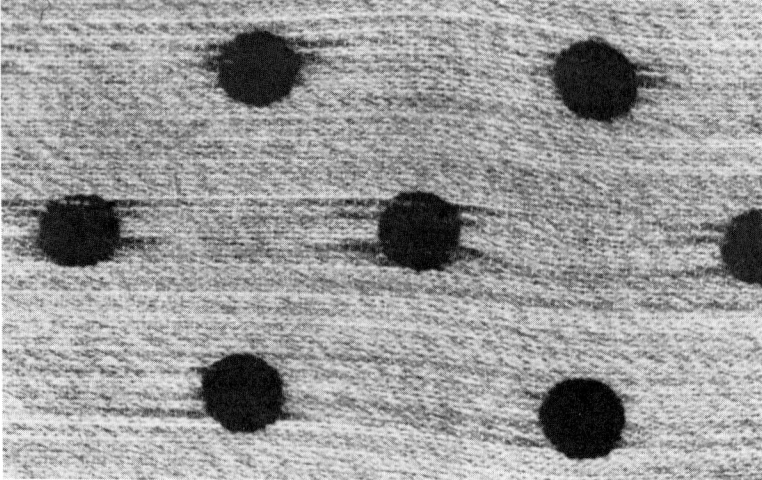

Figure 3-21 Yarn slippage from wear and cleaning, resulting in appearance of staining as though dye has bled.

Seam slippage occurs when yarns slip over one another at a line of stitching. This may be due to little or no twist in the yarns used to weave the fabric; a low number of yarns warp and/or filling — to an inch of fabric; or a gross imbalance of yarns between the lengthwise and crosswise direction of the fabric.

In laboratory testing for yarn slippage in a fabric, a pulling strain of known force is placed on the fabric, but there is a simple method frequently used to see if a fabric is susceptible to yarn slippage. Bring your thumbnails together. Place the fabric over them. With your two index fingers, pull the fabric in opposite directions. If the fabric is susceptible to yarn slippage, the yarns will separate or shift under the pulling strain.

The problem of slippage may be controlled in manufacture by adding more twist to the yarns or by establishing the correct balance of warp and filling yarns. When the fabric maker fails to observe these precautions, he constructs a fabric with very limited serviceability.

FABRIC COMBINATIONS

Various yarns may be used in combination with each other to make fabrics of enhanced aesthetic or performance characteristics. However, if careful attention is not paid to the properties of the yarns, a fabric with poor performance may result. Some fabric combinations have caused consumer dissatisfaction in wear even before cleaning. Sometimes the damage is not noted until after cleaning. For example, many beautiful fabrics are made with a smooth silk yarn in the lengthwise direction and a spun, yarn-dyed wool in the filling or crosswise direction. The fine silk yarns, which add strength, are usually invisible on the face of the fabric, and the heavier spun woolen yarns that are prominent on the surface give the fabric a woollike feel.

Pilling and felting of wool yarn may occur in wear because of abrasion and body moisture. Shrinkage and pilling in wear and cleaning may be attributed to yarn and fabric construction. In some fabrics the broken filaments of silk yarn protrude from the surface of the fabric at the edge of the cuffs, front opening, hemline, underarm area, across the shoulder, and on the seat of the skirt. Care must be taken in attempts to remove spots and stains by either the consumer or professional spotter. It is necessary to avoid any mechanical action such as brushing or tamping that may cause the yarns to shift or pill and the fabric to shrink or felt.

Also, lightweight summer fabrics made of cotton and nylon combinations or cotton and silk combinations can result in consumer dissatisfaction in wear and laundering or dry cleaning. In cotton-nylon combinations, the nylon fuses when the fabric is ironed with too hot an iron.

Some cotton-nylon fabrics are evidently being handled as though they were 100 percent cotton — perhaps because of lack of knowledge that a considerable amount of nylon is present. It is easy to fuse nylon when it is pressed with an iron at the cotton setting. The damage may appear as glazed areas, or the fused areas may break into a hole because of the stiffened, fused fibers.

Splitting may be traced to fabric construction. When a very fine (15-denier) nylon filament yarn is used in the warp and a highly twisted, fine cotton yarn is used in the filling, the fine nylon warp yarns are not strong enough to withstand strain in wear. They may break, causing a split across the warp yarns; the cotton filling yarns usually do not break.

CREPE YARNS

Creped yarns are used to make a variety of fabric constructions ranging from sheer fabrics to heavy crepes and crepe-backed fabrics. These have caused consumer dissatisfaction because of fabric damage caused by yarn slippage and seam slippage, as well as pulled threads, minor rips and tears that cannot be mended without showing, shrinkage, and stretching.

The exceptions are creped yarns made of man-made fibers that are properly heat-set.

STRETCH YARNS

Many different types of textured textile stretch yarns are used in making knitted and woven stretch fabrics. If the textured textile yarns are not controlled and the fabrics woven from the yarns are not properly finished, the degree of recovery of the stretch yarn may be lessened with wear and cleaning, and overstretching may result (see Figure 3-22). Many of the labels on garments made of textured textile yarns caution the consumer not to use a hot iron in combination with a moist cloth or steam.

If the stretch yarns are textured yarns, the tiny coiled filaments may be snagged in wear. When the filaments break, they may "ball up" on the surface and cause tiny "pills." As with any other fabric that may pill, the only known method of improving the condition is the use of a D-Fuzzit comb, carding comb, or brushing or shearing off the pills with a razor.

Stretch yarns, which are made of rubber, are easily identified.

1. Pull a lengthwise and crosswise yarn from a sample of fabric removed from an unexposed seam.
2. Note that the stretch yarn has a core of rubber. It is usually double wrapped with cotton yarn and stretches like a rubber band.

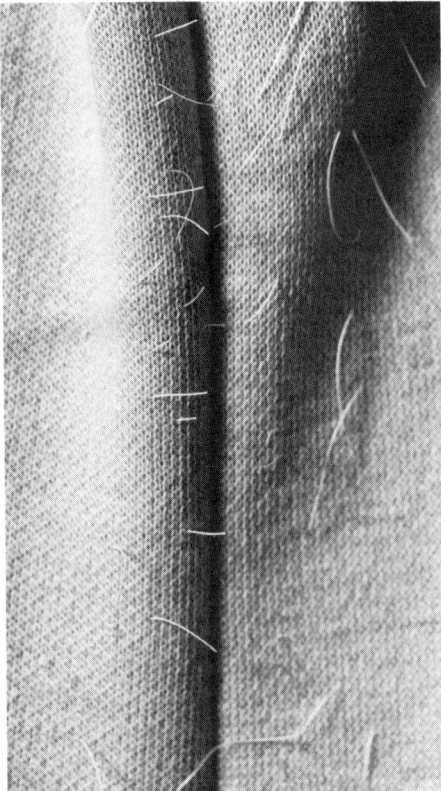

Figure 3-22   Example of an uncovered spandex yarn in a knit fabric that gave poor performance in use.

3. Pull the yarn to stretch it. When stretched, the wrapping of cotton opens in a spiral fashion.
4. Bring the yarn into the flame of a burning match. There will be a characteristic pungent odor of burning rubber.

Loss of elasticity of textile covered rubber core yarns may be due to several factors.

1. *Segmentation or cutting of rubber core yarn.* The fabrics that have caused complaints are made with a rubber core yarn wrapped with a textile yarn, usually cotton. When the fabric is stretched, the cotton yarn wrapped spirally around the core exerts a cutting action on it. This condition is not noted during wear or prior to dry cleaning. In dry cleaning, the natural rubber absorbs solvent and becomes swollen. During the flexing of the fabric during cleaning and drying, the core yarn breaks and this causes the fabric to relax and stretch.
2. *Deterioration of rubber core yarn.* There is sometimes evidence of a complete breakdown of the core yarn. It breaks up into a powdery substance, and the garment has an odor peculiar to rubber that has deteriorated. The scientific literature on rubber chemistry states that a very small amount of copper or brass in rubber can cause rapid deterioration. It is possible for small particles of copper or brass from the gears of the dyeing and finishing equipment to get into the rubber, and age will cause rubber deterioration. This is why rubber core yarn makers strongly recommend the use of sequestering and chelating agents in the dyeing and finishing of fabrics made of rubber core yarns. The agents combine with and neutralize the free copper.

BLENDS; HEAT-SENSITIVE YARNS

Perhaps one of the most baffling problems to consumers is heat damage to polyester blends. The problem is not new and peculiar to polyester, regardless of whether it is blended with wool, rayon, or cotton. The garment trade has seen this problem in connection with the cutting and sewing operations. Techniques for avoiding the problem have been circulated widely in the trade and, as a result, the problem has decreased. The garment trade has been informed that extra care must be given to cross-dyed and two-tone piecegoods to avoid discoloration in pressing, since they seem to be the most sensitive to heat. However, stock-dyed goods and fabrics dyed by other methods require extra care, too.

Improper finishing techniques can result in shine, moiré and streak markings, color migration, and fusing of polyester fibers.

Because polyester blends vary in fiber content, weight, and method of dyeing, they react differently to variations in temperature, pressure, and time in finishing.

If a garment is finished or pressed on the right side with a hand iron, the iron should be set on the rayon setting (225° to 300°F). Use only light pressure and move the iron quickly over the surface. The iron may be set at the silk setting (300° to 350°F) if you use a dry press cloth. With care, a steam iron may be used at the rayon setting. Since the heat of the iron is so critical in finishing these fabrics, it is advisable to check the setting of your iron from time to time. If extra care is not taken on double thicknesses such as seams, pockets, and pleats, shine may occur along the edges, and double impressions may be evident.

Many hand-knit yarns on the market today are made of heat-sensitive fibers that shrink excessively when exposed to heat in cleaning, drying, and finishing. Hand-knit items represent a large monetary investment in the yarn, a great amount of time and effort on the part of the creator, and much sentimental value. You may become disappointed and furious when something goes wrong with the handmade product if steam is used to block it or if it is sent for cleaning and blocking to a professional cleaner who has not been informed as to the fiber content of the yarn.

METALLIC

Many apparel and household fabrics containing metallic yarns can be dry-cleaned or laundered satisfactorily. However, some may cause problems. Consumer complaints may be classified as follows: loss of color; loss of metallic particles or coatings; perspiration damage; tarnishing; fabric damage from abrasion of the metallic yarns; shrinkage and puckering (in the majority of cases the textile yarns of the fabric shrink, or the metallic yarn shrinks because of the heat used in cleaning and finishing the fabric); and fabric damage in spot and stain removal. The majority of metallic yarns are not affected by carbon tetrachloride, perchlorethylene, fluorocarbon solvent, or Stoddard solvent. Some metallic yarns are affected by perchlorethylene and trichlorethylene. All metallic yarns are sensitive to abrasion and flexing. Therefore mechanical action in laundering or dry cleaning, tumbling, and spotting should be kept to a minimum.

Before attempting to remove spots or stains, the effect of the spotting agent on an unexposed seam should be observed. The color of metallic yarns may be affected in several ways: solvent-soluble dyes have a tendency to stain textile yarns; some dyes may fade to sunlight (under certain conditions, some dyes may leach out to water, synthetic detergents, and dry-cleaning solvents); the adhesive or bonding agent used to laminate metallic yarns may dissolve and cause a color change when attempting spot removal with water and a synthetic detergent; and colors and the metallic portion of the yarns may be affected by bleaching.

Metallic yarns made with a cellulose acetate butyrate film are affected by acetone and many spotting reagents that contain it or other solvents that similarly affect acetate.

The use of rust eradicator on metallic yarn will result in a dark discoloration because of a chemical reaction with the metallized pigments. Rust eradicator is hydrofluoric acid.

For safety, metallic fabrics should be pressed or finished at the temperature used to press acetate fabrics.

TEXTURED YARNS

Textured acetates have many good attributes, but they also have some limitations. Consumers complain that some textured acetate knits stretch and bag at the seat, elbows, and neckline. They do not bounce back with cleaning or pressing.

There are two explanations for this poor performance. In the first place, acetate itself is not an elastic fiber. Any excessive stretching action, as may occur at elbows, can cause an irreversible strain in the yarns. The natural elasticity of wool and nylon protect them against this. The only protection textured acetate knits have against excessive stretching is the structural elasticity inherent in highly twisted yarns and in the knitted structure itself. The second explanation is that textured acetate knit fabrics shrink excessively during pressing or finishing, and this gives them a tendency to elongate during wear and cleaning. Some manufacturers are using about 10 percent nylon with the acetate to give more fabric stability.

Other complaints are: delustering or dulling of the fabric during wear or in spot removal or finishing; shifting of yarns by improper spotting techniques; and shine during home pressing or commercial finishing.

Heat-setting of the yarn and fabric are very critical to the performance of garments in laundering, dry cleaning, drying, and finishing. If a textured yarn is not properly heat-set, it reacts like a stretch yarn. The fabric can shrink even when it is dyed. The more a fabric shrinks in dyeing, the greater must be the force to stretch or tenter the fabric. This can result in relaxation shrinkage.

LEARNING EXPERIENCES

1. Locate and mount fabric swatches that illustrate the following yarn structures: carded; combed; mercerized; filament; spun; woolen; worsted.
2. Find and mount fabric swatches along with a yarn taken from each that demonstrates the following: a single or simple yarn; a two-ply yarn; a four- or six-ply yarn; and "S" twist yearn; a "Z" twist yarn.
3. Assemble and mount fabric swatches along with yarn taken from each that illustrates various constructions of novelty yarn.
4. Analyze a fabric made of complex yarns. Analyze the yarn construction and explain the function of each. Identify and label the core, effect, and binder yarn.
5. Assemble and mount samples of stretch fabrics according to yarn construction; direction of stretch; and method of manufacture.
6. Explain the difference between a fabric made of a filament yarn and a fabric made of a blended filament yarn. Illustrate the difference.
7. Make a survey of your market area and determine the variety and composition of blended fabrics being used in different classes of wearing apparel. List six reasons why fabrics are made of blended yarns.
8. Define yarn slippage and seam slippage. Differentiate and illustrate.

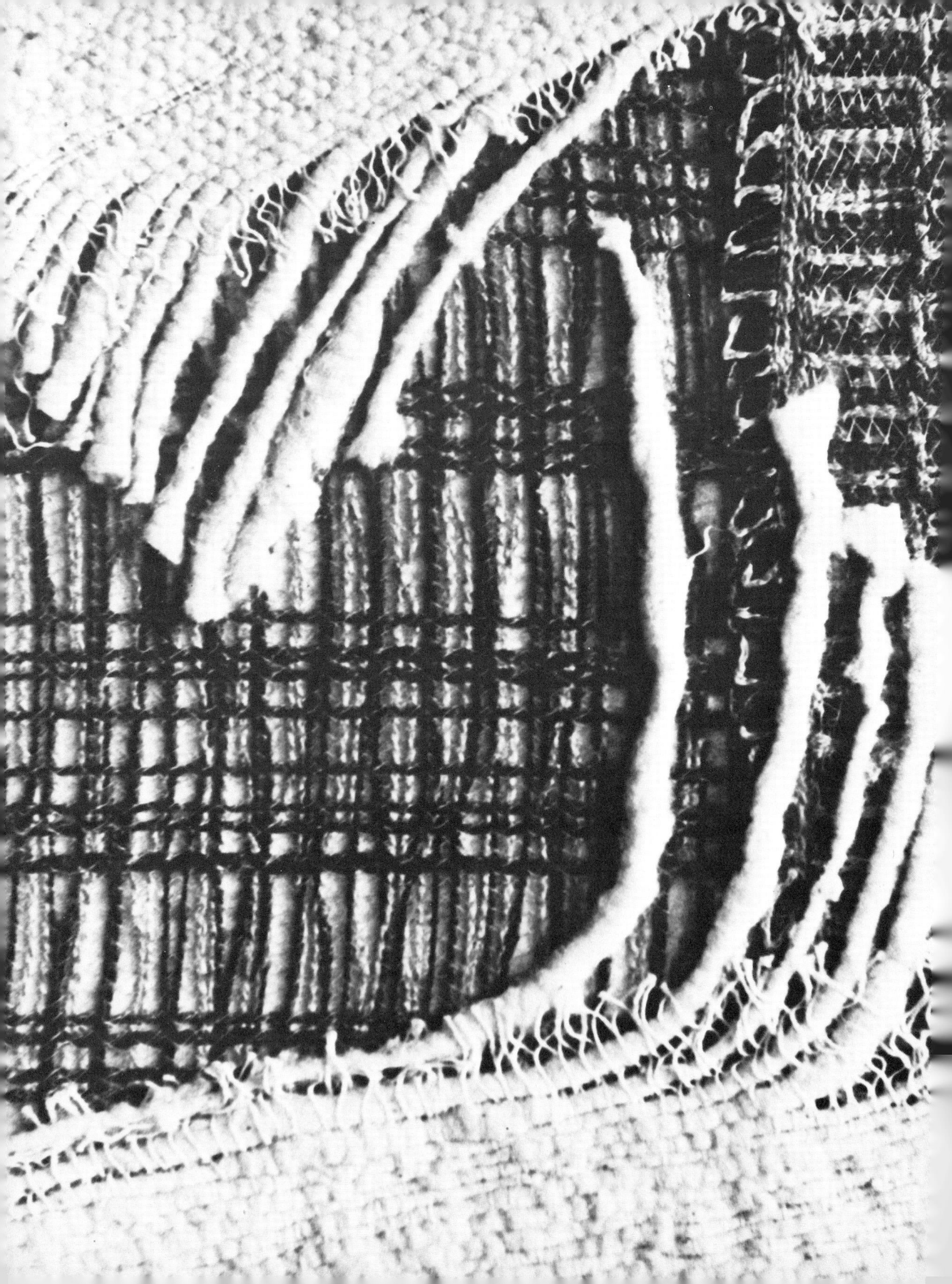

4

FABRIC CONSTRUCTION

PART I
FABRICS FORMED FROM
YARNS DIRECTLY

KNITTING

Authorities predicted that in the 1970s knits would dominate the fabric and fashion market. A leading fiber producer predicts knitwear production will double by 1980 and will comprise half of the apparel in the United States. The greatest growth will be in menswear. Knits have made the 1970s "the era of stretch." Doubleknits, jerseys, and full-fashion knits are lighter in weight and finer in gauge. Single jersey, warp, and Raschel knits are very significant in ready-to-wear. Knits will become more complicated with new fibers, textures, and mixtures.

Knit production is more flexible and faster than woven production. Knit machinery makes possible greater inventiveness. The industry changes rapidly, as illustrated by the technical skill of the new electronic knitting systems. An example is the advance pattern scanning and computer-programmed Moratronik knitting machines shown in Figures 4-1 to 4-3.

Producers of knit fabrics and garments are less inhibited by convention or tradition. Fiber producers and yarn texturizers

153

Figure
4-1 Computer-programmed Moratronik knitting machine.

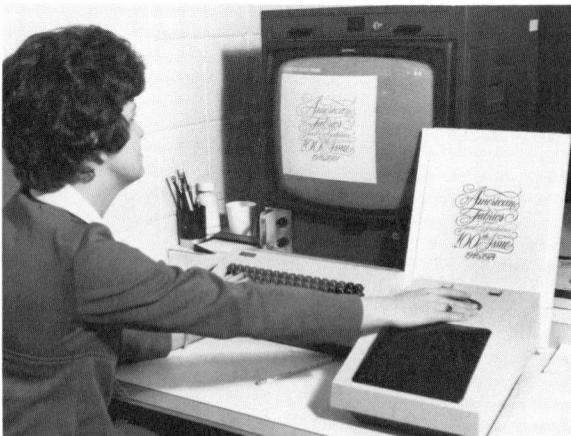

Figure 4-2 Video monitor for examination and correction by fabric designer prior to knitting.

Figure 4-3   Programmer setting up computer control data.

have given knitters new materials for varied textures and greater elegance. The popularity of travel and the revolt against old values have caused easy-care knits to boom. It is estimated that 85 percent of America's teenage girls sew some of their own clothes, and more and more young mothers sew. A 1969 DuPont survey of the home sewing development reveals home sewers spend $1,428,000 annually. In 1971 knits accounted for 30 to 33 percent of all fabric sold to home sewers. Another reason for the knit boom is a revival of handcrafts in America. Suppliers of knitting yarns are making it easy to knit and crochet.

It is predicted that once the novelty of knits wears off, there will be a 50/50 balance between knits and woven fabrics. Thus it is important to understand the structure of the knitting industry and the basic knit structures so as to identify fabric types and learn to properly relate performance and care characteristics with knit structures.

THE KNITTING INDUSTRY

The knitting industry is a unique and distinct part of the textile industry. In general, textile mills that manufacture knit fabrics do not manufacture woven fabrics. Exceptions to this are the vertical textile organizations, which produce knitted and woven goods. The knitting industry is not one industry but several. The hosiery industry, for example, differs in markets, styling, fabric type produced, and in other respects from the industry that produces double-knit fabrics.

The distinctive branches of the knitting industry exist because of the highly specialized machinery and technical skills required to produce the various types of knits. For example, machinery used to make sweater bodies cannot also be used to make hosiery, even though both are knitted products. The organization of the knitting industry tends to follow the lines of the specialized machinery used. Knitted fabrics and the machines that make them are inseparable.

The knitting industry is classified as: (1) the knitted yard goods industry, which produces fabric that is sold to apparel manufacturers, sewing center retail shops, and others; and (2) the knitted end products industry, which produces completed consumer products such as hosiery, sweaters, men's T-shirts and athletic shirts, and others (see Table 4-1).

Table 4-1   The Knitting Industry

Mill Type	*Knitted Yard Goods Industry* Products
Weft knitting	Single-knit jerseys, double-knits, interlock knits, knit terry, velour, etc., for dresses, sportswear, men's wear. Fake furs for coats, linings, hats, toys.
Tricot mills	Tricot jersey for loungewear, lingerie, blouses, skirts, dresses, three- and four-bar tricot for men's wear, sportswear, uniforms. Specialty items such as automotive upholstery fabric. Simplex fabrics, Milanese fabrics.
Raschel mills	Laces, power net, thermal underwear, thermal blankets, coat, suit, and dress fabrics, fish nets, netting.

Mill Type	*Knitted Apparel Producing Industries* Products
Hosiery mills	Fine-gauge seamless hoisery and panty hose.
Half-hose mills	Men's, women's, and children's coarse-gauge stockings.
Underwear mills	Men's and boys' athletic T-shirts, knitted shorts, ladies' and children's cotton and cotton blend panties and undershirts.
Full fashion mills	Full-fashioned sweaters and dresses.
Strip knitting mills	Sweaters, knit dresses, knit sport shorts.
Specialty knitting mills	Manufacture of knit hats, scarves, sweat shirts, neckwear, wristlets, etc.

Several factors are common throughout the knitting industry. First, practically all knit producers purchase yarn (the raw material of their products) instead of spinning or texturizing their own. In the weaving industry, producers usually spin and prepare their own yarn. Second, all knitters are either direct knitters or commission knitters. A direct knitter purchases yarn, knits products in his own plant and sells his merchandise under his own name or trademark. A commission knitter produces products for a second party who furnishes the yarn to the commission knitter and receives back the completed knit fabric or product.

Knitting is the construction of a fabric by forming loops of yarn with needles and drawing new loops through those previously formed. This definition is very simple. As you will see, knit structures can be very complex.

In all knit structures, there are certain terms to be aware of.

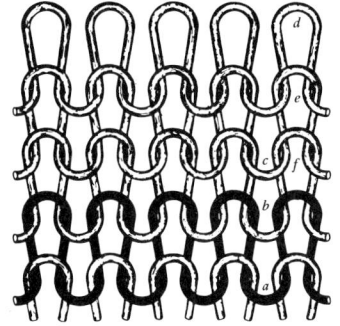

Figure 4-4   The loops that run crosswise of a knit fabric are called "courses."

1. *Courses.* The horizontal or crosswise row of loops made by successive needles (see Figure 4-4). It corresponds to the filling direction in a woven fabric. There are four courses in the illustration. The number of courses per unit length (courses per inch) of fabric is dependent on the height of the stitch loop. This depends on the distance the needle pulls the yarn when the loop is made.
2. *Wales.* The vertical or lengthwise column of interlocked loops made by the same needle (see Figure 4-5). It corresponds to the warp direction in a woven fabric. There are four wales in the illustration.
3. *Knit stitches.*   Knitted fabrics are formed by using large numbers of knitting needles. There are two types of needles used: (1) the latch needle, and (2) the spring beard needle (see Figure 4-6). Spring beard needles are usually used for finer, closer knit stitches. The way in which the actual knitting stitch is produced is illustrated in Figures 4-7 and 4-8.
4. *Gauge.*   The number of needles per inch on a warp knitting machine is called the gauge, and gauge determines the fineness of the knit. The higher the gauge (22, 24, 28), the finer the fabric; the lower the gauge (6, 8, 10), the heavier or bulkier the fabric. The exact relationship between needles per unit length and gauge is not the same for all types of knitting machines.
5. *Cut.*   Cut is the number of slots or cuts per inch in the flat needle bed of a weft knitting machine (e.g., 14-cut or 14 needles per inch).

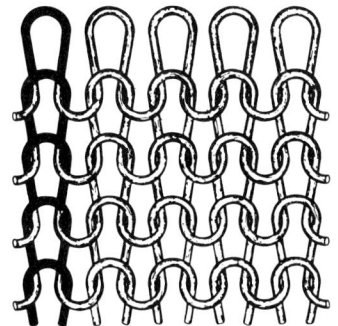

Figure 4-5   The loops that run lengthwise of a knit fabric are called "wales."

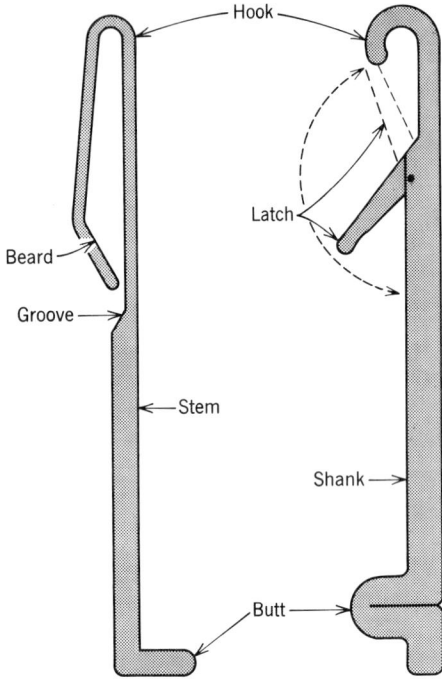

Figure 4-6 Spring beard needle (left) and latch needle (right) used in knitted fabric manufacture. (Courtesy: Fairchild Publications, Inc.)

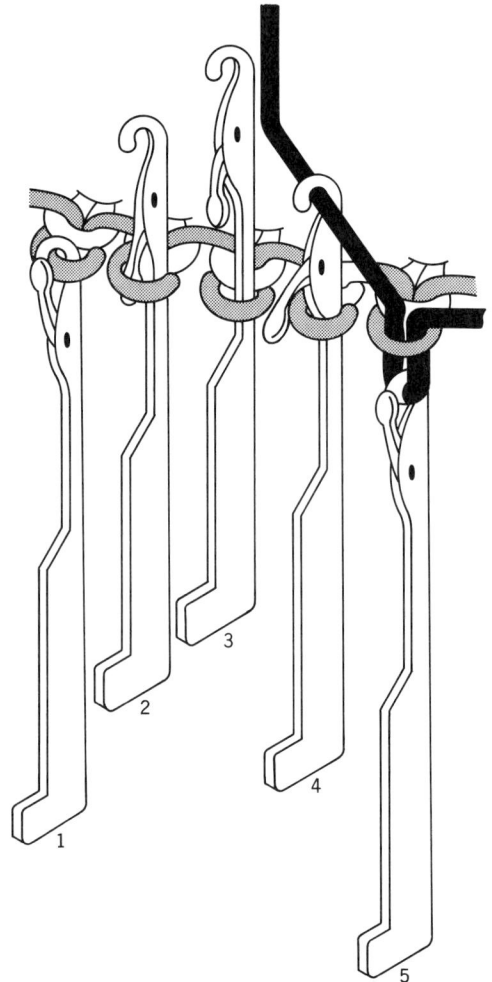

Figure 4-7 Forming knitted stitches with the latch needle. From left to right: (1, 2, and 3) The needle rises and, as it does, the previous loop opens the latch and slides down onto the needle shank. (4) As the needle begins to descend, a new yarn is fed onto the needle hook. As the needle continues to descend, the previous loop slides onto it and causes the latch to close. (5) The needle continues downward and the old loop slides off the needle completely (this is called the knock-over). In so doing, it becomes interlooped with a new loop, which has just been formed in the needle hook, thus creating the knitted fabric structure. (Courtesy: Fairchild Publications, Inc.)

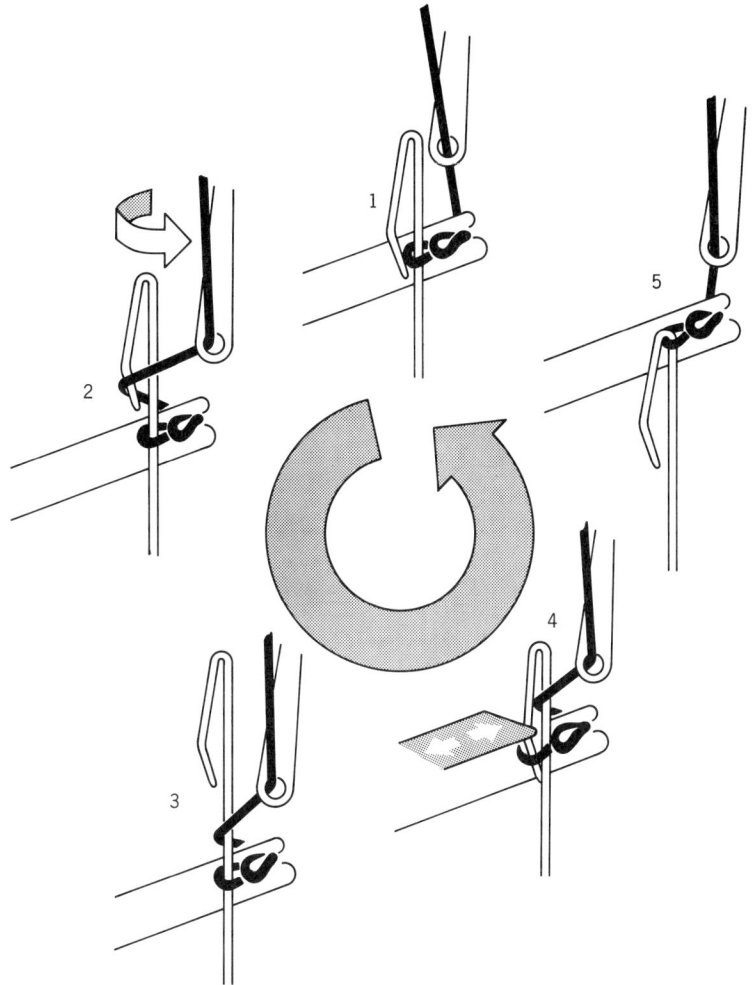

Figure 4-8 Forming knitted stitches with the spring beard needle. (1) As the needle moves upward, the previously formed loop slides down to the needle stem. (2) A new yarn is fed onto the needle through the action of the yarn guide. (3) The needle continues to rise and the new yarn slides under the beard. When the new yarn is under the beard, a presser bar comes forward and closes the beard. As the needle continues downward, the old loop slides onto the closed beard. The presser bar then moves back to allow the old loop to slide freely. (5) The needle continues downward and the old loop slides off the needle completely (this is called the knock-over). In so doing, it becomes interlooped with a new loop which has just been formed in the needle hook, thus creating the knit fabric structure. (Drawing by Ralph Kruse; Courtesy: Fairchild Publications, Inc.)

KNITTING STITCHES

There are four principal stitches used to make knit fabrics: (1) the plain stitch; (2) the purl stitch; (3) the miss stitch; and (4) the tuck stitch. These four basic stitches or combinations of them form the basis of all knitted fabrics.

Knit Stitch

This is the basic knitting stitch (also called plain stitch). The loop formation of the stitch is shown in Figure 4-9. It is also known as the jersey stitch.

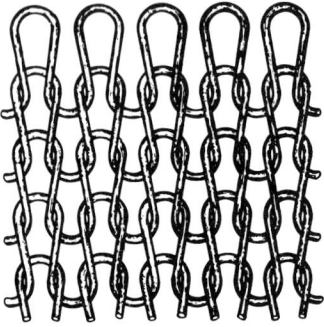

(a)

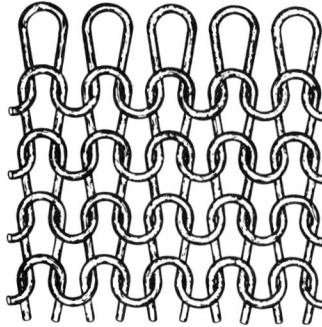

(b)

Figure 4-9 *(a)* The knit stitch or plain stitch. Face side of jersey shows necks of the loop. *(b)* Reverse side of jersey shows the heads of the loop. The purl stitch is reverse of the knit stitch. (Courtesy: National Knitted Outerwear Association)

Purl Stitch

This is actually the reverse of the knit stitch (sometimes called reverse knit stitch). The back of the plain knit fabric is a purl stitch structure. Purl fabric, in its simplest form, has the loops of one course intermeshed in the opposite direction, and so on, alternately. It produces a rounder, puffier stitch than a plain or jersey stitch.

The purl machine is sometimes referred to as "links and links" machine. The fabric looks the same on both sides (back of jersey heads of loop) and has more vertical than horizontal stretch.

Miss Stitch (Sometimes called Welt Stitch)

This stitch is made when one or more knitting needles are deactivated and do not move into position to accept a yarn. The yarn passes by and no stitch is formed. Follow the darkened yarn in Figure 4-10. The needle miss-knits. The missed or welted yarn floats unlooped on the reverse side of the fabric. This stitch is used effectively to produce color on the face of the fabric and then it can be floated to the reverse side of the fabric when it is not wanted on the face.

Tuck Stitch

A knitting needle holds its old loop and then receives a new yarn. Two loops collect in the needle hook. This action is repeated several times and eventually the yarn casts off the needle and is knitted. This results in an elongated wale. Tuck stitches appear on the back of the fabric and appear as an inverted "V" (see Figure 4-11). Blister or openwork effects as in lace or mesh are created by the use of this stitch.

Figure 4-10 Miss-stitch or welt stitch. Note the floating unknit yarn on the back of the fabric. (Courtesy: National Knitted Outerwear Association)

CLASSIFICATION OF KNITS

There are two basic categories of knit structures: (1) weft knits (sometimes called filling knits), and (2) warp knits. Each uses different and specialized machinery, and each produces different types of fabrics. Warp knits can be distinguished from weft knits (see Figure 4-12), usually by examining the face and back of the fabric. The face of a warp knit has clearly defined knit stitches running vertically (lengthwise) but slightly angled from side to side. The back of the fabric has slightly angled horizontal floats.

WEFT KNIT (FILLING KNITTING)

In weft knitting, a single yarn is fed into a number of needles in the horizontal direction. The fabric is made by building the loops on top of each other (see Figure 4-13).

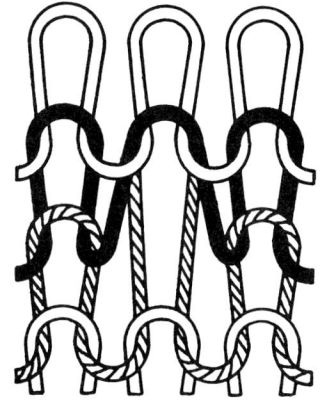

Figure 4-11 One-needle tuck stitch. Note the elongated wale on the back of the fabric. The tuck stitch on the face of the fabric looks like an inverted "V." (Courtesy: National Knitted Outerwear Association)

100% polyester double knit. Source: Inwood K.M.

100% polyester warp knit. Source: Fab Ind.

Figure 4-12 Warp knits can usually be identified and distinguished from weft knits by examination of the face and back of the fabric. The face has clearly defined knit stitches running vertically (lengthwise) but slightly angled from side to side. The back of the fabric has slightly angled horizontal floats.

Supply cone

Yarn
guide

Needles

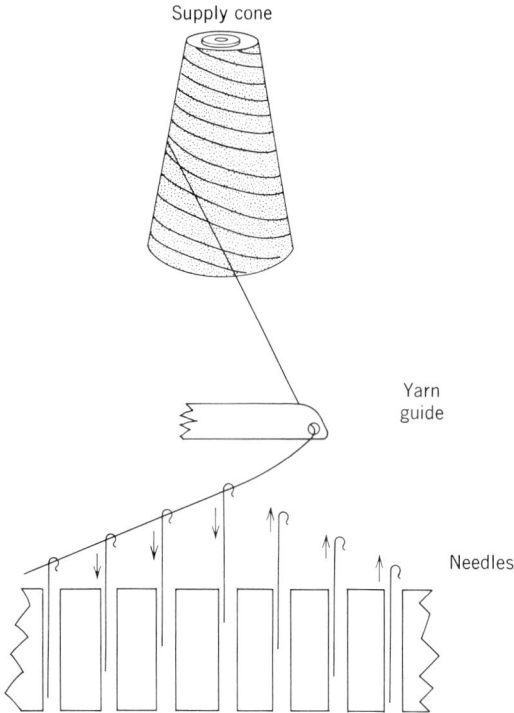

Figure 4-13 Weft knitting. One supply for all the needles. Needles move individually to receive the yarn. (Courtesy: E. I. du Pont de Nemours and Company, Inc.)

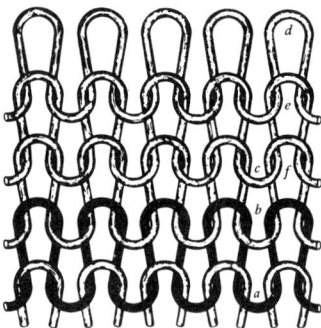

Weft knits may be made on either a circular or flat knitting machine. In making a circular knit, the knitting is done on a machine whose needle bed is a cylinder and produces fabric in a tubular form. In making a flat knit, the knitting is done on a machine whose needle bed is flat and produces fabric with a selvage on each edge. A diagramatic drawing of weft knitting is shown in Figure 4-14.

WARP KNITTING

In warp knitting a large number of parallel yarns are mounted on the knitting machine. In warp-knit fabrics the yarns run the length of the fabric. They form vertical loops in one course and then move diagonally to the next course to knit the next course. Thus the yarns zigzag from side to side along the length of the fabric. Each stitch in a course is made by a different yarn; a diagramatic drawing of warp knitting is shown in Figure 4-15. A diagram of a simple warp knit fabric is shown in Figure 4-16.

Figure 4-14 Diagram of weft knit shows direction the individual yarn assumes in the fabric — *horizontal.* (Courtesy: National Knitted Outerwear Association)

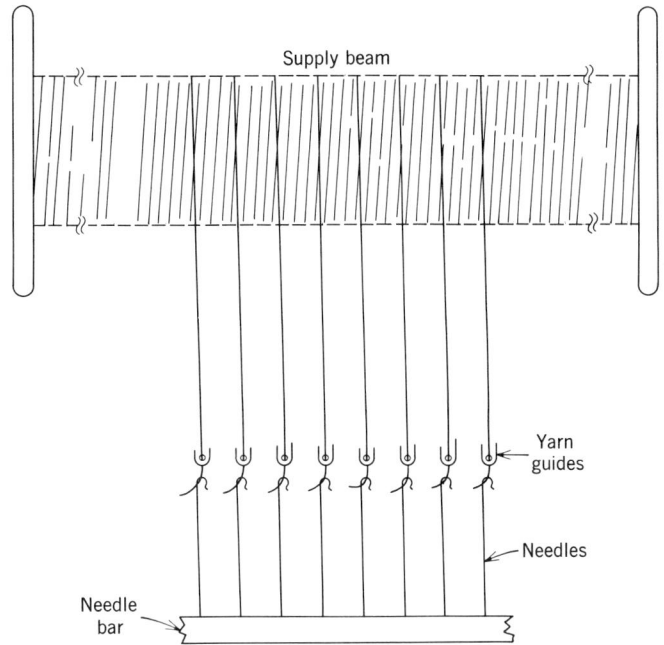

Figure 4-15 Warp knitting. Separate yarns supply for each needle. All needles move together in one motion. (Courtesy: E. I. du Pont de Nemours and Company, Inc.)

CLASSIFICATION OF WEFT-KNIT FABRICS

There are three general classifications of weft or filling knits. They are (1) plain knits; (2) purl Knits; and (3) rib Knits. There are variations of each of these methods of knitting.

PLAIN KNITS

Plain knits are sometimes called jersey or stockinette. Fabrics made this way have both vertical and horizontal stretch. The fabric front and back are different. Described another way, jersey is a single-faced knitted fabric with loops intermeshing in the same direction on the face side; semicircular loops on the reverse side (see Figure 4-9).

A simple jersey stitch can be varied by using different yarns; by using double-looped stitches of different lengths to produce plush, terry, and velour constructions; and lacing or transferring loops from the needle on which they are made to adjacent needles. Some fur pile fabrics are made with the jersey stitch, but with a sliver attachment on the machine that feeds the deep pile fibers into the knit fabric.

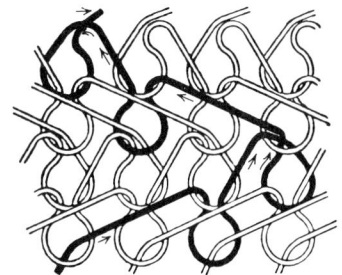

Figure 4-16 A simple warp knit fabric. This is the structure of a plain tricot jersey fabric. The darkened loops illustrate how, in a zig-zag manner, the warp yarn interlocks with other warp yarns in nearby wales to make a warp knit fabric. (Courtesy: National Knitted Outerwear Association)

Figue 4-17 It is fascinating to study designs in knitted fabrics. The concern for ecology is expressed in this red and white circular knit fabric.

The variations in jersey fabrics are endless. Different effects are achieved also by varying the methods of dyeing, printing, and finishing. Plain jersey, pattern wheel jersey, terry, and velour are all made with a basic jersey stitch. Designing knits is a study in itself — and a fascinating one (see Figure 4-17).

PURL KNIT FABRIC

Purl knit fabrics are those in which knit stitches and purl stitches alternate to the face and back of the fabric on successive courses. Simple purl fabrics look the same on both sides of the fabric. The simplest purl fabric is known as 1 × 1 purl in which one course has all stitches drawn to the face while the second course has all the stitches drawn to the back. This is repeated on the third course (see Figure 4-18). Purl knit fabrics are sometimes called "links and links" fabric because the machine on which they are made is called a links and links machine. They may be flat or circular machines and are very versatile, since they can be adapted to make plain and rib as well as purl fabrics.

RIB KNIT FABRICS

Rib knit fabrics are made on knitting machines that differ from those used for jersey knits. Rib knits have stitches drawn to both sides of the fabric, since the machine used to make them requires two sets of needles usually positioned at right angles to each other. Each set produces stitches, thus the fabric is formed between the two-needle holding beds. Rib knits are produced on flat as well as circular machines.

Rib knit fabrics are easily identified because there is a distinct lengthwise rib effect on both sides of the fabric. If one knit and purl stitch appears on one side and alternates with one rib and one purl on the other side, it is a 1 × 1 rib (see Figure 4-19). If two knit stitches and two purl stitches appear alternately on face and back, it is called a 2 × 2 rib. A 3 × 1 rib has three knit stitches and one purl on the face side of the fabric and one knit and three purl on the back. Many combinations are possible.

The rib knit has many variations.

1. *Cardigan.* This stitch is used to give increased weight and bulk to fabrics. Two versions of this stitch are the half-cardigan and the full-cardigan stitch commonly used to make sweaters.
2. *Interlock.* Interlock knit fabrics are a variation of rib knits. In rib knits columns of adjacent wales appear on the face and

Figure 4-18 1 × 1 purl fabric. Each successive course alternates 1 purl, 1 knit, 1 purl, 1 knit. (Courtesy: National Knitted Outerwear Association)

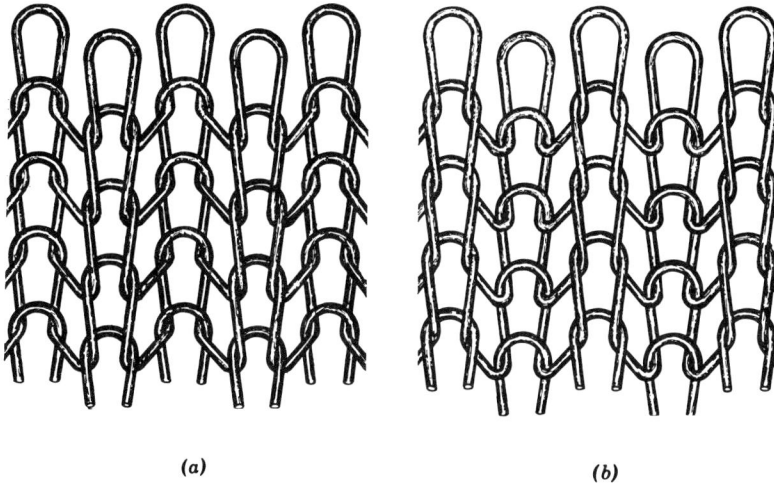

Figure 4-19 *(a)* 1 × 1 rib knit (face side of fabric). *(b)* 1 × 1 rib knit (reverse side of fabric). (Courtesy: National Knitted Outerwear Association)

back of the cloth. The back of any given knit stitch on the rib fabric will show the back of the fabric as purl stitch. On interlock knits, columns of wales are directly behind each other. The back of any given knit stitch on the interlock fabric will reveal another knit stitch directly behind it on the back of the cloth.

To determine if a fabric is an interlock or rib, hold the top of the fabric, spread it apart widthwise, and view the fabric wales carefully at the top edge of the cloth. If the knit stitches are one behind the other, the fabric is interlock. Another method is to put a pin through the center of a knit stitch on the fabric face, spread the cloth slightly widthwise, and view the appearance of the cloth where the pin comes through the other side. If the pin comes through another knit stitch, it is an interlock. If it comes through on a purl stitch, it is a rib fabric.

3. *Double Knit.* Double knit is a term used to describe a broad range of knits produced on rib machines. The fabrics vary from simple to very complicated structures. They are produced on machines having two sets of needles set at an angle to each other. The construction must have some variation of pattern and the cut must be greater than 15.

Some people classify an interlock knit as a doubleknit, but it does not meet the criterion of pattern variation. Ponte Di Roma knit is called a true double knit. Two feeds on the machine make a 1 × 1 interlock stitch, and two feeds make a plain jersey stitch. Blister knits are also classed as double knits. Pique, Milano rib, Ottoman, and Bourrelet are also examples of double knit structures.

A variety of different types of attachments can be added to circular or flat bed weft knitting machines to make complicated and beautiful jacquard knit fabrics. These include pattern wheels, perforated rolls, multistep drums, and continuous tapes and bands. Each one of these can be varied to produce complex designs such as jersey-jacquards and rib-jacquards.

VARIATIONS IN WEFT KNITTED FABRICS

DEEP OR HIGH PILE KNITS

Simulated fur pile fabrics or "deep pile" fabrics are made with a special type of jersey knit made by a procedure that involves feeding staple fiber in the form of sliver into the knit as the yarns are passing through the knitting needles while the fabric is being made. The fiber is caught in the knit structure and held between the knit stitches. These fabrics are also known as sliver knits.

In 1944 the first knitted high or deep pile fabrics were made on the sliver knit machine. Production speed was increased, and costs were decreased. The new method of production made it possible to pack more pile staple per unit area to create greater density and furriness of pile. Fabrics closely approach the appearance of the genuine animal pelt.

Any type of man-made or natural fiber, or blends of these, may be used for the pile. Modacrylic, acrylic, wool, mohair, rayon, polyester, nylon, and blends of these are widely used as the pile fiber. Modacrylic is the most popular fiber used. Cotton and polypropylene are the most widely used yarns for the knit backing.

In 1955 there were new developments in knitted fabrics made of acrylic and modacrylic fibers. They looked like genuine fur. Then the differential pile heights that created the "guard hair" look of genuine fur were born. This effect is achieved by using two different fibers that have differential shrinkages. The different pile heights are created by the finishing process, which shrinks one fiber to a lower pile height than the other.

In 1959 printed versions of animal furs on pile fabrics found public acceptance and rapidly gave them an identity of their own.

There is continuous experimentation with new fibers and new finishes. Research is being conducted in the field of finishing processes to improve resiliency and durability after dry cleaning. Research is also directed toward the use and adaptation of jacquard equipment to the sliver knitting machine. This would make possible the development of intricate patterns and sculptured effects through the use of different fibers with differential shrinkage. The whole area of color and design remains to be explored. To date, most designs have concentrated on duplicating the look of genuine pelts. The challenge is to break away from pelt designs and enter the area of original designs and colors.

Knitting and fiber technology in this field has made a major breakthrough with the introduction of the computer–programmed Moratronik knitting machine. The electronic pattern scanning permits the kind of realistic reproduction up to now available only in expensive woven imports.

Up to now, knitted deep pile fabrics were limited to a 2½ inch design grid which, when repeated either vertically or horizontally, resulted in a uniform appearance. The Morat system provides individual needle selection electronically enabling true reproduction of a natural random pattern such as a leopard, cheetah, ocelot, jaguar, lynx, black cross mink, and piece mink. Fiber content varies according to desired effects. Most of the spotted fur types consist of Verel modacrylic and Dralon, high-shrink acrylic.

KNITTED TERRY

These fabrics are knitted with two yarns feeding simultaneously into the same knitting needles. When the fabric is knitted, one yarn appears on the face, the other on the back. The method is known as plating. One of the yarns is called a ground yarn, the other a loop yarn. The loop yarns are pulled out by special devices and become the loop pile of the knitted terry fabric.

KNITTED VELOUR

These fabrics are made in the same way as the knitted terry. After the fabric is knitted, the loop pile is cut by a process called shearing, then brushed. Knitted velours have a soft, downy, suedelike texture, somewhat resembling velveteen.

WARP KNIT FABRICS

There are two general classifications of warp knit fabrics.

1. Tricot, a warp knit machine that produces vertical wales on the face of the fabric and crosswise ribs on the back.
2. Raschel, a warp knit machine that stitches or lays-in yarns and makes open and lacy fabrics or ridged or stretch fabrics.

TRICOT KNIT

Tricot fabrics are classified according to the number of sets of yarns used in their structures. Each set of yarns is controlled by a separate guide bar. A single guide bar fabric is relatively weak and unstable because each loop consists of only one yarn. Two guide bar fabrics are the most common all tricot knits; each loop is made up of two yarns, one from each guide bar. Three and four guide bar fabrics are more versatile, permitting more variety in design and weight of the fabric; each loop can contain three or four yarns.

The tricot knit construction has good abrasion resistance, high burst and tear strength, does not ravel, and has good stability, elasticity, and resiliency. Tricot fabrics may be made of acetate, nylon, polyester acetate, and triacetate. The main end uses are for lingerie, dresses and blouses, uniforms, and men's shirts. With the introduction of bonded and laminated fabrics, tricot became the dominant knit to be used as the backing fabric. Tricot knits are used widely for the backing of coated fabrics such as the simulated suedes and leathers and may also be coated with gold, silver, or colored pigments to make luxurious and glamorous blouse and dress fabrics.

RASCHEL KNIT

The difference between a tricot and raschel knit is that the raschel knitting machinery utilizes latch needles instead of spring needles and 2 to 48 guide bars. Because of the many guide bars, the raschel knit machine is very versatile because it can lay-in yarns while knitting through the use of multiple guide bars. Raschel fabrics can be produced with either filament or staple yarns and, since these yarns can be either standard or novelty types, it is possible to achieve design interest through surface texture. Fabrics range from openwork crochet looks to solid structures with three-dimensional effects.

Because the raschel knit machine is so versatile, it can be used for a wide variety of fabrics, ranging from beautiful nets and laces to dress, suit, curtain, and drapery fabrics, and including power net fabrics used in foundation garments (see Figure 4-20).

MILANESE KNITS

Milanese is knitted on flat knitting as well as circular knitting machines. The flat knit types use spring beard needles, the circulars use latch needles.

Milanese knits are characterized as a lightweight, fine fabric usually made from filament yarns. Milanese is used primarily for better types of lingerie and dress wear. The fabric is not very widely used compared with regular tricot constructions. It is stable, has excellent drapability, is more costly than regular tricot, and is considered a prestige fabric. It may be recognized by fine riblike stitches on the face and diagonal patterning on the back.

Figure 4-20 Knits are moving more into the foreground in draperies. This Raschel knit casement fabric is made by Joseph B. Hoffman of Monsanto Textile Company's SEF modacrylic fiber.

KETTENRASCHEL

Kettenraschel fabrics are made by a variation of the tricot knit using filament or staple yarns in coarse gauge. Many of the fabrics have raised pattern effects. Great variety in surface texture can be achieved by this construction.

SIMPLEX KNIT

A Simplex Knit is produced on a machine that is basically two tricot machines arranged back to back. It is a double tricot type fabric, and both face and back look like the face of tricot. The fabrics, which are heavier than tricot, find greatest uses in gloves, slip covers, and handbags.

LACES

Most laces are made on a raschel machine. The effect obtained depends on the number of latch needles and guide bars used. Many combinations are employed to make the great variety of nets and laces used in apparel fabrics. For example, pattern effects may be achieved by laying-in yarns. There are knitting machines with as many as 48 guide bars and, since each guide bar can direct the feed of a different yarn into the knitting machine, you get an idea how complex and versatile knitting can be.

FABRIC IMPERFECTIONS

Manufacturers of garments, retailers, and consumers have been dissatisfied with imperfections found in knitted fabrics. They are usually caused by lack of quality control in the knitting of the fabric, malfunctioning of the knitting machine, or imperfect yarns or improper finishing. The most common imperfections are listed and described in Table 4-2.

Table 4-2   Knitted Fabric Defects*

Barré. Streaks or bands in a fabric, caused by differences in yarn size, tension on yarns or fabric, color, luster, or shrinkage from one section of the cloth to the adjacent area. The bands are usually horizontal in weft knit fabrics and vertical in warp knit fabrics.

Birdseye or tucking defect. Unintentional tucking caused by a bent latch on the latch needle or the needle not being raised to the proper height for the old loop to be cast off.

Boardy.   Very harsh or stiff hand, caused by stitches being too tight or yarn being too large.

Bowing.   Design or line effect that curves across the fabric. The distortion is caused by the take-up mechanism on the knitting machine.

Broken filaments or yarn.   Mechanical breaks that cause separation.

Cockled fabric.   Fabric puckers and does not lie flat. It is caused by uneven stitches or uneven yarn size.

Drop stitch.   An unknitted stitch, caused by a stitch being too loose or the yarn carrier not being set properly.

Float.   Unwanted miss stitch(es) caused by needle(s) not raised to receive the new yarn.

Needle line.   Lengthwise marks or lines in the fabric resulting from a wale that is tighter or looser than the others. This is caused by a needle being tight in the slot or from a defective sinker.

Press off.   Large hole in the fabric, caused by a yarn breaking at a particular feed so knitting cannot occur.

Run or ladder.   A series of dropped stitches in a wale.

Skewing.   Design or line effect that is straight across the fabric but not perpendicular to the fabric edges.

Sleazy.   Term used to describe a flimsy or underconstructed knit fabric — one lacking ''body.''

Stop mark.   A horizontal fabric streak resulting when the knitting machine was stopped. It is caused by a tension difference in the yarns.

---

*See Manual of Standard Fabric Defects in the Textile Industry. Graniteville Company, Graniteville, South Carolina (1975) for other knitted fabric defects.

KNITS IN CONSUMER USE

SELECTION OF KNITTED FABRICS

Knitted fabrics have some positive advantages. They recover from wrinkling more readily than woven fabrics. Knitted fabrics, however, take a less sharp crease than wovens. Knitted fabrics mold and fit easily to body shapes and move easily with body movement. Woven fabrics are usually rigid (unless made with stretch yarns), do not mold to body shape, and resist body movement.

Bulky knit fabrics provide excellent insulation in still air but, because of open structure of knitted fabric, poor insulation in wind. Woven fabrics, when tightly woven, provide a high degree of wind resistance that knit fabrics cannot provide.

If two fabrics are otherwise equal (yarns and knit type) but of differing wales and courses per inch, their fabric properties will differ. The fabric with more wales per inch will be more stable and rigid in the width direction. The fabric with more courses per inch will be more stable and rigid in the length direction.

The fabric with both more wales and more courses per inch will, in addition to being more stable in both length and width, possess better ability to recover from stretching than one with lower wales and courses per inch.

The fabric with fewer wales and courses per inch will stretch easier (less rigid) and mold to body shapes and figures more readily, but it will have poorer recovery properties than one with higher wales and courses per inch.

The fabric with more wales per inch will tend to shrink less in their width direction.

The fabric with more courses per inch will tend to shrink less in their length direction.

CARE OF KNITS

Many of the new knits are designed for easy care at home, especially the acrylic and polyester knits. They can be machine-washed and dried in a home dryer and worn again without ironing. However, many have learned that dry cleaning preserves the appearance and prolongs the wear of "easy-care" knits. Professional dry cleaning is usually recommended on labels for luxury knits or expensive knit garments. The care method best for a particular item depends on fiber content, yarn construction, fabric construction, color and finish applied to the fabric, and design of the finished garment.

UNDERSTANDING PERFORMANCE OF KNITS

With the increasing popularity of knitted apparel and household textiles of all kinds, new performance problems have occurred in consumer use.

The International Fabricare Institute has found that performance problems with knits are related to one or more of the following.

1. Shrinkage and stretching.
2. Mechanical damage.
   a. Snagging.
   b. Pilling.
   c. Needle cut marks.
   d. Loss of pile.
3. Colorfastness
   a. Pigment prints.
   b. Screen prints.
   c. Sublimation of dye.
4. Garment design.
   a. Loss of pleats.
   b. Metallic trim.

SHRINKAGE AND STRETCHING

Knit fabrics made of polyester, acrylic, nylon, and other heat-sensitive fibers retain their size and shape in wear and cleaning if they have been properly heat-set in the textile mill. Yet many knit fabrics being sold today are causing complaints of shrinkage. Why? Perhaps it is because manufacturers are either unaware of the importance of precautions to be taken in carrying out the stabilization process or are failing to employ any process of stabilization whatever. The result is unsatisfactory performance of the garment.

Shrinkage has been noticed in men's polyester double knit suits. Evidence of such shrinkage is seen in the excessive fullness of the linings and the waviness of zipper tapes. In some cases, it is possible to steam the garment and stretch it back to shape, but this is only a temporary correction, and the fabric tends to revert to its shrunken dimensions after hanging for several hours. The home sewer can find some relief from this problem by preshrinking the fabric before making it into a garment. Shrinking and stretching has been noticed in some raschel constructions (see Figure 4-21).

Figure 4-21 The popcorn stitch Raschel-Crochet knit fabrics present several problems in wear, spotting, and cleaning. They may stretch in wear, stretch in dry cleaning, and distort and flatten in the removal of spots and stains.

MECHANICAL DAMAGE

Snagging

This is said to be the most common problem with knits. Knitting authorities explain that snagging is generally due to construction of the fabric, such as looseness of the loops, and that there are ways the knitter can minimize the problem. These include increasing yarn tension in the machine, setting the loop through heat treatment, bonding with an adhesive (thus preventing the yarns from pulling out), and applying an antisnag finish.

Reweavers, who can repair woven fabrics damaged in wear or cleaning, are reluctant to accept knit fabrics. About the only thing one can do is to take a needle or a needle threader with a fine wire loop and pull the loop the the wrong or underside of the fabric. If a hole develops in a knit, it is nearly impossible to mend it without its being visible.

Pilling

This problem ranks next to snagging. Depending on the type and construction of the yarn, the fiber ends tend to work to the surface and form small balls or pills. Natural fibers will break away, shedding the pills, but synthetic fibers are so strong that they do not break away readily from the fabric. Pills usually occur in areas that are especially abraded or rubbed during wear, such as in the underarm area.The condition can be accentuated by the action of laundering and dry cleaning. It is very difficult, if not impossible, to remove pills from synthetic fabrics satisfactorily.

Needle Cut Marks

Knits should be sewn only on a machine equipped with a ball needle especially made for knits. If the sewer is careless and allows a sharp needle to become dull or if he sews too rapidly, the needle may partially cut through the yarn along the line of stitching. At first, the damage is not noticeable. With wear and cleaning, the holes become obvious (see Figure 4-22).

COLORFASTNESS

Pigment Prints

This problem is not peculiar to knits, but this method of printing is used widely on knit fabrics, and complaints of loss of color due to pigment printing on knits are on the increase.

Figure 4-22 The needle cut marks from sewing are visible in the areas where the contrasting colored yoke is sewn to the bodice.

Screen Prints

Both hand and machine screen printing is used to produce designs on knitted fabrics. Some screen prints dry-clean beautifully; others have limitations. Some wet-clean or launder satisfactorily. Silk warp knits that are screen-printed must be handled with care. Some of them are printed with dyes that are very sensitive to water. There are limitations as to what you can or cannot do in removing spots.

Sublimation of Dye

Some yarn-dyed polyesters cause complaints because of sublimation of dye. Heat from a hand iron at a high setting or contact of the fabric with a hot surface may cause this damage. In a red and white polyester twill, the red dye may sublime, staining the white yarn. The damaged area is usually mistaken for a stain, and there is no way to restore the fabric. Therefore, keep a hand iron at the rayon setting.

GARMENT DESIGN

Loss of Pleats

Many knit fabrics made of 100 percent heat-sensitive fibers can be given a permanent pleat. But many knit fabrics combine heat-sensitive and nonheat-sensitive fibers (natural fibers and rayon) that cannot be given a permanent pleat that remains sharp through wear and cleaning. Fabrics made of textured yarns and novelty yarns are also difficult to pleat, particularly when the pleating is done on the bias of the fabrics. Many pleats in knit fabrics can be reset with careful hand finishing. However, when novelty machine pleats relax, they cannot be reset with hand finishing.

Metallic Trim

Current fashion favors increased use of metallic trims, studs, buttons, buckles, and chains. Some trims are removable; others are not because they are an integral part of the garment (see Figure 4-23), and some of the trims have very sharp edges that can snag or cut a hole in the knit fabric during the cleaning or drying cycle.

ADVANTAGES AND DISADVANTAGES OF SPECIFIC KNITTED FABRIC TYPES

A variety of effects may be achieved in knitted fabrics by varying the fiber content and using novelty yarns, and extra yarns or

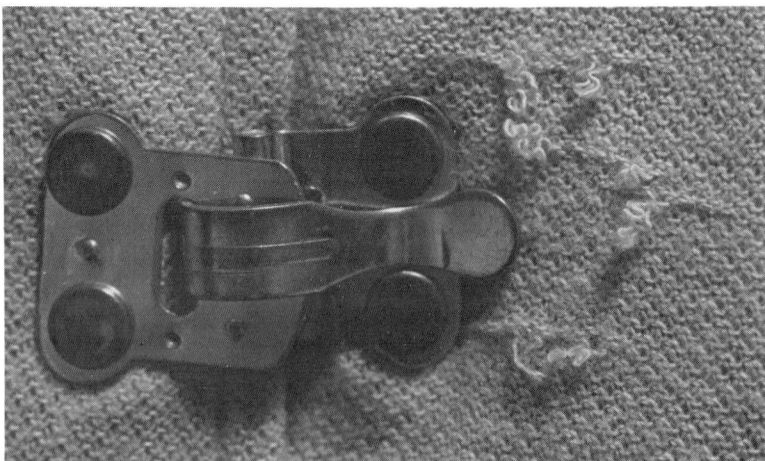

Figure 4-23 These brass hook and eye closures, set into the fabric with metal brads, are responsible for the snagging of the knit.

fibers may be knitted into the background fabric. Finishing techniques and printing may also be used to create interesting effects that change the appearance so that a knitted fabric often looks like a conventional woven fabric. In this discussion, we have classified knitted fabrics as follows.

1. Plain jersey knits.
2. Double knits.
3. Brushed knits.
4. Suede-finished knits.
5. Ribbon knits.
6. Simulated or deep pile fur fabrics.

Weft knits are made up of interlooped yarns in loops, each row caught in the previous row, and almost any fiber can be used.

Weft knits are offered in a wide variety of constructions and colors, and they are very comfortable to wear because they are elastic and porous.

Weft knits do not wrinkle easily; they pack and travel well; and most of them are easy to care for. They can be washed or dry-cleaned satisfactorily, depending on color, dimensional stability, and cut of the garment.

Some knit fabrics block and shape easily, while others do so with difficulty; some have places that are susceptible to forming a hole, and it is difficult to mend knit fabrics without the mend being obvious. Some knit fabrics made of synthetic fibers stretch with steaming and blocking and do not recover or respond to shaping.

Sharp objects such as pins or staples can cause fabric damage in a knit fabric. Some knit garments are difficult to alter because the line of stitching frequently leaves small needle holes in the fabric. It is very easy to cut a knit garment off grain in garment construction. This can result in an unsatisfactory appearance after wear and dry cleaning.

DOUBLE KNITS

Double knits, because of their double construction, can be classed as a two-faced fabric. The two-sided utility of the fabric offers the garment designer exciting possibilities for creating new color harmonies.

Double knits may be made of almost any fiber. They have a good appearance, hand, and feel, so they are comfortable to wear. They can be stabilized for shrinkage control by physical or chemical means. A well-balanced double knit construction that is stabilized for shrinkage control dry-cleans and launders satisfactorily. A double knit fabric that is improperly constructed and finished may sag or stretch with wear. Sometimes a resin is used for stabilization, but it can be removed in dry-cleaning solvent so shrinkage may occur.

Care must be taken in pressing or finishing double knit fabric made of the heat-sensitive fibers to avoid glazing, particularly on any garment detail where there is a double thickness of fabric.

BRUSHED KNITS

Knit fabrics can be given a finishing treatment that raises the fibers to the surface of the fabric. In brushed knits, loops cannot be seen on the face of the fabric. The fibers and yarns used to knit the fabric, the thickness of the fabric, and the degree of napping and brushing determine the texture and appearance of the fabric. Many interesting surface effects can be achieved. The majority of these fabrics dry-clean well, but many of them require special handling.

Some brushed knits are very susceptible to abrasion (rubbing) in wear and in dry cleaning. Long fibers in brushed knits have a tendency to "pill" in wear and cleaning, and the nap may be removed, leaving a bare spot. Some short fibers in brushed knits have a tendency to shed.

Brushed knit fabrics must meet the requirements of the Flammable Fabrics Act. The Flammable Fabrics Act is discussed in Chapter 9.

SUEDE-TYPE KNITS

Knit fabrics are given a mechanical finishing treatment that raises short fibers to the surface of the fabric. The fibers are sheared and pressed into the fabric. This gives it the appearance of suede leather. The loops of the background knit cannot be seen on the surface of the fabric. Suede-type knits may be made of almost any fiber.

This lightweight, durable fabric can be used for rainwear, sportswear, lightweight coats, dresses, and lounging garments. If shrinkage is controlled, suede-type knits are very serviceable and dry-clean satisfactorily. However, suede-type knits are susceptible to abrasion (rubbing) in wear. The nap may be removed, leaving a bare spot. Some of these fabrics are not treated to be dimensionably stable, so allowances should be made for shrinkage.

DEEP PILE FUR FABRICS

Man-made furs came into the consumer market in 1929. The fabrics were woven plush cloth simulating the look of genuine animal pelts such as Persian Lamb, broadtail, seal, and leopard. They were made of mohair, alpaca, or wool, often blended with rayon for luster. Between 1935 and 1938, woven high-pile fabrics of alpaca were developed and used as shells and liners, and there was a major technical advance that resulted in fabrics with denser pile, a more furry hand, better abrasion resistance, and new color interest.

As previously stated, the year 1944 brought the first knitted high-pile fabrics made on the sliver knit machine. The differential heights in pile was introduced in 1955. The printed versions of animal furs on pile fabrics arrived in 1959.

Fur type pile fabrics have a luxurious appearance and feel. They are intrinsically good and stand on their own merit. The fabrics are comparatively lightweight, warm to wear, and wear very well, yet the relative cost of furtype pile fabrics is less than genuine fur. Moths do not attack a clean fabric. These fabrics dry-clean satisfactorily, but they require special care. Some manufacturers recommend the furrier method of cleaning.

Some of these fabrics have a natural tendency to tuft in wear and in dry cleaning. (Tufting means the bunching together of fibers.) Some fabrics have a natural tendency to mat and flatten down. Both tufting and matting depend on the fiber content, fabric construction, finish, amount of wear, and method of cleaning. Some fabrics shed fibers that adhere to the woven fabrics with which they are combined in garment design. Fabrics made of heat-sensitive fibers may be damaged by excessive heat such as a cigarette burn or contact with a hot radiator.

FABRIC CONSTRUCTION — WOVEN

Woven fabrics are made by the interlacing of two or more sets of yarns at right angles to produce a fabric. The lengthwise yarn is called "warp," and the crosswise yarn is called a "filling" (see Figure 4-24). These correspond to the wales and courses in knitting. The warp yarns are parallel to the selvage. The face of the fabric forms the outside of a garment. A fabric is usually folded or rolled so that it forms the inner surface.

The three basic weaves are the plain weave, twill weave, and satin weave. All other weaves are variations or combinations of these three except for leno and weaves involving extra sets of yarns.

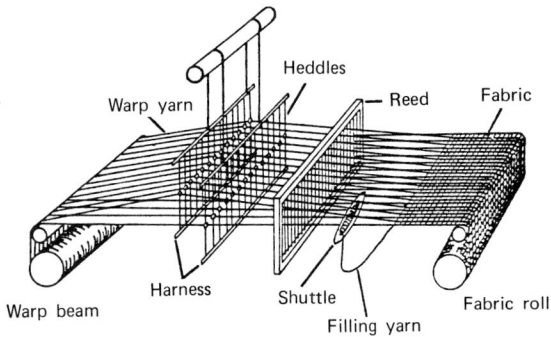

Figure 4-24 Diagrammatic sketch of a simple two-harness loom. *Warp Beam:* All the yarns to be used in the fabric are wound parallel to each other. *Harness and Heddle:* Warp yarns pass through harness that holds many thin vertical wires called heddles, each with an eye in the middle. Each warp yarn is threaded through the eye of one needle, controlled by the harness. The harness raises and lowers the warp yarns — called a shed. *Shuttle:* A boatlike device that carries the filling yarn through the shed. *Reed:* A frame with thin, vertical, nonmovable wires, resembling a comb that pushes the filling yarn tightly against the fabric on the fabric roll.

Figure 4-25 Plain weave.

PLAIN WEAVE

The simplest of all weaves is the plain weave. Each filling yarn passes alternately over and under each warp yarn. Each warp yarn passes alternately over and under each filling yarn. A plain weave fabric is reversible unless one side is printed or a definite face is made by finishing (see Figure 4-25).

Plain weave fabrics are usually firm constructions that wear well. They seldom ravel. They offer good backgrounds for printing, finishing, and surface designs. Some disadvantages are that they are sometimes uninteresting in appearance, have low tear strength, and show wrinkles very clearly.

Some examples of plain weave fabrics are buckrum, crinoline, chintz, chiffon, crepes, georgette, organdy, Mousseline de Soie, and shantung.

A more interesting surface texture may be given to plain weave fabrics by varying yarn twist and loom tension or by using crepe yarns. In crepe fabric, the nonlustrous, crinkly surface hides the fact that the crepe fabric is a plain weave. The filling yarns may be of high twist and the warp yarns of low twist, or vice-versa.

Rib Weave

This is a variation of a plain weave. The rib is produced by using heavy yarns in the warp or filling direction, by grouping yarns in specific areas of warp or filling, or by having more warp than filling yarns. Ribbed weave fabrics are reversible unless the face is printed or given a special finish. Examples are taffeta, faille, bengaline, ottoman, Gros-de-Loudres, grosgrain, rep or repp, barathea, and pique (see Figure 4-26).

Basket Weave

This is another variation of the plain weave. In this construction two or more yarns are woven as one in the warp or filling direc-

Figure 4-26 Rib weave.

tions, producing a basket effect. The fabrics are reversible unless the finish or print makes one side of the fabric the face. Examples of basket weave fabrics are monk's cloth, acetate sharkskin, oxford cloth, and hopsacking. The basket weave makes a pleasing decorative fabric. If the fabric is made of a relative low number of yarns per inch and if the yarns are low twist, they may be unstable in use and cleaning. They may stretch or shrink. They are difficult to sew (see Figure 4-27).

TWILL WEAVE

This is characterized by diagonal ridges formed by yarns that float on the surface. These ridges may vary in angle from a low slope to a very steep slope; they result because the float positions in the warp yarns progress up or down and in the filling yarns right or left in a regular manner.

Twill weaves are closer in texture, heavier, and sturdier than plain weaves and can be produced in many fancy designs. Common variations of the twill weave are wool broadcloth, Cavalry Twill, covert, foulard, gabardine, serge, sharkskin, surah, and whipcord (see Figure 4-28).

SATIN WEAVE

The satin weave is characterized by long, floating warp yarns that produce a high luster on one side of the fabric. In satin, warp yarns of low twist float or pass over four or more filling yarns in a regular pattern. The filling yarns that appear on the surface are spaced so as not to show a diagonal pattern (see Figure 4-29). The low twist and the floating of the warp yarns, usually filament fibers, give a high degree of light reflection. High-twist yarns may be used for the filling. There are many fabrics made of satin weave, but they are not called satin. The weave differs in the twist and combinations of yarns and weight of fabric. Some examples are antique satin; crepeback satin, charmeuse, messaline, slipper Satin.

The long floats of a satin weave produce a pleasing, lustrous surface on the fabric. They may also contribute poor wearing performance, since the floats are very susceptible to abrasion and snagging in wear, spot removal, and cleaning. The floats may snag, rough up, and even break. Care in selection of satin fabrics is very important. If the fabric is made with a high number of yarns per inch, good wearability can be expected because of high fiber density.

Sateens are a satin-type weave in which the filling yarns float and are visible on the surface of the fabric (e.g., cotton sateen).

Figure 4-27   4/4 Basket weave.

Figure 4-28   2/2 Right-hand twill weave.

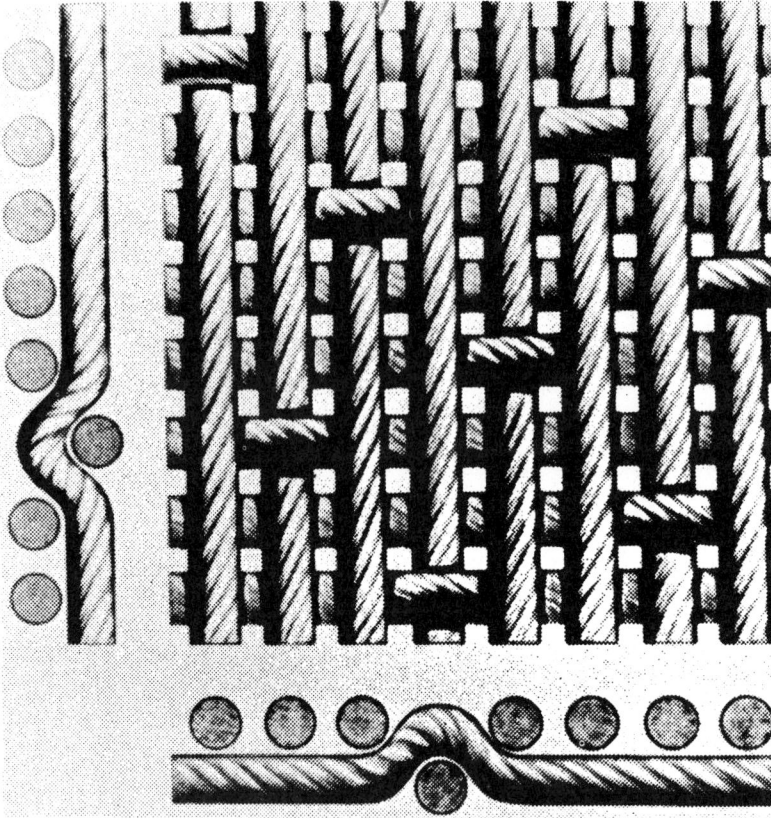

Figure 4-29 The satin weave is characterized by long warp floats on the face of the fabric.

DOBBY FIGURE WEAVES

Small designs can be woven inexpensively by placing a dobby attachment on a plain harness loom. Simple, small geometric designs or figures are repeated often throughout the fabric (e.g., honeycomb, bird's eye).

JACQUARD FIGURE WEAVE

Elaborate designs are woven on intricately constructed looms, called a jacquard loom (see Figure 4-30). It takes weeks to prepare the loom for intricate patterns. Examples are brocade, damask, tapestry, lamé, and matelassé.

Jacquard weave fabrics are usually purchased for their beauty, not their durability. Since the design unit frequently has long floats, the fabrics snag easily, are difficult to remove spots and stains from, and lack dimensional stability in laundering and dry cleaning.

Figure 4-30 Jacquard looms are complex. Cards for a particular weave are precut. The cards are strung up for the loom with the yarns that are released according to a predetermined jacquard pattern.

PILE WEAVE—DOUBLE CLOTH WEAVE

Corduroy, velveteen, plush, velour, and velvet are examples of the pile weave. The unique differences of corduroy and velveteen do not begin to take shape until the spun yarns are put into the looms for weaving. The yarns that will form the filling width of the fabric are first wound on bobbins. Those that will form its warp length are wound on beams and are stiffened for high-speed weaving with a coating of sizing, usually starch, in a process known as "slashing."

Weaving interlaces these warp and filling yarns by the action of a shuttle, which carries the filling, moving from side to side across the loom. It is the positioning of these yarns as they travel through the loom that determines the type of fabric being made. In the weaving of corduroys and velveteens, the yarns are positioned to produce the innumerable, tightly woven loops that will be cut and brushed together to form the pile.

Corduroy weaving interlaces the filling yarn, or "pile pick," with one or more warp ends and then "floats" it over three or more warp ends to form the loop. As the pile pick is floated over the same warp ends throughout the length of the fabric being woven, the parallel rows of loops are created that will form corduroy's characteristic rounded pile ribs when the loops, or floats, are cut.

As shown in cross section in Figure 4-31, the base or ground of the fabric is woven at the same time as the pile. The warp ends are closely interlaced with other filling yarns, called "binder picks," that are not cut, giving the fabric its strength and dimensional stability. In the finished cloth, the density of the ribbed pile will depend both on the number and coarseness of the pile or float picks and on the proportion of these to the binder picks — two, three, four, or more to one.

After weaving has been completed and the floats are cut to form the pile, the width of the rib will be governed by the length of the float. The longer the float, the wider the rib will be. When cut, the fibers tend to spring up and stand erect. They are brushed together to form the pile in ribs, cords, or wales in the finishing process.

The weaving of velveteen is similar, but here the ribs are woven so close together that when cut lengthwise and brushed crosswise, a solid pile surface is formed. The yarns used in making velveteen are usually much finer than those used for corduroy, and they are woven with two or three times as many picks to the inch. This accounts for velveteen's denser pile, more even coverage, more supple hand, and its lustrous appearance.

Velvets are woven primarily of yarns made of rayon, acetate, and nylon. Just as in the weaving of corduroy and velveteen in which the pile is made of the crosswise filling yarns, the lengthwise warp yarns form the pile in the weaving of velvet.

In weaving velvet, two layers of fabric woven simultaneously on a double shuttle loom form a kind of sandwich, with the vertical yarns as the filling. As the fabric comes off the loom, the two fabrics are separated by a horizontal knife traveling from side to side, cutting the vertical yarns to form two separate fabrics, each with an upright pile surface (see Figure 4-32).

The pile height is often slightly uneven; as the fabric leaves the loom, it is passed under the shearer, a revolving blade. This

(a)

Floats

Cut   Cut

Warp ends

Binder picks

(b)

Cutting rail

Slot

Guide wire

Circular knife

Cut fibers

Figure 4-31 *(a)* A cross section of corduroy or velveteen yarns before cutting. *(b)* Cutting of floats to create pile. *(c)* After cutting. *(d)* After brushing. (Courtesy: Crompton-Richmond Company, Inc.)

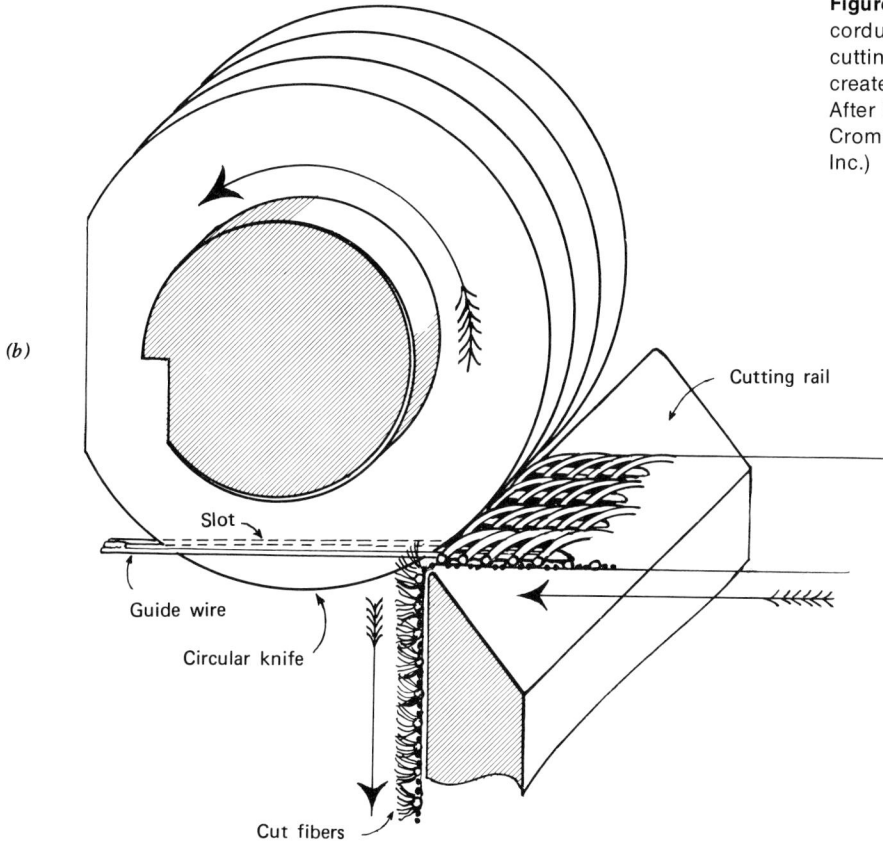

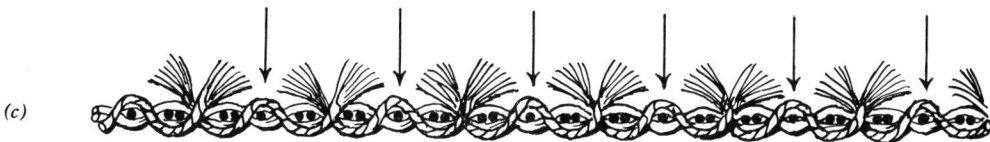

(c)

(d)

185

Double woven velvet before splitting

Cut

Pile tufts

Pile tension rods

Top take–up roll

Harness

Reed

Shuttles

Knife

Bottom
take–up roll

Pile feed rolls

Pile warp

Ground warp

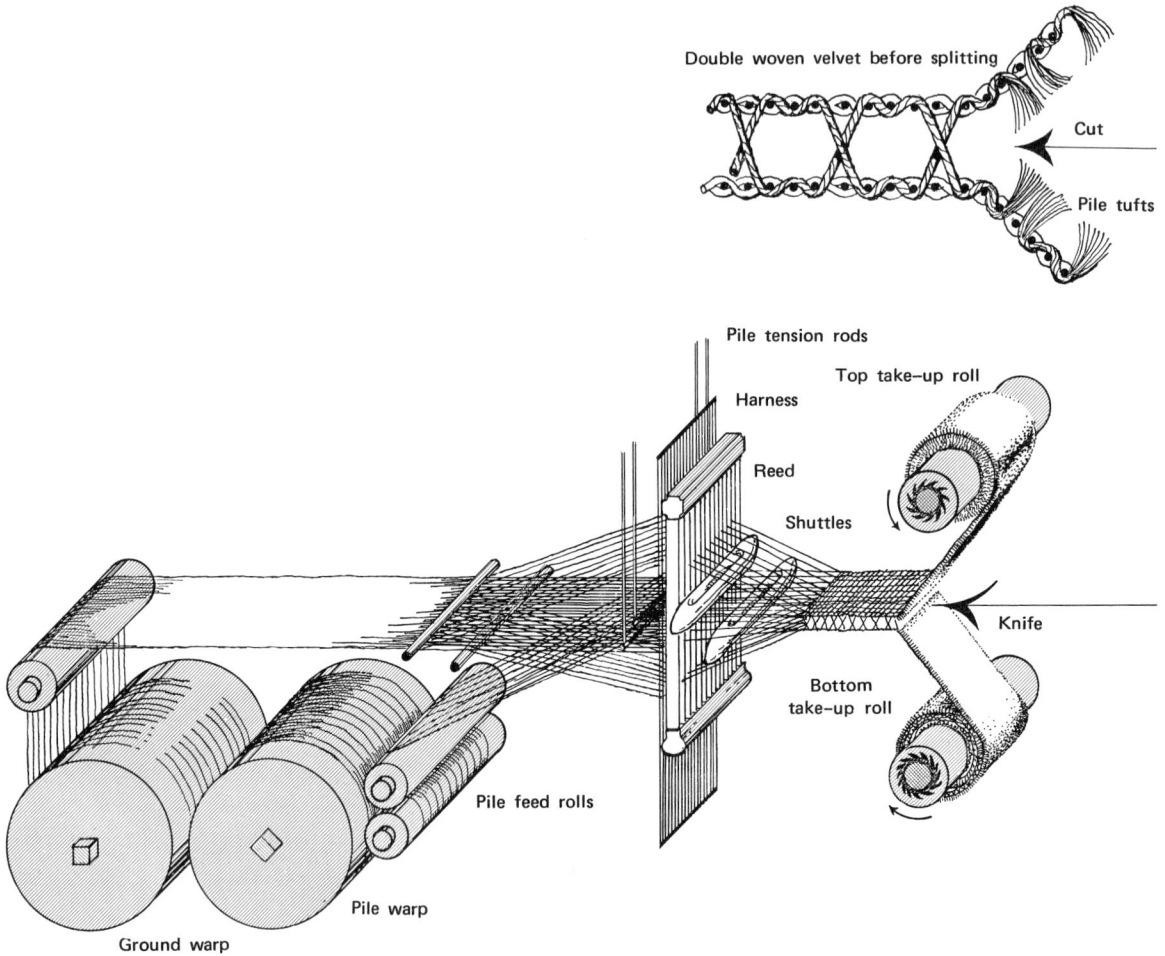

Figure 4-32 The weaving of velvet. As the fabric leaves the unique double action loom, the vertical filling yarns are severed, forming two separate fabrics, each with velvet's characteristic upright pile surface. (Courtesy: Crompton-Richmond Co. Inc.)

acts like a lawnmower, leveling the pile to a predetermined height and forming a smooth, uniform surface.

Consumers may classify pile weave fabrics as "V" and "W" construction. In a V construction, the pile yarn passes under only one yarn in the ground fabric before reemerging as a pile. For a W, the pile yarn passes under-over-under three yarns before reemerging as a pile. The fabric's pile looks like those pictured in Figure 4-33.

It can be seen from these drawings that the W interlacing is the more durable of the two, since the pile is held in place by three yarns. The back of the fabric may be a plain, twill, or satin weave.

When a pile fabric is made with two pieces of cloth woven at the

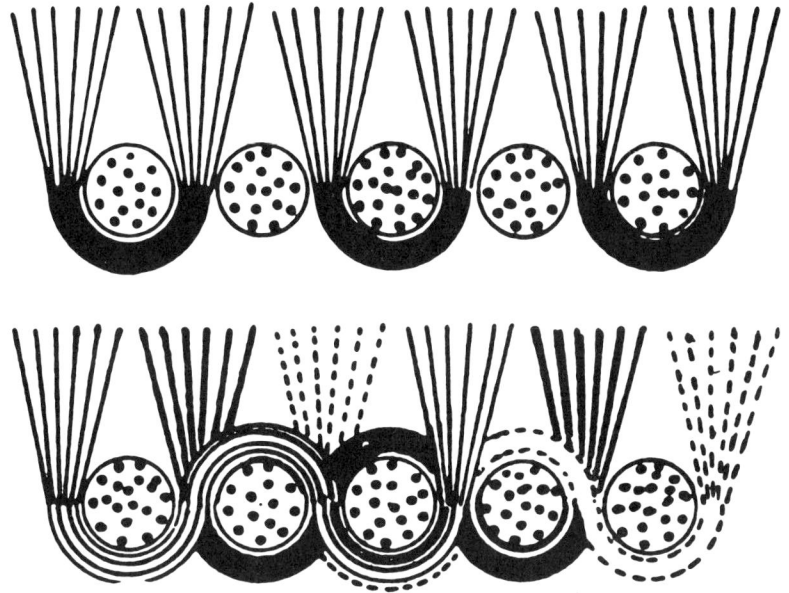

Figure 4-33 *(a)* Cross section of a "V" weave. *(b)* "W" weave velvet.

same time, face to face, with a fifth set of binding yarns to unite the two cloths and the fabric is not cut apart, it is called a true *double cloth* and the fabric is reversible (see Figure 4-34). An adaptation of a double cloth can be made of four sets of yarns in a reversible fabric; the four sets of yarns produce a fabric that is not reversible (matelassé). A reversible fabric may also be made with one warp yarn and two filling yarns (see Figure 4-35). Blankets, ribbon, coatings, and dress and jacket fabrics may be made of the double cloth variations.

In some fabrics like terry cloth and frisé the pile is not cut. It is also possible to have cut and uncut pile in the same fabric. Pile fabrics are very rich-looking and have good drape. Care must be taken in the cutting and sewing of pile fabrics so that the nap is cut in the same direction for all parts of the garment. A pile garment, after wear, may appear lighter or darker in areas, depending on the lay of the pile and the angle of light reflection. During periods of wear, pile garments should be stored so as not to flatten the pile. Fiber content such as acetate pile and finishes such as urea formaldehyde finishes for crush resistance can limit satisfactory performance in wear and care.

Double-faced fabrics may also be achieved through bonding (see Figure 4-36).

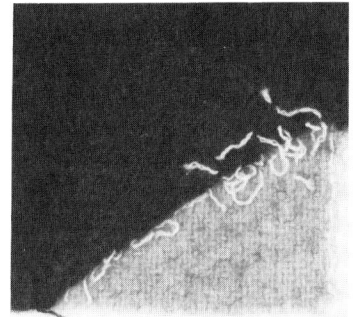

Figure 4-34 A double-cloth made with two distinct fabrics: a charcoal face fabric, 100 percent wool, and an off-white back fabric, 100 percent wool. The two fabrics are held together by an extra warp yarn.

Figure 4-35 Reversible satins and ottomans may be made with a warp yarn of one color and two filling yarns of another color. In this satin fabric, black yarns are thrown to one surface, gold yarns to the other.

Figure 4-36 A double-faced fabric is made by bonding two fabrics together with an adhesive. Fabric pictured is a 100 percent blue wool face and a 100 percent gold wool back.

Figure 4-37 Diagram of leno weave.

LENO WEAVE

A leno weave is made by a special attachment to the loom. The warp yarns do not lie parallel to each other. Instead, one yarn of each pair is crossed over the other to form a figure 8 before the filling yarn is inserted. The filling yarns in a leno weave are held in place firmly and cannot shift in the warp direction. But the warp yarns can shift in the filling direction. An example is marquisette (see Figure 4-37). The construction may be varied by the number of filling yarns inserted. If only one filling is involved in each crossing, the weave is an adaptation of leno and may be called gauze. This should not be confused with the staple name "gauze," a plain weave construction.

Fabrics made of the leno weave are open-textured and may vary from sheer to heavy. The leno weave may be combined with other basic weaves to make interesting patterned fabrics.

THERMAL WEAVE (ADAPTATION OF A LENO WEAVE)

Thermal-weave blankets are made according to a principle used in clothing worn in the conquest of Mt. Everest. It is the principle of thermal insulation (see Figure 4-38).

The way to keep warm when the air around you is cold is to preserve body heat. This is most effectively done by surrounding the body with a layer of still air. The air is warmed by your body and acts as an insulator.

This is the principle behind the whole concept of shell clothing worn by U. S. Army troops in cold weather and used not only in skiwear but in a great deal of winter outerwear. The outer shell of the garment acts as a windbreaker, while the inner lining traps air to preserve body heat.

In the thermal blankets, the cellular construction of the fabric traps the air around the body, while a lightweight outer covering or napped surface prevents it from being dissipated. Thus it is the construction of the fabric instead of the fiber itself that creates the warmth of thermal blankets.

In 1962 the first cotton thermal blanket, called Insulaire,* was offered for sale. It was merchandised as a blanket that keeps you cool in the summer and warm in the winter. Other manufacturers began to make thermal blankets, and each varied the construction slightly and promoted them under their own brand or tradename.

It is predicted that thermal-weave blankets will make up a large portion of total blanket sales. Some predictions are that napped synthetics will outsell cotton thermals. Some retailers are concerned with the cheaper qualities in the market, believing that they will affect sales of better quality thermals. Manufacturers state the product advantages of synthetic thermal-weave blankets are: warm, yet comfortably light; soft luxurious hand; shrink resistant; nonallergenic; permanently mothproof; mildew-proof; retains appearance; and resists pilling and shedding.

Research shows that thermal blankets can be laundered, dry-cleaned, or wet-cleaned by the professional dry cleaner. Air drying minimizes shrinkage. Light steaming after dry cleaning and brushing improves the appearance of the blanket.

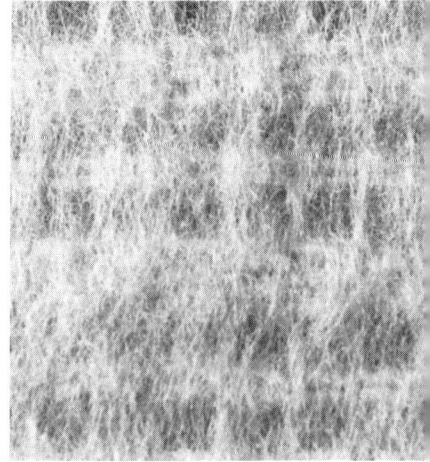

Figure 4-38 Close-up weave construction. The thermal weave air pockets insulate. It breathes for coolness, insulates for warmth.

FIGURE WEAVES

Simple figure weaves may be made by introducing extra warp or filling yarns. The looms are adapted to accommodate the extra yarns. The three variations are: (1) lappet; (2) swivel, and (3) dot or spot.

Lappet is a form of weaving in which extra warp yarns are introduced to create the design on the base fabric. As the loom attachment moves across the fabric surface to make the design, it forms floats on the back of the fabric. Long floats are usually clipped, leaving only the small design. If the floats are short, they sometimes are not removed. The lappet weave is durable and expensive. If long floats remain, they may snag easily. If the floats are clipped too short, the design may pull from the base weave.

The swivel weave is a form of weaving in which extra filling yarns are introduced to create the design on the base fabric.

*Morgan-Jones Division of Spring Mills, Inc.

Shuttles carries the yarn through the warp yarns in a predetermined design. As the attachment moves from pattern to pattern, extra filling yarns appear on the back of the fabric and are removed after the weaving is completed.

The swivel process can create a multicolored design with a raised appearance on both the face and back of the fabric. The yarns are securely fastened and will not pull out.

The lappet and swivel weaves are produced abroad.

Dot or spot weaves are made with either warp or filling yarns. The yarns are inserted the entire length or width of the fabric in the predetermined design patterns. The design yarns may be a different color and weight from the background fabric. If the long floats on the back of the fabric are cut, they are called "clipped spot designs." Spot or dot weaves in which the floating yarn is not cut are called "uncut spot designs." The latter is used to make border designs that may or may not be reversible. In both the cut and uncut weaves, the design yarns can be removed without destroying the basic weave. The durability of the design depends on the closeness or looseness of the background fabric. The design may be pulled out easily in a loosely woven fabric. Examples of the dot or spot weaves are dotted swiss; eyelash satin; and fringe fabrics.

STRETCH FABRICS

ORIGIN OF STRETCH FABRICS

At one time elastic fabrics were made only of rubber core yarns. They were popularly referred to as elastic fabrics. Today, elastic yarns are made by new yarn-making techniques using nylon, polyester, spandex, and the natural fibers. The term stretch is used as distinctive from the earlier rubber elastic fabrics. Stretch fabrics include all types of elastic yarns, regardless of fiber content (see Figures 4-39 and 4-40).

The elastic qualities of stretch fabrics can be provided by:

1. The physical modification of a textile yarn. (See previous discussion on textured filament yarns.)
2. The use of a rubber or a synthetic rubber core yarn wrapped with a textile yarn or stretch obtained by the use of a spandex yarn.
3. Stretch obtained in piece goods by chemical finishing (see Figure 4-41).

Figure 4-39 Stretch yarns are used in Stuart Nelson's stretch bicycle suit with pullover jacket to assure comfort and freedom of movement. Fabric is of "Antron" nylon and "Lycra" spandex. (Courtesy: Du Pont Company)

The first successful introduction of nonrubber-type stretch fabrics took place more than a decade ago in Switzerland. They became extremely popular in ski clothing. The fabrics were made of wool and a "textured" nylon warp yarn called "Helenca." Helenca yarns are made of nylon that is first twisted, heat-set in this twisted state, then untwisted. Today many different techniques of yarn manufactured are used to produce an elastic quality in almost any kind of thermoplastic fiber.

Italian designers are said to have been first to apply the stretch idea to dressy clothing, starting with a shantung-type material of

Figure 4-40 This chiffon-weight gown by Robert David Morton is made of ''Antron'' nylon and ''Lycra'' spandex — very packable and wrinkle-resistant. (Courtesy: DuPont Company)

Douppioni silk and stretch nylon. Now one sees beautiful knit and woven stretch fabrics of every description for both men's and women's clothing and for household use (e.g., contour sheets and slip covers).

Leotards and tight-fitting pants make up the largest volume of items for daily wear. A list of end uses for all kinds of stretch fabrics appears in Table 4-3.

CLASSIFICATION OF STRETCH FABRICS

Stretch fabrics may be classified in different ways. Regardless of the classification for determining fabric types, stretch fabrics that

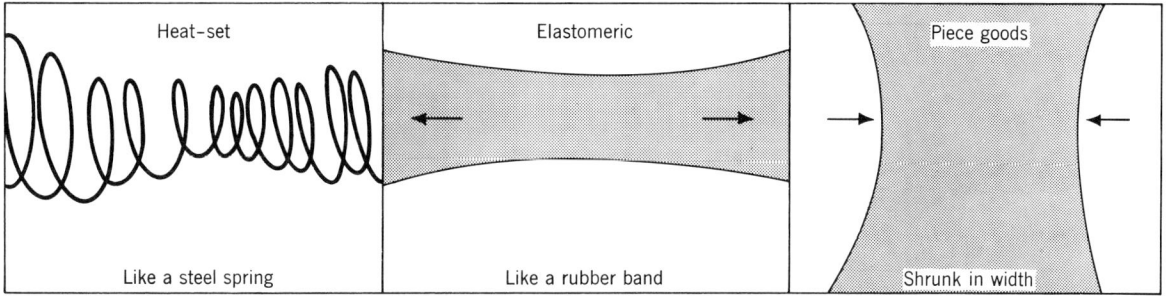

are to be laundered or dry-cleaned may be classified according to fiber content, fabric construction, color, garment design, and the degree of soiling. Since all stretch fabrics contain heat-sensitive fibers such as nylon, polyester, acetate, rubber, or spandex, they should be handled the same as any other fabric made of a thermoplastic fiber.

Table 4-3   End Use for Stretch Fabrics

Apparel Uses	
Slacks	Car coats
Jackets	Skiwear
Shirts	Spectator sportswear
Shorts	Dresses
Skirts and culottes	Men's suits
Leotards	Women's suits
Uniforms	Outerwear
Leisure wear garments	Gloves
Maternity dresses	Lingerie
Children's wear	Bathing suits
Snowsuits	Foam-backed stretch fabrics.
Playsuits	(Stretch warp and stretch filling fabrics for a wide range of apparel uses.)

Home Furnishings	
Drapery fabrics	Contour sheets
Upholstery fabrics	Mattress covers
Slip cover fabrics	

Classification by Construction

Stretch fabrics may be classified by method of fabric construction.

1. Any basic knit construction may be used to make a knitted stretch fabric by using appropriate fibers or yarns.
2. All of the conventional weaves used to make woven fabrics may also be made, using stretch yarns.
3. Laces and laminated fabrics may also be made of stretch yarns and fabrics.

Classification by Direction of Stretch

Such fabrics may be classified by the direction of the stretch.

1. *Warp stretch.* The stretch yarn runs lengthwise in the fabric.
2. *Filling stretch.*   The stretch yarns are woven crosswise in the fabric.
3. *Two-way stretch.*   Stretch yarns can be knitted or woven of all stretchable yarns. Two-way stretch yarns are being used in slip cover fabrics. The greatest uses of two-way stretch yarns are girdles and bathing suits.

Classification by Method of Manufacture

Stretch fabrics may also be classified by the way they are manufactured (see Figure 4-41).

Standards of Optimum Comfort — Performance

There are no generally agreed on standards of optimum comfort and performance in stretch fabrics. Experiments have shown that comfort improves rapidly up to 30 to 35 percent stretch and then levels off. For sleek-fitting slacks, the leveling point is higher, about 45 percent. It appears that performance properties of a fabric decreases with an increase in stretch. If performance is the primary requirement, as in men's suiting fabric, the optimum stretch level should be 20 to 30 percent. If comfort is the primary requirement, as in sportswear, the stretch level may vary from 25 to 40 percent, depending on end use. Since the primary requirement for slacks is comfort, the desirable stretch level is between 40 to 50 percent. It is obvious in building a garment that the optimum stretch may vary from the top to the bottom of a garment.

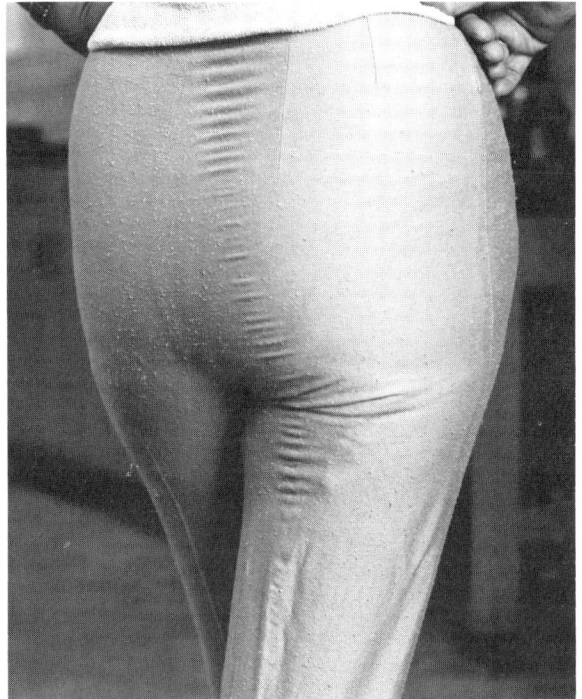

Figure 4-42 The fabric used in the stretch pants pictured is made with a rubber-core yarn wrapped with a cotton yarn. Note how the yarns have relaxed in the areas of stretch during wear.

Although stretch of the yarn is important, recovery of the yarn is equally important if one is to expect satisfactory performance of the garment. Lack of recovery will cause any stretch fabric to bag (see Figure 4-42).

How the body skin stretches and the optimum performance plus comfort are given in Tables 4-4 and 4-5 and Figure 4-43.

Figure 4-43 Ranges of body skin stretch. (Courtesy: American Fabrics and Fashions)

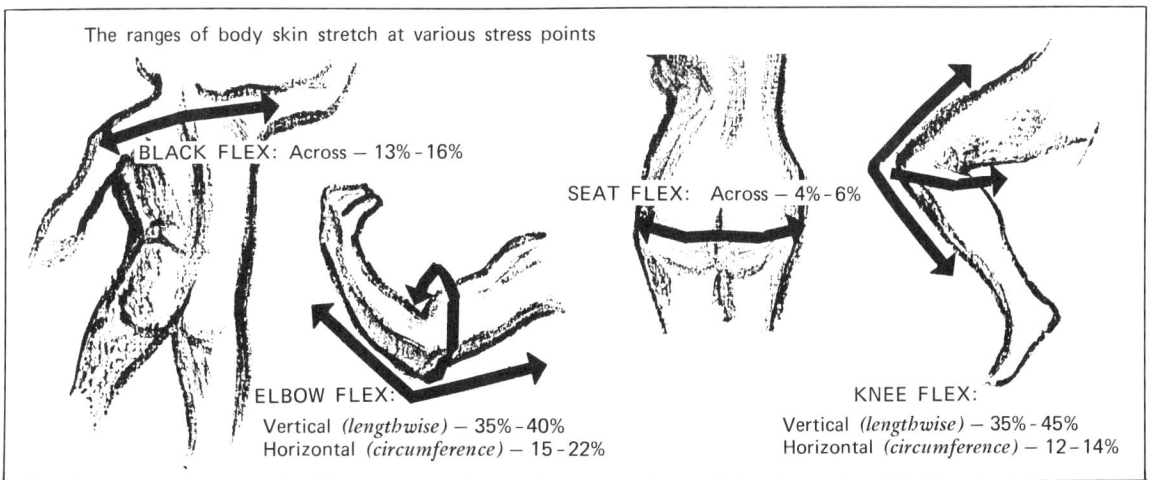

The ranges of body skin stretch at various stress points

BLACK FLEX: Across — 13% - 16%

SEAT FLEX: Across — 4% - 6%

ELBOW FLEX:
Vertical *(lengthwise)* — 35% - 40%
Horizontal *(circumference)* — 15 - 22%

KNEE FLEX:
Vertical *(lengthwise)* — 35% - 45%
Horizontal *(circumference)* — 12 - 14%

Table 4-4   How the Skin Stretches. (Courtesy: E. I. du Pont de Nemours and Company, Inc.)

Body Area	Movement	Horizontal	Vertical
Knee	Stand to sit	19-21%	41-43%
Knee	Stand to deep bend	28-29%	49-52%
Elbow	Straight to full bend	24-25%	50-51%
Seat — hip to hip	Stand to sit	15-20%	
Seat — hip to hip	Stand to bend	17-21%	
Seat — crotch	Stand to sit	35-42%	
Seat — crotch	Stand to bend	37-41%	
Seat — hip to hip	Stand to sit		27%
Seat — hip to hip	Stand to bend		34-35%
Seat — buttocks	Stand to sit		39-40%
Seat — buttocks	Stand to bend		45%
Back	Straight to forward, arm raised	31-35%	
Back	Elbows on table	28%	
Back	Elbow bending	14-16%	
Back	Shoe tying	47%	

Note. The range in percentages is the variation between men and women.

Table 4-5   Optimum Performance Plus Comfort. (Courtesy: E. I. du Pont de Nemours and Company, Inc.)

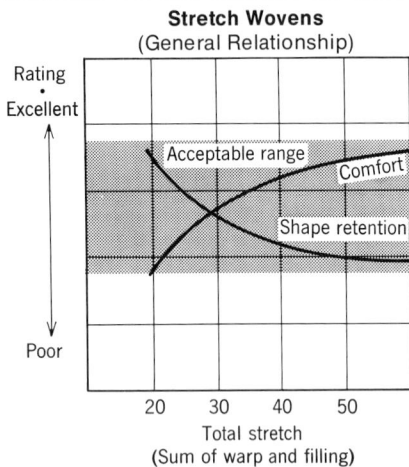

Stretch Wovens
(General Relationship)

This graph shows a schematic plot of the general relationship between fabric stretch level, comfort, and performance determined for slacks. The vertical axis plots wear-test ratings of poor to excellent performance and comfort. The horizontal axis shows the level of total stretch. Note that comfort improves rapidly up to about 35 percent total stretch and then tends to level off. Beyond this level, comfort continues to increase, but at a slower rate. On the other hand, shape retention diminishes with increasing available stretch. The range of overall acceptability is the shaded area.

In comparing one- and two-way stretch, it is important to use total (warp and filling) stretch values. Thus, a 22 percent filling-stretch fabric with only 8 percent stretch in the warp has 30 percent total stretch and should be comparable with a "two-way" fabric that has 15 percent stretch in each idrection.

KNIT/STITCH AND KNIT/WOVEN STRUCTURES

New methods of construction have been on the research and development drawing boards for some years. This is particularly true of constructions that combine conventional structures that we have known in the past such as knitting and weaving or knitting and stitching. There may be considerable time lapse between an inception of an idea, its commercial development, and acceptance by the consumer. In some cases, a well-known technique may be modified, and the resultant fabric appears to be a new development. An expected revolution may have a good beginning, only to fail to gain production or consumer acceptance. New developments that begin and are accepted abroad may stimulate monetary investment in the United States only to find no acceptance here. For example, Mali stitch-through fabrics raised great expectations for wearing apparel, but achieved acceptance in decorator fabrics instead. It was never expected that it would quickly replace weaving methods but, even so, expectations for Mali were not soundly based.

There is a difference of opinion as to how stitch-knit and stitch-woven structures should be classified. The textile industry in general classifies them with the regular knit constructions previously discussed. For our discussion, we will think of these structures in terms of consumer products: (1) the Mali fabrics; (2) the fiberwoven fabrics; (3) the fiber or nonwoven batt structures, formerly called "Arachne"; and (4) the warp or weftamatic knit fabrics. They have received their names from the machines on which they are manufactured.

MALI FABRICS

Heinrich Mauerberger developed the Mali process in East Germany in the late 1940s. The first power-operated machine to make it was developed in 1958. In the past 8 years, Mali has become important in the East German textile industry. In 1962 Klaus Bahlo, an American textile engineer, saw the machine at a trade show in Europe and sought distribution rights in the United States. The company he represented was not interested in it, so he resigned and set himself up as a United States Malimo Distributor. Later he joined with Crompton and Knowles of Worcester, Massachusetts, to form the C & K-Malimo Corporation. The machines are now offered on a lease and license arrangement. Mali fabric has been imported into the United States consumer market at the rate of many millions of yards each year.

The term Mali serves as an umbrella to describe three fabric types: (1) Malimo (three-dimension flat fabrics); (2) Malipole (short and long pile fabrics); and (3) Maliwatt (fortified, nonwoven fabrics). The latter is discussed on page 231.

MALIMO

When the new stitch-through system made a breakthrough, fabric developers accented these points about the system: fabric innovations possible by no other means; high productivity of the machine, but no immediate savings in cost; high durable press ratings; and performance similar to double knits. The system was successful for home furnishings and industrial fabrics, but what about apparel fabrics? There was a need to develop denser construction for apparel use, finishing problems had to be solved, and cutting and sewing techniques had to be learned.

WHAT IS A MALIMO STRUCTURE?

Mali is described as neither woven or knitted. Then what is it? The fabric consists of two layers of overlapping filling, a superimposed straight warp yarn, and a stitching thread. An interlocking tricot or chain stitch holds the two yarn systems together. The existence of a warp and a filling gives a woven characteristic to the fabric. Figure 4-44 shows the diagramatic method of construction. However, this basic structure can be modified into three characteristic structures.

1. A higher yarn count in the warp and filling with a fine stitching thread results in a fabric with a woven look.
2. An equal yarn count between all three systems produces the appearance of a woven look on the underside.
3. A fine warp and filling count and a very prominent stitching thread produces a fabric with a knit appearance but maintains woven characteristics.

These three basic structures may be varied by choice and arrangement of yarns used, or fabrics may be made using only stitching and filling yarns. Variation can also be achieved by choice of stitch — tricot or chain stitch. A jacquard Malimo construction is shown in Figure 4-45.

Physical properties of the fabrics depend almost entirely on the yarn or fiber components. The fabric behavior is more like that of woven fabrics than that of knits.

Observers expect this new method of fabric production to have far-reaching influence on the economics of fabric production. The production speed averages 2 to 3 yards a minute. The machine outproduces weaving, knitting, and even tufting — being 10 to 50 times as fast as a conventional loom, depending on the type of fabric production.

Although Malimo fabrics have found acceptance in the European market, they have been slow to find wide production and acceptance in the American market. In Europe one can purchase Malimo decorator and household fabrics, Malimo outerwear fab-

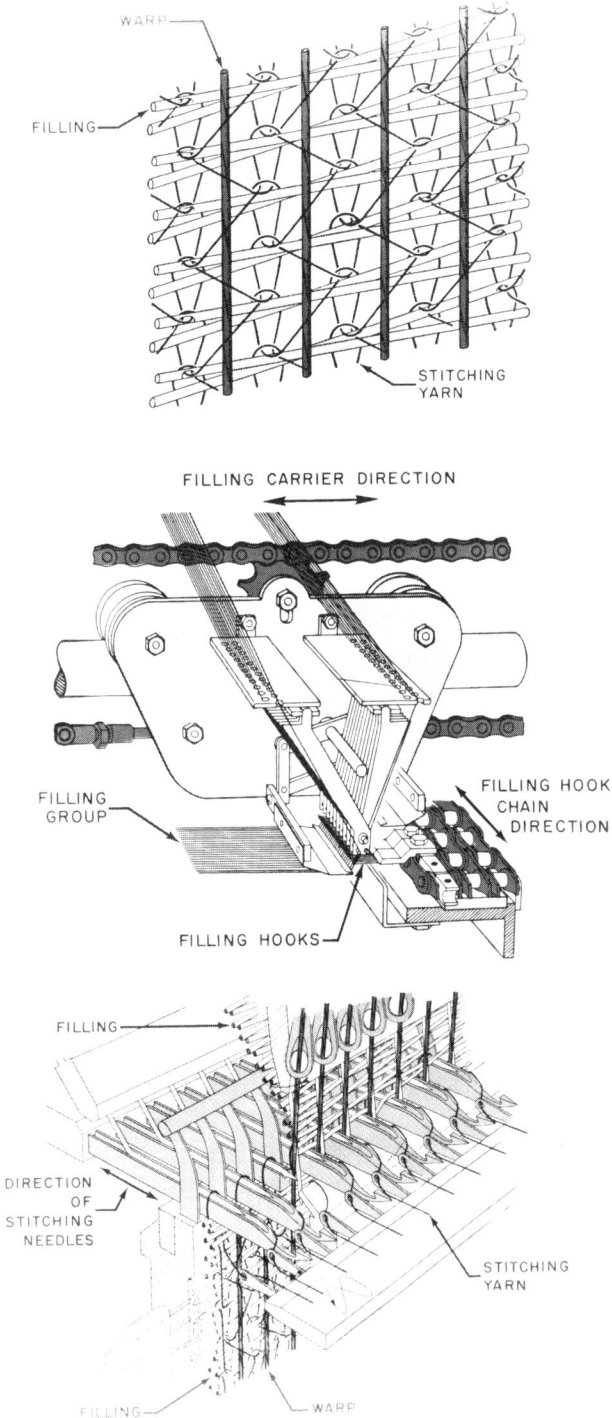

Figure 4-44 Malimo fabric elements. (Courtesy: Crompton & Knowles, Malimo, Inc.)

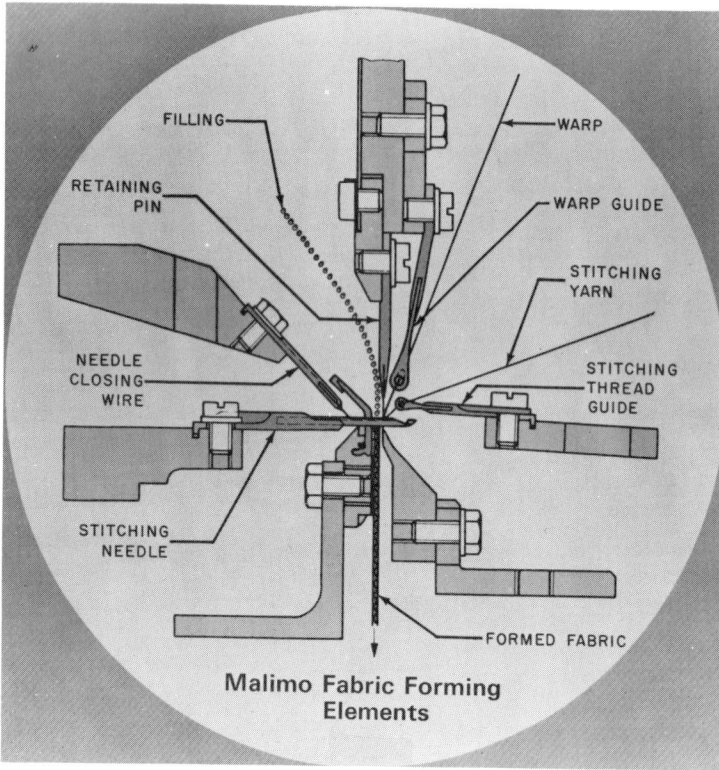

Figure 4-44 (Continued) Malimo fabric elements. (Courtesy: Crompton & Knowles, Malimo, Inc.)

Malimo Fabric Forming Elements

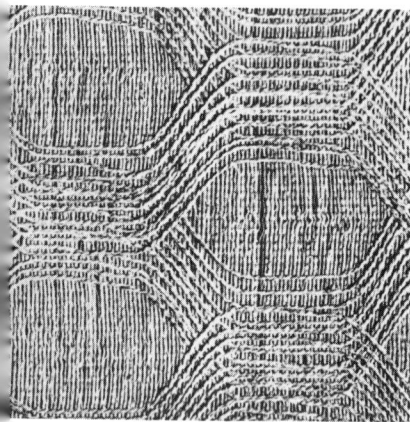

Figure 4-45 Very fine SEF modacrylic yarns are intricately joined into a geometric jacquard design produced by Malimo machinery. Offered for contract drapery use mainly in natural tones, some in two colors. (Courtesy: Polylok)

rics designed for both women's and men's apparel, Malimo prints for dresses, and Malimo beach and casual wear fabrics.

PERFORMANCE OF MALIMO FABRICS IN USE

In the United States, Malimo fabrics have found their widest use in drapery fabrics. The manufacturer states that Malimo's three-dimensional construction makes it possible to produce decorative fabrics with an open sheer construction that are more resistant to yarn slippage and distortion than sheer woven fabrics, because the yarns are bonded or locked in place by a knit stitch of transparent nylon or polyester monofilament yarn. However, any fabric with an open structure must be protected to avoid snagging or yarn cutting by sharp, rough, or jagged surfaces. At the present time, Malimo drapery fabrics are used in draperies for hotels, motels, banks, and the like, and they are being sold to interior decorators, retail stores, and mail order houses for home decorator fabrics in increasing volume.

Malimo fabrics dry-clean or wet-clean satisfactorily. By the manufacturer's preferred method (dry-clean and air-dry), there are essentially no failures in shrinkage in drapery length. When shrinkage occurred in cleaning, it is greater in the fabrics that are tumble-dried. Shrinkage is almost exclusively confined to open construction and the crosswise direction. The majority of Malimo fabrics have an acceptable surface appearance after dry cleaning and do not require pressing or finishing; other fabrics can have their appearance restored with slight steaming.

Malimo fabrics have good strength and stability and should be generally designated as durable but, as may be expected from any sheer or open weave fabric, Malimo fabrics are affected by mechanical damage such as pulls or snags, breaks, or yarn separation caused by the breaking of the binder yarn.

MALIPOL

The Malimo machine has been varied to form single-faced pile fabrics. See Figure 4-46, which is a diagram of how Malipol fabrics are made. Also study Figure 4-47, which shows how the pile in a Malipol fabric is held to the base fabric.

Figure 4-46 Malipol fabric forming elements. (Courtesy: Crompton and Knowles)

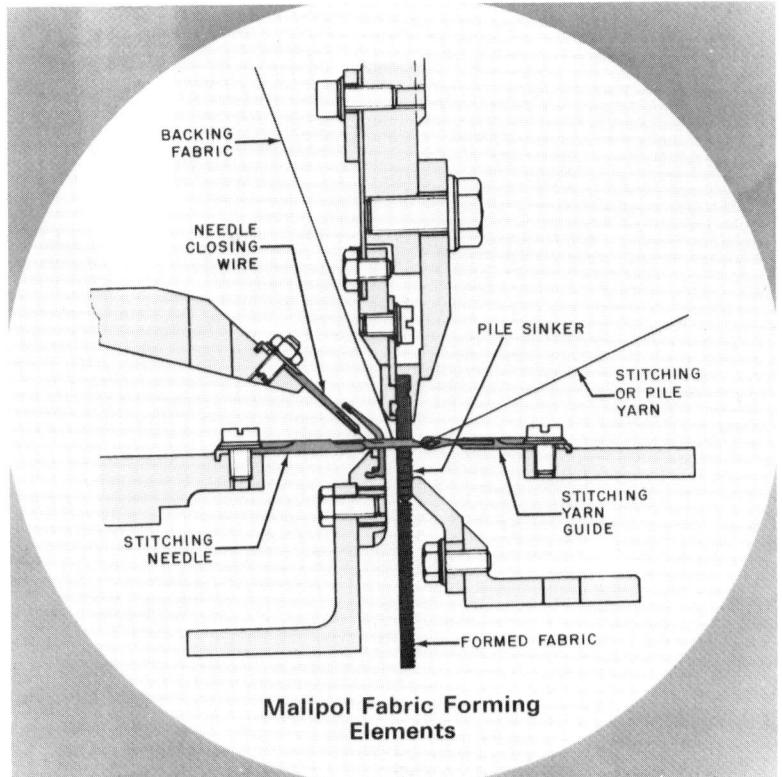

Malipol Fabric Forming Elements

Figure 4-47 Close-up of a simulated fur pile fabric made on a Malipol machine. Note how the pile is held by a chain stitch.

The versatility of the Malipol machine can be illustrated by the wide range of fabrics produced: outerwear and winter coatings similar to high-nap woven fabrics; pile lining materials for outerwear; imitation or simulated fur; floor covering; blanket materials; upholstery; and plush. Most simulated fur fabrics you see are made by knitting or weaving the pile and base cloth together in one operation. A new way of making simulated fur fabrics is by use of a Malipol machine.

We do not know whether there is more than a very limited production of simulated crushed velvet and fur Malipol fabrics being sold for apparel and upholstery fabrics, and whether more of it is produced abroad than in the United States. We do know that more of it has been produced for upholstery use than for apparel and that there has been some disappointments or failure of the product in dry cleaning.

Figure 4-48 Close-up of the underside of a Malipol crushed velvet fabric. The pile is stitched with a chain stitch into the base fabric.

CRUSHED VELVET — MALIPOL CONSTRUCTION

These short pile fabrics are made on the Malipol machine. Tiny tufts of pile fiber are punched through a base fabric of scrim or sheeting, resulting in a short pile surface on the face side and closely placed rows of chain stitching on the back (see Figure 4-48). Then a coating of adhesive is spread on the back side to anchor the stitches in place. The face side is "polished" to lay the pile in the lengthwise direction. This last treatment is what gives it the "crushed panné velvet" look.

IDENTIFYING MALIPOL FABRICS

In knitted or woven simulated fur fabrics the pile yarns are locked into place as the cloth is woven. In Malipol fabrics the tufts of yarn are punched into the background fabric. They would pull out easily from the back if they were not held in place with an adhesive coating. The adhesive in the Malipol fabric dissolves in the solvent, or at least is softened somewhat.

Looking at the back of a Malipol fabric, you can see that it is covered with closely placed rows of chain stitching, each representing a tiny tuft of pile on the opposite or face side. The entire back of the fabric is usually coated with an adhesive material. Touch some perchlorethylene to the back of the fabric. If it feels tacky, beware (see Figure 4-48 and 4-49).

MALIPOL FABRICS IN CONSUMER USE

Garments of these fabrics are made for all apparel uses — men's women's, and children's — and they come in every hue of the rainbow.

Figure 4-49a Close-up of the underside of a Malipol slack fabric showing loss of pile from a scrim background fabric after wear and dry cleaning.

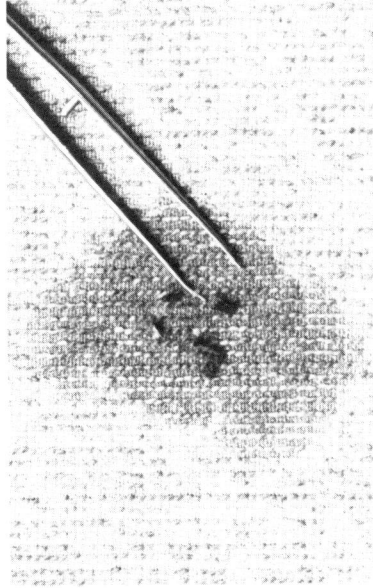

Figure 4-49b Perchlorethylene applied to the back of the fabric causes the adhesive coating to become tacky. The pile is easily removed with a pair of tweezers.

Malipol crushed velvet has a high, glossy, almost shiny appearance because of the final finishing or heat polishing step in the textile mill. This treatment lays the pile smoothly in the lengthwise direction of the fabric; however, this mechanical finish can be disturbed in wear and cleaning. Anything that disturbs the pile causes a difference in light reflection. This is why a consumer may complain that the pile surface appears changed.

The fabric manufacturer uses an adhesive or coating on the underside of the fabric to hold the pile to the backing so that in the dyeing and finishing processes the pile will not pull away. The amount of adhesive used may vary from a very light to a very heavy application. This is determined by the looseness or closeness of the weave of the base fabric as well as the end use for which the fabric is intended. For example, a manufacturer may consider the ability of an adhesive to withstand dry-cleaning solvents in making a fabric for wearing apparel, whereas this performance property would not be important in making an upholstery fabric.

Consumer complaints may be classified as: (1) change in appearance of the fabric surface; (2) change of the fabric's hand or feel; and (3) loss of pile in wear and dry cleaning. Sometimes loss of adhesive in dry cleaning can make a Malipol crushed velvet feel limp; in other cases the effect of dry cleaning and drying on the adhesive leaves the fabric stiffer than it was originally.

The loss of pile from Malipol fabrics is attributed to three causes.

1. Construction of the background fabric; for example, a loosely woven scrim would lose pile more readily than densely woven backing.
2. Kind and amount of adhesive applied to the back of the fabric.
3. Wear alone, or wear in combination with dry cleaning.

Research has shown that Malipol crushed velvets performed satisfactorily through three consecutive dry cleanings in Stoddard solvent, perchlorethylene or fluorocarbon solvent. This shows that dry cleaning in itself is not damaging to Malipol crushed velvet. However, loss of pile may occur after wear and dry cleaning. The flexing action in wear causes some types of adhesive to break loose so that the tufts are no longer firmly anchored to the base fabric; then, when the fabric is dry-cleaned, the solvent affects the adhesive more readily. Perchlorethylene softens the coatings more than Stoddard or fluorocarbon solvents do.

WEFT INSERTION KNITS

Weft (filling) insertion on warp knits combines the properties of knitting and weaving in the production of wearing apparel and household fabrics. Some knitted fabrics have drawbacks such as lack of dimensional stability, poor resistance to abrasion, pilling, snagging, and instability during cutting of a garment. Developers of weft insertion knitting say it will overcome some of these undesirable features.

To put it simply, weft insertion on warp knitting is a process utilizing a conventional tricot machine that can introduce a filling yarn across the width of a course. This is accomplished by adding a rotating creel to dispense the crosswise yarn that is inserted into the tricot knit fabric as it is being knitted. Technically, the process is quite complex (see Figure 4-50). A diagram of the weft insertion structure is shown in Figure 4-51. A fabric made of the construction is pictured in Figure 4-52.

Although this method of fabric construction is new in the United States, it had its beginning as early as 1791 and, during World War II, the British produced blankets by this technique.

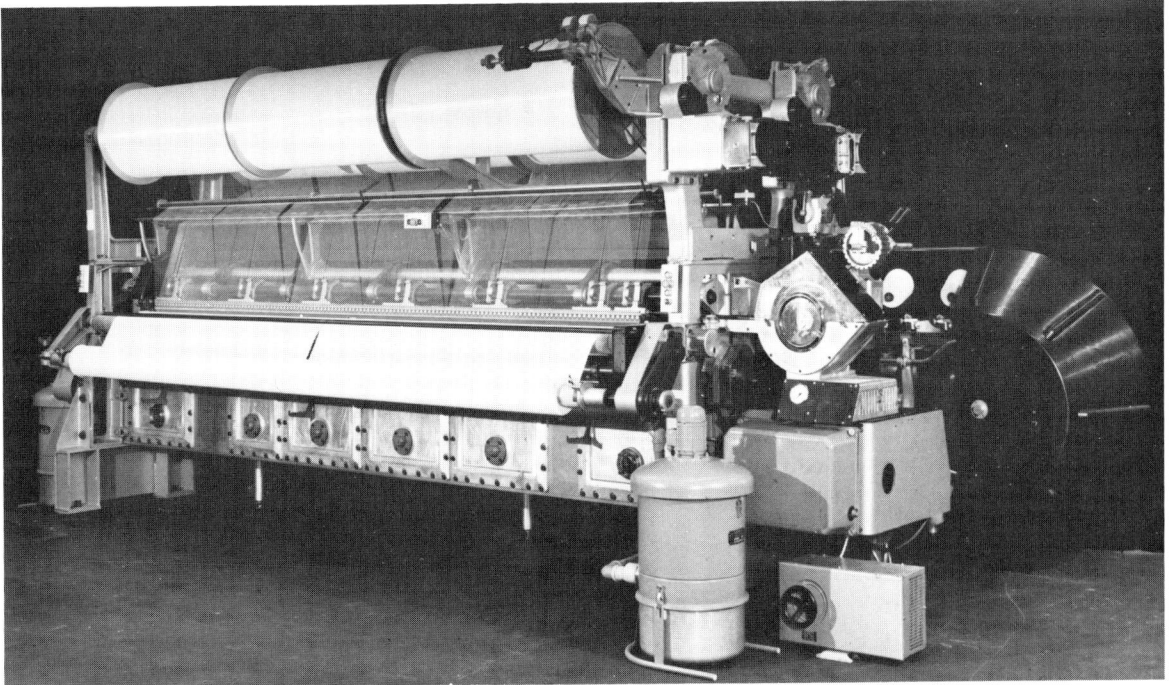

Figure 4-50 Tricot weft insertion machine, Type KMS3 130. (Courtesy: Mayer Textile Machine Corporation)

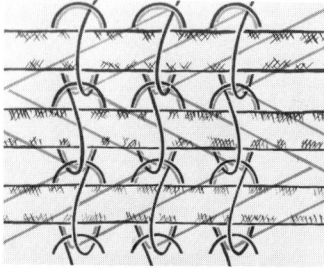

Figure 4-51 A diagram showing how the filling yarn is inserted across the width of each course. (Courtesy: Mayer Textile Machine Corporation)

Figure 4-52 This Weftamatic apparel fabric is made of 76 percent polyester and 24 percent wool warp knit in a plaid of red, yellow, white, and blue.

But very little was done with the idea until 1964, and the first full-width machine was delivered in 1969.

ADVANTAGES OF WEFT INSERTION KNITS

There apparently are many production advantages. But the chief advantages to consumers are:

1. Fabrics have new aesthetics and fashion potential. The method provides the introduction of spun, textured, or slub yarns to be incorporated into warp knit fashions.
2. Various degrees of stability can be introduced into fabrics, depending on the physical properties of the insertion yarn and the finishing techniques employed.
3. Stitch formation can be designed to make warp stretch fabrics: textured or stretch yarns can be used to make filling stretch fabrics; a combination of both allows production of two-way stretch fabrics.
4. Slippage of warp or filling is overcome to a larger degree than can be accomplished on a weaving loom.
5. Fabrics may be produced that are similar to other knits in some respects but are lighter in weight.

PART II
FABRICS FORMED FROM COMBINATIONS

LAMINATED AND BONDED FABRICS

Some authorities refer to this class of fabrics as "multicomponent fabrics." This kind of fabric has a structure in which an outer (or face) fabric is laminated to a backing fabric by means of a third layer or bonded to the backing fabric with adhesives. "Bonded" or "laminated" are often used interchangeably or together.

Lamination involves the combining of the outer and backing fabrics with a layer of foam. The surfaces of a layer of urethane foam are melted, the face and backing fabrics are applied to the foam while its surfaces are still molten, and they adhere together during cooling.

Wet adhesive bonding is the other basic process used in fabric-to-fabric bonding. An adhesive, usually a water-based acrylic compound, is applied between the fabrics and is heat-cured. This creates a permanent bond.

There are many advantages to laminated and bonded fabrics. They broaden the range of fashion fabric construction. Open weaves, laces, and slubby fabrics often have a weak structure of themselves, but become practicable when bonded. They are virtually self-lined, and thus save time and money for both cut and sew operators and the home sewer. Because they are stabilized, they lay out well on patterns and are easy to work with.

LAMINATED URETHANE FOAMS

There are three basic methods used in bonding fabric to foam.

Open Flame Method (Fusion Laminated)

This technique simply melts the foam by passing it over a gas flame or an electric bar with temperatures high enough to bring the foam to the melting point. The foam is then immediately pressed against the fabric by passing through a roller, and the bond is made (see Figure 4-53).

It is estimated that about 80 percent of all foam fabric laminations are done on open-flame equipment. The advantages claimed are:

1. Better bonding results.
2. This method leaves the final fabric porous, while chemical bonding does not.

207

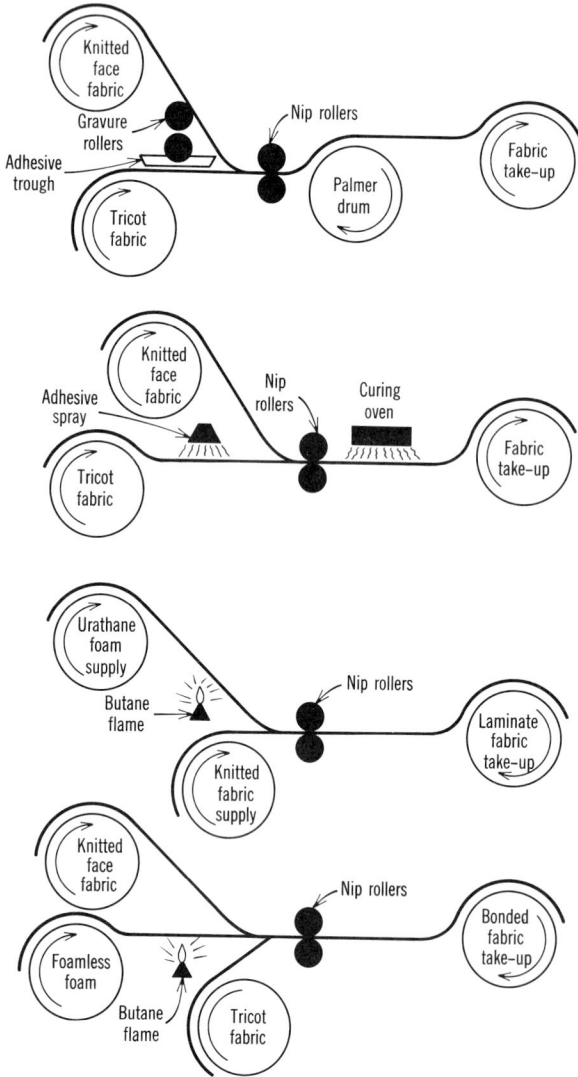

Figure 4-53 Bonding and laminating methods.
(Courtesy: National Knitted Outerwear Association)

Chemical Adhesive Method

The chemical industry is manufacturing many adhesives for use in laminating urethane foam to fabric. They range from cold-setting, water-based rubber to high-temperature curing resins.

The chemicals used in bonding can be coated on the fabric by a roller or a knife, or they may be sprayed or printed onto the fabric (see Figure 4-53). A laminated fabric is shown in Figure 4-54.

Vulcanizing Method

This method is still in the experimental stage. Vulcanizing foam to fabric is a radical departure from the present lamination methods. The technique currently used on some rug foaming operations would involve a method for the actual foaming of polyurethane directly to the fabric.

FILM, FOAM, FABRIC COMPOSITE

A new type of fabric with unusual design characteristics has been developed by Rohm and Haas Company. The trademark name is Ayrcryl. It consists of a base substrate that has been treated with crushed acrylic foam and laminated to a transparent acrylic film preprinted with a photograph or design on its back. Although printed on the back, the design is visible through the top surface of the fabric, achieving a three-dimensional effect. The process is applicable to a wide range of substrates, making possible a variety of fabrics for skirts, coats, suits, jackets, other wearing apparel, and accessories. The development is new and has not been evaluated for consumer performance.

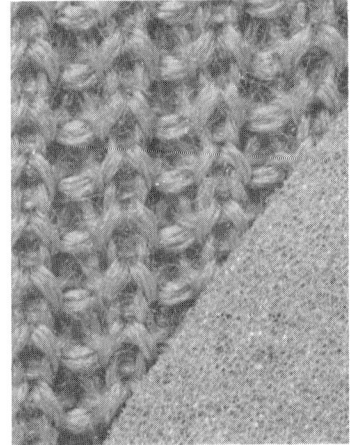

Figure 4-54 A knitted fabric laminated to foam.

BONDED FABRICS IN CONSUMER USE

Fabrics laminated to urethane foam by either the open flame method or chemical adhesive method made their appearance in 1960. Fabric bonded to fabric came into the market in 1963. The fabrics were usually bonded to acetate or nylon tricot.

Laminated urethane foam fabrics provide warmth with less weight and less bulk. The foam does not support growth of bacteria or fungi. It is odorless and nonodor-retaining. The foam will not bunch, mat, shrink, or stretch. It is perspiration-proof, nontoxic, and nonallergenic. The foam may be coated with a reflective finish. Fabrics that were never designed for such uses may now be laminated and used for outerwear garments. Urethane foam eliminates the conventional interlining of outerwear garments. Laminating fabric to foam improves the stability of a fabric in some instances. Sandwiched foams (a fabric laminated to each side of the foam) are readily adaptable to reversible garment designs.

Most urethane laminated foam fabrics dry-clean and launder satisfactorily. Although some of the early laminates showed partial or complete separation of the fabric from the foam in dry cleaning and wet cleaning, improvements are being made to minimize this problem. The foam is unaffected by the heat of pressing.

The performance of urethane foam laminated fabrics depends to a great extent on the performance characteristics of the particular woven or knitted fabric.

Tricot is desirable as a backing fabric because of the following fabric properties: (1) elasticity and a controllable degree of stability; (2) resiliency; (3) crease resistance; (4) drapability; (5) abrasion resistance and high tear strength; (6) soft to touch, hence comfortable; (7) runproof and nonraveling; and (8) can be pleated by heat setting.

The tricot fabric serves to stabilize loosely woven or knitted fabrics, lace, or leno constructions. Tricots may lend a color contrast to open or transparent constructions. There are infinite possibilities for combining different colors and textures of face fabrics with different colors of tricot backing fabrics.

The basic criteria for a good bonded fabric are: (1) the bond must withstand washing and dry cleaning; (2) fabric drape or hand must not be affected; (3) no stiffening of the fabric; (4) no odor; (5) must resist discoloration; (6) no chemical breakdown of the fibers; (7) no strike-through of adhesive; and (8) shrinkage of the two fabrics must be compatible to avoid puckering. Shrinkage should not exceed 3 percent for woven and 5 percent for knitted fabrics. Heat-setting and finishing techniques have been developed to the point where today's shrinkage control of nylon tricot can be kept within 1 percent, but acetate tricot cannot be stabilized to this degree.

CHEMICAL QUILTING

The next development by textile manufacturers in bonded fabrics was chemical quilting. A face and backing fabric were quilted to either a urethane foam or a fiber batt. In the case of the chemically quilted urethane foam fabrics, the foam held the face fabric to the foam. In the fabrics bonded to a fiber batt and chemically quilted, an adhesive held the face fabric, fiber batt, and tricot together in the selected quilted design. In wear and use dissatisfaction resulted from the complete or partial loss of design in wear and cleaning.

POLYURETHANE FILM-BONDED TO FABRIC

One of the newer ideas in "wet look" apparel is a "see through" effect made by bonding a sheet of clear plastic film to finished fabric so the color and pattern is visible. It is popular in ladies wear and provides a plastic protection that does not hide the fabric, but enhances it.

The film-bonded fabric is made of clear polyurethane film bonded by an adhesive to the face side of a woven or knitted fabric.

Although the film itself is not affected by dry-cleaning solvent, satisfactory performance in dry cleaning depends on the adhesive's resistance to solvent, the bond's effectiveness, and the nature of the backing cloth. The fabric bond must be strong enough to prevent separation of film from fabric. Some films discolor or yellow after exposure to light.

FILM TO FABRIC

COATED FABRICS

The first "coated fabric" was probably "oilcloth." Since the production of this fabric by relatively simple means, the coated fabrics field has expanded to a large and important segment of the textile industry.

Coated fabrics are made by three processes: (1) knife coating; (2) soild film coating, and (3) cast or transfer coating. Knife coating is the oldest method used. Since knife coating works in a medium of liquids, the processes can vary greatly. Solid film coating can be made to exact specifications in an infinite variety of patterns, strengths and thicknesses. Urethane film has opened up many ways to achieve a variety of coated fabrics. In the transfer coating process, the solution is cast onto a specially treated urethane grade paper and dried in an explosion-proof oven. A second "tie" coat is applied over the dry first coat. The second coat may be based on the same resin as the first coat. Fabric is brought into contact, under pressure, with the second coat while it is still wet. The paper coating-fabric laminate is dried in an explosion-proof oven. Following this final oven drying, the release paper is immediately stripped from the coated fabric and rolled for reuse, while the coated goods are rolled separately. There is no way a consumer can distinguish the method of coating used on the fabrics purchased.

The fabrics that fall into this classification are varied, but they are classed for our discussion as follows.

1. Fabrics used for dresses or trim.
    a. Smooth or textured surface simulated leather.
        (1) Coated method.
        (2) Expanded vinyl method.
        (3) Laminated method.

2. Rainwear fabrics for coats, capes, and jackets.
   (a) Synthetic rubber coating.
   (b) Vinyl coating.
   (c) Microporus finish.
3. Reflective linings for coats and jackets.
4. Drapery linings.
   (a) Reflective.
   (b) Opaque.
5. Aero-cellular acrylic.
6. Self-lined drapery fabrics.

METALLIC PLATED FABRICS

Nylon or acetate tricot knit fabrics are coated on one side with silver, gold, or colored pigments in a resin binder. This produces a soft, luxurious fabric. It cannot be abused in wear. These plated fabrics are quite expensive; therefore they are used in high-style and unusual garment design. Plated fabrics may be considered fragile, requiring extreme care in dry cleaning, stain and spot removal, and finishing.

Plated fabrics abraid easily. This may occur as light streaks on some areas. Creasing of the fabric may also result in streaks. Color changes may result from perspiration. Some of the spotting agents used to remove spots and stains will also remove the metallic particles. The brightness of the fabric may be lost in wear and cleaning. The fabric cannot be ironed on the right side as the iron will stick to it.

SMOOTH OR TEXTURED SURFACE SIMULATED LEATHER (COATED METHOD)

Simulated leather is a term used to describe a coated fabric that has the look, feel, and pliability of genuine leather. The base fabric may be knitted or woven from a variety of fabric constructions. Originally, these coatings were a nitrocellulose product called pyroxylin but, for a number of years, vinyls have been used for apparel and upholstery applications. Various leather simulations are achieved by embossing.

Simulated leather is adaptable to a wide range of garment constructions for men, women, and children. Simulated leather serves as an effective trim with a variety of woven and knitted fabrics. It is used widely to reinforce sleeves, elbows, and knees of active sports garments.

Performance satisfaction depends on fabric combinations and garment constructions. Simulated vinyl leather garments should be wet-cleaned.

Simulated vinyl leather cannot be dry-cleaned. Dry cleaning removes the solvent-soluble carrier for the resin that is used to coat these fabrics. Manufacturers are making improvements in the performance of the smooth surface simulated leathers. Some manufacturers claim their product is drycleanable.

SMOOTH OR TEXTURED SURFACE SIMULATED LEATHER (EXPANDED VINYL METHOD)

A smooth surface, expanded vinyl fabric is made by applying the coating with foaming agent. This expands the material into a spongelike cellular structure with a soft, pliable hand. This material is bonded to a knitted background. The surface can be embossed to resemble the many different markings of grain leather.

This group of fabrics may be used to make coats, jackets, vests, caps, and gloves. It may be combined with woven or knitted fabrics in a variety of garment designs. The fabrics are soft and pliable. They have a good appearance and hand. Smooth or textured leathers of the expanded vinyl type should be wet-cleaned unless labeled dry-cleanable.

Garments that combine dry-cleanable fabrics with smooth or textured expanded vinyl fabric may present a problem in cleaning. Shrinkage of the dry-cleanable fabric may occur in wet cleaning. If excessive shrinkage occurs in the expanded vinyl fabric, it is impossible in most cases to shape it back to size. Some stains such as dye, ink, and lipstick are difficult if not impossible to remove without causing damage to the surface of the fabric.

SMOOTH OR TEXTURED SURFACE SIMULATED LEATHER (LAMINATION METHOD)

Smooth or textured simulated leathers are made by laminating a sheet of vinyl film with an adhesive to a woven or knitted background fabric. The surface of the film may be embossed to resemble the grain of any genuine leather. This is done by calendering or fusing the two parts together.

Simulated leathers made by the lamination method may be used for rainwear, jackets, and hats. They are used widely for making shoes and handbags. Laminated simulated leathers may be combined with dry-cleanable fabric in garment design or be used as trim. The fabrics have a good appearance and hand. They are less expensive than genuine leather.

The laminated leathers should be wet-cleaned. Laminated simulated leathers should not be dry-cleaned. Dry cleaning may cause stiffening in some fabrics and partial or complete separation of film from fabric in others.

COATED OUTERWEAR FABRICS

Medium-weight fabrics, usually cotton, are coated on the back with a rubberized coating or a vinyl coating to make the fabric weather-resistant. These fabrics are lightweight and warm. Although they keep the wearer warm and dry, they do not permit air to pass through the surface of the fabric; this can eventually lead to a clammy feel or sensation. Many vinyl coated fabrics stiffen in dry cleaning. They can be wet-cleaned.

Rubberized coatings are best cleaned by the petroleum solvent method of dry cleaning. These coatings may be affected by some of the spotting chemicals used to remove spots or stains.

COATED RAINWEAR FABRICS

Fabrics of cotton, silk, rayon, nylon, and polyester are thinly coated on the front to impart water resistance to the fabric. Some of these fabrics are lightweight. They are comfortable to wear and pack easily. Many attractive colors and designs are available.

Some of these fabrics are warm and uncomfortable in warm weather and cold to wear in cold weather. Some crack and yellow with age. The tear strength is low by comparison with many fabrics used in outerwear garments. They tear easily. These fabrics cannot be dry-cleaned, because they stiffen in cleaning. They can be wet-cleaned.

REFLECTIVE WEARING APPAREL LINING FABRICS

Conventional suit and coat lining fabrics such as satin, taffeta, twill, and plain weave lining fabrics are coated on one side with metallic or colored flakes in a resin binder. It is claimed that this type of lining is warmer in cold weather, cooler in the hot sun and, therefore, comfortable to wear all year. These linings have eye appeal and sales appeal. Reflective linings can give good serviceability in wear and cleaning if the aluminum coating is applied to a firmly woven lining fabric and if the conditions of applying the aluminum particles are properly controlled.

Wear and dry cleaning may alter the appearance of the treated side of the lining fabric. Cases are on record where some of the metallic particles have been removed in one dry cleaning. More particles may be removed in successive dry cleanings. This alters the appearance of the coated side of the fabric. This may or may not be objectionable, depending on the attitude of the wearer. If the metallic particles are removed from the lining fabric and transferred to a lighter coating fabric, a graying of the outer coating fabric may occur.

REFLECTIVE DRAPERY LINING FABRICS

Conventional cotton drapery linings such as sateen, brocade, and print cloth (a plain weave cotton) are coated on one side with metallic or colored flakes in a resin binder. This type of fabric may be sold under various tradenames.

The shiny surface of the drapery fabric placed against the window reflects the rays of sunlight. This, it is reasoned, deflects the sun's rays and does not permit their penetration of the drapery fabric. This reduces the chance of fabric damage and color damage to the draperies and curtains, as well as other household fabrics in the room.

Dry cleaning may remove some of the metallic particles. The degree of removal is closely related to the background fabric. A lining fabric of a loosely constructed weave will flake off more particles than a lining fabric with a tightly woven weave. This flaking often alters the appearance of the reflective side of the lining fabric.

OPAQUE DRAPERY LINING FABRIC

Conventional drapery lining fabrics such as sateen or print cloth are coated on one side with a vinyl resin material to make the fabric opaque. This type of coated fabric comes in white, silver, or black, allowing selection according to use.

The coating serves to shut out light and prevent it from entering the room. At the same time, the coating stops the light inside the room from being seen on the outside. Coated fabrics serve as a good blackout material in rooms used to project movies. Coated fabrics serve a useful function as a blackout fabric in case of emergencies, such as war.

Vinyl coated drapery lining can be cleaned satisfactorily in petroleum solvent. Dry-cleaning in a synthetic solvent causes some of the coatings to separate from the lining fabric; still others may stiffen and crack. One manufacturer has improved his product so that it can be cleaned satisfactorily in both petroleum and synthetic solvent.

AERO-CELLULAR ACRYLIC LINING

The manufacturer claims that the aero-cellular acrylic coating serves as a lining and, in addition, that the finish dampens outside noises effectively without distorting sound inside the room; insulates against cold wintry drafts — keeps rooms warmer in winter; defies the sun's heat; keeps rooms cooler in the summer; gives more depth and dimension to the surface of the drapery fabric for a much more luxurious appearance; assures privacy, since the drapery is almost completely opaque; and is guaranteed against sun rot and fading for years.

There are two types of finishes: (1) foamed acrylic on the window side of the fabric; and (2) a layer of foamed acrylic coating bonding a nonwoven fabric with the face fabric.

Both are dry-cleanable. But, like many coated fabrics, the new foamed acrylic thermal-lined draperies require special handling when hung to air-dry to prevent possible damage to the backing. Both fabrics are also machine washable, as outlined on care labels permanently attached to the drapery panels.

PLASTIC LAMINATED DRAPERY FABRIC

A conventional drapery fabric may be laminated with a vinyl film. The film is bonded to the underside of the fabric with an adhesive compound.

A vinyl film applied directly to the surface of a drapery fabric eliminates the need for a separate lining. It is called a self-lined drapery fabric. The film has a reflective property to sunlight and, therefore, blocks out light. The film has an insulation value, because air cannot pass through the plastic layer of the fabric. It is said to be effective in maintaining room temperature. The film makes the fabric 100 percent blackout. It also has acoustical values.

Manufacturers state the film of the fabric should be wiped with a damp cloth and the fabric side vacuumed. Wet cleaning may result in excessive shrinkage and separation of film from fabric. Dry cleaning results in excessive shrinkage. The fabric stiffens. There may be partial separation of the film from the fabric. Exposure to excessive heat over a long period of time may cause yellowing of the vinyl film.

FIBER TO FABRIC

FLOCKED FABRICS

Research and development in the flocking industry has resulted in many fashion fabrics for men's and women's apparel and home furnishings. Flocking used to be confined to design applications, but no longer! Research and development has been done to produce flocked fabrics that are dry-cleanable, washable, breathable, colorfast, flame-resistant, and abrasion-resistant. Wovens are the main base fabric but knits are being used as base material in the hope that they will provide competition in weight and cost. Flocked fabrics are made to look like velvet, crushed velvet, wide and narrow wale corduroys, and simulated suedes. Experiments are underway to make flocked lace and tire cord flocked with nylon (a flocked yarn). The latter is woven into tapestry cloth as a decorative component. Research in cross-dyeing is underway to achieve two-tone effects in various color combinations when processing natural colored flock of different fibers in the same dye bath. There is also experimentation in developing sculptural pattern surfaces.

FLOCKED VELVETS

The early flocked velvets were made by bonding small particles of fibers, called flock, to a base fabric. They were usually made into ribbons and used as trim for collars, cuffs, belts, decorative designs on dresses, negligees, housecoats, and suits.

Today, two basic constructions are used to make flocked velvets in garments and household items: (1) rayon flock held to a woven background fabric by an adhesive coating, and (2) rayon flock held to a urethane foam that is bonded to a knit or woven fabric.

Flocked velvet is used in a variety of garments for adults and children: dresses, coats, jackets, pantsuits, vests, trousers, and the "nonconstructed" easy suits. Colors run the rainbow. Some fabrics are treated with water-repellent finishes.

FLOCKED VELVETS IN CONSUMER USE

Consumer complaints on performance in use and care fall into definite patterns: (1) loss of flock in wear and cleaning; (2) separation or peeling of foam from the background fabric along with the tearing away and loss of foam; and (3) loss of color caused by solvent-soluble dye (see Figure 4-55 and 4-56).

FLOCKED SUEDE FABRICS (COATED METHOD)

A flocked fabric is made by binding small particles of fibers (called "flock") to the entire surface of a woven fabric. This type of fabric construction permits a wide variation in achieving different surface effects. A fine, short flock on the surface may be used

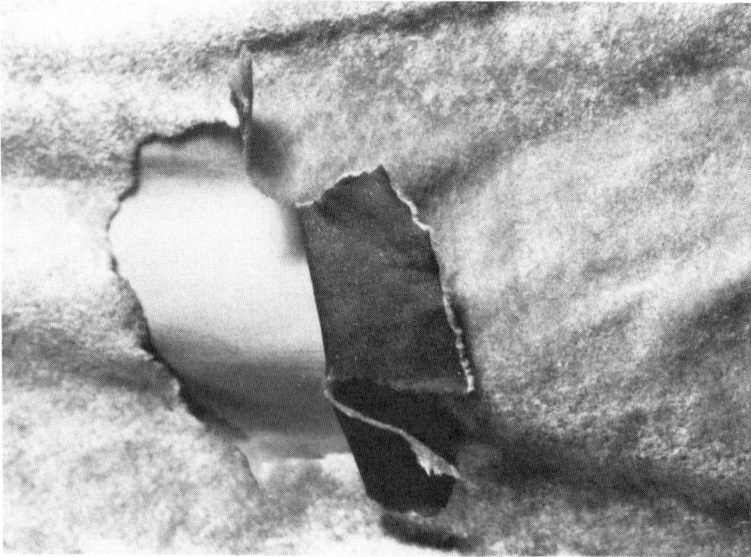

Figure 4-55 Flocked foam separates, peels, and tears away from the base fabric in dry cleaning.

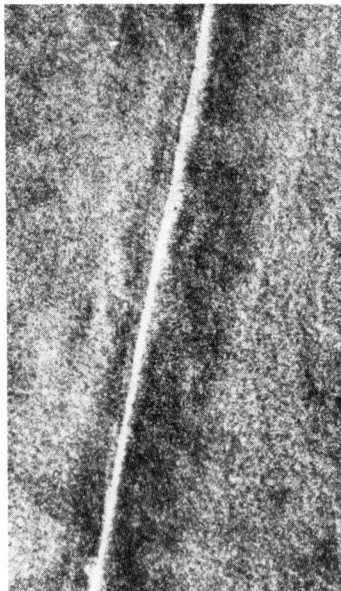

Figure 4-56 Loss of pile in a flocked velvet caused by edge abrasion during wear.

to create a suede effect; a long flock may be used to create the effect of a deep pile upholstery fabric.

Some flocked fabrics are used in dry-cleanable garment constructions, such as jackets, lining fabrics in coats and jackets, and skirts and jumpers. Flocked pile fabrics may be used as trim and for shoes and bags.

A great improvement has been made in the performance of flocked surface suedes by using an acrylic adhesive to bind the flock to the base fabric.

Some flocked suedes made with a neoprene adhesive have caused problems: change of color, loss of flock, loss of tensile strength, and stiffening. There is a limit to what can be done to remove spots and stains, since some of the reagents needed to remove many types of stains also remove the flock from the base fabric.

FLOCKED SUEDE FABRICS (EXPANDED VINYL METHOD)

A flocked expanded vinyl fabric is made by heating a vinyl or plastic material. This expands the material into a spongelike cellular structure with a soft, plastic hand. This material is bonded to a knitted background fabric. Short lengths of cotton or nylon, called "flock" are bonded to the surface. The fabric has the appearance of genuine suede.

Expanded vinyl suede fabrics are used to make coats, jackets, vests, caps, dresses, jumpers, suits, slacks, and shorts. Knitted and woven fabrics may be combined with expanded vinyl suede in a variety of garment designs.

Expanded vinyl suede has a good appearance and hand. It is less expensive than genuine suede. Nylon flock gives an extra factor of durability because of its resistance to rubbing and abrasion. A garment made of knitted or woven fabric combined with expanded vinyl suede presents a problem in cleaning. Shrinkage may occur in wet cleaning.

FIBER TO FOAM

NONWOVEN URETHANE FOAM CONSTRUCTION

Nonwoven blankets, in beautiful colors with a soft, velvety feel, are now being made for institutional use and home use in sizes ranging from the baby crib to the king-size bed. They can be dry-cleaned, but certain precautions are necessary. The new patented process for making nonwoven blankets is called Vellux by West Point Pepperell, Inc.

The main insulating component of a Vellux blanket polyurethane foam is not a textile product at all, but a soft, flexible, plastic substrate. However, thin-gauge polyurethane foam lacks some of the characteristics required of a blanket. The sheet of foam elongates and breaks under tension, and its rubbery hand and drab appearance make it unappealing. The deficiency is overcome by bonding a special nylon mesh between two thin layers of foam so that the resultant foam laminate is very strong and stable (see Figure 4-57). Next, both sides are flocked with carefully screened fine nylon fibers that are held to the foam

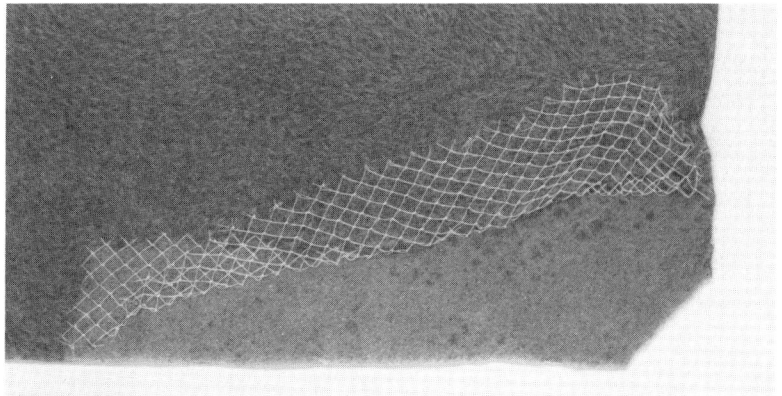

Figure 4-57 Two pieces of foam are bonded to nylon net; this provides dimensional stability and adds tear strength. The foam provides warmth without weight. Reversible blankets are made with a printed design on one side and a solid flocked surface on the other, which also serves as a binding.

substrate with an acrylic adhesive. (The adhesive also contains the dyes that give the foam substrate its permanent color.)

As they fall toward the foam, the fibers pass through an electrostatic field that aligns them in a position vertical to the blanket. The electrostatic field then repels the fibers and forces them into the adhesive, where they become embedded. At the same time, beater bars vibrate the foam substrate, causing the fibers to embed more deeply in the adhesive layer. The adhesive is then cured to fasten the fibers permanently to the foam. The performance of the flocked material depends in large part on the adhesive that holds the fibers in place.

Nonwoven blankets are available in different solid colors — pink, blue, green, gold, and white. Some blankets are made to be reversible: solid white on one side and a printed floral design on the other. The top and bottom edges of the blankets are bound with nylon satin or are self-hemmed. The manufacturer claims these nonwoven blankets look and feel like velvet after more than 50 washings, and that they are resistant to shrinking, pilling, shedding, and are lightweight yet warm. They claim the blankets are dry-cleanable and completely machine-washable and machine-dryable.

This fabric is also used for robes, jackets, skiwear, linings, gloves, and bunny slippers.

FIBER TO YARN FABRIC

QUILTED FABRICS

Quilting is the stitching together of two or more fabrics with a layer of padding or batting of fibers inside the outer fabrics. This type of construction offers a wide selection of fabrics for wearing apparel and household items. Many of the quilted fabrics give warmth without weight. Many of the quilted fabrics wear, launder, and dry-clean satisfactorily.

The type and length of the stitching thread contributes to serviceability. If the stitches are long and floating, they catch readily in use and cleaning, causing loss of design. Some battings tend to mat and bunch up in wear and cleaning. If the fabrics that are quilted are not preshrunk, shrinkage may occur. In some of the battings, dark-colored waste fibers are used, so in wear and cleaning the dye may bleed and stain the outer fabric (see Figure 4-58).

Figure 4-58 A conventional quilted fabric using thread.

PINSONIC QUILTING

A method of producing quilted fabrics has been developed jointly by Crompton and Knowles Corporation and Branson Sonic Power Company.

Pinsonic quilting is the result of a combination of ultrasonics and machinery manufacturing skills (see Figure 4-59). This new system can produce seven times the amount of quilted material that conventional quilting machines do at one tenth the cost. The

Figure 4-59 Pinsonic quilting is accomplished by passing face, batting, and back between the pattern role and ultrasonic heads. Quilting is accomplished by heat fusion. (Courtesy: Branson Sonic Power Co.)

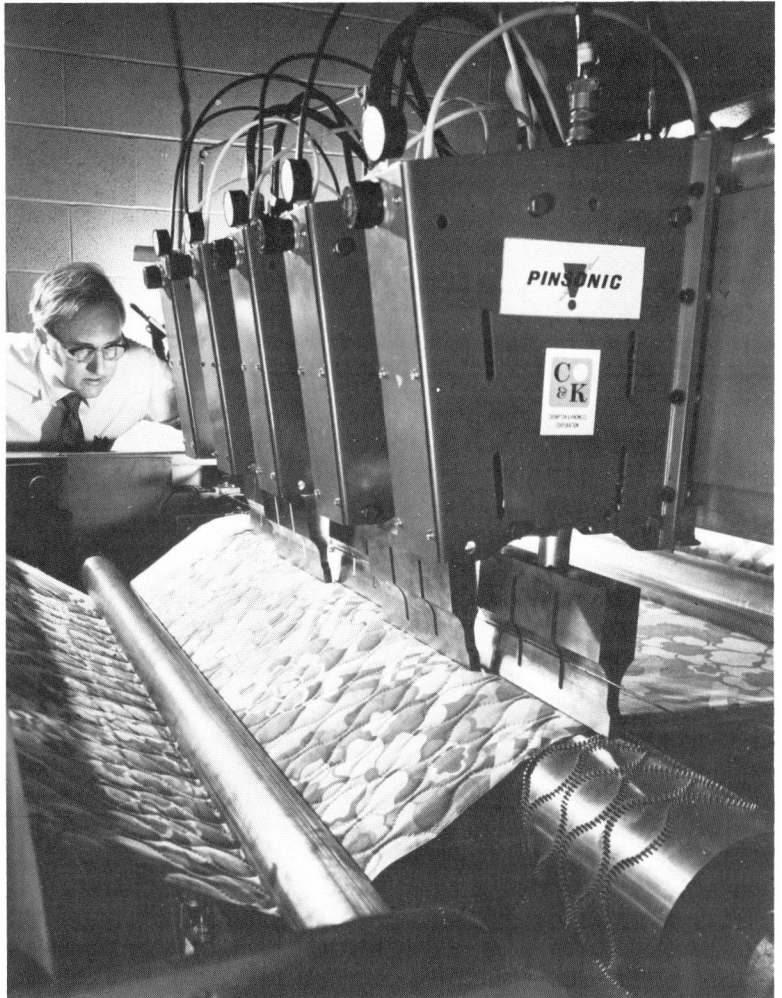

method produces quilted fabric with thermally bonded joints, completely eliminating the stitching threads.

The Pinsonic process is performed by passing the fabrics to be joined — face, batting, and backing — between a pattern roll and the ultrasonic heads. All welds across the fabric width are made simultaneously, permitting operating speeds of 20 feet per minute or more.

This method of quilting provides versatility because each weld is independent of the other. This eliminates the need for continuity of pattern lines, a limiting factor in traditional quilting — complicated scroll patterns, shell patterns, and unconnected motifs all run as easily as conventional diamonds or onion patterns. Claims are made that the Pinsonic system not only eliminates the use of costly stitching threads but also eliminates the cost of product failure in quilted structures — the breaking of the stitching threads.

YARN TO FABRIC

TUFTING

Machine tufting originated in 1940 and its first market was tufted bedspreads, then robes. In 1950 tufted carpets and rugs made their appearance. And now tufted fabric production is widely used for household textiles such as bedspreads, draperies, and upholstery.

Tufting is a process of manufacturing pile fabrics by inserting loops into an already woven ground fabric. This ground fabric may be of any type and composed of any fiber; jute (burlap) historically provided the base fabric for tufted carpeting, but polypropylene background fabrics are seriously challenging jute now. The tuft yarns may also be of any fiber; cotton, rayon, wool, acrylic, polyester, nylon and acetate fibers are all popular in tufted fabrics.

Pile loops, cut or uncut on the face, are inserted with needles and held in place by a special coating applied to the back or by untwisting the tufted yarn and shrinking the base fabric. Tufted fabrics are less costly than their woven fabrics of comparable or similar constructions and appearance. By controlling the amount of yarn being fed to each needle, the size of the loop is determined; this in turn produces variations in texture and design. Loops can be cut or uncut, and combinations of both are used to create interesting designs.

Identification of tufted fabrics is comparatively simple if the back of the yarns are visible. However, some tufted constructions are bonded to another fabric (secondary backing) to increase dimensional stability and prevent damage, or they are coated with a heavy layer of adhesive. These backings make it difficult to see the characteristic tufted structure but, if it can be seen, tufts run in the lengthwise direction, and the underside shows the back loop of the tufts as a separate yarn, not an integral part of the weave.

PART III
FABRICS FORMED FROM FIBERS DIRECTLY

FELT

Felt is a compact, thick fabric made by compressing wool and sometimes other fibers, with the addition of heat, moisture, and pressure. Felt can be made in different grades and weights from very light to very heavy.

Felt is an unusual fabric when compared with woven or knitted fabric. It has many apparel and home furnishing applications, and it may be combined with other fabrics in many interesting garment constructions. Felt fabrics offer a wide selection of colors, from solid shades to the iridescent felts achieved by the blending of dyed fibers, usually wool and rayon. Felt fabrics offer a wide selection of fabric designs, such as printed, painted, or flocked, and the addition of sequins, feathers, metallic yarns, and embroidered designs. A 100 percent wool felt is more expensive than blended felts. However, it gives the best service for money invested.

Felt fabric may be given special finishes to improve the appearance, such as a starch finish to impart stiffness or a wax finish to make it smoother and more lustrous. Felt fabrics dry-clean satisfactorily, but they require special care. Some felts shrink in steam finishing, but they may be pressed satisfactorily without steam. Combining felts with woven fabrics in a garment makes dry-cleaning and spotting more difficult.

Low- and medium-quality felt fabrics cannot withstand a great strain, because thin areas in the fabric break. They cannot be mended satisfactorily, are susceptible to abrasion, and rough up in wear and in dry cleaning. Some felts are not relaxed in manufacture; therefore they may shrink in dry cleaning and finishing.

Some iridescent fiber dyed felts possess poor colorfastness to moisture. Spilling water or a beverage on the fabric may cause dyes to bleed, staining the surrounding area. The wax finishes are solvent-soluble, leaving the fabric less lustrous after dry cleaning; on removal of a starch finish, the fabric is less stiff. Some of the printed, painted and flocked designs are affected adversely in dry cleaning. Inferior felt is hard, coarse, shiny, and lacks body.

224

REINFORCED FELT

Lightweight felt with a net base differs from the regular felt. It has a nylon net in the center with wool and rayon fibers felted to both sides of the netting. See discussion of Needlepunched Fabrics, page 231. This type of felt construction is adaptable to many uses, such as skirts, dresses, jumpers, jackets, and coats. The fabric is lightweight, yet strong. The fabric is supple and looks like a fine broadcloth. It drapes and tailors well and retains its shape. It may be given special water-repellent, stain, and spot-resistant treatment.

A fabric made of this construction is susceptible to abrasion in wear, and undue strain may result in tears that cannot be mended without being visible. This fabric is dry-cleanable with care.

MOLDED FABRICS

Thermoplastic fibers such as the acrylics, modacrylics, polyesters, and polyolefins, by themselves or in certain specific blends with other fibers, can be molded into shapes having form and dimensional stability in use by the application of heat and force.

Knitted, woven, nonwoven fabrics and felts of thermoplastic fibers may be molded.

Heat-shaping may be accomplished by three methods.

1. *Plug-molding.* In this method a cooled or heated mold of any shape or design is forced into a fabric that has been pre-heated.
2. *Modified vacuum forming.* The fabric is preheated to a pliable or formable temperature and is deformed into the desired shape. An elastic impermeable membrane is placed on one side of the fabric with vacuum on the other side to achieve the closest conformation to the shape of the mold. A plug assist may be used to keep the fabric to conform to the molded shape.
3. *Compression forming.* Two molds — male and female dies — may be used to make more complex shapes and designs. The process is similar to that of plug molding. Because of the pressure developed, the shaped product is usually stiffer and glossier than those formed by the plug or vacuum method.

Either male or female molds may be used. Imagination is the only limit in the use of this new method of creating designs and shapes for consumer products ranging from molded hats to molded carpeting.

NONWOVENS

Glazed wadding, the forerunner of today's nonwoven fabrics, was made as early as 1860. Today, hundreds of patents cover techniques and processes for the manufacture of nonwoven fabrics. Nonwovens came into their own in the late 1960s. Today, it is well over a $1.2 billion market.

Nonwoven fabrics may be described or defined in different ways. A scientist or researcher might define a nonwoven fabric as a structure composed essentially of textile fibers that have been bonded, interlocked, or both by mechanical, thermal, solvent, or chemical means or by some combinations — but without weaving or knitting. Some people prefer to define nonwovens by the manufacturing process. This is sometimes difficult, because the machinery and techniques are very complex. The manufacturing classification includes: (1) stitch through (Arachne and Maliwatt); (2) needlepunch; (3) carded webs; (4) air-laid products; (5) wet-laid products; (6) composite paper products; (7) spun-bonded products, and (8) spun-laced products. Still others may define nonwovens according to manufacturers (fiber producer and/or mill producer), market, or end-use product.

There is a growing trend to define nonwovens as "durables" or "disposables." A "durable product" is defined as one that has multiple uses. A "disposable product" is one that is made to be disposed of after one use. However, some of the disposable products can be laundered. This can be confusing. The key appears to be the intended purpose or end use of the item instead of durability.

Regardless of manufacturing process, the steps in manufacturing nonwoven fabrics are: (1) preparation of the fiber; (2) formation of the web; (3) bonding the web; (4) drying and curing the fabric; and (5) dyeing, printing, and finishing.

Of the steps listed above, web formation is one differentiation of the final fabric end use. There are three ways by which webs are formed.

1. *Random.* The spreading and laying of fibers by controlled air currents (sometimes called isotropic structures) that produces

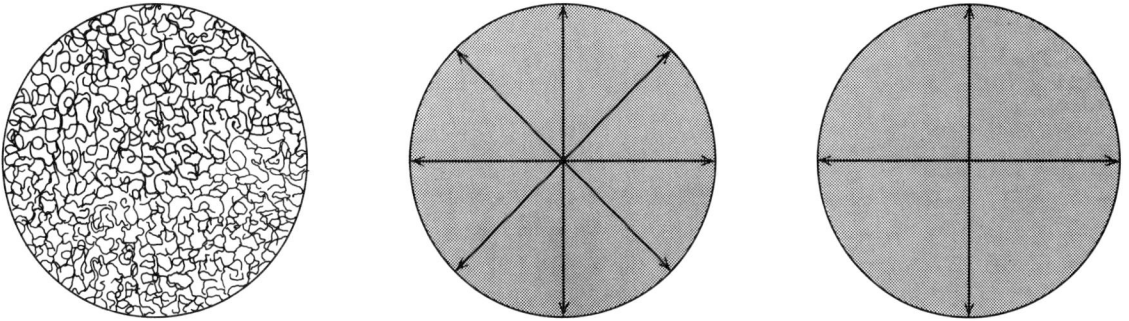

Figure 4-60 There are three methods of making nonwoven fabrics: (Left) A diagram of man-made fibers randomly distributed, bonded by heat and chemical binders. It will not ravel because of multidirectional strength, it is porous, long-lasting, nonshrinkable. (Center) All-bias polyester nonwoven for medium-weight fabrics, especially knits, because of "give" in all directions. (Right) Regular nonwoven of straight fibers, no "give," for stabilizing flat areas.

a fabric that has equal strength in all directions. At this time it is the most popular method of manufacture.

2. *Cross-directional.* Two layers of fibers are laid at right angles to each other. In fabric form the crosswise direction is stronger than the lengthwise direction.
3. *Oriented web or unidirectional structures.* Where the fibers are parallel to the longitudinal axis. In fabric form the lengthwise direction is stronger than the crosswise direction (see Figure 4-60).

Fiber webs may be bonded together by: (1) the use of thermoplastic fibers, heat, and pressure; (2) discontinuous bonding applied in strips or points so that most of the fabric is not bonded; (3) saturation of the complete web or mat with the adhesive; or (4) spraying the carded webs or mats with an adhesive or solvent and drying without pressure.

The two major systems for making nonwoven fabrics are shown in Figure 4-61.

Classified as to fiber content, durable nonwovens are made of polyester/polyethylene/polypropylene; rayon; nylon; modacrylic; acetate; vinyon; and wool. Disposables are made of rayon (85 percent); polyester; cotton; acetate; vinyon; and modacrylic. Rayon is a good fiber for nonwovens because it is absorbent, soft, easy to dye, easy to bind, and is biodegradable. Its disadvantage is low strength. Polyester is strong and thermoplastic, but it is not absorbent, is difficult to bind, and is not biodegradable.

Tradenames, method of manufacture, and uses of some nonwoven fabrics are given in Table 4-4.

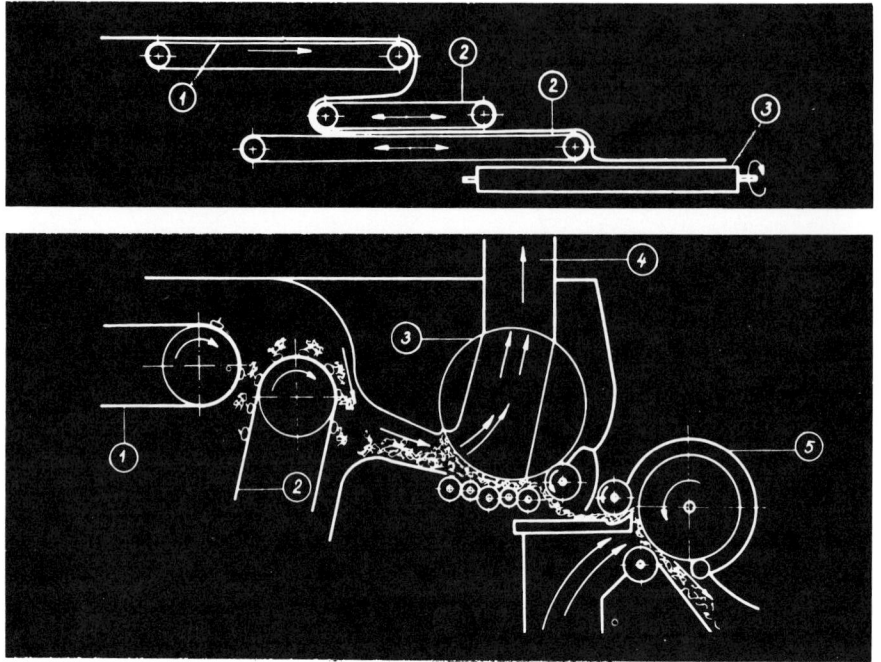

Figure 4-61 Two major systems for making nonwoven fabrics. (Top and center) Two dry-laid systems of making nonwovens. (Top) Cross-directional construction with the web laying on a horizontal web layer in a continuous production line. (1) Feed conveyor, (2) Swinging layer conveyors. (3) Delivery conveyor. (Center) The Rando-Webber machine system makes isotropic (multidirectional) nonwovens. (1) Stripping conveyor. (2) Inclined feed conveyor. (3) Screen drum with cover. (4) Suction. (5) Opening mechanism. (Bottom) Spunbonded system, polymer to web. (1) Spinnerettes. (2) Draw-off rollers. (3) Electrostatic fiber charging. (4) Air feed. (5) Delivery conveyor. (6) Battle plate. (Diagrams from "Manual of Nonwovens" by Dr. Radko Krcma) (Courtesy: American Fabrics and Fashions)

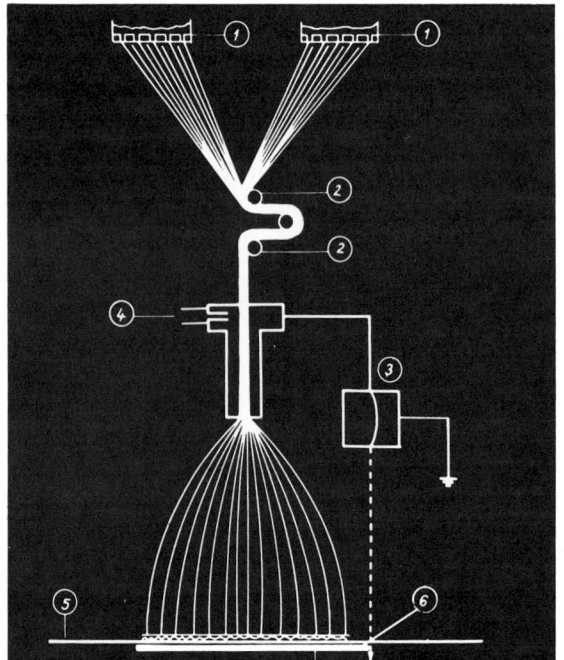

Table 4-4   Nonwoven Fabrics*

Tradename and Manufacturer	Method	Uses
Kyron (J. P. Stevens)	Saturated air-laid polyester	Interlinings, waistbands, interfacings.
Poly-Kyron (J. P. Stevens)	Lightweight version of Kyron	Women's collars, cuffs plaquettes
Bondaire (J. P. Stevens)	Spray-bonded polyester fiberfil batt	Bra padding, filter media
Needleweb (J. P. Stevens)	Made of polyester, Nomex, and other fibers for needlepunch products by the method	
Nexus (Burlington)	A spun-laced sheet of staple fiber achieved by air entanglement. No binder used. Du Pont produces the goods. Burlington dyes, prints, embosses, and naps the fabric.	Home furnishings (bedspreads, draperies). Aprons, cover-ups, robes, nightgowns
Spun-bonded (Du Pont)	Sheets of filament fibers achieved by air entanglement. Sold under following tradenames	
(1) Reemay	Polyester fibers randomly arranged, dispersed and bonded.	Interlinings, carpet backing, furniture, bedding, shoe interlinings
(2) Typar	High-strength sheet produced by spinning and bonding continuous filaments of polypropylene.	Carpet backing, furniture and automobile construction
(3) Tyvek	Tough, durable sheet formed by spinning a very fine polyethylene fiber and bonding under great pressure.	Tags, labels, signs, banners, books, and wall coverings
Cerex (Monsanto)	Nylon spun-bonded	Underlay for carpets acting as sandwich between foam rubber and carpet. Quilting materials, filters, cargo flares, parachutes

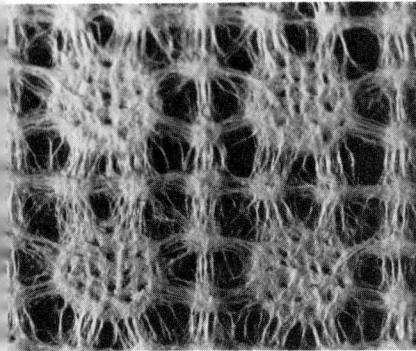

Figure 4-62a Nexus 100 percent polyester spun-laced in blue for nightgowns and peignoirs. (Courtesy: Burlington Formed Fabrics)

Table 4-4 Nonwoven Fabrics (Con'td.)

Tradename and Manufacturer	Method	Uses
Pellon (Pellon Corp.)	Over 300 variations. Random fiber distribution bonded by heat and chemical binders	Interlinings, interfacings, fusibles
West Point (Westpoint Pepperell)	Dry-laid	Needlepunched products for shoe interfacings and coating substrate
(1) Landtuck	Dry-laid	Interlinings, interfacings for apparel
(2) Lanapress	Dry-laid	Shirt interlinings, cuffs, etc.
(3) Interlon	Dry-laid	Over-the-counter sales

*Partial listing.

SPUN-LACED FABRICS

This is the latest and newest of nonwoven fabrics. It is singled out for discussion because it is predicted that it will have an impact on the fashion apparel and home sewing market. The fabric is manufactured by Du Pont under a patented spun-laced process. It entangles staple fibers in a predetermined repeat pattern to form soft, sophisticated fabrics without an adhesive binder. The fabrics are made by passing extremely fine high-pressure jets of liquid through various screening devices on to a special fabric web. The impact of the fluid jets entangles the end of the fibers throughout the web and controls the pattern. The continuing impact of the fine droplets of fluid entangles the fibers to such a level that the entire fabric is held together by fiber-to-fiber friction, as in a spun yarn instead of by a chemical or thermal bond in a spun-bonded fabric or conventional nonwoven. Burlington dyes, prints, and finishes the fabric and markets it under the tradename Nexus (see Figure 4-62).

NONWOVENS IN CONSUMER USE

Fabrics ranging from very lightweight to heavyweight are available in many colors. Nonwoven fabrics are claimed to have good stability, good shape retention, and are porous and flexible for

Figure 4-62b Nexus 100 percent polyester printed drapery. (Courtesy: Burlington Formed Fabrics)

comfort in wear. The fabrics do not ravel and can be cut in any direction. The fabrics are sold as dry-cleanable. Some are sold as washable.

Thin, lightweight, nonwoven fabrics have relatively low tensile strength. Undue strain may result in tears that cannot be mended. Some of these fabrics lose their stiffness in wear and dry cleaning or wet cleaning. They may also rough-up on the surface. Some of the fabrics stiffen and yellow with age. They absorb soil and dyestuffs readily from either a water or solvent cleaning system.

Some of the press-on fabrics become loose from the outer fabric in dry cleaning or wet cleaning. This is related to the surface of the fabric to which the nonwoven fabric is bonded instead of the method of cleaning. If a press-on, nonwoven fabric is loosened from the fabric to which it is bonded, it may be resealed in some cases — flat surfaces more readily than curved surfaces.

Some of the earlier fabrics stained the outer fabric placed next to it. In most cases the stains could be removed by a special dry-cleaning treatment, but this usually entails taking the lining out of the garment.

NEEDLEPUNCHED FABRICS

Needlepunched fabrics are made with a barbed needle pushed through a fleece of fibers. As some fibers are forced through the fleece, they remain displaced when the needle is withdrawn. If enough fibers are thus displaced, the fleece can be converted into a nonwoven fabric.

There are three main classes of needlepunched materials, along with the fibers used: (1) fleece without scrim, using polyester, nylon, and blends for thermal insulation, underfelts, filters, and waddings; (2) fleece with scrim, using wool, acrylics, nylon, polyester, rayon, and blends for blankets and outerwear; and (3) fleece with scrim impregnated with resin, using nylon and polypropylenes, for floor coverings.

One of the systems, Fiberwoven, is used to make blankets. The process is shown in Figure 4-63.

Needlepunched fabrics are used for jacket interlinings, insulation, upholstery backing, shoe parts, and substrates.

STITCH-THROUGH FABRICS

Functionally, the fabrics made on the Maliwatt and Arachne machines are the same. However, the Arachne machine is more versatile because of the stitching variety.

FIBERWOVEN PROCESS

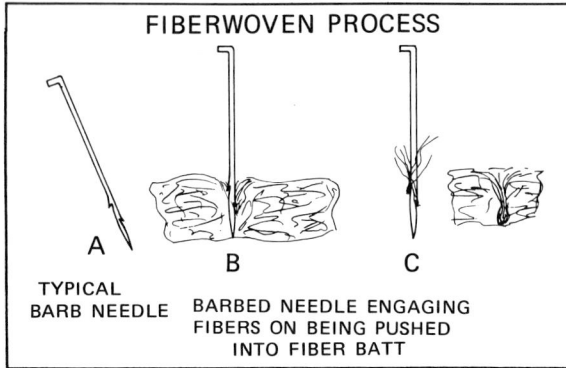

A
TYPICAL
BARB NEEDLE

B C
BARBED NEEDLE ENGAGING
FIBERS ON BEING PUSHED
INTO FIBER BATT

(a)

FIBERWOVEN PROCESS

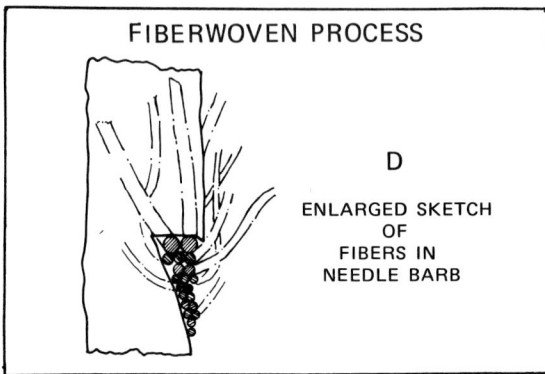

D
ENLARGED SKETCH
OF
FIBERS IN
NEEDLE BARB

(b)

FIBERWOVEN PROCESS

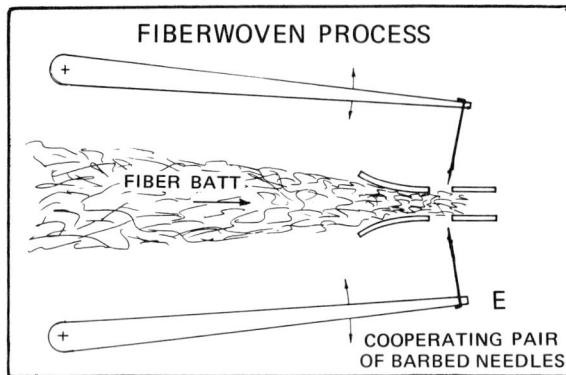

FIBER BATT

E
COOPERATING PAIR
OF BARBED NEEDLES

(c)

Figure 4-63 Steps in Fiberwoven process. *(a)* Pointed needle with two barbs is pushed through fiber batt, catches up number of fibers as in B and C. *(b)* Shows different-sized fibers hooked by barb of a needle. These are the interrelated factors that influence probability of fiber pickup: fiber orientation, fiber crimp, fiber-to fiber friction, previous needling, density and thickness of fiber batt, needle-barb size, barb shape, and barb location relative to point of needle. All affect fiber pickup, influence fiber entanglement. *(c)* Shows arrangement of pair of cooperating needles mounted on rocker arms. These move together. Needles penetrate batt alternately in synchronized movement of fiber batt to orient fibers into chains of entanglement.

(d) Motion of needle pair and synchronized sequence of Fiberwoven process shown here. Action is: (1) Top needle picks up and carries fiber downward and withdraws. (2) Fiber batt advances slightly. (3) Lower needle picks up fiber, passes it through fiber loops positioned by partner needle, withdraws. (4) Fiber batt again advances slightly. Procedure repeated, resulting in continuous chain of interlooped, entangled fibers resulting from action of the two needles. (e) Multiply above by more than 13,000 pairs of cooperating, closely spaced needles arranged in four needling stations and you have an idea of how Fiberwoven fabrics are made. (f) Fiberwoven process lends itself to making blankets of a layered structure. Fiber type, denier, and quality can differ in the layers. (Courtesy: Beacon Manufacturing Company)

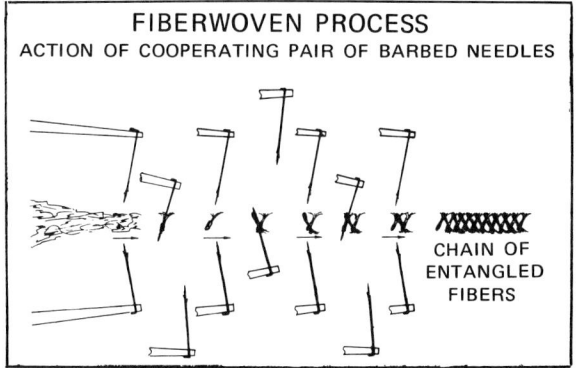

FIBERWOVEN PROCESS
ACTION OF COOPERATING PAIR OF BARBED NEEDLES

CHAIN OF ENTANGLED FIBERS

(d)

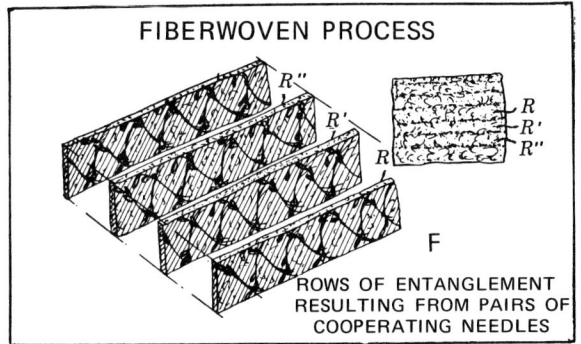

FIBERWOVEN PROCESS

ROWS OF ENTANGLEMENT RESULTING FROM PAIRS OF COOPERATING NEEDLES

(e)

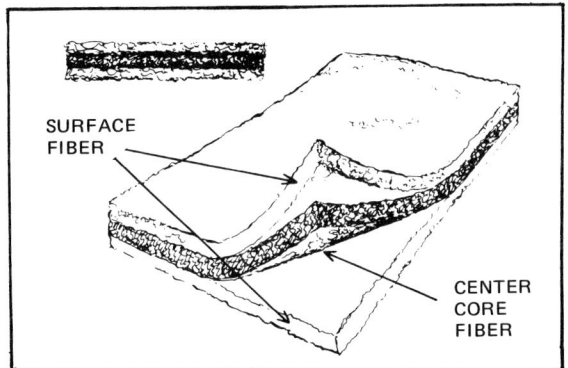

SURFACE FIBER

CENTER CORE FIBER

(f)

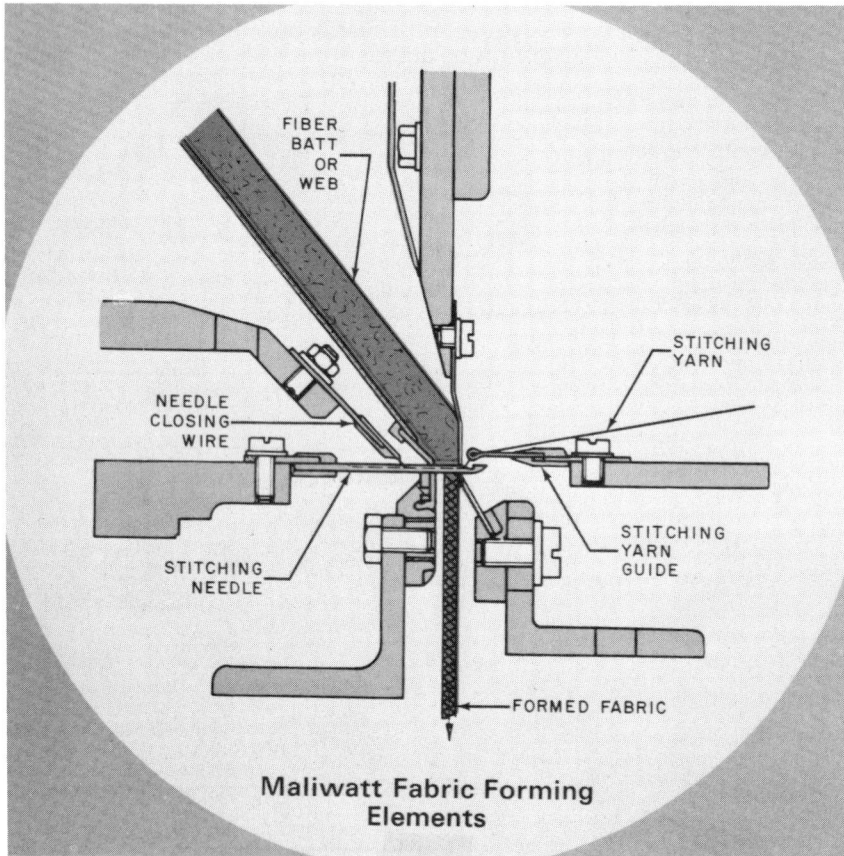

FIBER
BATT
OR
WEB

STITCHING
YARN

NEEDLE
CLOSING
WIRE

STITCHING
YARN
GUIDE

STITCHING
NEEDLE

FORMED FABRIC

Maliwatt Fabric Forming Elements

Figure 4-64 Maliwatt is a variation of the Malimo machine that substitutes a nonwoven batting web for the warp and filling yarns and stitches the batting together with an interlocking tricot stitch. (Courtesy: Crompton and Knowles)

Maliwatt and Arachne are referred to as "stitch-bonded" fabric. Fabrics from 6 ounces up are used for draperies, table linens, upholstery, linings, insulating, coated fabrics, blankets, rugs, and apparel.

Maliwatt and Arachne fabrics are said to have an extremely high tear strength and a relatively high bulk per unit weight; therefore they have good insulating ability and a hand between knitted and woven fabrics. They can be piece-dyed, printed, or resin-finished.

A description of the Maliwatt stitching element is shown in Figure 4-64. In making a Maliwatt fabric, a nonwoven batting web substitutes for the warp and filling yarns in a woven fabric, and it is stitched through with an interlocking tricot stitch.

PART IV
FABRIC FORMED FROM
NONFIBROUS MATERIALS

NONSUPPORTED PLASTIC FILM

Films are used today in wearing apparel and household uses. They are not considered a textile, even though they are made from the same chemicals as the man-made fibers. Instead of being extruded as filament, they are made into lightweight flexible films of different weights and uses.

Such films have found use as interlinings in jackets because the film serves as a good wind breaker. These films are waterproof and so are made into many types of rainwear garments and shower curtains.

These films resist soiling and can be cleaned readily by wet cleaning. They are *not* machine-washable. Nonsupported plastic films should *not* be dry-cleaned. Some of the films become yellow, brittle, and boardy with age. Some plastic films, if dried with heat, stiffen and shrink.

FLOCKED URETHANE FOAM THAT LOOKS LIKE SUEDE

A new nonwoven fabric, imported from Japan, has been created to look and feel like genuine suede. Ultrasuede™ is not genuine suede, although when you see and feel the downy, soft napped, nonwoven fabric it is hard to believe — it looks and feels like suede. Ultrasuede™ fabric, distributed exclusively by Skinner®, a division of Spring Mills, is a nonwoven fabric made of 60 percent polyester and 40 percent nonfibrous polyurethane. Skinner says it took 7 years and $14 million to develop.

According to Skinner, Ultrasuede is colorfast (not possible with real skins); will not crock, nick, pill, fray, or wrinkle; will not water-spot or stiffen — remains soft and supple all the time; will retain its shape — no stretching or bagging; can be dry-cleaned by regular cleaning methods, not costly suede techniques; and can be ironed with a steam iron on synthetic setting. It is machine-washable and tumble-dryable.

ULTRASUEDE IN CONSUMER USE

There are several considerations to be aware of in the wear and care of garments made from Ultrasuede.

Ultrasuede has a definite nap direction like many other pile fabrics. In home sewing and in ready-to-wear clothing, it is important that every section of the garment is cut with this factor in mind. Otherwise, different sections of the finished garment may appear to be different shades because of differing lay of the nap.

The nap may also be important in spot and stain removal. An expensive, full-length Ultrasuede coat with a few spots on it was sent to a professional cleaner and the garment cleaned up perfectly. The second time the garment was taken to the cleaner it was stained quite badly with grease spots. These were not surface stains as the others had been, and they were not removed by dry-cleaning. Soaking the stains did not touch them, so the cleaner used a solution of one third dry-cleaning detergent and two thirds solvent and tamped the stains very lightly with a brush. This disturbed the surface — raised the nap some — so those sections spotted on the coat were different in appearance from the rest of the coat. The color difference in spot removal is due to a difference in light reflection because of changing the direction of lay of the fibers on the fabric surface. The difficulty in removing deeply embedded grease stains may be attributed to the nonwoven polyurethane structure of the fabric. It is quite different from removing a grease stain from a knitted or woven structure.

Another consumer got her coat caught in the door of a car, resulting in a tear. Ultrasuede cannot be mended like a woven or knitted fabric. It must be mended by application of mending tape to the underside of the garment. Care must be taken to bring the torn edges together before applying heat to the mending tape. Remember, since Ultrasuede is made from polyester and non-fibrous polyurethane, it can be damaged by high heat.

Ultrasuede is susceptible to mechanical damage by careless use of pins and machine stitching. Pin holes and needle marks will show forever, as they do in real leather. This is a very important consideration in altering a garment made of Ultrasuede.

PART V
MINOR FABRIC CONSTRUCTIONS

BRAIDED FABRICS

Narrow braids are used for trim. They also can be joined together to make rugs.

Three or more yarns are doubled back and interwoven, one yarn over another, to form a fabric. They are characterized by a diagonal surface effect. An early example of braiding is the handmade braided rug. Today, complex braids are made and used as trim or fashioned into unusual garments. Circular braids are used to make shoelaces and insulation for wires. Horsehair and saran braids are used for shaping items.

BRAIDS IN CONSUMER USE

Many braided fabrics have stretch in length and some have stretch in width. Sometimes this causes a problem in applying braid as a decorative trim.

Braided rugs, because they are made up of narrow bands of braid, should be dry-cleaned. They lack strength to withstand the mechanical action of washing.

Horsehair was originally used in making upholstery and lining fabrics. Today, horsehair nets and braids may be made of man-made fibers such as nylon or saran.

Horsehair nets and braids offer a selection of open weave fabrics that are very stiff. These fabrics are very important in creating the bouffant look. Combined with braids and laces, horsehair braid can be made into unusual garment designs. These fabrics are dry-cleanable and require special care.

The yarns are very stiff and therefore uncomfortable to wear unless lined with a woven fabric. Because the yarns are so stiff, they break readily with bending and flexing in wear and cleaning. The yarns are so fine, stiff, and wiry that they have a tendency to shift with strain, pull, and fray at the seams.

LACES AND NETS

Laces developed into a fine art in Italy between 1300 and 1500. The bobbinet machine was invented as early as 1808. Lace was first made by machine in 1831. There are many books on lace making. We will not discuss the methods by which lace is made, but mention that there are many different kinds of machine-made laces that are used for all-over garment designs, insertions, flouncing, and beadings. Their distinctive feature is that their construction (of knotted, twisted, or looped yarns) varies from simple to complicated and fine to coarse constructions. Several of the most common types of machine-made laces sold today are:

Leaver method. Alençon, Chantilly, Cluny, Filet, Maline, Milan, tulle, Valenciennes.
Bobbinet method. Commerical nets, Filet, Maline, net appliqué, point d'esprit, tulle.
Nottingham method. Filet, net, Nottingham lace.
Schiffli method. Breton, Cluny, Point de Venise, Richelieu.

And, of course, there are many types of handmade laces.
Some of the terms used to describe definite parts of lace are:

A'jour. The open-work design that forms the pattern.
Cordonnet. The heavy thread or yarn that outlines the design.
Ground. The inside part of the design.
Mesh. The net part made by a needle or bobbin.
Picot. The little loops on the surface of the design or along the edge of the lace.
Réseau. The background as distinguished from the prominent design.

NETS

A net fabric may be fine and sheer or coarse and open. There are three basic types of constructions resulting in fabrics with square, hexagonal, and octagonal meshes: rachel, tricot, and bobbinet. Nets may be made of nylon, cotton, polyester, silk, rayon, acetate, and other man-made fibers. A number of different finishes may be applied, depending on use. The softer nettings are made of heat-setting fibers. Others may be finished with starches or plastic-type resin finishes. Manufacturers may have special tradenames to describe their nettings. Those that are used most widely may be classed as follows.

Bobbinet

Depending on the size of the yarn, bobbinet may be very thin and transparent like bridal illusion bobbinet or heavier and transparent like cotton bobbinet. These are made primarily in England and France.

Fish Net

This is a coarse open mesh fabric made by knotting meshes similar to a fisherman's knot.

Maline

A very, very fine open diamond-shaped mesh net.

Tulle

A fine, small, hexagonal mesh net fabric lighter in weight than bobbinet, made by the tricot method.

LACE AND NETS IN CONSUMER USE

LACE

Lace lends itself to many beautiful formal garment designs. It also has many applications in household items. Lace can be given special finishes to create interesting effects. For example, Repausse lace is heavily starched, then embossed by ironing to raise the pattern. Ciré lace is given a shellac finish.

Lace requires special care in use and in cleaning.

Lace fabrics that are sized with water-soluble or solvent-soluble sizings may become limp in use and cleaning. In many cases it is possible to resize lace after dry-cleaning. Lace is very susceptible to snagging or breaking in use because of the many loose yarns, floats, and loops that can get caught. Once lace is torn, it cannot be mended satisfactorily because the mend shows.

NETS

There is a wide selection of net fabrics that are suitable for formal wear. They create an airy, bouffant illusion that is not achieved by any other method of fabric construction. Net fabrics require special care in wear; they are delicate because of their construction. Net fabrics are dry-cleanable and require special care.

Net fabrics that are sized with a water-soluble sizing become limp in wear and cleaning. Once the sizing is lost, the meshes may distort, resulting in sagging of a garment. The majority of nets can be resized after cleaning. Net fabrics, once torn, cannot be mended satisfactorily; the mend shows.

LEARNING EXPERIENCES

1. Analyze and report why the knitting industry is divided into so many branches and subbranches. Explain the difference between a direct knitter and a contract knitter.
2. Illustrate and explain the terminology used to describe the lengthwise and crosswise direction of a knit fabric.
3. Mount a single knit and doubleknit fabric swatch. Explain the difference.
4. Find, mount, and label fabric swatches that illustrate the four basic stitches: plain, purl, welt, and tuck.
5. Make a fabric swatch chart illustrating the classification of weft knit fabrics and some of its variations.
6. Make a fabric swatch chart illustrating the classification of warp knit fabrics and some of its variations.
7. Explain why some knit fabrics should be folded and placed in a drawer or on a shelf and others may be placed on hangers. Demonstrate how knit garments should be folded or hung on a hanger.
8. Assemble knit garments that have given dissatisfaction in use or care. Analyze the problem. Discuss what caused it. How might the problem be remedied?
9. List the advantages and disadvantages of knit fabrics. Explain why some shrink while others stretch. Why do some knits provide warmth and comfort to the wearer while others give little protection?
10. Why has the Malimo apparel construction been successful in Europe and unsuccessful in the United States?
11. Demonstrate how you may identify a Malimo construction and a Malipole construction.
12. Locate, mount, and label fabric swatches that illustrate the three basic weaves and their variations.
13. Illustrate the difference between a dobby figure weave and a jacquard figure weave. Explain the difference in aesthetics and cost.
14. Assemble samples of pile fabrics: velvet, velveteen, velour, and corduroy. Explain the differences in construction. How is construction related to consumer performance?
15. The leno weave may be used alone or in combination with other weaves. Find, mount, and label a true leno weave construction; an adaptation of a leno weave; and a leno weave combined with another basic weave construction. Analyze and describe the advantages of each.
16. Illustrate with fabric samples the differences between a true doublecloth; an adaptation of a doublecloth; a reversible fabric and a double-faced fabric.

17. Make a list of the advantages and disadvantages of the following constructions: fiber to foam; fiber to fabric; and yarn to fabric. Give examples.
18. Assemble, mount, and label representative nonwoven constructions. What is the future of nonwoven structures?

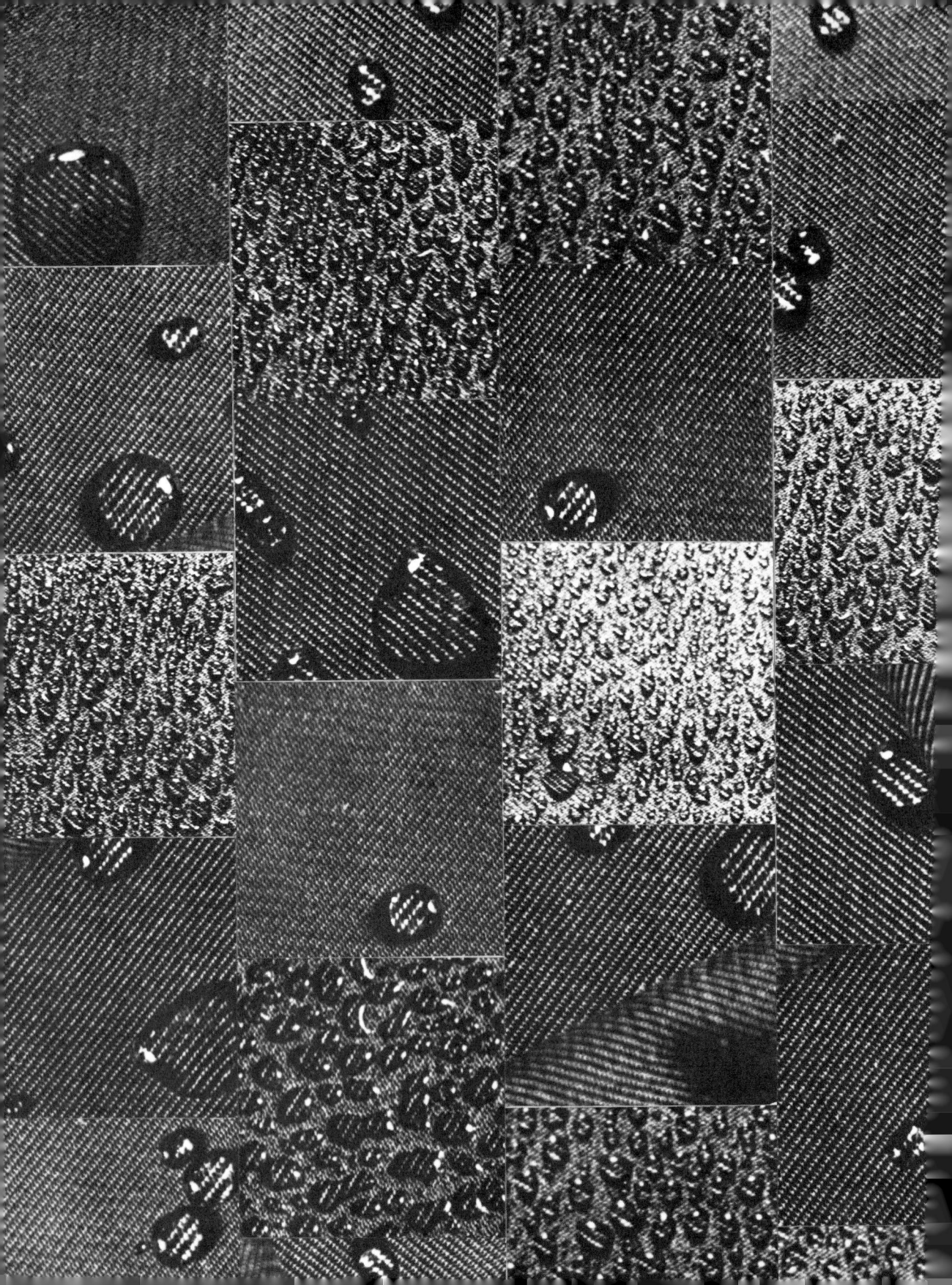

5
FABRIC FINISHES

IMPORTANCE FOR THE CONSUMER

Special or functional finishes are directly related to the end-use requirements of a particular textile item. The purpose is to enable the fabric to perform a certain function more effectively by adding to the aesthetic, comfort, ease of care, or even economic attributes of textiles. The consumer who clearly visualizes the end-use requirements for a fabric and is familiar with the special finishes available will be in a good position to match end use and finish. For example, the consumer who is purchasing a wool blanket that will be stored for several months of the year should consider a moth-resistant finish, while the consumer selecting towels for a warm, humid climate should consider a mildew-resistant finish.

In the evaluation of a special finish, the following questions might be considered.

1. Will the finish provide the required property? For example, will a spot- and stain-resistant finish resist both water and oil stains if it is likely to be subjected to both?
2. Will the finish require special care in laundering, wet cleaning, or dry cleaning? For example, will the resin finish discolor if the fabric is bleached with a chlorine-type bleach?
3. Is the finish durable or permanent, semidurable or temporary? Finishes are classified as durable when they will successfully withstand normal wear and care for the expected life of the product.
4. Is the finish water-soluble or solvent-soluble? A water-soluble finish will not be durable to normal laundering procedures. A solvent-soluble finish will not be durable to dry-cleaning procedures.
5. Is the finish guaranteed to be durable to laundering, wet cleaning, or dry cleaning? Or, is it semidurable, requiring the fabric to be retreated after laundering, wet cleaning or dry cleaning?

243

Many of the special finishes applied by the textile finisher do not have names that are used in promotion to the consumer, and labels or hangtags may not indicate which finishes have been applied to the fabric. Some special finishes do have trademark names that appear on labels or hangtags and are used in advertising to the consumer.

CLASSIFICATION OF FINISHES

Authorities differ as to the definition of "finishing." Some include the cleaning operation to rid fabric of soil, oil, and additives before dyeing, printing or finishing. They include wet processing (boil off), dry cleaning (solvent scour), carbonizing, singeing, bleaching and, in some cases, the application of optical brighteners.

We will consider finishes to include all the processes after fabric construction until it is ready for use. Finishes contribute so much to the final character and appearance of the fabric that it is often said, "It's the finish that makes the fabric." Some authorities classify finishes into two groups: (1) special or functional finishes that give an added quality to a fabric; and (2) general or routine finishes. This presentation on finishes is unorthodox in that we have grouped those finishes that give fabrics a distinctive surface effect or design in Chapter 6. In this chapter we will group and discuss special or functional finishes that give aesthetic properties; those that add durability; finishes that provide added comfort, safety, and improved care performance; and finishes that provide environmental and biological resistance. The general or routine finishes are discussed alphabetically.

FINISHES THAT PROVIDE AESTHETIC VALUES

CALENDER FINISH

This is the simplest of all finishes used to give a good appearance to the finished fabric. It consists of passing the fabric between the heated cylinders of a calendering machine. It is simply ironing a fabric to make it smooth and give it a lustrous surface. The round yarns are flattened, hence reflect more light. It is a temporary finish, since the yarns revert to their round shape with steaming, laundering, and dry cleaning. Examples of calendered fabrics are sheeting, poplin, and broadcloth, both cotton and wool.

SPECIAL CALENDERING (BEETLING)

This is a process in which linen or cotton cloth, wrapped on a wooden core, is pounded to give a flat effect. Instead of wood, an iron core may be used to produce a moire effect. The result is a soft, full, thready finish that gives cotton goods the appearance of linen.

Beetling gives a beautiful luster to the fabric. The flattened yarns reflect light. This is a temporary finish and can be lost in laundering. Pressing with a hot rotary iron can improve the appearance after laundering.

GLAZED FINISH

This finish is achieved by passing a fabric through a friction calendering machine. It produces a high glaze or polished effect on the face side of the fabric. One highly polished steel cylinder rotates at a much higher speed than the fabric passing between the steel cylinder and the lower roller.

Before the fabric goes through the calender, it is treated with starches, waxes, or resins that fill the spaces between the yarns and contribute to the degree of glaze produced on the fabric surface. Starches and waxes give a temporary finish; resins give a durable one to laundering and dry cleaning. Examples are glazed chintz and polished cottons.

LUSTER — DELUSTER

As discussed previously, the degree of luster can be controlled by the amount of pigmentation entered into the spinning solution before extrusion of the filament. But luster and delustering can also be achieved in finishing.

The natural sheen of synthetic yarns may be reduced or eliminated during finishing by using various chemicals. Lustering is a mechanical finishing process making luster on yarns or cloth by heat and pressure, with or without chemical aids.

SIZING

This is a general term for compounds that, when added to yarn or fabric, form a more or less continuous solid film around the yarn and individual fibers. Sizing may be applied to increase strength, smoothness, stiffness, or weight.

Some textile finishes used to impart certain characteristic finishes to fabrics, such as gelatin, starches, gums, and glues, are removed by any contact with water in spotting, dry cleaning, wet cleaning, or laundering. Many of these finishes can be replaced by the dry cleaner (see Figure 5-1).

Chemical finishes are applied to cotton, rayon, and nylon sheers to make them stay crisp during wear, laundering, wet cleaning, and dry cleaning. Such finishes will also help to keep corners of sheer fabrics from rolling.

FINISHES TO SOFTEN FABRICS

A good hand or feel is an important aesthetic property of knitted and woven fabrics. To achieve this property, manufacturers may use reagents called softeners. Materials may be used in warm sizing or fabric finishing to impart a soft, mellow hand to the fabric. This is achieved by the use of sulfonated oils, glycerine, waxes, and silicones. Some softeners may be removed in dry cleaning and wet cleaning. When this occurs, the fabric may have a harsh hand or feel.

Some of the softeners used are quite durable. There are durable types of cationic softeners that remain in the fabric after laundering or dry cleaning.

NAPPING

This is a mechanical finish used on fabrics made of staple fibers where a lustrous nap is desired. The fabric is fed into a machine where a "teaseled" covered cylinder raises the fiber ends to the surface of the fabric, thus producing a soft nap. The nap may be

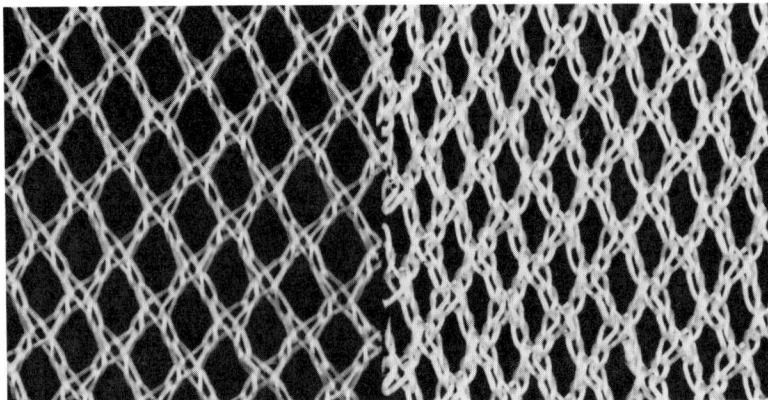

Figure 5-1 Removal of water-soluble sizing may result in distortion of a net fabric. (Left) Original fabric. (Right) Net fabric after immersion in water.

full and upright or it may be pressed flat to give a lustrous surface. Napped fabrics have a soft hand. In some cases, they provide insulation because the fibers can entrap dead air. They are subject to pilling and abrasion in wear, particularly at the edge of collars, cuffs, elbows, and the seat of a garment. Some napped fabrics give good performance in use; others must be considered as luxury fabrics with limited serviceability. Flattening in wear may sometimes be restored with brushing (see Figure 5-2).

FINISHES THAT ADD TO DURABILITY
ABRASION-RESISTANT FINISH

Abrasion resistance is defined as the ability of a fiber to withstand rubbing in use and care. Fibers possess different degrees of resistance to abrasion. Manufacturers can combine or blend fibers with low and high abrasion resistance for the performance they wish to achieve in the end product. The manufacturer can also achieve abrasion resistance by the application of thermoplastic resins to either the yarn or the finished fabric. The resin binds the fibers together, thus imparting abrasion resistance to the fabric in use. This property is desirable in trouser, slack, and lining fabrics.

ANTISLIP FINISH

This finish is applied to a fabric to keep the yarns in place so that they will not slip over one another. This finish has received wide

Figure 5-2 A soft appearance is given to this knit by napping the surface of the fabric.

application in fabrics made of the synthetic fibers. This finish also serves to keep seams from fraying.

The textile manufacturer has many products available to impart this finish; of these, the resin finishes give the best performance in consumer use. Unfortunately, tradenames are seldom merchandized to the consumer.

ANTISNAG FINISH

With greater use of knits, consumers became increasingly aware of the snagging of doubleknits. Du Pont has developed a multiaction chemical finish (ZePel) they claim not only reduces picks, pulls, and snags, but also provides three additional features: antistatic properties, water repellency, and oily stain resistance with repeated washings and dry cleanings.

FINISHES THAT PROVIDE ADDED COMFORT

ABSORBENT FINISH

Absorbent finishes are sometimes applied to fabrics designed for toweling, diapers, underwear, sportswear, and other items where moisture absorbency is an important factor. Recently, development efforts have been concentrated in the area of woven and knitted polyester fabrics used in clothing. For example, a manufacturer wishing to give a 100 percent polyester fabric properties close to those of cotton uses a process that actually changes the molecular structure of the fiber's surface. The finish will also work on polyester and cotton blends but not with fabrics treated with certain durable press or resin finished, water-repellent fabrics. The process makes 100 percent polyester fabrics cooler to wear, easier to wash, and more like cotton than normal. The finish breaks up the moisture into small particles that disperse into the fabric and evaporate readily, since the fabric dries quickly.

ANTISTATIC FINISH

The winter months generally bring a rash of static and lint problems, and static and lint are related. Static charges in a fabric attract and hold lint and even soil. To overcome this problem, manufacturers have sought and applied chemical finishes to reduce or eliminate this problem.

Static is an electric charge consisting of a large accumulation of excess electrons remaining in one place because the fabric is dry.

This gives the material a negative charge. Some materials become positively charged. When one material gets an excessive number of electrons, it has to take them away from another material. The material that has lost electrons is positively charged. Whenever two different materials are brought into close contact, electrons will flow from one material to the other. If the materials are suddenly separated, one of them will be negatively charged because of the extra electrons it has captured, while the other is positively charged. So long as they are kept apart and insulated, the charge will persist.

Under normal conditions, these charges are too tiny to be detected because of the small area of contact. Detectable charges are encountered only when the area of contact is very large and the number of contacts and separations is multiplied many times. A very common example of this is walking down a long hotel corridor on a carpeted floor in dry weather; an individual can become so charged that he draws a spark when he touches the elevator button. The large number of contacts of shoes with the dry fibers in the pile of the rug and the subsequent separation produces the charge. The dry atmosphere prevents the charge from "leaking off" and provides insulation until the finger approaches the elevator button. The charge then leaps to this conductor in a spark discharge.

Because static electricity is a real problem for the consumer, manufacturers have developed antistatic finishes. One or more basic concepts are taken into consideration in the application of these finishes: (1) conductivity, whereby the charged electrons move to the air or are grounded; (2) absorption of water by the finish provides a conductive surface on the fabric that carries away the static charge; and (3) the principle of neutralizing negative and positive charges. The most effective finish combines all three concepts.

Labels do not give consumer information on these finishes. Most of them are cationic surface active agents based on quaternary ammonium compounds; some are nonionic. They are not durable to laundering and need to be replaced. Permanent antistatic effects are obtainable by modification of the man-made fibers.

WATER-REPELLENT FINISHES

These finishes resist the penetration of water into or through the fabric and permit the passage of air. The fabric breathes and is comfortable to wear. The concept is that the yarns, not the fabrics, are coated with the chemical finish; therefore air can pass between the yarns of the fabric. The water remains on the surface of the fabric instead of being absorbed. Sometimes the water-repellent finish is used to make the fabric suitable for rainwear; sometimes it is used to make it resistant to spots.

These water-repellent finishes, applied in finishing, are divided into two classes: durable finishes and nondurable finishes. Dry cleaning, wet cleaning, or laundering removes the nondurable type, but the durable finishes are not removed by either dry cleaning or laundering. This does not mean that all fabrics containing a durable water-repellent finish remain satisfactorily water-repellent after washing or dry-cleaning. Although the finish is not removed, the detergents used have a wetting-out action that masks the effect of the finish. The effectiveness of water repellents depends as much on the fabric construction as on the finish itself. A finish applied to a tightly constructed fabric is more effective than the identical finish applied to a loosely constructed fabric.

Unfortunately, all garments containing a durable, water-repellent finish are not labeled as such (e.g., names of durable finishes such as Zelan, Norane, Permel, Ranedare, Hydropruf, and many others). Most of the so-called durable, water-repellent finishes lose their water repellency when dry-cleaned. This is something the dry cleaner cannot avoid in practical plant operations. One of the main virtues of the durable finish is that after dry cleaning, their water repellency is retained when retreated, while other fabrics usually do not.

WATERPROOF FINISH

This finish is made by applying rubber, lacquer, linseed oil, or a synthetic resin to a fabric. These materials close the pores of the fabric and do not permit it to breathe and, therefore, are incompatible to wear. Some of these materials stiffen in dry cleaning. Fabrics so treated should be wet-cleaned or laundered.

MICROPOROUS WATERPROOF FINISH

A microporous film is applied to the back of the fabric. Although the film appears to be solid, it has millions of tiny cells called "micropores." These cells are too small to permit wind and rain to penetrate, but they do allow passage of moisture vapor. This finish is used for rainwear and outerwear fabrics.

FINISHES THAT PROVIDE SAFETY

FLAME-RETARDANT FINISHES

Flame-retardant finishes are selected and applied to fabrics to reduce flaming, charring, and afterglow of fabrics. This is done by: (1) releasing of gases or foams that reduce flaming; (2) formation of acids at flaming temperatures that accelerate the dehydration of cellulose to carbon and water, thus inhibiting flaming; and (3) releasing substances that hasten the degradation of cellulose with the release of volatile products that reduce flaming. From the standpoint of durability, flame-retardant finishes range from temporary or nondurable to semidurable to durable finishes (see Table 5-1).

Table 5-1   Flame-Retardant Treatments and Processes

Nondurable	Ammonium acid phosphates, borax/boric acid, inorganic sulfamates, bromides, and tungstates. Organic: urea derivatives, amine phosphate, alkylamine bromides
Semidurable	Antimony oxide plus PVC or chlorinated paraffins; tungstate-tin chloride codeposits
Durable	Tetrakis (hydroxymethyl) phosphonium chloride (THPC) and hydroxide (THPOH) plus amines, ammonia; nitrogen-containing phosphonate, chloroalkyl-phosphinic acids; titanium and antimony oxychlorides; metal oxides and their hydrates; proprietary processes

The greatest amount of research on flame-retardant finishes to date has been directed to cotton and rayon fabrics. Since 1970, research has been directed toward man-made fibers and blends of natural fibers with man-made fibers.

The nondurable finishes are generally achieved by the application of certain inorganic salts or simple organic compounds. These are water-soluble materials that are completely removed by laundering or dry cleaning.

Semidurable finishes are achieved with mixtures of phosphate salts and such chemicals as urea or guanidine. These finishes require a cure at an elevated temperature; if the cure is carried out under optimum conditions of time, temperature, and pH, a fairly durable finish is achieved on cotton.

The term "durable" flame-retardant finish is reserved for those achieved with an organic phosphonium salt or base combined with an amine resin former. These materials react chemically with cotton to form a complex phosphorous-nitrogen resin that is resistant to washing and dry cleaning.

What About Synthetic Fibers?

Everything covered so far refers to cotton fabrics only, and to some degree to rayon. The amount of research on flame-retardant finishes for nylon, polyester, and acrylic fibers and blends with natural fibers is quite limited when compared with cotton. Formulations designed for the treatment of cotton fabrics may be quite ineffective on these thermoplastic fibers. Even the test methods used for cotton fabrics may not be valid for thermoplastic fibers. However, topical finishes are being applied to nylon and nylon blends as well as to polyester and polyester blends.

A nitrogenous resin has been introduced as a flame retardant for use on nylon fabrics in woven, nonwoven, and molded constructions. The retardant is claimed to be compatible with fluoro-chemical, antistatic, and fluorinated soil release finishes. It is also said to have permanency to dry cleaning and washing.

A flame-retardant finish for 100 percent polyester yarns and fabric can be applied during the dyeing operation. It is applied in conventional machines used for fiber, package, and jet dyeing. The emulsion is based on the use of an organic bromine. The success of the system depends on application techniques.

General purpose finishes that use propylene glycol resin burn readily. However, resin systems containing triethyl phosphate (TEP) result in increased flame retardancy on synthetic fibers. Furthermore, a 50 percent addition of alumina trihydrate greatly increases flame retardant properties. The best overall polyester system consists of a formula of resin, alumina trihydrate, and triethyl phosphate. Consumer performance research is not available on these new finishes.

Manufacturers have also found that in addition to the finish, flame retardancy can be affected by fabric weight, construction, and surface texturing. Tightly woven or knitted heavy fabrics burn more slowly than sheer, lightweight, loosely constructed fabrics. Napped fabrics with air spaces between loose, fine fibers will ignite more readily than smooth-surface materials. Fabrics with short pile and great density burn less readily than those with high puffy pile and, finally, tailored, fitted garments are less flammable than those with loose, flowing sleeves, ruffles, and lace trim.

The Consumer's Dilemma

The Flammable Fabric Act (See Chapter 9) has brought the following problems to the consumer.

1. *Cost.* Prices on the new garments will average $1 more per garment and as much as $3 more on robes.
2. *Care.* Unless elaborate special instructions are followed when laundering the garments, their flame-retardant properties can vanish in the wash.
3. *Style.* The new fabrics require styling modifications that may make the garments less attractive.
4. *Comfort.* Much of the new flame-retardant fabric is far less pleasant to the touch than untreated material. Allergic reaction to some fabrics has been noted.
5. *Wearability.* In some fabrics, the strength is decreased with the addition of the chemical treatment.

Consumers who purchase the new flame-retardant garments find complicated washing instructions on the labels. Unless those instructions are followed, the flame-retardant properties of the clothes may disappear.

The basic rules manufacturers are giving consumers to follow in laundering flame-retardant cotton fabrics are:

1. Use a phosphate-based detergent (if allowed in your area).
2. Do not use bleach.
3. Do not use soap or soap powder.
4. Do not use hot water.
5. Read and follow the washing and drying directions given by the manufacturer on the "care" label of each garment (certain flame-retardant fabrics require specialized attention).

The following suggestions are for consumers in areas where phosphates are banned.

1. Use soft water, if possible.
2. Use a heavy-duty liquid laundry detergent — following directions on the container.

Certainly there is need for research on care methods in relationship to flame retardancy whether it be home washing, commercial laundering, or dry cleaning. For example, statements have been made that flame-retardant nightwear should not be washed in soap or sent to a commercial laundry because all commercial laundries in the United States use acid sours and they destroy flame-retardant properties of a fabric. Lee Johnston of the International Fabricare Institute (IFI) points out it is the combination of soap and hard water that causes trouble, not the soap alone, and most laundries use high-quality water softeners. He further points out that all laundries do not sour every time; therefore a label saying "do not sour" would be sufficient. He feels labels saying "do not send to a commercial laundry" are unnecessary and discriminatory.

There appears to be a difference of opinion on the use of a sour or acid rinse. A USDA report to consumers states that there is a simple way to protect flame-retardant finishes. They recommend that cottons be rinsed in a mildly acidic solution during laundering by adding about 1 cup of white vinegar to the rinse cycle of home washing machines.

FINISHES THAT IMPROVE CARE PERFORMANCE

CREASE-RESISTANT FINISH

Crease-resistant finishes are used on cotton, rayon, and linen because these fibers wrinkle easily. They are resin finishes that involve saturating the fabric with resin and then curing the resin at temperatures of about 360°F. The fabric usually becomes stiffer, less absorbent, and more resistant to wrinkling. Sometimes the strength and abrasion resistance is lowered in the cellulose fibers. Some of the finishes are semidurable or durable, depending on the percentage of resin take-up of the fabric.

WRINKLE-RESISTANT FINISH

This finish is applied to a fabric to make it resistant to wrinkling and to help it recover rapidly from wrinkling after wear. The effectiveness of the finish depends on the fiber content of the fabric, the construction of the fabric, and the particular chemical formulation applied to it. Some of these finishes are combined with water-repellent finishes and seem to have the power to resist waterborne stains and soil. They iron or finish more easily. This property may work to a disadvantage. A garment may fail to take a press, making the seams, collars, cuffs, and hemline look wrinkled instead of pressed. Some of these finishes have been known to cause loss of strength to some fabric constructions.

DURABLE PRESS/WASH/WEAR FINISHES

Durable press (sometimes called permanent press) is a concept based on the use of finishes and processes that give wearing apparel and household textiles properties that resist wrinkles and retain creases and pleats through many wearing and cleaning treatments. Two basic systems are used to achieve durable press: (1) heat setting of thermoplastic fibers, and (2) resin treatments. Both systems impart a memory in the fabrics. They return to the original shape when they are heat-set or cured.

As far back as 1949, manufacturers permanently pleated nylon. Methods for permanently creasing wool were worked out by chemical treatments. Attempts to produce similar effects with cotton using resins lead just to "easy care" and "minimum care," but some ironing was still needed. Heavier resin treatment caused cotton to suffer a strength loss; 100 percent cottons treated to be permanently pressed have to be of such heavy construction for satisfactory durability that they are too heavy for many uses. It was found that cotton blended with synthetic fibers permit lightweight fabrics that give satisfactory durability and durable press characteristics.

There are several methods of producing permanent press garments.

1. Postcured permanent press, also called deferred cure permanent press. The fabric is first impregnated with a resin and dried at low temperature so that little or no curing occurs in a finishing plant. The fabric is then shipped to an apparel manufacturer who cuts, sews, and presses the garments to remove wrinkles and press in creases and pleats. The garment is cured in an oven at about 325°F for 5 to 15 minutes, depending on the fabric and garment. The curing sets the garment in the shape it was in when it entered the oven.
2. Precured permanent press. The fabric, which consists of a blend of a thermoplastic fiber and a cellulosic fiber, is impregnated with resin and cured at the finishing plant. The fabric is then sold to a manufacturer who cuts, sews, and presses finished articles. The pressing is done with a special hot head press that has enough heat to set the thermoplastic portion of the blend.
3. Recured permanent press. This method starts in the same way that precure permanent press does. The thermoplastic cellulose blend is impregnated with resin and cured. Simultaneously, it is impregnated with a chemical that will later cause the breaking of the cured resin molecules in the presence of steam. The fabric becomes temporarily uncured. Further heating causes recurring of the resin and setting of the thermoplastic fiber, providing permanent press characteristics.

4. No-cure permanent press. This method depends entirely on thermoplastic fibers. No resins are used and no curing of fabric is involved. The permanent press characteristics are obtained in final garment pressing with a special hot head press. This process requires that the fabric contain at least 90 percent thermoplastic fiber.

Consumer Problems with Durable-Press Finishes

There are a few problems with permanent creased fabrics that have not been solved yet.

1. *Alterations.*   When alterations are being made, there is no known method to remove a durable-press crease from cotton or from a fabric containing cotton. A dry cleaner can remove an unwanted crease from durable-press wool, but only by special treatment.
2. *Shrinkage.*   Some garments are oversized to accommodate shrinkage in curing. If further shrinkage occurs in laundering, dry cleaning, or finishing, consumers may complain of improper fit, which cannot be corrected.
3. *Color change by abrasion.*   Dark-colored fabrics may appear grayed or lighter in shade after repeated dry cleanings or washings. This may be noted along crease, pleat, and hem lines.
4. *Permanent set wrinkles.*   If wrinkles are pressed into a garment and cured, they cannot be removed.
5. *Garment construction and design.*   When permanent creases or pleats are put into sections of a garment, this causes a problem in the shaping, sewing, and pressing the final garment. As with any garment, it is necessary to use compatible components that will stand up under high temperatures, wear, dry cleaning, wet cleaning, and washing (i.e., zippers, waistbands, sewing thread, elastic, and shoulder pads).
6. *Odor.*   Some improperly applied finishes can cause an odor problem in the fabric.
7. *Skin irritation.**   Some consumers have reported skin irritation from durable-press garments after wear and dry-cleaning. They think residual solvent, detergent, or other cleaning material may be the cause, but research has determined the cause of irritation in these cases to be formaldehyde-type resin compounds present in the garments. The remedy is to launder the garment to remove residual chemicals in the

*Journal of the American Medical Association, Vol. 194, p. 593, November 8, 1965.

fabric. Persons who have sensitive skin should wash durable-press garments before wearing them.

SHRINK-RESISTANT FINISHES

Dimensional stability of any textile material depends on fabric geometry, fiber surface characteristics, and friction between fibers and yarns, as well as physical and chemical properties of the fiber and its morphological structure. Shrink-resistant finishes are designed to restrain dimensional change in spite of other changes that occur during wear, laundering, or dry cleaning.

In view of the previous discussion of "felting shrinkage" in wool fabrics and "heat shrinkage" of fabrics made of heat sensitive fibers, the following pertains to relaxation, residual and progressive shrinkage, and swelling shrinkage.

Relaxation Shrinkage

Yarns woven or knitted to make a fabric are stretched and sized during the weaving or knitting operations. Further shrinkage may occur during finishing, but the fabric is stretched during tentering to regain any length and width lost. Then, when the fabric is dry-cleaned, wet-cleaned, or laundered, the fabric relaxes to its original, normal position. Some manufacturers take this relaxation shrinkage out of fabrics. It is good practice to look for the label that indicates minimum shrinkage. Fabrics not pre-shrunk or stabilized against shrinkage may shrink during dry cleaning, wet cleaning, or laundering, and laundering usually causes more shrinkage than dry cleaning. Knit garments, particularly, may show relaxation shrinkage, but they stretch back to size when put on and worn.

PROGRESSIVE SHRINKAGE

Some garments cleaned once or twice remain in good condition but, after the fourth or fifth cleaning, they have shrunk one size. Such shrinkage may be controlled by slack drying compression shrinkage or chemical treatment. Slack drying involves over-feeding a fabric onto a drying frame and simultaneously applying stretch in the crosswise direction of the fabric. Compression shrinkage involves application of controlled compression forces parallel to the surface of the fabric, pushing together the warp yarns to release weaving strains. Fabrics so treated may have less than 2 percent shrinkage in the warp and filling direction. Chem-

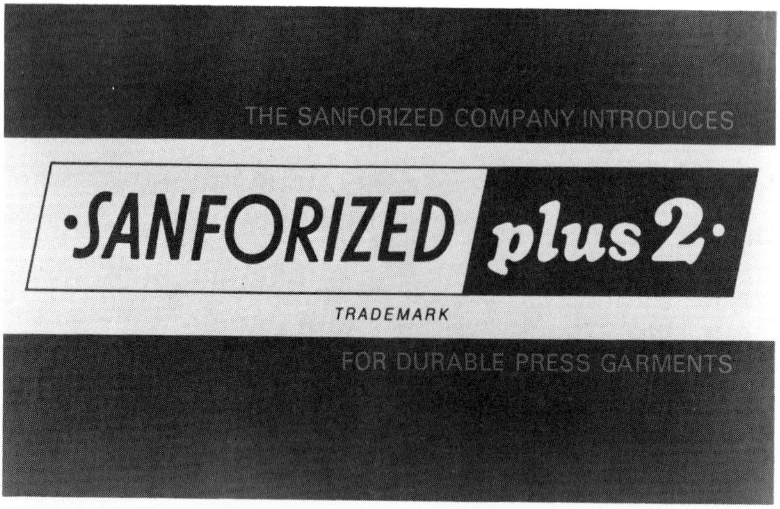

Figure 5-3a

Figure 5-3b

Figure 5-3c

SANFORIZED
PLUS 2
Cluett, Peabody & Co., Inc., permits use of its trademark "San-forized" only on fabrics that meet its rigid shrinkage requirements under its regular inspection. Such fabrics will not shrink more than 1 percent by the government standard test.

SANFOR KNIT
(Trademark of the
Sanforized Company)
They permit use of the trademark Sanfor Knit only on knit garments that meet its comfort performance requirements.

SANFOR SET
(Trademark of the
Sanforized Company)
They permit use of the trademark Sanfor Set only on fabrics that meet rigid requirements. Such fabrics will not shrink more than 1 percent in length or width by AATCC Test Method 135-1970 IIB.

Figure 5-3 Hangtags may give consumers assurance against shrinkage.

ical treatments involve mercerization, resin impregnation, and acetylation. Resin impregnation is the most frequently used chemical treatment. The degree of shrinkage control is directly related to the amount of resin applied to the fabric and the heat conditions of setting.

Manufacturers that preshrink fabrics use tradenames to convey information to the consumer (see Figure 5-3). The consumer is then responsible for interpreting percentages to inches and satisfaction in wear and care as shown in Table 5-2. Some methods manufacturers use to stabilize fabrics are given in Table 5-3.

Table 5-2 Shrinkage Percentage Interpretations (Given: dress length — 50 inches; width at waist — 26 inches)

Residual Shrinkage	Percentage Given On A Label			
	1	2	3	5
Shrinkage in garment				
Length	½ inch	1 inch	1½ inch	2½ inch
Width	¼ inch	½ inch	¾ inch	1 inch
Results	Shape is retained	Feel is tight	Look is gone	No longer wearable

Table 5-3   Some Methods of Stabilizing Fabrics

Fiber Type	Method	Description of Method
Cotton	Mechanical	Slack or compression methods
Cotton	Chemical	Mercerization
Cotton	Chemical	Resin impregnation — cross-linking
Rayon	Chemical	Resin impregnation. Cross-linking with acetal (a) Cellulose ether and formaldehyde Glyoxal reacts with urea to form dihydroxyethylene urea plus formaldehyde to create dimethylol — dihydroxyethylene urea
Nylon	Physical	Heat setting
Polyester	Physical	Heat setting
Acrylics	Physical	Heat setting
Wool	Mechanical	Steaming or sponging
	Chemical	Chlorination
	Chemical	Impregnation of resins (acrylic, nylon, synthetic rubber polymers) plus radiation with Cobalt 60 or atomic particle accelerator.

SWELLING SHRINKAGE — HYDROPHILIC FIBERS

Fibers that pick up moisture will swell. This can cause shrinkage in rib-weave fabrics and in rib variations. These include some failles, Gros de Londres, epingles, grosgrains, bengalines, and ottomans. Shrinkage is usually greatest in the rib-weave fabrics made of wool, rayon, cotton, acetate, or a combination of any of these. Shrinkage of rib-weave fabrics is due to two causes: (1) the fabrics are not relaxed, and (2) the fiber content and weave construction makes them susceptible to swelling shrinkage. Usually rayon or acetate yarn is used in the warp or lengthwise direction of the fabric. The heavy crosswise rib is usually made of rayon and cotton. These rib fibers swell more than acetate when wet. When they swell, they pull the ribs close together, and shrinkage occurs (see Figure 5-4).

Shrinkage may occur when these garments are dry-cleaned, wet-cleaned, or laundered. Some may shrink even when steam is used in finishing them.

Fabrics may be preshrunk by methods available in modern textile finishing plants, although the relaxation of rib-weave fab-

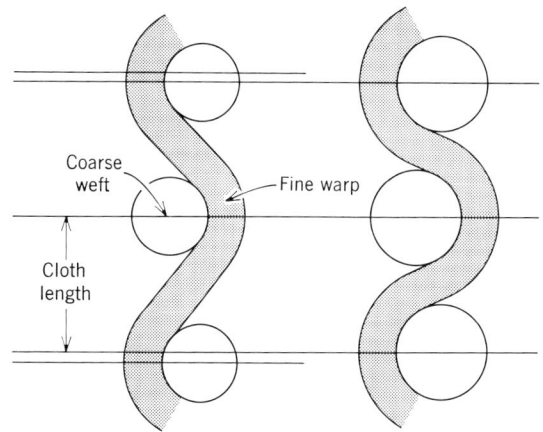

Figure 5-4 A cross-sectional view of three ribs in a rib-weave fabric. The left diagram shows the fabric in a normal condition. In the right diagram, the rib yarns have increased in moisture content and swelled, causing shrinkage.

rics is more difficult than that of others. This group of fabrics should be cleaned in solvent with low solvent relative humidity. Wet-cleaning or laundering results in the risk of excessive shrinkage.

SOIL RELEASE FINISH

All fibers become soiled, but most can be washed with good results because water, detergents, and optical brighteners can penetrate the fiber. The development of soil release finishes became necessary after growth of permanent press, because the high percentage of resin and the presence of polyester fiber results in a fabric with very low absorbency. Soil release finishes permit relatively easy removal of soils (specially oily soils) in laundering. The polyester fiber and the resin are hydrophobic (resist water and are oleophilic), like oil. Soil release finishes aid in making the fiber more absorbent (hydrophilic), thus permitting better "wetability" for improved soil removal. Several added benefits result from the use of soil release finishes in permanent press fabrics. These include improved antistatic properties, improved fabric drapability, and somewhat greater comfort in hot weather.

When soil release first came onto the market, it was quickly confused with soil repellency, and sometimes it still is. The 3M's Dual-Action Scotchgard is the only soil release system on the market today that is also promoted as a soil repellent system. Actually, soil repellency may work against soil release. For example, the original Scotchgard tended to hold stains if they were rubbed in but, if the stain was merely a surface contact stain, it could be blotted off.

At the present time, soil release systems are of two types: a film and a charged surface. The film protects the fiber so that oil and waterborne stains never get to the fiber itself, and water will float the soil away. The charged fiber surface is the result of the soil release finish, causing a chemical reaction with the fiber so that the surface attains a hydrophilic character (likes water); the two systems approach the problem from different directions, but achieve the same goal. Some claim soil redeposition is a problem and that soil release systems need to contain an antisoil redeposition component. Two systems are claimed specifically to attack soil redeposition with good results. Most other companies have made soil redeposition claims, and they state their soil release systems are good at attacking the soil release problem. A baffling consumer problem results when a finish attracts and holds soil (see Figure 5-5).

Static is the cause of much soil deposition in all-polyester or in high-polyester blends. Some feel that any soil release system is bound to fight static because it makes polyester or polyester blends hydrophilic and thus antistatic.

There are many claims being made on the effectiveness of soil release systems in the removal of stains. Perhaps what has been overlooked is that each stain has its own individual method of removal. Aging and heat setting make stain removal more difficult. Stain technology is a bit behind the finishes themselves.

A standard working method of testing the stain and soil resistance of various fabrics is needed. The American Association of Textile Chemists and Colorists is working with 13 participating laboratories to develop test methods for the measuring of soiling and soil removal in textiles.

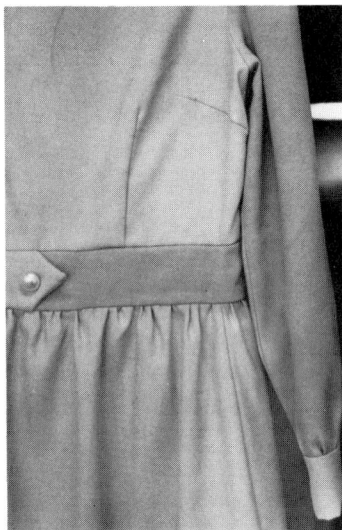

Figure 5-5 In recent years, consumers have encountered a peculiar type of greying that stops at the seam between two panels of a garment. This problem has been traced to certain acrylic finishes that were incorrectly cured. Note the belt and sleeve, which show soil redeposition in this polyester crepe dress. This same phenomenon may also occur on cotton and wool fabrics.

STAIN AND SPOT RESISTANT FINISH

It has been known for a long time that water-repellent fabrics are also resistant to staining by waterborne stains. Only recently, however, have we seen the advent of fabric finishes that are resistant to oil-staining materials. It became possible with the advent of fluorinated hydrocarbons, or "fluorocarbons," as they are called.

Stain-resistant finishes are conveniently classified according to chemical type. The following are five general classes.

1. *Wax.* These include all of the common wax emulsion non-durable water repellents. They are resistant to waterborne stains.
2. *Resin.* Thermosetting resins normally used in finishing cotton fabrics are not water-repellent, but special water-repellent resins are obtained by mixing stearamides or similar repellent compounds with the resin monomer and curing them together. These are durable and resistant to waterborne stains.
3. *Pyridinium.* These are the durable water repellents of which "Zelan" was the prototype. This type is resistant to waterborne stains.
4. *Silicone.* These compounds are hydrocarbon derivatives of silicic acid and form durable water-repellent finishes that are resistant to waterborne stains.
5. *Fluorocarbon.* The fluorinated organic compounds from durable finishes on textiles that are resistant to both oil and waterborne stains.

Some of the commercial stain-resistant finishes are identified in terms of the above classification (see Table 5-4).

There is considerable consumer advertising and promotion of stain-resistant finishes. Producers of the finish often supply hangtags and labels to the garment manufacturer. Some manufacturers of the finishes have set up quality control and testing programs. However, there is much to be desired in the clarification of the language used to describe these finishes. It is not meant to imply that manufacturers misrepresent performance of the finish. In many instances, there is a failure to qualify the finish. Terminology is important to the retail store, since it serves as a safeguard against overselling, which could lead the consumer to expect more than reasonable performance.

For example, a label may read, "Stain-resistant." The finish may be resistant to all nonoily stains. Some promotions seem to imply that if a fabric is treated with a stain-resistant finish, it does not require cleaning. Some promotions state "Launder or Dry-clean Occasionally."

Time, pressure, abrasion, temperature, and impact are definite circumstances of soil contact that influence the degree or extent of staining. Fabrics may repel stains or spots on the surface (spilling of substances), yet the staining substances can be carried into the fabric by pressure or abrasion (sitting on the staining substances).

Table 5-4   Spot and Stain-Resistant Finishes and Water-Repellent Finishes Used as Spot and Stain-Resistant Finishes

Registered Tradename	Resistant to Stains	Chemical Classification	Durable-Nondurable	Manufacturer
Aerotex	Nonoily	Silicone	Durable	American Cyanamid Co.
Aquagard	Nonoily	Silicone*	Durable	Solvol Chemical Co.
Aquanon	Nonoily	Wax emulsion	Semidurable	Solvol Chemical Co.
Cravenette	Nonoily	Wax and metallic salts	Nondurable	Cravenette Co.
Cravenette Super	Nonoily	Silicone	Durable	Cravenette Co.
Cravenette Long Life	Nonoily	Pyridinium	Durable	Cravenette Co.
Cravenette Plus	Nonoily	Resin	Durable	Cravenette Co.
Drilene	Nonoily	Silicone, resins, and wax	Durable	Refined Products Co.
Drusil	Nonoily	Silicone*	Durable	Drew Chemical Product
Hydropruf	Nonoily	Silicone* and polysiloxanes†	Durable	Arkansas Co.
Norane	Nonoily	Silicone		
Permel (Cyana)	Nonoily	Melamine resin	Durable	American Cyanamid Co.
Permel Plus (Dyana)	Nonoily	Silicone	Durable	American Cyanamid Co.
Paramul (DC1 & DC2)	Nonoily	Wax and metallic salt	Semidurable	American Cyanamid Co.
Paramul (115)	Nonoily	Wax and salts	Nondurable	American Cyanamid Co.
Quarpel	Nonoily	Fluorocarbon compounds with pyridinium or resin	Durable	U.S. Quartermaster Corps
Unisec	Nonoily	(not identified)	Durable	United Piece Dye Work
Ranedare S	Nonoily	Silicone	Durable	Metro-Atlantic, Inc.
Ranedare Plus	Nonoily	Resin	Durable	Metro-Atlantic, Inc.
Syl-mer	Nonoily	Silicone	Durable	Dow Chemical Corp.
Scotchgard	Nonoily, oily	Fluorocarbon	Durable	Minnesota Mining Co.
Zelan	Nonoily	Pyridinium	Durable	E.I. du Pont de Nemours & Co., Inc.
Zepel	Nonoily, oily	Fluorocarbon	Durable	E.I. du Pont de Nemours & Co., Inc.

*May appear at the consumer level under the Syl-mer label if the fabric passes the Dow Chemical Corporation's specifications.

†May appear at the consumer level under General Electric label.

Some chemical finishes used to make fabrics resist waterborne stains actually increase their tendency to pick up oily stains. For example, some rainwear fabrics are heavily soiled at the neckline or collar area, which touches the neck, and at the bottom of the cuff, which contacts the hand and wrist area. The treated fabric has an unusual affinity for body oils from the skin. Yet, at the same time, the fabric resists waterborne stains.

FINISHES THAT PROVIDE ENVIRONMENTAL RESISTANCE

FUME FADE-RESISTANT FINISH

These finishes are used on acetate and triacetate to prevent color changes caused by nitrogen oxides in the atmosphere. Fading or color change is counteracted by changing the physical surface properties of the acetate fiber.

Some finishes are fairly durable; others are removed in laundering and dry cleaning. Some manufacturers regard application of an antifume finish as a method of cutting corners. They claim best protection is achieved through proper selection of dyes that contain an inhibitor.

OPAQUE FINISH

These finishes are fomulated coatings applied to the back of drapery lining fabrics to resist the transfer of light through the fabric. Fabrics with this finish can be dry-cleaned by a petroleum solvent method of cleaning. Cleaning by a synthetic solvent method may result in removal of the coating, stiffening of the fabric, or both.

INSULATION (THERMAL) FINISH

Manufacturers of drapery fabrics use coatings or finishes to give an added performance property such as: softening outside noises effectively without distorting sound inside the room; insulating against cold, wintry drafts to keep rooms warmer in winter; defying the sun's heat to keep rooms cooler in the summer; giving drapery fabric a fuller hand; improving light control by making fabric more opaque; and protecting against sun rot and fading.

Metallic or aluminized finishes, foamed acrylic or aerocellular acrylic, vinyl resins, and synthetic rubber finishes may be used (see Figures 5-6 and 5-7 and Coated Fabrics, page 211).

FINISHES THAT PROVIDE BIOLOGICAL RESISTANCE

ANTISEPTIC FINISH

The use of bactericides in fabric finishing or retreatment of fabrics after cleaning is relatively new. It is claimed that such

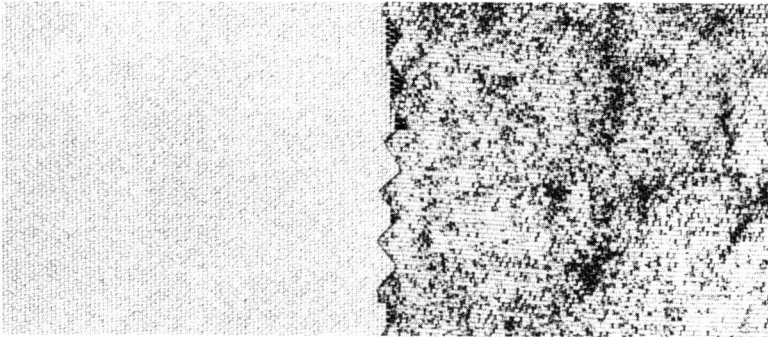

Figure 5-6 Some reflective lining fabrics lose their metallic particles in drycleaning.

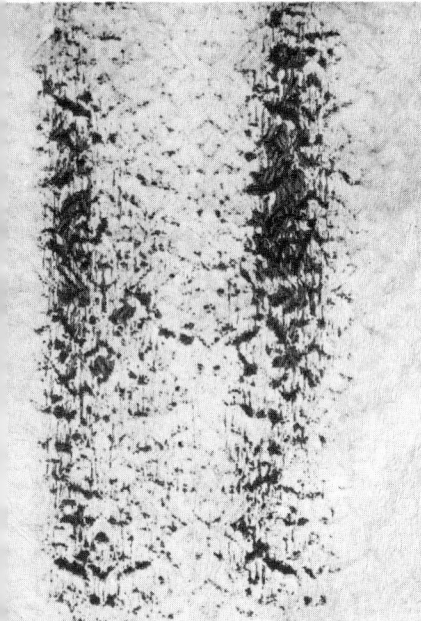

Figure 5-7 This acrylic coated fabric became tacky in both dry-cleaning solvent and water. The coated surfaces should not be in contact because they stick together. When you try to separate them, damage can occur. The coating may also be affected by light and storage. Improvement in the performance of these coatings are being made.

finishes inhibit bacterial growth and the formation of perspiration odors.

To discuss the general subject of sanitation accurately, some terms should be carefully defined. Infectious diseases are caused by microorganisms (germs).

There are many different kinds of germs capable of causing disease. Two of these, bacteria and viruses, are the major ones that cause diseases that are transmitted by direct contact between an infected person and one who is not infected.

Bacteria are unicellular microorganisms, ranging in size from 0.5 to 50 microns. There are 25,400 microns in 1 inch. For comparison, the clay particles that predominate in airborne dust range below 2 microns. Therefore bacteria are relatively coarse in size and can be filtered from liquid suspensions. Some cause disease, while others perform such useful functions that they are essential to life on earth.

"Viruses" are parasites that can only reproduce inside of a living cell. They are smaller than bacteria, from 0.01 to 0.3 microns, too small to be filtered out by filters. Viruses cause many of our most serious diseases in both plants and animals.

A "disinfectant" is an agent that destroys disease-producing germs. It will not necessarily destroy the spores of these germs. The term is the proper word for use in connection with treatment of fabrics.

Disinfectants vary widely in their power and range; therefore the fact that a chemical product is approved by the U.S. Department of Agriculture for labeling as a "disinfectant" should not be construed to mean that it will necessarily destroy every kind of bacteria and virus. In fact, many products sold as disinfectants have been tested only against bacteria, not viruses. As a result, broad claims made for disinfectants should be regarded with some skepticism.

"Germicide" means almost the same as disinfectant, but it is a broader term. It is not limited to disease-producing germs (microbes) or to application of the agent to inanimate objects only.

When a chemical product has been tested only against bacteria, it should be called a bactericide, and this is the term chosen for use in this text.

Do Cleaning Processes Remove and Destroy Germs?

It has been generally thought for a long time that both laundries and dry-cleaning plants did a satisfactory job of sanitizing textiles because of the nature of the processes. In laundering, the use of 160°F or high wash temperatures, chlorine bleach, and hot-heat presses should certainly provide adequate disinfection.

In dry cleaning, continuous filtration is used, and bacteria are large enough to be detached from the fabric by the cleaning process and filtered out of the solvent. The surviving ones are later exposed to steam presses, or steam-air forms.

Research studies show that:

1. All the processes in a cleaning plant operation remove bacteria to some degree: cleaning, drying, and especially steam pressing.
2. Articles that receive prolonged steam pressing, such as blankets, will be disinfected.
3. Conditions and processing practices differ so much between plants that no general conclusions about the degree of disinfection are warranted.
4. Although various stages in cleaning combine to kill or remove the majority of bacteria present on a fabric, it is still possible for bacteria to be transmitted from one article to another and to survive all steps of the process under certain conditions.
5. Further studies of this matter would be desirable.

Do Bactericides Render Fabrics Self-Sterilizing?

It is often claimed that the presence of a bactericide on a fabric will insure that any bacteria that subsequently impinge on the fabric will be killed. This claim is based on a bacteriological test in which a sample of treated fabric is placed on an infected culture medium and the effect of the fabric inhibiting the growth of bacteria is observed over a period of time. It has been shown that this test is invalid.

There is one exception. If garments are treated with formaldehyde, dry bacteria deposited on them will be killed. This is presumably because the fabric slowly releases gaseous formaldehyde.

Aside from fabrics treated with formaldehyde or fabrics capable of releasing formaldehyde through some chemical mechanism, claims of self-disinfecting fabrics should be regarded with skepticism.

Can Treatment of Garments with Bactericides Prevent Perspiration Odors?

It has long been known that perspiration odors on clothing are caused by bacterial attack on perspiration residues and sebum residues. Therefore it seems logical to many people that the solution to this is to treat the garment with a bactericide. However, recent work has shown that the main location of the bacterial attack on these residues is not on the garment, but on the skin of the wearer; therefore disinfection of the garment is ineffective, because the fabric picks up the odorous products from the skin.

What Kinds of Chemicals Act as Germicides?

A great variety of chemicals are good germicides. They include phenols, alcohols, and iodine; chlorine and many chlorine compounds; and some metals and their compounds, such as mercury, silver, and copper. Others are the quaternary nitrogen compounds, called simply "quats" by the chemists. This class of compounds is most frequently derived from ammonia or pyridine. Some of the quats have good germicidal properties, although their bactericidal spectrum is limited. Also included in this group are most of our cationic wetting agents, softeners, and detergents. While all cationic detergents may not have germicidal properties, a number of them do.

MOTH-RESISTANT FINISH

Moth larvae and carpet beetles are known to attack fabrics made of the animal fibers or blends (see Figures 5-8 and 5-9).

Will they eat synthetic fabrics? This question is asked occasionally. An advantage often claimed for man-made fabrics is that they are mothproof. But, under certain conditions, insects may attack them, too. Research has shown that the presence of synthetic fibers in a garment is not in itself assurance that the garment will not be attacked by insects. Some people suggested that insect holes might be caused by crickets, silverfish, or similar

Figure 5-8 Testing fabrics for moth resistance. Moths may attack fabrics other than 100 percent wool.

insects instead of by the usual moths or carpet beetles. Crickets and silverfish are known to damage cellulose, for example, particularly when starch, glue, or food stains are present. Carpet beetles and moth larvae have been known to chew through a nonwoolen material to get at food underneath. There is no proof that carpet beetle larvae would actually eat a man-made fabric.

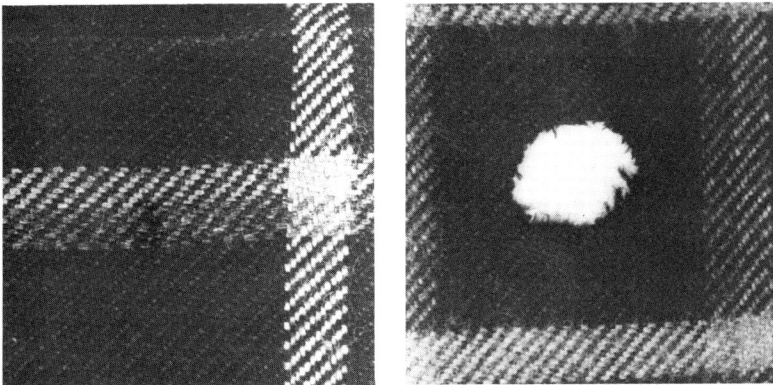

Figure 5-9a (Left) A rayon-acetate blend. (Right) Identical fabric damaged by carpet beetle larvae.

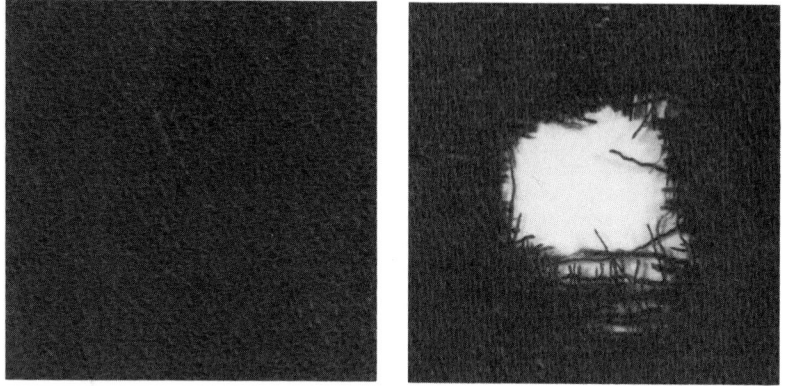

Figure 5-9b   (Left) A 100 percent acrilan fabric. (Right) Identical fabric, showing considerable insect damage.

Commonsense precautions should be taken by consumers to avoid any chance of damage. A good rule to follow is never to store soiled garments for any length of time. If garments are to be stored, they should be stored clean.

Moth-resistant finishes may be classed as durable or non-durable. The latter term means that the finishes are removed by laundering or dry cleaning and must be replaced or renewed. There are two basic kinds of moth-resistant finishes: (1) those for home use, which give off an odor that repels the moth so that eggs are not deposited on the fabric; and (2) those that give off a gas toxic to the moth or larvae.

Some products are added to fulling or dyeing processes of the fabric and are promoted as durable finishes. Others are chemical products such as fluorine that are applied from a water bath, are removed by water, and must be reapplied or renewed.

It is advisable to ask retail sales personnel these questions when purchasing fabrics treated with a moth-resistant finish: "How long will it last? Does the fabric require special care?" Some dry cleaners can retreat garments and household items to give them a moth-resistant finish.

MILDEW-RESISTANT FINISH

This is a chemical finish applied to a fabric that is susceptible to mildew. It may be combined with other finishes, such as water repellents.

PERSPIRATION-RESISTANT FINISH

This is a chemical finish applied to a fabric to make it resistant to the damage caused by body perspiration. It finds widest use in the garment lining field (see Antiseptic Finish).

GENERAL OR ROUTINE FINISHES

These finishes may be classified as mechanical or chemical. They are used to produce a certain characteristic associated with definite fabric construction. Routine finishes may or may not influence performance of the fabric in wear or method cleaning. In many cases, they cannot be seen or felt. However, they are there to impart the desired end-use property in the finished fabric. These are discussed in alphabetical order.

Bleaching

Bleaching is a chemical process whereby the finisher whitens the fabric and removes impurities by the use of chemicals such as peroxide, chlorine bleaching compounds, or sulfurous acid.

If bleaching is not controlled, fabric damage in use and care may occur. Sometimes even colored or printed fabrics may be bleached and redyed or printed to the season's fashion color. If the reducing bleaching process is not controlled, the color in the fabric may revert to its original hue by reoxidation or reaction with the oxygen in the atmosphere.

Brushing (or Teaseling)

This is a mechanical finishing process in which circular brushes raise a nap. This finish is applied to fabrics made of staple yarns.

Calendering

This is a mechanical finishing process of pressing fabric between rollers. There are different types of machinery. Various conditions of heat, pressure, and tension will produce different effects. It may be used with chemical treatment to obtain special surfaces (see discussion of Surface Applied Designs, Chapter 6).

Carbonizing

This is a chemical treatment to remove vegetable matter from wool. When wool is dry, the carbonized matter "dusts off" in a mechanical crushing operation. The process is also used on reused wool.

Crabbing

This is a mechanical wool-finishing process to prevent creases or other forms of uneven shrinkage in later stages of finishing. The fabric is treated with boiling water to set or fix the yarns permanently.

Decating or Decatizing

This is a mechanical finishing process applied to fabrics to set the material, enhance luster, and improve the hand. The cloth is wound around a perforated drum between layers of a blanket, and steam is passed through from the inside to outside layers. The action is then reversed, and the steam is removed by a vacuum pump on completion of treatment. This process may help overcome uneven or blotchy dyeing.

Degumming

This is a scouring operation that removes the natural gum from silk in a hot soap solution. Degumming is usually performed after the yarn has been woven or knitted.

Fulling

This is a mechanical finishing process in the woolen industry that involves the application of moisture, heat, friction, and pressure.

When wool fabrics come from the loom, they are loose and hard in texture. To make the fabric soft and compact, the fabric is subjected to controlled moisture, heat, friction, and pressure that causes the yarns of the fabric to shrink together with the desired soft hand or feel.

Heat Setting

Heat-sensitive or thermoplastic fabrics are usually heat-set to retain their shape or to make them dimensionally stable. Each fiber has its own melt and flow temperature. At this point, the fibers can be shaped. The fabric is then cooled. Any subsequent reshaping or resetting must be done at a temperature higher than that used initially. This fiber characteristic makes permanent designs on fabric surfaces possible (see Chapter 6 on Surface Applied Designs as well as garment designs such as pleating).

Consumers must exercise care in laundering fabrics made of heat-sensitive fibers. If the flow or melt temperature is exceeded in washing or drying, smooth fabrics may become permanently wrinkled.

Mercerization

This is one of the most important of all cotton finishes. This finish imparts luster to the cotton, increases its strength by nearly 25 percent, and improves dye affinity, producing brighter shades than unmercerized cotton. The finish consists of treating the material with a cold, concentrated sodium hydroxide solution while under tension. Both fabrics and yarns can be mercerized. It is a permanent finish (see discussion, page 94).

Scouring

This is done to remove natural waxes, dirt, finishing oils, and sizes used on yarns or fabric. In some cases, bleaching and scouring are done in the same operation.

Shearing

This cuts and removes undesirable surface fibers so that the weave of the fabric is visible. The process can be adapted to make a nap uniform or to cut designs into pile fabrics to produce sculptured effects.

Weighting

This is the addition of substances to add weight to a yarn or fabric or to act as a filling agent to the fabric (e.g., imported weighted silk velvet).

Tentering

Tentering is a mechanical straightening operation and drying of a fabric. In a finishing plant the fabric is handled in a ropelike form, winding its way through each of the many finishing processes at a speed of 300 yards a minute. There is a strain on the fabric as it is hauled, tugged, or yanked through vats, wringing devices, and guides. It is very easy for the fabric to get off grain.

Two problems — bow and skewness — occur as the fabric is handled in these high speed operations.

"Bow" occurs when the crosswise yarns curve toward the outer edges of the fabric. "Skewness" means that one selvage leads the other in passing through the machinery (see Figure 5-10).

It is very difficult to detect or remedy these distortions at high speed. To correct this defect would require slower production and, therefore, higher cost of the finished fabric. Consumers have said they would be willing to pay an additional cost to have fabrics with a straight grain, and they complain bitterly when they have no choice but to purchase off-grain fabrics.

Consumers know that for good clothing construction, whether it is a man's shirt or a woman's dress, the lengthwise yarns of the fabric must be at right angles to the crosswise yarns. If they are not, the fabric is off-grain and difficult to cut and sew, whether the garment is made commercially or in the home. Such garments have poor shape retention in wear and after dry cleaning or laundering.

Figure 5-10 (a) Skewness in fabrics occurs as one selvage leads the other selvage in passing through the machinery. (b) Bow in fabrics may be seen at the center of the goods as cross yarns lag behind the outer edges.

(a)

(b)

LEARNING EXPERIENCES

1. Assemble fabric swatches that have a gloss or luster achieved by beetling, calendering, and glazing. Cut each sample into two parts. Keep one piece for comparative purposes. Wash and dry the other samples. Mount the original and washed samples of each fabric. Compare and record your observations.

2. Locate a net or woven cotton that is highly sized or starched. Cut the sample into three parts. Keep one sample for the original. Place one sample in warm water and the other in perchlorethylene dry-cleaning solvent. Allow to stand for an hour. Remove the samples. Dry. Mount and record observations. How may sizing be reapplied in the home? Locate a dry cleaner that reapplies sizing to fabrics. Ask him to allow you to observe the process. What problems are involved?

3. Locate a sample of cotton batiste and a nylon fabric that has been given a finish to soften the fabric. List the reasons textile finishers use softening agents.

4. Find samples of a fabric that has been given a napped finish and a brushed finish. How do they differ? What properties do these finishes give to a fabric? What are their limitations in use and care?

5. How can the textile finisher achieve abrasion resistance and antislip and antisnagging properties in a fabric?

6. Assemble swatches of toweling, diaper and underwear fabrics, and pieces of blotting paper and bond paper. Place some food color in water. With a medicine dropper, put one drop of colored water on each sample. Record your observation on absorbency when you do the experiment and after you allow the samples to dry.

7. Demonstrate static electricity. Tear a piece of paper into small bits. Take a glass rod and rub it with a piece of wool fabric. Then hold the glass rod to the edge of a piece of paper. Record your observations. Explain why a textile finisher applies antistatic finishes to some fabrics.

8. Survey your market area and mail-order catalogs. List the merchandise treated with a water-repellent and water-proof finish. Record tradenames, information on care, and guarantees of assurances of durability of the finish.

9. Make a market survey. Determine the availability of fabrics treated with flame retardant finishes. List tradenames, cost, and care instructions. Compare and decide which is the best buy in terms of performance and ease of care.

10. Take cotton and nylon woven fabric swatches and a polyester knit fabric swatch. Press identical pleats in each swatch. Record observations immediately after pressing and at the end of one week. Cut the samples into two parts. Immerse one set of samples in water and the other set in perchlorethylene dry-cleaning solvent. Allow to stand 1 hour. Remove. Dry. Record observations on crease and pleat retention.

11. Make a consumer survey in your community to determine consumer satisfaction or dissatisfaction with permanent press garments. Assemble and examine garments that gave poor performance. Analyze and record the reasons.

12. Assemble three sets of 2 × 3-inch swatches of closely woven cotton or woolen fabric, rayon crepe, cotton net, and matelassé. Retain the first set as the original. Immerse the second set in lukewarm water and the third set in perchlorethylene dry-cleaning solvent. Remove after an hour and dry on paper towels. Make a chart and mark three rows of 2 × 3-inch blocks in the crosswise direction and mark out three rows of 2 × 3-inch blocks under the rows marked crosswise on the lengthwise direction. Mount the original samples in row 1, the samples wet out in water in row 2; and the samples wet out in solvent in row 3. Record your observations.

13. Assemble a group of fabrics that you may wish to test for dimensional stability. Include both knitted and woven fabrics. If fabric is available in sufficient yardage, each sample cut should be at least 24 × 24 inches. Mark a 20 × 20-inch square within the 24 × 24-inch sample. If fabric for testing is limited, each sample cut should be 14 × 14 inches. The marked square should measure 10 × 10 inches. Determine the number of samples you will need for the data you wish to collect. One is needed for each method of laundering — hand wash or machine wash; one for dry cleaning (either coin operated or professional dry cleaning); and one for pressing or steam finishing. Label each sample for method of cleaning and finishing. Mark warp and filling direction.

> W — Warp or lengthwise measurement in woven fabrics; wales in knitted fabrics.

> F — Filling or crosswise measurement in woven fabrics; courses in knitted fabrics.

Measurements should be taken three points in the lengthwise and crosswise direction on the fabric and averaged for the final measurement. Shrinkage and stretch is calculated as follows. The average figure is subtracted from the original measurement (20 inches or 10 inches). The result is divided by the original measurement and multiplied by 100 percent to achieve the percentage change in dimensions. Examples:

$$\begin{array}{r} 20.0 \\ -18.5 \\ \hline 2)\overline{1.5} \end{array} = 0.75 \times 100 = 7.5\%$$

$$\begin{array}{r} 10.0 \\ -8.5 \\ \hline 10)\overline{1.5\%} \end{array} = .15 \times 100 = -15.0\%$$

Use the symbol − (minus) for shrinkage and + (plus) for stretching. Accuracy of data depends on the accurate marking of the shrinkage square and the accurate measuring of the square after processing. Always examine your data and recheck your measurements if a discrepancy occurs. Also observe and record observations for change of hand, feel, color, and general appearance.

14. Cut 4 × 4-inch square of faille, grosgrain, and ottoman fabrics. Immerse the samples in warm water for an hour. Remove from water and dry. Record and explain your observations.

15. Prepare a stain strip, as illustrated, on an untreated fabric and a fabric treated with a stain-resistant finish.

STAIN STRIP

1	5	9	13
2	6	10	14
3	7	11	15
4	8	12	16

1. Linseed oil
2. Nail polish
3. Blue lacquer
4. Egg white
5. Grapefruit juice
6. Lipstick
7. Mascara
8. India ink

9. Ball-point ink
10. Violet ink
11. Red ink
12. Yellow paint (latex)
13. Argyrol
14. Gentian violet
15. Mustard
16. Coffee

Allow stain strip to age 1 week. Launder each sample. Observe and record your observations.

16. Explain why soil release finishes became necessary. How do they differ from stain- and spot-resistant finishes? Explain the similarities and differences between stain- and spot-resistant finishes and water-repellant finishes.

17. If your laboratory is not equipped with a gas fading chamber or laboratory equipment, enlist the cooperation of the chemistry department to help you observe gas or fume fading of acetate fabrics. Place a petri dish or small beaker containing 5 milliliters of nitric acid in the bottom of a desiccator. *Caution:* DO NOT SPILL THE ACID OR IN-HALE THE FUMES. Suspend small samples of acetate fabrics on a wire under the lid of the desiccator. Allow to stand 6 to 8 hours. Make observations and record them.

18. Make a collection and mount fabrics with opaque and insulated finishes. List advantages and care methods for each.

19. Collect home products that may be used to protect wearing apparel and home furnishing fabrics from moth damage. Study and compare recommendations for use, claims made, and costs.

20. Survey the local market and study mail-order catalogs for labels or information on moth-repellant finishes, mildew-resistant finishes, and perspiration-resistant finishes. Record your observations.

21. List the problems that consumers may experience if textile finishers overbleach fabrics; do not properly heat set thermoplastic fabrics; and tenter fabrics off grain.

6

APPLIED SURFACE DESIGN

Fabrics have eye appeal because of their construction, finish, applied surface design, and color. The methods by which fabrics get a design have always been of interest.

Construction design effects discussed are those achieved by:

1. The combining of colored fibers to create a particular effect such as tweeds and cross-dyed fabrics for color effects (fiber dyed).
2. The combining of yarns to make a particular design such as stripes, checks, and plaids (yarn dyed).
3. The introduction of novelty type yarns such as metallic and bouclé yarns.
4. Making weave designs, such as the dobby and Jacquard patterns.
5. The introduction of a yarn or yarns to form a design on the background weave such as leno or figure weaves.

Designs may be achieved by dyeing and printing fabrics in various ways after it has been made (see Chapter 7).

Surface designs will be discussed in this chapter because they are distinct and often unusual. Most authors call these "special finishes." However, "surface applied designs" appears to be a better description, since they can be readily recognized; they have a special aesthetic appeal and specific performance properties in use and care. They will be presented alphabetically.

281

Figure 6-1 The beige silk organdy flowers, stuffed with pink tinted cotton, are appliqued to a tan satin fabric with gold embroidery.

APPLIQUÉ

Figures or designs are cut from one fabric and are sewn, embroidered, or otherwise attached to the fabric. Usually, a three-dimensional effect is achieved (see Figure 6-1).

BURN-OUT PRINTS

A burn-out print uses certain chemicals to dissolve (burn out) fibers in a fabric to create a design in a fabric made of two fibers. The chemicals may be selectively applied to burn out one fiber, leaving a sheer area. For example, a fabric made of 20 percent nylon and 80 percent rayon may be burned out by using phenol. The phenol dissolves the nylon, leaving a sheer rayon that forms the design. In a fabric of acetate and rayon, acetone may be used to burn out the acetate fibers (see Figure 6-2a).

In fabrics made of a single fiber, burn-out techniques may be used to make eyelets or other holes to create a design (see Figure 6-2b). In this case, the chemicals burn out all the fibers and fuse the edges around the holes so as to prevent raveling of the fabric. An adhesive or flocking may also be used to prevent raveling.

The technique of burn-out printing makes possible many interesting designs. Fabrics printed in this manner are launderable, wet-cleanable, and dry-cleanable, depending on the fabric and garment design. However, if the chemical process is carried too far, fabric weakening may shorten the fabric's wear life. Also, unbound eyelets and holes, if caught, tear readily, and they also may fray around the edges of the hole.

Figure 6-2a This fabric is made of 20 percent nylon and 80 percent rayon. Phenol dissolved the nylon (dark areas) leaving the sheer rayon (light areas) to form the design.

CIRÉ

Ciré is a special calender finish applied to fabrics and laces to produce a very high, patent leatherlike luster. There are two methods used to create this effect.

1. Wax or a thermoplastic resin is applied to the fabric under heat and pressure. This finish has limited durability.
2. Fabrics made of heat-sensitive fibers may be polished or embossed to create a high luster finish on the surface of the fabric. This finish is durable.

EMBOSSED DESIGNS

Embossing is a term used to describe a method by which a design may be achieved on the surface of a fabric. There are two methods of making embossed designs in fabrics.

1. *Mechanically.* The design is pressed into a fabric under conditions of heat, moisture, and steam.
2. *Chemically.* The design is pressed into a fabric that has been pretreated with a resin.

Embossed designs may be found on cotton, rayon, silk, acetate, nylon, and other synthetic fabrics of many different types of construction (plain weaves, satin, rib weaves, etc.) (see Figure 6-3).

This method of fabric design results in many interesting textured effects. Variety and beauty of design are achieved.

With the introduction of the use of heat-setting resins and the use of heat-sensitive fibers, embossed designs can now be achieved that are permanent in relation to wear and cleaning.

EMBROIDERED DESIGNS

A fabric is stitched on a Schiffli machine with one or more threads to make a design. Designs may range from very simple to very elaborate. The design stands in relief to the ground fabric. In some patterns, the fabric may be cut away to form scallops, divided motifs, and designs (see Figure 6-4).

FLOCKED DESIGNS

In flock printing, a fabric is first printed with an adhesive, then dusted with flocks (short fibers, hair, or metallic particles) that adhere to the adhesive to form a design that stands in relief to the

Figure 6-2b Burn-out design on 100 percent acetate taffeta with a satin stripe.

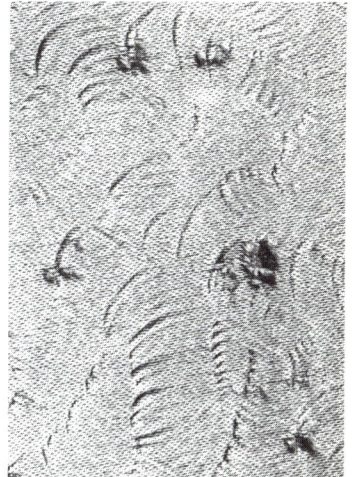

Figure 6-3 The engraving roller used to create this embossed design has cut the yarns of the fabric. Sometimes this damage does not become evident until after the fabric is cleaned.

Figure 6-4   A white embroidered design on a blue linen fabric.

surface of the fabric. Some flock prints are made by an electrostatic method. The flock is actually pulled through the surface of the fabric and stands perpendicular to it (see Figure 6-5).

Flock printing offers a wide selection of interesting fabric designs. These designs are made on a variety of wearing apparel and household fabrics, from sheer curtain and dress fabrics to very heavy dress and drapery fabrics. Some flock-printed fabrics are wet-cleanable; others are dry-cleanable; others may be washed or dry-cleaned.

Performance of flock prints in wear and cleaning depends on:

1. The basic fabric; a firmly woven fabric provides a good base for the flock; a loosely woven fabric does not always provide a good base.
2. The type of adhesive used; some are soluble in dry-cleaning solvents; others will withstand both solvent and water action.
3. The conditions of the heat-setting of the adhesive in manufacture; these conditions must be properly controlled to produce satisfactory flock prints.
4. The degree of abrasion in wear and in cleaning.

GLUED DESIGN

Many types of materials may be used to form a design on the surface of the fabric. These designs are held to the fabric's surface by a glue or an adhesive (e.g., felt cut-out design glued to a felt skirt or chenille or sequin dots glued to a fabric surface). The adhesive used may be solvent-soluble, and the design will be removed in dry cleaning (see Figure 6-6 in color section).

Figure 6-5   A black flocked design on a yellow mousseline de soie.

GLAZED

Chintz and polished cottons are terms applied to a large group of gaily printed or solid-colored, highly glazed fabrics. The better qualities are made of a firmly woven cotton fabric having a hard, twisted warp yarn and a coarse, slackly twisted filling yarn. Some of the fabrics are "fully" glazed; some are "semiglazed." There are two methods of producing a glazed finish on this group of fabrics.

1. *Nondurable.*   The fabric is given a wax and starch finish and then pressed between hot rollers.
2. *Durable.*   The fabric is treated with a resin (urea or melamine) under patented methods of applying and curing.

There is a wide selection of quality, color, design, fully or semiglazed surface, and degree of crispness in this class of fabrics. Chintz and polished cottons are adaptable for many wearing apparel and household items. The finish imparts a certain degree of wrinkle, soil, and spot resistance to the fabric. Chintz and polished cottons are wet-cleanable and dry-cleanable, depending on the finish that has been applied. Some are washable. It requires special care in use and cleaning. The nondurable-type finish is lost in laundering, wet cleaning, and dry cleaning. In fabrics that have a heavily applied finish, the fabric develops white streaks when it is bent or flexed in use or in cleaning. Once this occurs, there is no known cure.

LACQUER PRINTS

Lacquer printing is a method of roller printing in which insoluble pigments are mixed with a lacquer carrier to form a printing paste and then applied to an already finished piece of goods (e.g., a taffeta or a faille). The design does not stand out in relief to the surface of the fabric. This type of print is difficult to distinguish from a pigment-resin print and designs that are made by a roller printing method using dye pastes.

A variety of designs may be applied to current colors and fabrics of a particular season. Some lacquer prints may dry-clean satisfactorily; some perform unsatisfactorily in dry cleaning.

Performance of lacquer prints in wear and cleaning depends on the fiber content, construction of the fabric, and the carrier used to carry the pigments. Lacquer prints are easily affected by abrasion in wear and in dry cleaning. The pigments used to make these prints are affected by the dry-side spotting reagents required to remove many types of spots and stains.

LACQUER STENCIL PRINTS

In lacquer stencil printing, insoluble, finely ground pigments are mixed with a binder and a thickener to form a printing paste. This is then applied to the fabric in a variety of designs. The design stands in relief to the background fabric. They actually look like paint designs.

Attractive and unusual designs may be applied to a variety of fabrics such as satin, taffeta, plain weave fabrics made of cotton, rayon, and acetate, and other fibers.

A great improvement has been made in lacquer stencil print designs. Some lacquer stencil prints dry-clean satisfactorily;

Figure 6-7 Some lacquer stencil prints dry-clean satisfactorily. Others are affected by dry-cleaning solvents. The plasticizing oils are removed, leaving the fabric in a shriveled condition, as illustrated.

others wet-clean or launder satisfactorily; and still others perform unsatisfactorily to wear and dry cleaning.

Performance of lacquer stencil prints in wear and dry cleaning depends on the fiber content and the construction of the fabric, the type of binder used to carry the pigment, and the conditions of the "curing" and "setting" of the binder and pigment after the application (see Figure 6-7).

METALLIC OVERPRINTED DESIGNS

Technically, overprinting is "application" or "direct" printing. It may be compared to applying a design on a wall with a roller paintbrush. No attempt is made to dye the base fabric. The goal is merely to cover part of the surface of the fabric with another color. When gold or metallic particles are used, a binder is used to fix the metallic particles to the fabric.

Entirely new effects can be created by overprinting a fabric. Properly cured prints can now be made that will withstand laundering, wet cleaning, and dry cleaning. The addition of a resin finish to the fabric helps to seal in the design and to increase the dimensional stability of the fabric; it also adds a glittering effect to the fabric. If the binder is not properly selected and cured, metallic overprinted designs may be removed in wear and dry cleaning.

MOIRÉ

Moiré is a term used to describe several methods by which a design may be achieved on the surface of a fabric. There are three distinct types.

1. *Bar moiré.*   The wavy designs form rows or bars. This is a mechanical method depending on moisture, heat, and pressure.
2. *Scratch moiré.*   The yarns are deflected to produce a variety of simple designs. (A mechanical method as described above.)
3. *The H-process.*   A combination of chemical and mechanical processes that may result in a larger and more complicated design.

Moiré designs may be found on cotton, silk, rayon, acetate, nylon, and other synthetic fabrics of many different constructions. Ninety-five percent of all moirés on today's market are bar moirés.

Many interesting and beautiful designs can be produced by moiréing and, with the introduction and use of resin finishes and

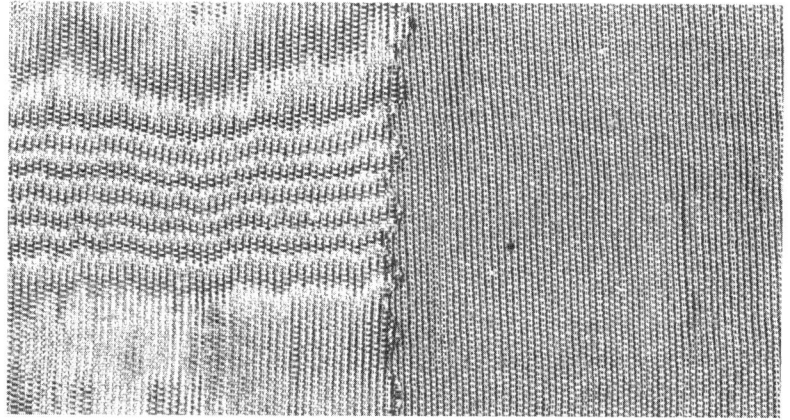

Figure 6-8 A moiré design made on cotton, rayon, silk, or a combination of these fibers is removed by water or steam unless the fabric is treated with a resin to make the design permanent. (Left) Original. (Right) After dry cleaning.

thermoplastic fibers, moiré designs can be made that are permanent to laundering, wet cleaning, and dry cleaning.

Moiré designs made on nonthermoplastic fibers without the use of a resin to make them permanent, may be removed by moisture and heat, such as perspiration, spilling water or a beverage onto a fabric, steam pressure used to finish the fabric after dry cleaning, or wet cleaning, or the use of moisture to remove a spot or stain (see Figure 6-8).

HAND-PAINTED DESIGNS

The design may be painted on a section of a garment before it is made or applied to a finished item. Painted designs on fabric sold by the yard may be found occasionally. Sometimes the painted design is reembroidered with a yarn to emphasize the design. Other applications are hand-painted designs on blouses and painted designs on ties. Some painted designs dry-clean satisfactorily; others are partially or completely removed in dry cleaning (see Figures 6-9 and 6-9*a*).

PLEATED FABRICS

A pleated fabric is one that has folds arranged with a predetermined pattern. There are several methods of pleating.

1. *Form pleating.* The fabric is put into a paper pattern form and steamed or cured in a steam box or autoclave. Examples are sunburst, circular, and fancy pleats.

Figure 6-9 A white painted design on pink linen. The design is embroidered with a pink cord to give emphasis to the design. The painted design was removed in dry cleaning. The fabric could not be wet-cleaned or laundered because of excessive shrinkage.

2. *Machine pleating.* There are three types of machine pleating.
   a. *Conventional.* The fabric is fed into a pleating machine that folds the fabric into knife or box pleats.
   b. *Random or ripple.* This is a trick method of pleating whereby the fabric is pushed together mechanically, forming an irregular ripple pattern.
   c. *Embossed pleats.* Pleats are pressed into the surface of the fabric in the form of scallops, squares, or corrugations.

The various methods of pleating offer a wide selection of beautiful fabrics and garment designs. Some fabrics made of the heat-sensitive fibers can be given durable pleats. Some fabrics that are first treated wtih a resin finish before pleating can be given durable pleats, too. In most cases, pleats following the grain of the fabric give better pleat retention than pleats on the bias. Pleated fabrics require special care in handling, regardless of the method used to clean them.

Many pleated fabrics lose their pleat sharpness and smooth appearance with wear and cleaning. The pleats separate and must be reset. The degree of separation depends on:

1. The fiber content of the fabric. Heat-sensitive fibers give better pleat retention than fabrics of nonheat-sensitive fibers, unless given a special finishing treatment.
2. The construction of the fabric. A closely woven or knit fabric gives better pleat retention than a loosely woven or knit fabric. In general, woven fabrics give better pleat retention than knit fabrics.
3. The method of pleating used. Generally, the autoclave method produces better pleat retention than the steam box method.
4. The conditions of pleating regardless of the method, such as temperature, time, or rate of cooling.
5. Garment design. A tightly fitted garment will result in a greater degree of pleat separation than a loosely fitted garment.

Novelty pleated fabrics cannot be reset unless the garment is taken apart and repleated by a pleating firm (see Figures 6-10 and 6-11).

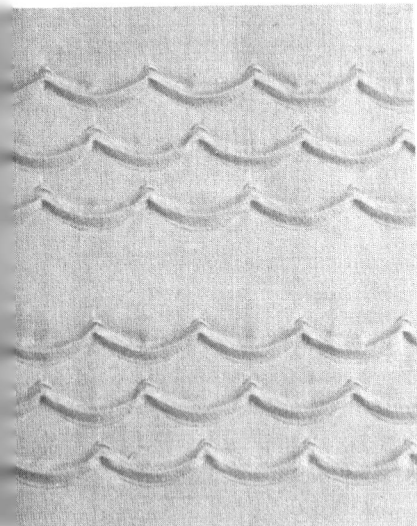

Figure 6-10 Novelty embossed pleats are pressed into the surface of the fabric to form a scalloped design.

PLISSÉ PRINTS

Plissé printing is a process that does not use color. Designs are made by the use of chemicals. The fabric passes between rollers

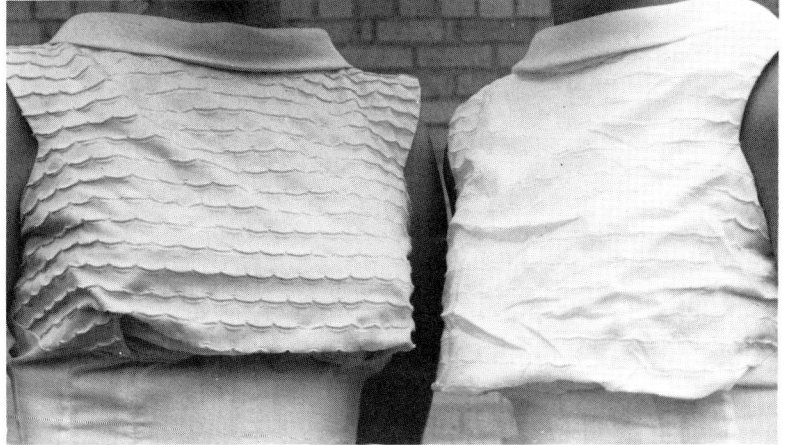

Figure 6-11 The bodice is made of the same fabric as the skirt of this garment, but it has been pinch-pleated. The pleated section is lined with a cotton lining fabric treated with a plastic-type sizing, the purpose of which is to prevent the pleats from relaxing in wear and cleaning. (Left) Before cleaning. (Right) After cleaning.

that permit a caustic solution to contact certain areas of the fabric where a puckered design is desired. Sometimes this is accomplished by protecting parts of the fabric with a resisting solution, then putting the fabric through a caustic bath. The unprotected areas of the fabric then pucker.

SONIC FOIL EMBROIDERY

Finely detailed or simple sonic stitching can now be produced in vibrant color. Fabric can be decorated in color with an endless variety of stitch patterns. Expensive designer touches can be added at very little cost to any item where color can enhance the product.

When sonic foil (one-half mil polyester film coated with thermoplastic pigment) is fed with fabric into the sonic sewing machine, a permanent colored stitch is produced. Changing stitch color is simply a matter of feeding a different color of sonic foil with the fabric (see Figure 6-12). The manufacturer states there was no sign of deterioration after repeated test launderings (detergents, enzymes, or bleach), machine dryings, and dry cleanings.

SCHREINERIZED DESIGNS

This process is similar to embossing. A calender roll is engraved with a series of fine lines, about 250 per inch and at an angle of about 20 degrees to the fabric construction. The finish produces a soft luster on cotton and linen fabrics and an opaque finish on nylon and polyester tricot knits.

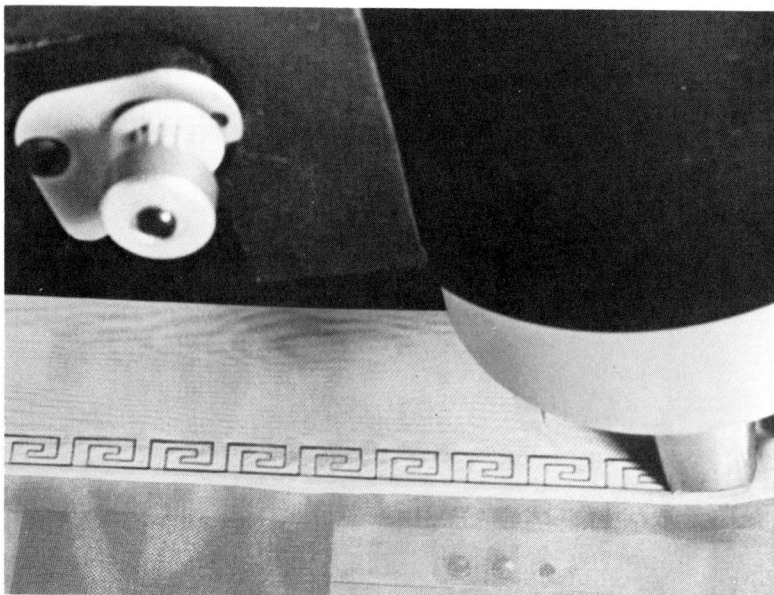

Figure 6-12 Detail shows 100 percent polyester curtain material as it is simultaneously seamed, decorated, and colored with ultrasonics and Swift sonic foil. Material can also be cut in conjunction with this operation by adding a cutting wheel. The stitch pattern is provided by an anvil or stitching wheel whose circumference is machined in the desired design. (Courtesy: Branson Souri Parver Company)

TRANSPARENT FINISHES AND DESIGNS

To produce a transparent finish or design on cotton fabrics, such as organdy, the fabric is immersed in a sulfuric acid solution under controlled conditions and then quickly neutralized. This can be done to the entire fabric to make it transparent. To make designs, the fabric surface is first printed with an acid-resistant substance and then treated as outlined above. Designs can be developed to have transparency or opaqueness.

LEARNING EXPERIENCES

1. Mount fabric swatches with embossed designs. Describe the fiber content, weave construction, and method of making the design. Can you predict performance based on this information?

2. Mount a fabric swatch that illustrates the two methods of making a flocked design. List the variable of production that influences performances of the flocked designs that we wear and care for.

3. Survey your market and study mail-order catalogs to determine the availability of durable and semidurable glazed chintz. Compare claims in relation to cost and recommended care procedures.

4. Assemble garments and accessories or illustrations of hand-painted designs. Determine if they are washable or dry-cleanable.

5. Assemble examples or photos of pleated fabrics. Classify them as to method of pleating. List the variables that determine performance of pleated fabrics in wear and care.

6. Place a sample of a laundered, lightweight cotton fabric on paper toweling. Immerse a glass rod in sodium hydroxide solution. Make dots or stripes on the swatch. Allow to dry. Observe and record results. Relate the experiment to the method of printing. (*Caution*. DO NOT SPILL THE SODIUM HYDROXIDE ON SURROUNDING SURFACE OR ON YOUR SKIN.)

7. Place a sample of a laundered, lightweight cotton fabric in a beaker or glass containing a sulfuric acid solution. When you observe a change in appearance, quickly remove the sample with a pair of tweezers and plunge into a glass of water to rinse it. Dry. Observe and record results. Relate the experience to a method of design application. (*Caution*. DO NOT SPILL THE SULFURIC ACID ON THE SURROUNDING SURFACE OR ON YOUR SKIN.)

7

HOW FABRICS RECEIVE COLOR—DYEING AND PRINTING

It is most difficult for the consumer or retailer to get information on the performance of colorfastness properties of modern fabrics. Colors are generally considered fast when they resist the deteriorating influences to which they are subjected in use and care. This does not mean that tests are not available for testing colorfastness properties. Nor does it mean that manufacturers do not test for colorfastness (many do), but the information is not usually conveyed to consumers on hangtags or labels.

The American Dye Manufacturers Institute, Inc., is an association of manufacturers of dyes and pigments. The dye industry has been the main force behind the increased use of color in every facet of our lives. Their program includes testing and quality control programs as well as working with governmental agencies and educational and other groups.

The American Association of Textile Chemists and Colorists (AATCC), through its numerous technical committees, has developed 41 laboratory test procedures that indicate the fastness of colors and predict their performance in end use to 18 different manufacturing, wear, and care conditions. The details of the test methods are published in the Technical Manual of the American Association of Textile Chemists and Colorists.

WHAT IS GOOD COLORFASTNESS?

All dyes and prints do not have the same degree of colorfastness. Some may have good colorfastness, others fair, and still others poor. Good colorfastness means that a dyestuff or pigment will retain its original color with conditions of wear or use, cleaning or washing, and storage.

The type of fabric selected and the purpose for which it will be used will determine the degree of colorfastness desired in a fabric. For example, the best colorfastness properties for an eveningwear garment might not be necessary. However, in an active sportswear garment, good colorfastness properties are a necessity.

FACTORS THAT INFLUENCE COLORFASTNESS

Many factors influence the fastness of the dyes and pigments used today. Perhaps the factor of greatest importance is the interest of the manufacturer in the selection and application of the color to the fabric. Dyeing and printing involves complex technology that is of great concern to the manufacturer but that seldom enters the mind of the average consumer. Yet it is very important to develop an understanding of the factors that affect performance in wear, use, and care.

The variables in color application to fabrics are:

1. *The chemical structure of the fiber.* Dyes that work satisfactorily on protein fibers such as silk and wool are not effective on cellulosic fibers. Most dyes that work satisfactorily on silk, wool, cotton, and rayon are not effective on man-made fibers (see Table 7-1).

Table 7-1   Fiber Content — Dye Classification.

	Classes of Dyestuffs Predominantly Used
Acetate	Disperse dyes
Acrylic	Basic dyes
Acrylic	(modified)-Acid dyes
Cotton	Direct dyes, sulphur, azoic, vat, reactive
Linen	Same as cotton
Nylon	Acid dyes
Nylon	(modified)-Basic dyes
Polyester	Dispersed dyes
Polyester	(modified)-Basic and dispersed dyes
Rayon	Direct dyes
Rayon	(modified)-Acid dyes
Silk	Acid, direct, reactive
Wool	Acid

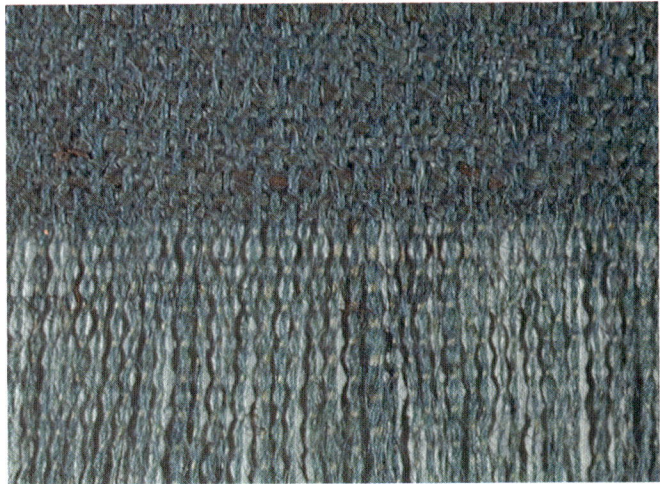

Figure 1-4. When unravelling burlap fabric, it will be noted that at the point where the crosswise yarn goes over or under a lengthwise yarn, light areas appear. This indicates poor dye penetration.

Analogous or Related Harmony

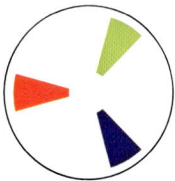

Triad Harmony

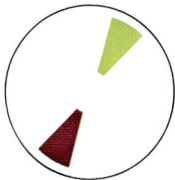

Complementary or Opposite Harmony

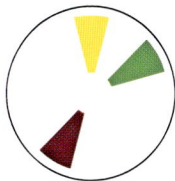

Split Complementary Harmony

575 nm
YELLOW

YELLOW-ORANGE

YELLOW-GREEN

600 nm
ORANGE

500 nm
GREEN

RED-ORANGE

BLUE-GREEN

700 nm
RED

475 nm
BLUE

RED-VIOLET

BLUE-VIOLET

VIOLET
400 nm

Figure 1-13. *Analogous or Related Harmony* uses any three adjoining colors on the wheel. They flow and blend together. *Triad Harmony* consists of any three colors equally spaced on the color wheel. *Complementary or Opposite Harmony* utilized opposite colors on the wheel for a most dramatic and contrasting effect. *Split Complementary Harmony* is a variation of opposite harmony. Instead of the true complementary being used, the colors on either side of the complementary colors are introduced. *(Courtesy: Pittsburgh Paints)*

Figure 6-6. The applied surface designs of sequins lost their color in dry cleaning. Note the contrast in the shirt with the design of the trousers. *(Courtesy: International Fabricare Institute)*

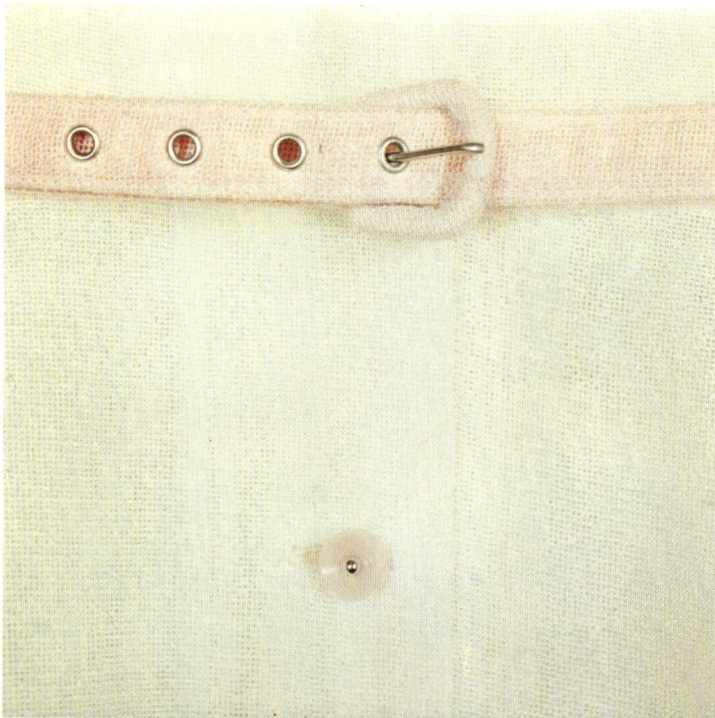

Figure 7-1. The pink dye used to color this fabric was completely solvent-soluble. The belt, which was not dry-cleaned, is the original color of the fabric.

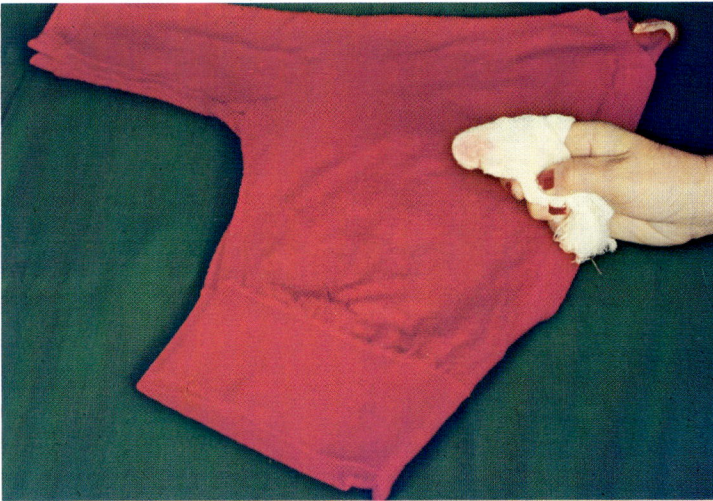

Figure 7-2. Crocking of dye may usually be determined by a simple test. Moisten a piece of cheesecloth with solvent. Rub over the colored fabric. Any transfer of dye to the white cloth indicates crocking. The same test can be made using water instead of solvent.

Figure 7-3. The original blue color of this printed fabric is shown in the area of the opened pleats. This area was protected from light. The unprotected areas of the garment faded.

Figure 7-4. Note that this fabric has weakened only in the yellow areas. The yellow dye has accelerated the sunlight's tendering action on the fabric.

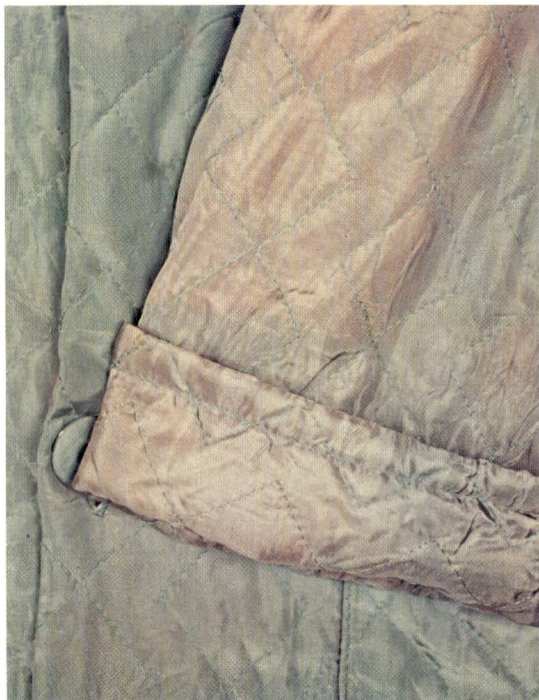

Figure 7-5. (above left) The pink discoloration of the sleeve of this blue quilted robe is typical of the color change that occurs in dyes sensitive to certain gases generally present in the atmosphere. These gases come from the burning of coal, oil, and gas. The color change is called "fume fading," "gas fading," or "atmospheric gas fading."

Figure 7-6. (above right) A dress made from two different lots of fabric. The original color of the dress was melon. The yellow component of the dye was removed in cleaning, leaving the skirt a pink color.

Figure 7-7. (right) Loss of color from cold wave solutions may not be noted on a fabric at the time of contact. Color loss may develop several months later.

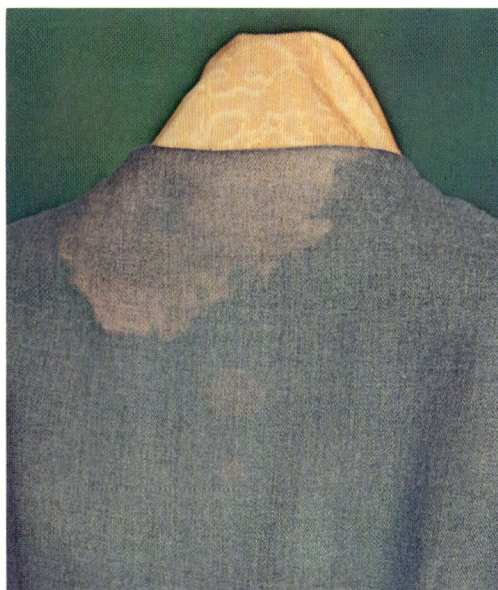

Figure 7-8. (above) Shown is a dyeing machine, in which packages of yarn are dyed at high temperatures under pressure. These machines have capacities up to 2000 pounds with a dyeing cycle of 2+05 hours (depending on yarn type, color, procedure, etc.). *(Courtesy: National Spinning Company, Inc.)*

Figure 7-9. (left) The men are examining skeins of yarn at the dryer that were dyed in the kettles in the foreground. Dyeing is accomplished by controlled circulation of the dye bath around the skeins hanging therein. Drying eliminates moisture and plumps the yarn. *(Courtesy: National Spinning Company, Inc.)*

Figure 7-11. (*a* and *b*) (above) Commercial batiks are usually blue, but some are available in browns or greens as well. *(Courtesy: Ameritex)*

Figure 7-12. (right) A Pantograph operator transfers a pattern from an etched zinc plate to a coated copper roll, which is then acid etched for roller printing. *(Courtesy: Arnold Print Works, Inc.)*

Figure 7-14. (left) Flat bed screen printing. *(Reproduced by courtesy of American Association of Textile Chemists and Colorists)*

Figure 7-15. (below) Rotary screen printing. *(Reproduced by courtesy of American Association of Textile Chemists and Colorists)*

Figure 7-16. (right) Many screen prints clean satisfactorily. However, the original color of this screen-printed fabric was lost in the first dry cleaning. (Left) Original color. (Right) After dry cleaning.

Figure 7-20. (below) To celebrate the Bicentennial, Riverdale Fabrics, inspired by the Grandma Moses paintings, translated three of her most popular early New England farm scenes onto fabric. *Early Springtime* shows a New England farm, the snow still on the roofs of outbuildings and trees, but now in patches on the ground. A happy wagonload of people is pulling into the barnyard, passing a flock of geese, farmers going about their chores, children at play, and meandering livestock. Bright, gay graphic vistas . . . perfect for draperies, bedspreads, upholstery, slipcovers, and pillows. Fifty percent polyester and 50 percent cotton, with Scotchgard-Plus finish. Copyright: Grandma Moses Properties, Inc., N.Y. *(Courtesy: Riverdale Fabrics)*

2. *The chemical structure of the dye or pigment.* The dye or pigment must have a chemical structure so that it can be applied to the fabric and reflect light.

3. *The addition of chemical additives or substances that aid in the dyeing or printing of the fabric.* Oxidizing and reducing agents can regulate the amount of oxygen that is needed to produce color. Exhausting agents can be added to a dye bath to slow down the dye take-up of the fabric, and swelling agents are used with polyester to help it take up the dye. These help to produce a uniform color.

4. *Variation of methods and techniques of color application.* There are many methods and techniques used to "fix" colors to make them permanent. Each process has a technical name such as mordanting, diazotizing, developing, and aftertreating.

COLOR IN CONSUMER USE

All fabrics must be cleaned by one method or another. Fabrics are thought of as being washable or dry-cleanable or both. Methods of washing and dry cleaning vary, so dyes and pigments must be chosen with this in mind. For example, delicate fabrics that require hand washing may be dyed with colors that will withstand warm water and a mild detergent, while an active sportswear fabric requires a more rigorous washing procedure; therefore the fabrics must be dyed with colors that withstand hot water, detergent and, in some cases, bleach. Colorfastness to acids and alkalies is important in fabrics such as those used for industrial uniforms, which are sent to commercial launderies.

Colorfastness properties closely related to care practices include resistance to bleeding in laundering, dry cleaning, ironing, or pressing (see Figure 7-1 in color section). Another consideration is the colorfastness of a fabric to the usual methods used in spot and stain removal. Steam used in pleating fabrics can cause some colors to change.

Colorfastness to perspiration, deodorants, and antiperspirants is an important consideration in wearing apparel. Perspiration is acid when it is first given off by the body. With decomposition by the bacteria, it becomes alkaline.

The greater the alkalinity (the greater the decomposition of perspiration), the greater and quicker the fabric damage.

Contaminated perspiration or normal perspiration, besides producing strong odors, causes fabrics to rot and lose strength. Color and finish of fabrics may also be affected.

Equally important is colorfastness to crocking or rubbing off of color. This property is desirable in wearing apparel and slipcover and upholstery fabrics. If a fabric crocks in wear and use, it will continue to crock even after laundering or dry cleaning (see Figure 7-2 in color section).

Colorfastness to light is expected from all fabrics but is most important in home decorator fabrics — curtains, drapes, upholstery, slipcovers, and rugs (see Figures 7-3 and 7-4 in color section). Several additional factors affect colorfastness to light: (1) source — daylight, incandescent, fluorescent; (2) type — direct, indirect; and (3) spectrum — ultraviolet content plus temperature and humidity. The majority of colors become lighter in hue when exposed to light. Some become darker in hue. The Fade-Ometer is a standardized testing device used to measure colorfastness of fabrics.

Few realize that air contaminants or heat can cause some colors to change. For example, heat can cause vaporization of dyes that may condense in other cooler parts of the fabric; this is called dye sublimation. Oxides of nitrogen in the atmosphere, produced by the combustion of gasoline, coal gas, or oil burners, may cause colors to change; this is called fume fading or gas fading. Ozone in the atmosphere is sometimes responsible for colors changing.

A blue may turn to pink, a brown to red, a purple to pink, a green to yellow, and a gray to pink. Or there may be a change in intensity — a dark blue may turn to a light blue or a dark green to a light green. Articles do not always fume fade evenly. Garments fade most noticeably over the shoulders, down the length of the sleeves, and in lengthwise streaks along the sides of the skirt. Draperies may fade along the folds (see Figure 7-5 in color section).

Bathing suits may change color because of salt water or chlorine-treated water. Even clothing that is exposed to an ocean spray may change color.

Some systems of printing may cause consumer complaints, but great improvements have been made in many cases. Some pigment prints dry-clean satisfactorily, others wash and wet-clean satisfactorily, and still others are unsatisfactory in either. Performance of pigment prints in wear and cleaning depends on fiber content, construction of the fabric, type of binder used to carry the pigment, type of pigment, and the condition of "curing" after printing. Some pigments used to make these prints are solvent-soluble; therefore they are affected by dry-side spotting agents required to remove many types of spots and stains.

Some of the binders used to make pigment prints are affected by light, and it is thought that this affects their colorfastness to dry cleaning and wet cleaning (see Figure 7-6 in color section).

Carelessness during wear may cause color change in garments. For example, Cold wave solutions damage or change the color of many dyestuffs (see Figure 7-7 in color section).

Perfume applied directly to clothing may result in dye rings, color removal in the fabric, a resinous stain that cannot be removed, or a disagreeable odor upon aging after storage of the fabric. Modern perfumes are so manufactured that the odor lingers for a long period. When they are applied to fabrics, the odor may not disappear from a garment even after dry cleaning.

CLASSIFICATION OF DYES

Dyestuff chemists say there are as many as 4000 different dyes or combination of dyes being made and used today. They may be classified as to origin, chemical composition, method of application to fibers or fabric, and nature of the reaction necessary to produce color.

Dyestuffs classified according to origin are either natural or synthetic. Before 1856, there were only natural dyestuffs. These included coloring matter derived from insects, plant life, shellfish, and minerals. Some students of the arts and crafts still use these materials to achieve the color effects they desire.

In 1856, Henry Perkins, an undergraduate student, discovered how to make mauve from coal tar; this was the beginning of synthetic dyestuffs and, incidentally, the start of the petrochemical industry.

CHEMICAL CLASSIFICATION

Modern chemical dyes change constantly to meet the demands of new textile technology.

ACID DYES (ANIONIC)

The acid dyes form a very large and important group of dyestuffs. The dyes are derived from organic acids; therefore they are usually applied as solutions in acetic, formic, or sulfuric acids.

Acid dyes are used for dyeing wool, silk, nylon, acrylic, and some modified polyester, spandex, polypropylene, and olefin fibers.

However, performance of acid dyes are unpredictable; some possess excellent colorfastness to light, while others are fugitive, and their performance to washing, dry cleaning, and perspiration varies.

Colorfastness of acid dyes may be improved by adding metallic salts such as chromium, aluminum, cobalt, nickel, and copper in an aftertreatment, and they are called metallized dyes. The addition of those metallic salts improves colorfastness performance to laundering, dry cleaning, and light.

BASIC DYES (CATIONIC)

Basic dyes were the first synthetic dyes made of coal tar derivatives. Today, they are being used successfully with some of the newer man-made fibers.

Basic dyes are derived from an organic base, hence the name basic. Their wide use is attributed to their low cost.

Basic dyes with a mordant such as tannic acid are used to dye acrylics, modified nylon, and polyester. They are also used to dye basic-dyeable variants of nylon and polyester. Basic dyes are used to dye hemp, jute, and the like, because the dyes are cheap.

DIRECT DYES; SUBSTANTIVE DYES

Direct dyes are water-soluble dyes and are applied directly without the use of a mordant or binding agent. They comprise the largest group of commercial dyes used, because they are easy to use and they are relatively inexpensive.

Direct dyes can be used on cotton, linen, rayon, wool, silk, and nylon. The colors are not as brilliant as those of basic dyes, but they have good colorfastness to light. Unless treated with finishing compounds, they possess poor colorfastness to washing. Colorfastness of direct dyes can be improved by aftertreatments (diazotized and developed). Although these treatments give very good colorfastness to washing, they result in poor colorfastness to light.

AZOIC DYES; NAPHTHOL DYES

Azoic dyes, also called Naphthol dyes, are developed in the fiber by applying two chemicals (both colorless) successively. The two chemicals react to form the finished color. These dyes are used mainly on cellulose, but also on nylon, acrylic, polyester, and polypropylene.

The azoic dyes are used primarily for bright red shades (most other classes of fast dyes lack good red dyes), and they have good colorfastness to laundering, alkalies, bleaching, and light. However, azoic dyes have certain disadvantages: poor colorfastness to crocking or rubbing and a tendency to bleed in dry-cleaning solvents.

VAT DYES

Vat colors are reduced chemically in an alkaline solution to a soluble substance that is not the same color as the original dye. The soluble substance is reoxidized after being absorbed in the fiber and reverts back to its original color, which is insoluble and therefore gives very good colorfastness performance to laundering. Vat dyes are used on cotton, linen, rayon, and nylon.

Research studies have shown that indirect and direct rays of sunlight can cause holes in fabrics printed or dyed with a certain yellow vat dye. Sunlight, plus moisture present in the fabric and atmosphere, causes formation of hydrogen peroxide, which weakens the fabric in the printed area and results in hole formation.

These weakened areas may not always be visible before washing or cleaning, but the mechanical action causes the weakened yarns to break. This type of damage is most common in fabrics made entirely or in part of cotton, rayon, silk, and nylon. Nylon and silk are more quickly affected than rayon and cotton. Silk is more quickly affected than nylon.

SULPHUR DYES

Sulphur dyes are used on cotton, linen, and rayon. Colors from sulphur dyes are not very bright and have poor resistance to sunlight, but they have excellent resistance to washing. If not neutralized with alkalies, the acid formed can cause the fabric to become weak and tender.

REACTIVE DYES

Reactive means what the term implies. The dyes react chemically with cotton, linen, wool, silk, rayon, nylon, and acrylics to produce bright colors. Reactive dyes have very good colorfastness to laundering and dry cleaning, but they can be damaged by chlorine bleach. They have good colorfastness to crocking or rubbing off, and they are resistant to fume or gas fading.

An entire spectrum of colors is available in this class of dyes, and they can be used for dyeing and printing by a variety of methods.

DISPERSED DYES (ACETATE)

The poor affinity of acetate for most dyes used for cottons and rayons was a great problem to the dye industry. After much experimentation, it was found that acetate could be dyed with dispersed dyes. This group includes certain insoluble azo dyes or anthraquinone vat dyes kept in a colloidal suspension by sulfonated oils or soaps. They are dispersed during dyeing in a mildly alkaline solution and absorbed by the fiber.

It is now possible to dye acetates, nylons, acrylics, and polyesters in a range of colors with good fastness to light, laundering, dry cleaning, and perspiration. There is not, however, the wide range of colors in this class with superior fastness that is found in vat dyes. Some colors in this class of dyes possess poor colorfastness to fume or gas fading. Classes of dyestuffs predominantly used for specific generic fiber classifications are given in Table 7-1.

METHODS OF DYEING

Synthetic dyestuffs used today and their application is a complex technology. The discussion that follows is presented to develop an understanding of dyeing modern fabrics.

There are five basic methods of dyeing fabrics determined by the various states of textile production. They are: stock or fiber dyeing; top dyeing; solution dyeing; yarn dyeing; and piece dyeing.

STOCK OR FIBER DYEING

In this method, natural fibers are dyed before they are spun or blended into a yarn and then woven into a fabric. Modern stock or fiber dyeing machines generally involve the principle of a rotary drum holding the fibers and turning them in a bath of dye. Some methods keep the fibers stationary and circulate the dye liquid with precision pumps. Baths provide uniform dyeing of the fiber. Fiber dyeing is used to produce mixtures and heathered effects in fabrics.

TOP DYEING

This method of dyeing is applied to wool that is combed into slivers and wound into cheese-shaped tops. The tops are placed in a can that fits into a tank, and the dye solution is pumped through the cans. After dyeing, different colored tops may be blended together to produce special color effects in yarns and fabrics.

SOLUTION DYEING

Man-made fibers may be colored as chemically spun to give colored fibers with remarkable resistance to fading when exposed to sunlight, salt water, perspiration, soot, washing, and weathering. The dye is added to the spinning solution before it is extruded, and the color becomes a part of the fiber. When a reduced luster is desired in man-made fibers that have a high natural luster, dulling agents may be added to the fiber-forming substance before spinning. Fibers that have dye added before spinning may also be called "spun-dyed" or "dope-dyed." The advantages of solution dyeing is color uniformity and good color-fastness properties. The disadvantage is limited color range.

YARN DYEING

Different methods are used to dye yarns.

1. Yarn is wound onto a wheel to form skeins (called skein dyeing) for dyeing.
2. Yarn is wound onto a perforated spool (package method), and dye is forced through it in and out (see Figures 7-8 and 7-9 in color section).
3. Yarn is wound onto a perforated warp beam, and dye is forced through the beams.

Yarn dyeing makes possible the construction of yarn-dyed fabrics such as checks, plaids, stripes, or herringbone. The use of one colored yarn in the warp or lengthwise direction of a fabric and another colored yarn in the crosswise direction produces a changeable or irridescent effect.

SPACE DYEING

Space dyeing, a form of yarn dyeing, is a term used for the dyeing of yarns at intervals spaced along the length of the yarn. The use of space-dyed yarns in the warp or filling of a fabric can produce interesting and unusual effects. Modern processing methods can achieve complete dye penetration, fast color, and washability, whether applied to coarse or finely twisted yarns. The effect achieved is comparable to warp printing.

OMBRÉ DYEING

Ombré means shaded in French. A shaded or graduated color effect may be made either by dyeing, printing, or weaving. One color may range from a dark shade to a light shade across the width of the fabric; or the selvage edges of the fabric may be a dark shade ranging to a very light shade in the center of the fabric. In weaving or printing more than one color may be used, but shading ranges from light to dark shades, giving a striped effect.

PIECE DYEING

Dyeing a fabric in the piece after it has been woven or knitted is the most common method in use today because it is economical. It is a preferred method because:

1. Converters do not have to commit themselves to big yardages as in yarn-dyed fabrics.
2. There is more flexibility to fashion changes in color.

Piece-Dyeing Classifications

Union-dyed fabrics are woven of two or more fibers and yarns. Dyeing is done in one bath, and the identical color is implanted uniformly to all fibers.

Cross dyeing is based on the different reactions of two or more fibers to the same dye. For example, a dyer may take a fabric made of rayon and acetate and put in a blue dye. The acetate may pick up the blue dye, and the rayon remains white. The fabric may be passed through a second dye bath (e.g., red). The rayon absorbs the red dye, while the acetate remains blue. The result would be a red and blue pattern without yarn dyeing. Cross dyeing may also be used to achieve more than one color effect from a single dye bath (see Figure 7-10).

POLYCHROMATIC DYEING

Polychromatic dyeing is a new dye technique whereby a variety of colorful patterns may be made on a fabric. There are two methods used: the flow-form method and the dry-weave method.

In the flow-form method, different colored dye solutions flow directly onto a moving fabric and are then crossed with other colors, thus developing the design; the strength of the dye solutions, positioning of or flow duration fiber-to-dye exposure, and fabric movement determine the final pattern on the fabric. In the dye-weave method, the colored dye solutions run down an inclined plane instead of running directly onto the surface of the moving fabric, and some dye mixing on the inclined plane can be arranged for.

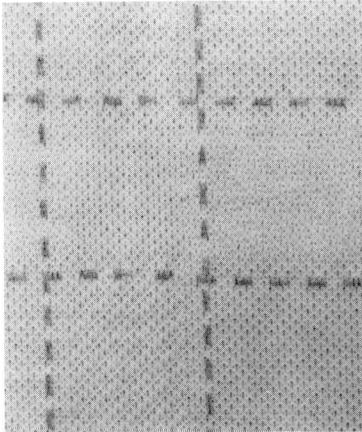

UNDYED GREY GOODS
WHITE: Type 610. Disperse.
WHITE: Type 640. Cationic.
BOX: Type 671 (B). B/W Heather.

WHITE: Type 610. Disperse.
BLUE: Type 640. Cationic.
BOX: Type 671 (B). B/W Heather.
DYE: Cationic Blue only.

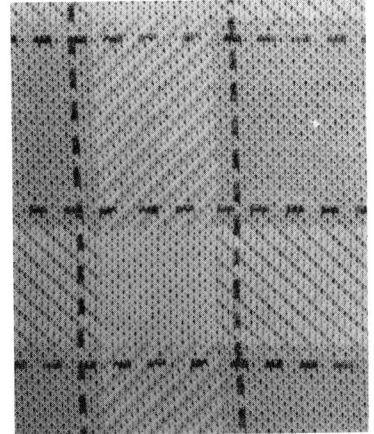

LT. GREEN: Type 610. Disperse.
GREEN: Type 640. Cationic.
BOX: Type 671 (B). B/W Heather.
DYE: Disperse Green only.

GREEN: Type 610. Disperse.
BLUE: Type 640. Cationic.
BOX: Type 671 (B). B/Gr Heather.
DYE: Disperse Green & Cationic Blue.

BLUE: Type 640. Cationic.
HEATHER: Type 674. Contrast Blue/W.
BOX: Type 671 (B). B/W Heather.
DYE: Cationic Blue only.

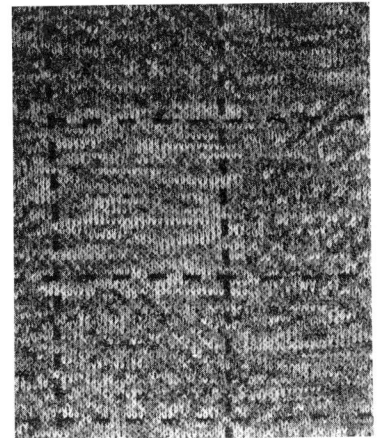

BOX: Type 640. Cationic.
BLUE/WHITE: Type 674.
GREY: Type 671 (B). B/W Heather.
DYE: Cationic Blue only.

Figure 7-10 One fabric—five styling variations produced by piece dyeing. The flexibility of the new Trevira polyester yarn variants is clearly demonstrated in the knits shown. In each of the six swatches, the pattern is the identical three-color jacquard design, made on a 20-cut Moratronik knitting machine. In each, the finish color pattern was developed through piece dyeing. Fabric No. 1 is grey goods. The color differences between fabrics Nos. 2, 3, and 4 were achieved simply by changing the dyestuffs. In fabrics Nos. 5 and 6 a contrast yarn (Type 674) replaced the Disperse yarn (Type 610). Fabric No. 6 has the same ingredients as No. 5, but the yarns are in different positions. The yarn components and dyestuffs used in each case can be readily seen. (Courtesy: Hoechst Fibers, Inc.)

GAS DYE PROCESS

A new method of dyeing may be the answer to the pollution problem from dye factories. The new process developed in Japan may be described as "gasification dyeing because it takes advantage of sublimation of dispersed dyes." The experimental process consists of a tubular circulator containing a dispersed dye and a package of yarns or fabrics and connected to a vacuum pump. The circulator is placed inside an oil bath, and the dispersed dye is gasified by sublimation vacuum evaporation at temperatures of 150 to 200°C in a vacuum and condenses on the yarn or fabric. This method has been used experimentally with success on nylon, polyester, and acrylic fibers; coloration was uniform, and the fabrics exhibited good colorfastness properties.

RESTRICTED DYE APPLICATION

A new method of dyeing developed by the U.S. Department of Agriculture's Southern Regional Research Center makes it possible to dye one side of a cotton fabric one color and the other side an entirely different color. The process, which involves piece dyeing, is said to be another dimension to imparting colors to cotton textiles. One side of the fabric is treated with a modified Wash 'N Wear formulation, then the fabric is dyed with a cotton reactive dye. The dye has no effect on the treated side, but it colors the untreated side. After the dyeing process, the fabric is washed in an acid bath to hydrolize and remove the "resister." The fabric, now free of chemicals and dyed on one side, is dyed again, resulting in a two-colored fabric. Screen printing one side can result in a surface applied design.

CONTINUOUS SOLVENT DYEING

A continuous solvent dyeing system for polyester woven fabrics has been developed by Teijin Ltd., Tokyo. The newly developed method is a closed system in which the solvent is recycled almost permanently and therefore eliminates the problem of pollution. In the new process, a fabric is dyed with a mixture of solvent and disperse dye using superheated steam. Then cleansing is done by trichlorethylene, followed by recovery of solvent and dye for recycling. There are four main advantages of the new system. They are: (1) no water pollution; (2) recovery and recycling of solvent and excess dye; (3) simple operation in changing dyeing colors; and (4) automation in color matching and tone adjustment with the use of a computer system and automatic weighing system.

PRINTING OF TEXTILES

Printing of fabrics has existed from time immemorial — such as the use of wood or metal blocks, and tie and dye resist printing. These were hand methods and production was slow, but they are still used in arts and crafts courses. Handmade Indonesian batiks (usually in 6- or 8-yard lengths) are imported, but the commercial batik is preferred for informal women's sportswear, men's evening jackets, and home decorating (see Figure 7-11 in color section).

ROLLER PRINTING (DIRECT PRINT)

Roller printing has been so perfected and mechanized that modern machinery can produce printed fabrics in as many as 16 colors at a rate of up to 200 yards a minute (see Figure 7-12 in color section and Figure 7-13). In roller printing, the design is engraved on a metal roll. Each color of the design is on a separate roll. Areas of the design that are not to be used to produce color are coated with a chemical resist print, and the roll is dipped into an acid bath that etches out the areas not coated. The coating is then removed and the roller polished.

The engraved rolls (as many as 16) are placed and locked into position around the padded main cylinder of the printing machine. Each roller passes through its own color trough to pick

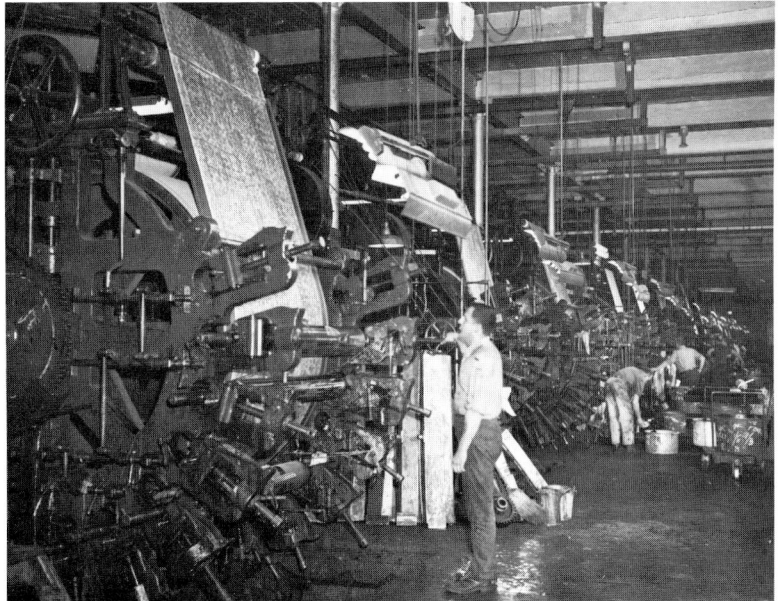

Figure 7-13 Roller print room. These machines are capable of printing a maximum of 14 colors. (Courtesy: Arnold Print Works, Inc.)

up the colored dye, and excess dye is removed from the roller by a "doctor" blade. After the design is printed, the fabric moves through a drying oven. Modern printing machines are controlled electronically to produce even, clear, and matched or in-register color prints.

VARIATIONS IN DIRECT PRINTING

Discharge Printing

It is a method by which some of the dye of the base of background fabric is removed, thus creating a white design on a colored fabric. Another dye may be applied at the same time the original dye is removed.

Duplex Printing

This is a method of printing the same design on the face and back of the fabric in two distinct operations to achieve the effect of a woven fabric design.

Pigment Printing

Pigment printing is a method of roller printing in which an insoluble pigment is mixed with a resin binder and thickener to form a printing paste. The printed fabric is treated at high temperature to cure the resin binder, and the print is difficult to distinguish from designs made by a roller printing method using dye pastes. A variety of attractive designs may be applied to nearly every fabric construction made of cotton, rayon, acetate, or combinations of these fibers.

Photographic Prints

These prints are made by using photoengraved rollers whereby photographic effects are transferred to the fabric. Several different processes are in use. Many colors can be obtained by using the three primary colors: red, blue, and yellow.

Resist Prints

A design is printed on a white or light-colored fabric with a chemical that resists dye. Then the fabric is piece-dyed. The "resisted" patterns stay uncolored against a colored background, and the fabric may then be direct-printed to insert colors in the uncolored areas.

Warp Prints

Warp yarns are printed after they have been set up on the warp beam of the loom. The printed warp yarns are woven with a plain, colored filling yarn. A soft, indistinct, shadowy or muted design is achieved.

SCREEN PRINTING

Screen printing is an ancient art but, because of low productivity, hand screen printing is used today in only a limited way for making scarfs, towels, and other small items. However, screen printing has been mechanized. Flat bed screen printing and rotary screen printing are shown in Figures 7-14 and 7-15 (in color section).

Rotary Screen Printing

Automatic rotary screen printing combines some of the advantages of both roller printing and screen printing. The rotary screens, which are made from metal foil instead of fabric, are extremely lightweight, considerably less costly than copper rollers, usable for small or large repeat patterns, and are able to achieve a color depth associated with flat screens.

Rotary screen printing is continuous, and its rate of production is higher than that attained by the flat screen method, which necessitates stopping and starting again at intervals. Rotary screen printing does not achieve the production speed of roller printing, but the downtime during pattern changeover is less than that for roller printing.

Both the rotary screen printing and flat bed screen printing are similar in that the fabric is fed into a conveyor belt where it is run under the cylinder screens — one for each color — before being fed into a dryer.

Screen prints show variable performance in both laundering and dry cleaning. Some pigments are removed in cleaning (see Figure 7-16 in color section).

HEAT TRANSFER PRINTING

A dry printing process was introduced to this country in 1968. Today there are seven major companies doing heat transfer printing. By 1980 it is predicted that 600 million yards of fabric will be printed by this method. It is a system of printing whereby dyes sublime from paper and transfer to fabric by vaporization achieved by rolling the paper and fabric together under high heat (200°C) and pressure for a few seconds. After printing, no subsequent treatment of the fabric, such as scouring or steaming, is required (see Figure 7-17 and 7-18).

The main advantages of heat transfer printing are:

1. Better registration and clarity of design because the print goes directly down onto the fabric, line for line, color for color, pattern for pattern.
2. Rapid adaptation of design in any size or color, faster than any other printing process, to meet quick changes in fashion.
3. Easier handling of knits to achieve registered prints.
4. Marked savings in production because of quick training of operators and lower labor costs.
5. Saving of time in printing (1 percent compared to 8 to 12 percent in rotary screen or roller printing).

Roller or rotary screen printing cannot achieve clarity and sharpness of design because of wicking of paste into the fabric. Other methods require many steps: printing, drying, steaming, scouring, drying, and rolling for shipping. These methods also require four people per unit as against one person per unit by the heat transfer method.

Figure 7-17 Printing of fabric by the heat-transfer process. (Courtesy: Sublistatic Corporation of America)

Fabric   Finished fabric

Printed paper   Waste paper

Figure 7-18 The heat-transfer process transfers the design made on paper to the fabric.

There are some disadvantages to heat transfer printing. The system works well on polyester, nylon, acrylic, triacetate, and high-polyester cotton blends. It does not work well on rayon, acetate, cotton, and wool. It is predicted that in 3 to 5 years cottons will be printed by this method.

Designing is another disadvantage, but this can be overcome by hiring designers or purchasing exclusive designs. Another disadvantage is speed. One can obtain 40 to 42 yards per minute by rotary screen printing and 35 yards per minute by roller printing, as against 10 to 15 yards per minute by heat transfer. Still another big problem is paper disposal.

There are four ways to make heat transfer paper: (1) gravure; (2) offset; (3) flexographic; and (4) converted rotary screen prints. The gravure, utilizing steel or copper cylinders, accounts for 75 percent of the business. Flexographic, which utilizes rubber plates, is used widely in Britain and will no doubt be used in the United States. The most interesting development is the conversion of rotary screen machines to this new printing technique.

The latest development of heat transfer printing includes a single transfer paper that prints solid colors. This method may make inroads into the piece dyeing of fabrics. It is predicted that by 1980 about 20 percent of the printed fabrics will be produced from heat transfer systems.

CYMATIC PRINTING

KBC (Koechlin Baumgartner and Cie AG), a giant textile combine that has been called the General Motors of the European print industry, has developed a process called cymatic printing that catches the oscillations of a musical chord on a quartz plate and photographs the vibrations. The result is a startling group of print patterns of unusual variety and originality. Special colors have been utilized to highlight the fragile beauty of the designs. The new technique makes it possible, for example, to reproduce the vibrations of any particular chord from any particular symphony, thus literally making the music visible.

The cymatic process was the brainchild of Dr. Hans Jenny, who studied natural sciences and medicine and developed a passionate interest in oscillations and photography that ultimately led to the cymatic process. KBC owns exclusive rights to cymatic for the textile field. The initial prints were used on DuPont's Qiana nylon. However, the company now plans to use the prints on fabrics made of other fibers.

People may wonder why cymatic printing has been confined to the Old Masters instead of to chords from the Beatles or the Rolling Stones, who are known for their rock and roll music. Making designs from rock music would pose a problem. In printing with sound, anything is possible, except for the royalties one would have to pay. It is much cheaper to use the Great Masters.

NEW SYSTEMS OF PRINTING

A number of firms experiment and develop new systems of printing. For example, Du Pont introduced Dybln, a colorfast system for polyester/cotton blends. There are three components: (1) a line of new dyes called "Dybln" dyes; (2) special chemicals used in the fixation process, also carrying the "Dybln" trademark; and (3) technology. Both fibers in the blend are dyed with one dye in a single fixation step. In printing, the system's advantages are good colorfastness to washing, abrasion, and frosting.

ART INSPIRES PRINTED DESIGNS

It should be apparent that inspiration for the designs on fabrics is often inspired by art. The study of fabric design is fascinating. An excellent example of art-inspired fabric is shown in Figure 7-19 and Figure 7-20 (in color section).

QUALITY CONTROL OF DYEING

Dyeing of fibers, yarns, and fabrics has become a science. Color matching and color formulation for dyeings may be carried out using an IBM computer system. This system matches the color automatically, giving a choice of alternate dyestuff formulas. It

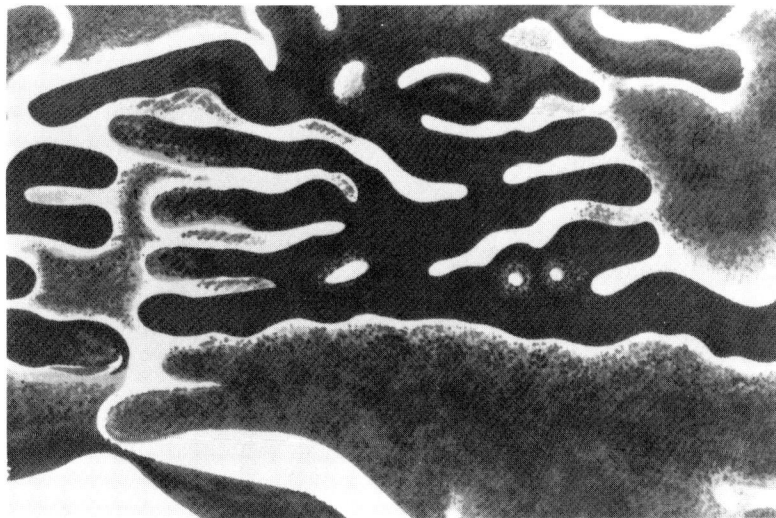

Figure 7-19 Cymatic print. Seventy-fifth bar of the seventh symphony, second movement by Ludwig Van Beethoven. (Courtesy: Stelmar Trading Corporation)

also computes the cost of each formula (often there is a difference of as much as 15 cents per pound of dye between formulas) and indicates how the color match will appear under different lighting. In addition, the computer is doing in minutes a job that used to take a week: the task of going through some 24,000 different samples of dyed yarn in order to find a match.

Basically, the computer matches colors the way an artist does on his pallet, except that it uses numbers to represent colors and makes the calculations in millionths of a second. Since the computer is not color-sensitive, standard dyes and the samples to be matched must be analyzed first by a spectrophotometer. As a prism does with light, the spectrophotometer breaks colors down into their component hues. Recording the hues on a numerical color profile of the sample, the computer then "blends" potential matching formulas from standard dyes in combinations of three or four at a time.

The process uses a bank of information on standard dyes and details any one of these dyes to react with different fibers at different concentration levels. Once the best color match is calculated and tested in the laboratory, the computer documents the formula. The computer also keeps track of the dyestuff inventory.

EVALUATION OF COLORFASTNESS PROPERTIES

Evaluation of colorfastness is carried out by standard test methods developed by the American Association of Textile Chemists and Colorists, which currently has about 40 colorfastness tests that are added to or modified as needed. The AATCC manual, updated and issued annually, gives details of the test methods and how to interpret results. The evaluation ratings are commonly expressed in numbers, but words corresponding to the numbers are also given.

These same words may be used by the consumer to describe colorfastness properties when a color failure is experienced in use, washing, dry cleaning, pressing, spot removal, or storage.

COLOR MEASUREMENT

Colorimeters, Spectrophotometers

Colorimeters and spectrophotometers are two instruments used to measure color of fabrics. Such instruments are no better than trained humans at detecting small color differences, but they are unbiased, untiring, and are not subject to human vagaries. When teamed with today's fast computers, they are invaluable in the dyehouse.

Either instrument can specify a color in three-dimensional color space so that the dyer and color-matching computer know precisely what the target is. The spectrophotometer can also tell the relative contribution made to the total color by each part of the visible spectrum — a very helpful capability when working with new dyes or fabrics.

LEARNING EXPERIENCES

1. List and illustrate the factors that influence colorfastness of fabrics.
2. Demonstrate the effect of perspiration, deodorants, and antiperspirants on colored fabrics.
3. See Figure 7-2. Assemble colored swatches of fabric. Place white cheesecloth over the index finger and rub the fabric surface 10 times. Observe any transfer of color from swatch to cheesecloth. Observe and record results. Repeat with cheesecloth dampened with water. Repeat with cheesecloth dampened with perchlorethylene. Record your results.
4. Explain the colorfastness properties you desire in the following: an evening dress; a sports dress; a bathing suit; a curtain or drapery.
5. Explain the application of color to fabrics by dyeing and by printing with pigments. List the variables that control the performance of pigment printing in wear and use.

6. Explain and illustrate the principles of fluorescent dyes and tints. If a fluorescent white dye changes color, can it be corrected?

7. Explain why it is important to examine an item under different lighting systems as well as daylight. Explain the phenomenon when color differences occur.

8. Why is it necessary to have so many different classes of dyestuffs? Give examples.

9. Explain the difference between piece dyeing and duplex printing. Can you distinguish between the two methods of color application? How is it possible to achieve variation of color and styling in a piece-dyed fabric?

10. Assemble and mount fabric swatches to illustrate direct printing, discharge printing, resist printing, warp printing, and screen printing.

11. Explain the advantages and disadvantages of heat transfer printing. Why is it predicted that this method will make conventional printing methods obsolete?

12. Make a market survey to determine the amount and kind of colorfastness information that the consumer is given on hangtags and labels. Are any guarantees given? Report on your findings.

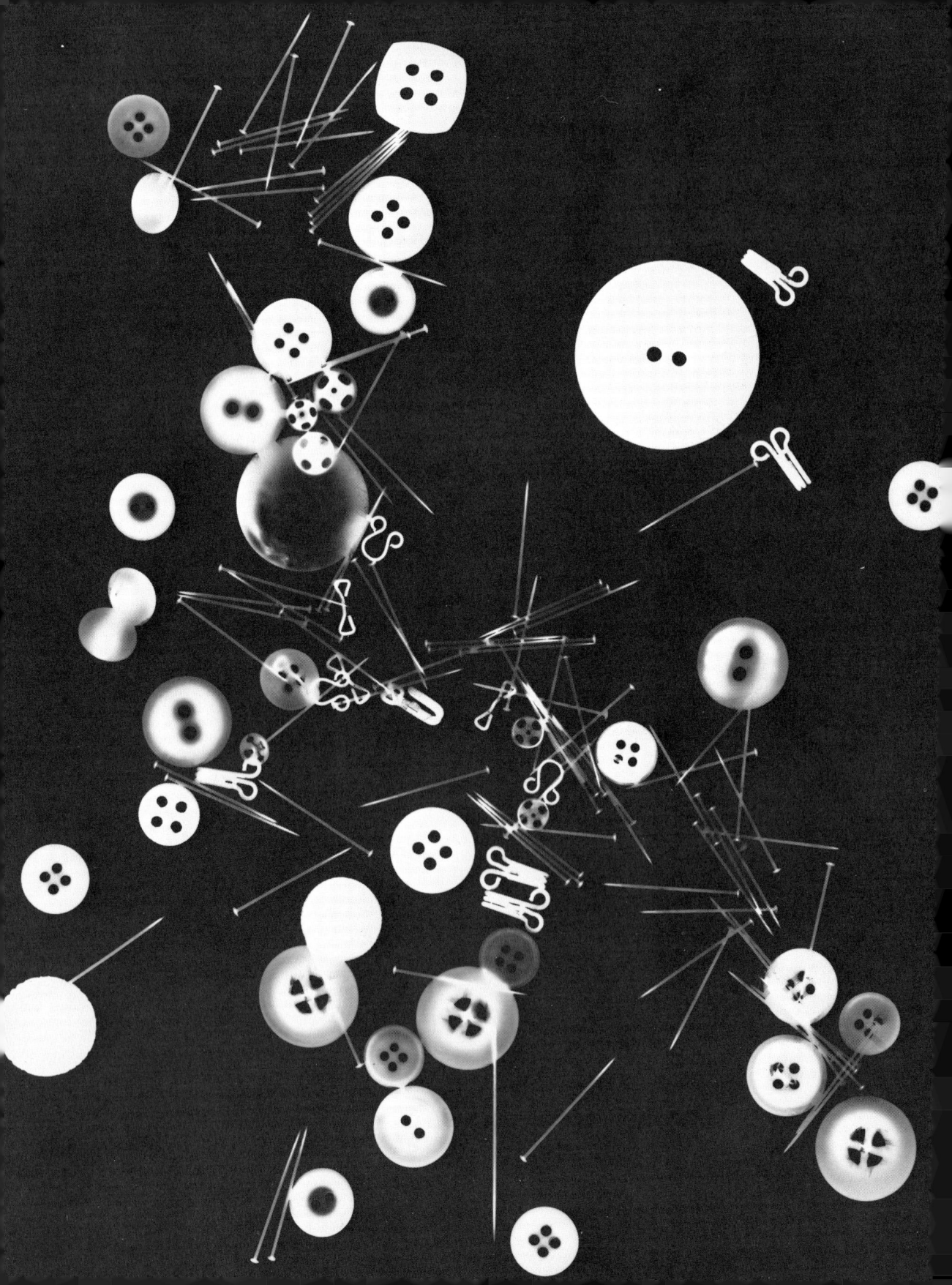

8
COMPONENT PARTS

We are living at a time when all methods and equipment used in the needle trade to make clothing and household items are changing rapidly.

The most recent demands from the apparel industry have been for equipment to deskill production operations and yet offer a degree of flexibility. Industry acceptance of highly sophisticated equipment has been slow, with most activity taking place for less complex automated systems.

Some pioneers, however, have taken the giant step and are ordering items such as numerically controlled sewing machines, fabric transfer systems, computer-operated laser beam fabric-cutting systems, and computerized marker-making systems.

NEW METHODS OF CONSTRUCTION

NEW CUTTING METHOD

Garments can now be individually cut by laser beams far more speedily and accurately than any other method has been able to cut through 100 layers of the same thing. The laser, a pure form of light that is as bright as the center of the sun, burns a line through the fabric sharper than any cut of a knife (see Figure 8-1).

A single layer of material is unrolled from a bolt and moved along a conveyor until it is directly under the positioning device. Turned on by a computer, the laser's beam — but not the laser itself, which is stationary — is automatically directed to follow the pattern lines as stored in the computer.

The concept of cutting one layer of fabric at a time instead of many layers is a revolutionary change in the established methods

315

Figure 8-1 The laser beam burns through one layer of fabric at 40 inches per second, directed by computers. (Courtesy: Genesco)

of apparel production. It means that any size, model, or type of garment, in any ordered sequence or quantity, can be cut, one at a time, with efficiencies and economies matching those of multiple-layer cutting.

STITCHLESS SEWING (JOINING BY FUSION)

Stitchless sewing is the technique used to bond fabric to fabric by heat-sealing alone or heat-sealing in conjunction with an adhesive or heat-sensitive web. Stitchless sewing can be used to make coat fronts, collar linings, facings, cuff bottoms, flap and breast darts, side seams, zipper insertions, welts, hems, appliques, and trim. It is even used for mending. At present it is used in men's and boys' suits, rainwear, and a limited number of ladies' garments (see Figures 8-2 and 8-3).

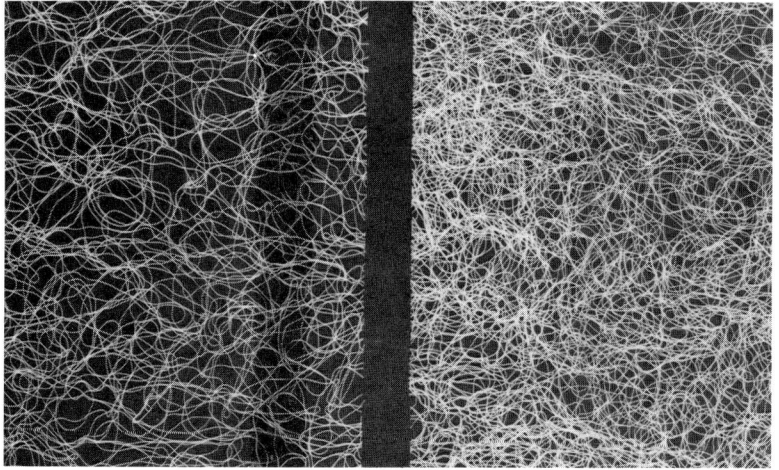

Figure 8-2 A thermoplastic web of fibers is used to join fabric by heat-setting.

Different techniques have been developed by the manufacturers who have pioneered stitchless sewing to production reality. They may be described as follows: (1) fusion is achieved through the use of thermoplastic synthetic fibers, adhesives, powders and, in some cases, with the material itself, which is thermoplastic; and (2) the use of a nonwoven web of 100 percent polyester, which is a hot melt adhesive in fabric form. The strip is inserted between two fabrics or between a doubled fabric and heat applied through usual pressing. The manufacturers who have converted to fusing cite production advantages. One firm in Pennsylvania states it has helped to eliminate 12 to 17 traditional stitching and basting operations in the production of men's and boys' sport coats and suits, but it requires changes in quality control procedures, since the fusing operation must be rigidly controlled.

CONTINUOUS FUSION

The concept of continuous fusing utilizes a conveyor to feed the garment pieces automatically nonstop through the fusing machine. Because the conveyor runs continuously, production is virtually unlimited, depending only on how fast the operators can load and unload the machine (see Figure 8-4).

SONIC SEWING

"Sonic sewing" is a new method used in garment construction and in applying decorative designs to wearing apparel and

Figure 8-3 Some clothing manufacturers are fusing interlinings in coat fronts. Occasionally, the face fabric separates from the lining fabrics. The fabrics cannot be resealed with pressing.

(a)

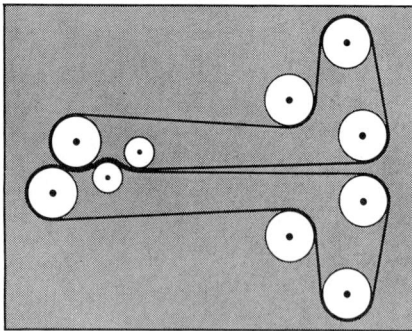

(b)

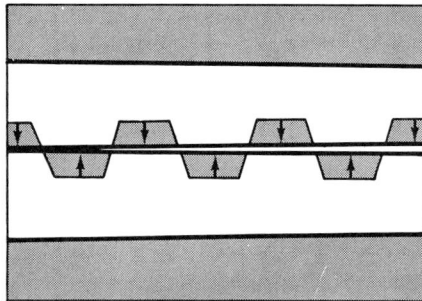

(c)

(d)

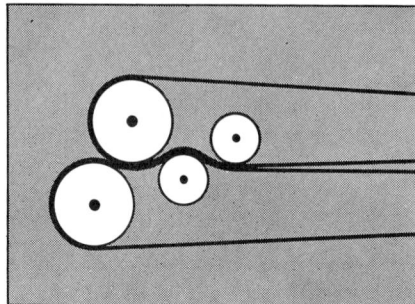

(e)

Figure 8-4 *(a)* Union special—reliant rolamatic continuous fusing system feeds garments through the machine nonstop, resulting in higher production and better quality. *(b)* Garment part is fed between two synchronized conveyor belts. *(c)* Heating modules apply heat evenly from top and bottom. *(d)* Fusing temperature, pressure and time are accurately controlled. *(e)* Two specially designed rollers apply pressure on a continuous line contact basis. (Courtesy: Union Special)

household items. Its use right now is limited, but its existence should be known so that it can be recognized.

Sonic sewing machines can join knitted, woven, and nonwoven synthetic fabrics and thermoplastic film and even blends up to 35 percent natural fibers without the use of needle or thread at rates up to 50 feet per minute (see Figure 8-5). These machines emboss material with decorative patterns and also trim and seal edges simultaneously.

Ultrasonic energy (high-frequency vibrations) is generated and channeled into a sewing tool or horn. When fabric or film is fed between the vibrating horn and a specially designed stitching wheel, frictional heat created by the horn bonds the pattern of the chosen stitching wheel. Wheels are available in a wide variety of patterns (see Figure 8-5).

LININGS, INTERLININGS, INTERFACINGS

LININGS

The outer fabric and the lining fabric must be compatible. If the outer fabric is dimensionally stable to laundering or dry cleaning and the lining fabric shrinks, this causes the outer fabric to pucker; this makes it impossible to finish or press a garment for satisfactory appearance. The reverse is also true. If the outer fabric shrinks and the lining fabric is dimensionally stable, the dress fabric remains smooth, while the lining fabric puckers and sometimes hangs out at the hemline and edge of the sleeves.

Obviously there must not be any difference in shrinkage when two different fabrics are seamed together. If there is, unsightly puckering results. The only way this can be prevented is by the selection of compatible fabrics in garment manufacture.

PRESS-ON LININGS

Composite fabrics consisting of face fabrics with woven, press-on linings are relatively new. They should not be confused with press-on interfacings or the double face fabrics.

The manufacturers of both fabrics and garments with press-on woven linings see two definite advantages: (1) the press-on lining helps to stabilize the fabric against shrinkage or stretching; and (2) the press-on lining fabric serves as a built-in interlining.

Although many of the fabrics and garments clean satisfactorily, there are some instances when consumers have been disappointed because of (1) separation of the press-on lining from the face fabric; (2) seam slippage and pulling away of the press-on

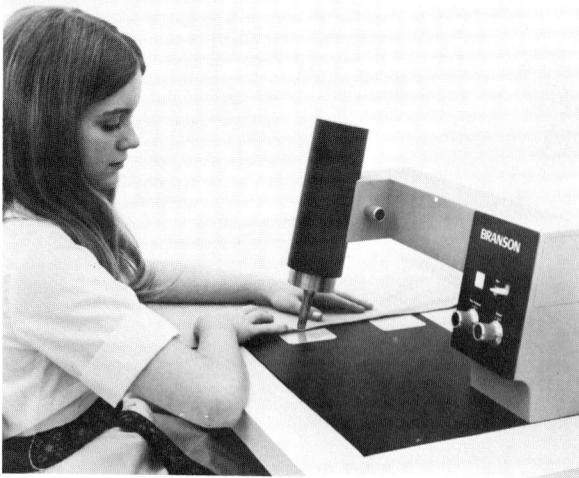

(a) — The Sonic Sewing Machine, developed by Branson Sonic Power Company, Danbury, Connecticut, sews synthetic materials without needle or thread.

(b)

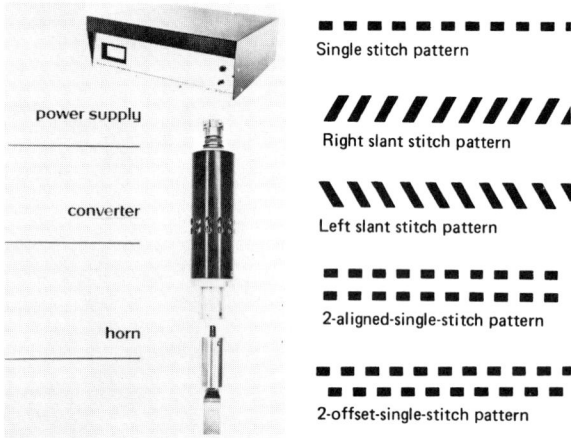

power supply

converter

horn

Single stitch pattern

Right slant stitch pattern

Left slant stitch pattern

2-aligned-single-stitch pattern

2-offset-single-stitch pattern

Blanks may vary in width

Knurled pattern

(c)

Dot stitch pattern

Dot-stitch, single-stitch pattern

Zigzag pattern

Serpentine pattern

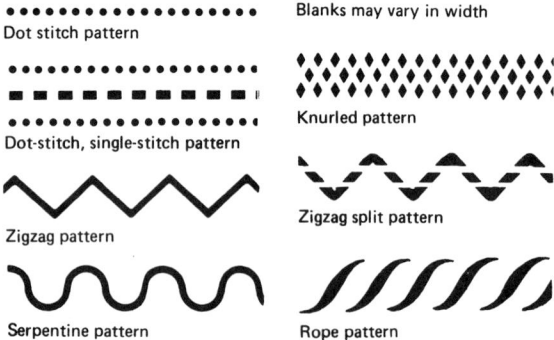

Zigzag split pattern

Rope pattern

Figure 8-5 *(a)* A sonic sewing machine. *(b)* Structural parts of the machine. *(c)* The stitches it can make. (Courtesy: Branson Sonic Power Company)

lining from the seams; and (3) shrinkage in some novelty curl-knitted face fabrics.

INTERLININGS

Interlinings are a necessary portion of garments, since they give support to tailoring details, impart stiffness or body, and enhance the drape of the finished garment. Interlinings are usually of cotton; they may be of canvas, buckram and, in some instances, of coarse materials not unlike burlap. Interlining is usually found in collars, cuffs, facing, or waistbands, and it is usually sewn between the outer fabric and the lining or between two thicknesses of the outer material. It is very important that the interlining is dimensionally stable and have permanent-type finishes and good colorfastness to laundering and dry cleaning. Otherwise a consumer may be dissatisfied when it becomes limp because of loss of finish or loses dye to stain the outer fabric (see Figure 8-6).

PRESS-ON INTERFACINGS

Until 1961, the nonwoven interfacings were cut and sewn into a garment like a woven interfacing. Nonwoven fabrics are now made with an adhesive (thermoplastic resin) on one side that melts with the heat of an iron to form a bond with the outer fabric. A press-on facing eliminates the need for basting or temporary stitching in clothing construction. The adhesive, if not properly formulated and applied to the interfacing, may leach through to the face fabric and stain it (see Figure 8-7).

PRESS-ON BINDING

Press-on bindings are woven edge rayon tapes with a patented heat-activated bonding agent. They may be used for hemming dresses, skirts, trousers, shirts, curtains, and draperies. The manufacturer points out the following advantages for press-on bindings: (1) requires no sewing — hems can be made without a needle or thread merely by applying an iron to the tape and fabric to be hemmed; (2) saves time — hems can be made in 10 minutes with press-on binding instead of the hour or more sewing takes; (3) easy to use — even an inexperienced person, if he knows how to use an iron or pin a hem, can produce a professional-looking hem with a press-on binding; (4) permanent bond — it will withstand dry cleaning and washing; (5) easily removed — when fashion dictates a changing hemline,

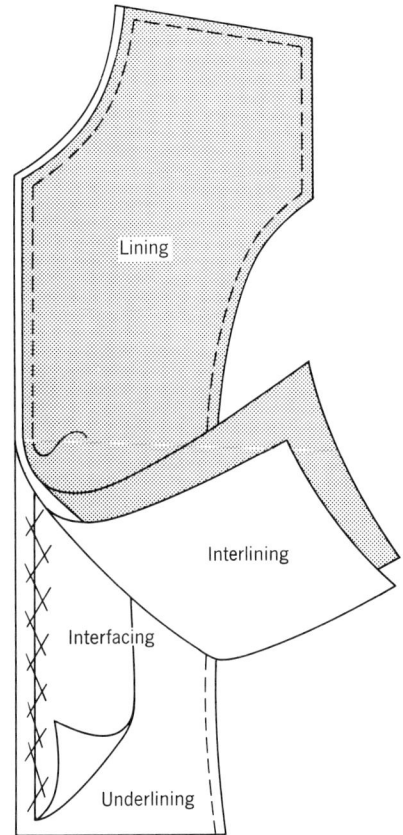

Figure 8-6 Today, manufacturers of wearing apparel are heat-fusing underlinings, interfacings, interlinings, and lining components.

Figure 8-7 The collar on this raincoat is discolored from the nonwoven press-on interfacing. The discoloration looks like mildew staining.

press-on binding can be removed with a heated electric iron; and (6) nonshrink, colorfast — the wide range of available colors are guaranteed to be colorfast and nonshrinkable.

Many press-on bindings will dry-clean satisfactorily. In some cases, there might be a partial or complete separation of the binding from the fabric if the binding has not been properly applied or the bond is broken because the fabric is one that does not permit the temperature required to obtain a good bond.

SEWING THREAD

Sewing thread and seam construction have taken on a new meaning. In addition to contributing to the satisfactory performance of wearing apparel and household items, they are now recognized as important considerations in the flammability of clothing and household textiles.

Choosing the right thread for sewing is more complicated than a person might think. Before synthetic threads came on the market for use with modern fabrics (e.g., stretch, bondeds, and durable press), the only concern was in choosing between silk and cotton, selecting the right size, deciding on how many spools to buy, and getting a good color match. Now the fiber content of all fabrics must be considered.

Today's thread label yields a wealth of information. In addition to size, color, and price, it tells how much thread is on the spool (the amount often differs from manufacturer to manufacturer). Now the choice has widened to include nylon, cotton-covered polyester, and even 100 percent polyester thread.

Also, if read carefully, it will be found that there is a choice among mercerized, glazed, waxed, and silicone finishes, or a combination of several.

CLOSURES

Metal zippers have been with us a long time but, today, manufacturers are turning a large share of their production to the manufacture of a filament coil zipper made of nylon or polyester, and molded zippers out of a plastic called Delrin. The coil zipper is used in skirts, blouses, dresses, and trousers. This new type of closure is not yet used widely in household items.

Change usually occurs as a result of research. The coil zipper is considered the most important advance in zipper technology in more than 60 years. This new development represents years of joint research by the producers of nylon and polyester and the manufacturers who make the fiber product. The new closure eliminates the individual metal teeth mounted on both sides of the fabric tape. If one metal tooth of the metal zipper is broken, flattened, or lost, the metal zipper is useless. The new closures have no teeth, just continuous coils.

The new closures, because of their unique construction, are said to be highly resistant to snagging, since there are no sharp edges to catch thread or frayed fabric. In addition, they are lightweight, narrow in width, and very flexible. This makes them suitable for application on every weight fabric, from sheer to heavy.

LOOPED FASTENERS

The looped fastener, called Velcro, is used in place of buttons or conventional slide fasteners on men's and boys' outer jackets, skirts, and sweaters. This fastener has found wide use in clothing for the handicapped. The fastener is different in appearance from conventional fasteners and trim.

The fastener is made of nylon loops and polyester hooks that interlock. It is available by the yard or precut lengths, dots, and squares. One strip is sewed into one side of the garment and the other strip to the opposite side. The two strips stick together tightly when merely pressed together, and they can be separated by pulling them apart with a "peeling" action. They resist sidewise pulling; therefore, the fastener does not open accidentally in use.

According to the manufacturer, the fastener operates on the "cocklebur" principle. One strip of the fastener has myriads of tiny hooks that engage the mass of loops on the opposite strip, much as the hooks on a cocklebur snag the fibers of any fabric that brushes against it.

The looped fastener presents no unusual problems in wear and care. Some hooks may break off without diminishing the holding quality of the fastener.

BUTTONS

Buttons may be functional or decorative. Functional buttons are used as a form of closure. They are simple in shape and design and usually are very serviceable. Many functional buttons are subjected to tests in order to determine their serviceability and durability. Decorative buttons are made for fashion appeal. Some carry approvals, such as replacement or refunds of money, by commercial testing laboratories.

To obtain satisfaction of performance in wear and care, consider the following questions at the time of purchase. Is the dyestuff or surface applied color colorfast to dry cleaning, wet cleaning, laundering, and light? Will the button itself or the finish applied to the surface dissolve in dry-cleaning solvent? Will the button crack, peel, or craze in wear? Will the button warp out of shape, blister, or melt with heat? Will the paper filler of which the button is made stain the fabric? With wear, will the button become whiter, darker, cloudy, or even rust? Will the irregular shape or surface cause abrasion to the fabric of the garment? And what about the shank? Some break very easily.

BELTS

Cleaners are well aware of the problems in cleaning belts. Consumers become irate when a cleaned dress is returned with a half-cleaned or dirty-looking belt. Cleaners have learned from past experience that there are a few belts that can be dry-cleaned and do not present a problem. Some belts are labeled "hand-cleanable." These are handled or cleaned by hand on the spotting board. But some belts cannot be dry-cleaned by any method with satisfactory results because of: cardboard, artificial leather, or paper backings that disintegrate in dry-cleaning solvents; rubberized interlinings that dissolve in solvent and stain the outer belt covering; buckram, facings, and linings dyed with fugutive dyes; back of belts and buckles fastened with a solvent soluble adhesive or glue; and decorative trim of glass and metal that cannot withstand the mechanical action of the dry-cleaning process.

When purchasing a garment look for a label stamped on the back of the belt that indicates the manufacturer's name, patent or license number, and the statement "Wash or Dry-clean."

SHOULDER PADS

Shoulder pads are used when fashion dictates their use. And fashion moves in cycles, so there are periods of time when they may not be used and other periods when they are a component part of garment construction.

The majority of shoulder pads used in the past have given satisfactory performance in use and care. Exceptions have been sponge rubber pads that deteriorated in wear and cleaning; spontaneous ignition of sponge rubber shoulder pads when drying in a tumbler; and bonded wool pads that develop hydrochloric acid in wear and care, causing a color change on the outer and lining fabric in shoulder area and deterioration of the pad.

BEADS, SEQUINS, PLASTIC TRIMS

Trims of many types are used to add a decorative treatment to garment design. Many dry-clean satisfactorily, but others do not and can ruin an otherwise dry-cleanable garment.

BEADS

Some silver-coated beads turn black because of oxidation of the metal. Some coated beads with a black porous center cause stains because the black material bleeds and leaches out onto the dress fabric. Polystyrene beads dissolve partially or completely in solvent (see Figure 8-8).

SEQUINS

Cellulose acetate sequins curl and melt with heat of pressing. Some dyes used to color the sequins bleed and stain the dress fabric.

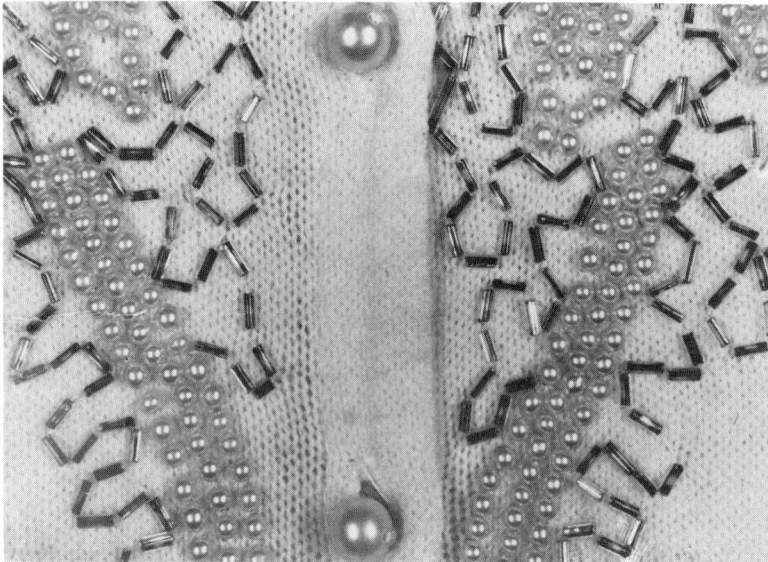

Figure 8-8 The silver sparkling buggle beads on this sweater were discolored in dry cleaning. Oxidation of the silver coating makes the beads look black in color.

PAILLETTES

Some paillettes curl and turn dull with steam in pressing. Metal clamps used to hold the paillettes to the fabric may tear the dress fabric.

PLASTIC

Some plastic trim cracks because of stress from improper curing of the resin. Some plastic beads become dull from steam. Condensation of the steam on the bead can delusterize some fabrics. Plastic filaments used to shape pleated and fluted sections of a garment can break in wear and cleaning, causing a loss of shaping.

Every part of a garment must dry-clean, launder, or wet-clean satisfactorily. If one part does not clean like all the other parts, it makes the garment unserviceable.

LEARNING EXPERIENCES

1. If possible, make an appointment to tour a garment manufacturing plant to observe how fabrics are cut and shaped into garments.
2. Read the textile periodicals and report on new developments in garment fabrication.

3. Describe situations in which the lining, interlining, and interfacing may give a consumer satisfactory or unsatisfactory performance.
4. Assemble and describe different linings, interlinings, and interfacings and list their specific uses.
5. List the reasons why a seam puckers. What determines seam strength? Explain how the stitching thread must be compatible to fabric type for optimum performance in use and care.
6. What factors influence the choice of a closure? Mount and describe different kinds of closures. Point out their advantages and disadvantages.
7. Examine ready-to-wear belts in your stores and shops. Try to determine their construction. Are they labeled as to proper method of care? Collect old belts and dissect them to determine how they are constructed. Why is it so important that a belt made of the same fabric as the dress be washable on a washable garment; dry-cleanable on a dry-cleanable garment?
8. Shoulder pads move in and out of the fashion cycle. Are shoulder pads being used today? Of what materials are they made? Are they washable? Dry-cleanable?
9. Assemble examples of decorative trims used in today's fashions. Experiment and determine if they can be washed or dry-cleaned.

9
FABRIC PERFORMANCE AND LABELING

Consumers become annoyed when clothing or household fabrics perform unsatisfactorily during use, storage, or when laundered or dry-cleaned.

Some years ago Dr. Jules Labarthe, Senior Fellow of the Mellon Institute, pointed out that in order to establish justification of a consumer complaint or consumer dissatisfaction, it is necessary to set up a system of standards of serviceability and attitude measurements. He suggested that consumers ask themselves the following questions.

1. Why did I buy the item to begin with?
2. What did I expect it to do by way of performance?
3. How long do I feel the item should have lasted?
4. What did the store's salesperson or representative tell me about it?
5. Did I misuse or mistreat it, or has it failed to live up to my expectations?

Of the complaints Dr. Labarthe studied, he found that 66 percent were not the fault of the merchandise. This means that in general the consumer, the laundryman, or the dry-cleaner had misused or mistreated the textile item, causing its early failure, and that the fabric itself was not at fault.

The Mellon Institute studies show that women's wear accounts for the greatest number of returns (71.3 percent), followed by men's wear (13.4 percent), children's wear (8.3 percent), and all other types of textiles (7.0 percent).

329

Over the years, the International Fabricare Institute's Textile Analysis Laboratory has compiled textile damage statistics that indicate that the service industry is responsible for one fourth of the complaints, the consumer for one fourth, and the manufacturer for about one half. There are cases where responsibility cannot be assigned. Typical types of damage and responsibility assignments are shown in Table 9-1.

Many times there is no easy answer as to who is responsible when textile damage occurs. The circuitous route through which textile items travel from fiber to consumer is a complex one. Sometimes it is impossible to pinpoint the responsibility.

Responsibility for satisfactory performance of textile items in end use is four fold.

1. Control at the source. The manufacturer should produce merchandise that will give consumer satisfaction.
2. Control by the retailer. The retailer should purchase goods for resale that will give satisfactory consumer performance.
3. Remedy of soil and stain conditions. The service industries should study and develop proper methods of handling and cleaning of textile items, recognizing the fact that some merchandise requires special processing techniques.
4. Prevention and care in use. The consumer should exercise discrimination in the selection of textile merchandise, to use the article as it is intended to be used, giving it the proper care in wear, cleaning, and storage.

Progress is being made in developing test methods and specifications that more accurately predict fabric performance under conditions of use. The Bureau of Standards, the American Society for Testing Materials, the American Association of Textile Chemists and Colorists, and the American National Standards Institute are interested in and working toward tests that more accurately predict fabric behavior in end use. Such efforts will result in greater satisfaction on the part of the consuming public.

It is difficult and sometimes impossible to separate the characteristics of fiber, yarn, and fabric in analyzing why a fabric performs as it does in end use. The addition of color, finish, and design complicates the problem more.

In Chapter 2 we pointed out that fiber properties depend on length, cross section, shape, twist or crimp, and contour of the surface. In Chapter 3, we discussed how fiber properties influence yarn construction and how yarns can be designed taking advantage of fiber properties. But just as important is the manner in which the yarn is designed to give the effect wanted in the fabric. In Chapter 4 we talked about the endless ways the

Table 9-1 Types of Damage and Responsibility Assignments*

Consumer	Manufacturer	Service Industry
1. Mineral acid damage	Shrinkage — other than bonded fabrics	Mechanical damage
2. Oxidized oil stains	Color loss — pigment prints	Heat damage
3. Insect damage	Solvent-soluble dyes or pigments	Alkaline color change
4. Caramelized sugar stains	Color loss — sun fading	Stains from dry-cleaning bath
5. Mechanical damage	Stiffening of plastic	Soil redeposition
6. Cold wave damage	Fluorescent dye discoloration	Color loss from pre-spotting
7. Color loss from bleach	Blistering or separation of bonded fabrics	Carbon stains
8. Fused fibers	Water-soluble dye	Prespotter stains
9. Dimensional change	Loss of finish	Color loss from spotting
10. Contact dye stains	Stretching	Delustering
11. Streaks in drapes	Fabric construction defects	Chafing
12. Color loss caused by perfume	Shrinkage — bonded	Acid color change
13. Albumin stains	Foam laminate deterioration	Nonvolatile material
14. Scorch	Fume fading	Shrinkage (wool felting)
15. Oxycellulose	Silk splits	Color fading — glass fabrics
16. Ink stains	Color change by acid	Chemical damage to fabric
17. Medicines	Damaged velvets	Color loss from wet cleaning
18. Adhesives	Soil-prone finish	Stains from wet cleaning
19. Chemical damage to acetate	Pilling	Nap or pile distorted
20. Chloride damage to silk	Low strength	Acrylic fiber yellowed
21. Metallic stains	Sun-tendered drapes	Metallic stains
22. Blood and perspiration stains	Foam laminate yellowing	Stretching
23. Carbon	Rubber-lined jackets	Dye bleeding
24. Paint	Alkali-sensitive dyes	Loss of pleats
25. Abrasion	Salt-sensitive dyes	Color fading — wet cleaning

*Ranked from highest to lowest number of complaints as recorded in 1975 by the International Fabricare Institute's Textile Analysis Laboratory.

construction of the fabric can be varied and the properties controlled by fiber and yarn structure. Finally, finishing of the fabric by the many techniques available can completely alter end-use performance.

How does a knowledge of all these variables help a consumer make a wise selection in relation to wear and care? There are very few guidelines, even through laboratory testing, that can give fairly reliable data on the fabric itself. But there is little or no relation or correlation at the moment between laboratory test methods and end-use performance. Then there is a large gap of measurements of subjective feelings of psychological reactions as applied against physical and chemical measurements.

APPEARANCE

Appearance is an aesthetic value and has been illustrated in Figure 1-8 to 1-11.

Hand and drape of a fabric are interdependent. The hand of a fabric may vary from very pliable to very stiff (flexibility); from very soft to very hard (compressability); from very limp to very springy (resilience); from rigid to a high degree of stress (extensability); from very smooth to very rough (surface contour and mass); and from slippery to very harsh (surface friction); and it may feel very cool to very hot to the wearer (thermal characteristics).

CREASE AND WRINKLE RESISTANCE

Crease and wrinkle resistance is another property that is very difficult to control because of the interrelationship of fiber content, yarn construction, fabric construction, finish, and garment design. Some authors contend that good wrinkle recovery is achieved by long, staple fibers and filaments, and short fibers produce poor wrinkle recovery. This is not always true in consumer use. It is debatable, too, that actual shape and fiber diameter and the degree of twist of a yarn in itself produces poor or good wrinkle recovery. Crease and wrinkle resistance is perhaps more related to human factors. You can take the identical fabric made into garments and put it on two or more people and you will obtain different results in crease and wrinkle resistance because of the wear factors of the individual as well as the fit of the garment. A person who sits, bends, flexes, and builds up body heat and moisture and wears tight clothes will vary greatly from an individual who wears a loose-fitting garment and is inactive during the wear period.

DIMENSIONAL STABILITY

The dimensional stability of a garment is planned to resist reduction or expansion to a smaller or larger fit, and can be controlled by manufacturing influences on the fiber, yarn, and fabric and to the inherent characteristics of the fiber itself. Most fabrics, unless specially treated or processed, tend to undergo dimensional losses. Depending on the kind or amount of dimensional loss that takes place, such loss can sometimes be recovered by renovation techniques in some cases but, in most cases, cannot be entirely recovered. The mechanisms or types of shrinkage are discussed on pages 103, 257 to 261.

DURABILITY

Many factors contribute to the durability of a fabric. Some fibers are strong; others weak. But this in itself does not serve as a guide. Weaker fibers may have induced strength by virtue of yarn and fabric construction.

Strength is a generic term for the ability of a material to resist strain or rupture induced by external forces during use or wear. Tear strength or the force required to start or continue a tear in a fabric under specified conditions is just as important.

ABRASION

Abrasion is the wearing away of any part of a material by rubbing against another surface. *Flat abrasion* is the rubbing away of fibers from a flat surface. This may occur in wear, stain and spot removal, laundering, or dry cleaning. Flat abrasion is usually associated with pile flocked fabrics where the protruding fibers are subjected to a rubbing action (e.g., across the shoulder, at the elbow, and at the seat of the garment). The manner in which the yarns are constructed and woven into a fabric can also influence its ease of abrasion. For example, long, smooth floating yarns in satins, brocades, and Damask may rough up and break with rubbing action. Softly napped fabrics, pile, and flocked fabrics abraid easily.

Edge abrasion is shown in Figure 4-56. This is the removal of fibers along the edges of collars, cuffs, front closings, and fell seams.

Flex abrasion is associated with the removal of fibers, color, or sizings from the fabric by flexing or folding action on itself or other fabrics in wear, laundering, or dry cleaning. This usually results in the formation of light streaks or crow's feet on the surface of the fabric.

Frosting is a change in color in a limited area of fabric caused by abrasive wear. Frosting may be the result of differential wear, as in multicomponent blends in which the fibers do not match in shade, or of the abrasion of single-fiber constructions in which there is a variation in penetration or an incomplete penetration of dyestuff.

PILLING

Pilling is the bunching together of surface fibers into a ball. This is usually more noticeable in knit than woven fabrics. Soft fibers such as wool and cashmere pill readily, but the small balls break away from the fabric because the fiber is soft, so that one is unaware of them. Pills on fabrics made of synthetic fibers are strong, adhere to the surface of the fabric, and are difficult to remove. Pilling may occur during wear; it is accentuated and aggravated by laundering and dry cleaning.

SNAGGING

A snag or a pull may be defined as a yarn that protrudes from the basic background fabric but has not been broken. It may, in some cases, be brought back into alignment by applying tension in pressing or finishing. Snagging is more apparent in knit fabrics. Mechanical devices have been offered to consumers to work the pulled yarn back into the fabric. A needle threader or a fine crochet hook also can be used for this purpose.

COMFORT

Comfort factors involve the psychological reaction to textiles. For example, some people say they are allergic to wool. Others claim they cannot stand heavy fabrics. What is comfortable to one individual may be uncomfortable to another.

THERMAL PROPERTIES

Systems related to thermal properties include: (1) variables such as metabolism, sex, and level of activity; (2) environment, such as temperature, relative humidity, air currents, and radiation intensity; and (3) the variable components of the fabric, garment design, fit, and number of layers.

Thermal properties depend on (1) conduction or transfer of heat from the body to the air; (2) conversion or loss of heat from the body by the air that moves over and around the body; (3) radiation or the loss of body heat when the air temperature is below body temperature; and (4) moisture transport or heat loss caused by the loss of evaporation of the moisture from the body.

We can select clothes and household textiles to adapt to climatic conditions. In warm climates we can select fabrics made of smooth, fine yarns, loose weaves, and light colors. In cold climates we can select soft, fluffy, napped, dense, or double-faced fabrics that entrap air and help the body retain its heat. Or we might select fabrics with an insulated finish that keep cold air out and warm air in. We may also combine and layer fabrics in the garments we wear. During energy crises, thermal properties of garments and household textiles take on new import.

AIR PERMEABILITY

This characteristic is most important for body comfort and protection against moisture. It is closely related to thermal properties. If a fabric has good air permeability, it carries heat from the body by the air that moves over and around the body; a fabric with low permeability prevents loss of heat by air movement. Air permeability is influenced by fiber, yarn, and fabric construction (e.g., fabrics of low thread count and fine yarns are more air permeable than fabrics of high-thread count and dense fabric construction). A double-knit of 100 percent polyester may have poor air permeability, while a 60/40 cotton polyester blend may have excellent air permeability.

ABSORBENCY

Absorbency of a fabric is in direct relation to its ability to take up moisture (absorb), hold moisture (adsorb), or give up moisture by capillary action (wicking). These are complex phenomenons and, unfortunately, the consumer is given little or no help of this property on labels and hangtags.

To summarize the facts already presented, hydrophilic (water liking) fibers like and take up moisture and release it more readily than hydrophobic (water-hating) fibers. Fabrics made of staple or spun yarns take up and give up moisture through wicking more readily than filament yarns. Loosely woven fabrics will take up (adsorb) and give up (transmit) moisture more readily than densely constructed fabrics. Finishes applied to fabric may aid or change the ability of a fabric to take up and give up moisture. So the problem of absorbency can become complex, depending on the possible fiber content, yarn construction, fabric construction, and finish combinations. And all these factors work together to make a fabric comfortable or uncomfortable to wear. For example, a 100 percent polyester fabric may have poor absorbency; a 60/40 cotton polyester blend may have excellent absorbency. A selected finish may be applied to a nylon or polyester fabric to give it an excellent rating in absorbency.

It is very difficult for consumers to understand the complex concepts of adsorption, absorption, and wicking actions of fabrics. By experience, consumers have learned that wool can absorb a lot of moisture before it feels damp; terry cloth toweling absorbs water easily because of the soft looped yarn surface of the fabric; linen takes up moisture readily but also releases quickly and drys quickly, and some synthetic fabrics do not release body moisture; therefore the fabric is uncomfortable.

IMPLIED SERVICEABILITY — LIFE EXPECTANCY

Very little consideration has been given in published textbooks to developing an understanding of implied serviceability designations and life expectancy rates of wearing apparel and household textiles. This is of special importance to the consumer who experiences disappointment in the performance of the goods she purchases, wears or uses, launders, or has dry-cleaned.

A GUIDE FOR ARBITRATING COMPLAINTS

The International Fair Claims Guide for Consumer Textile Products was first introduced in 1961 as an adjustment formula for the settlement of damage claims. Its success was immediate and far-reaching. It is widely used today by dry cleaners, launderers, insurance adjusters, retailers, Better Business Bureaus, civil authorities, and others in many countries.

In 1964, the Guide was expanded to include criteria for determining responsibility for damage to consumer textile products. This called for a special body of information on terminology, labeling, causes of damage, and new concepts of product classification unavailable from any other source. For this reason, the document has come into wide demand for educational uses as well as for arbitration purposes.

The document is now formally presented by the International Fabricare Institute for voluntary use in all countries because: (1) all apparel products exported to the United States must comply with the FTC Care Labeling of Textile Wearing Apparel (1972) rule, and (2) the Guide has achieved wide international acceptance for its criteria on textile performance questions in general.

The guide introduces the concept of life expectancy for clothing and textile products (see Table 9-2). Estimates are given as

Table 9-2   Implied Serviceability Designations and Life Expectancy Rates

Item	Renovation Method	Rate (Years)
MEN'S AND BOYS' WEAR		
1. BATHING SUITS	Hand wash	2
2. COATS AND JACKETS		4
Cloth, dress	Dryclean	
Cloth, sport	(See #20)	
Pile (Imitation fur)	Dryclean. Cold tumble only. No steam.	
Fur	Fur Clean	10
Leather and Suede	(See #7)	
Plastic	(See #10)	
3. FORMAL WEAR	Dryclean	5
4. GLOVES		
Fabric	Med. Wash; dryclean	1
Leather	Leather Clean only	2
5. HATS		
Felt and straw	Clean by hat renovation specialists only. Water resist.	2
Fur	Fur Clean	5
6. JACKETS (See #2 or #11)		
7. LEATHER JACKETS AND COATS		5
Suede and grain leather products require special care in cleaning. Colors normally subject to fading and some loss in cleaning. Suedes and most grain leathers restorable by application of color and finishing products.		
8. NECKTIES	Dryclean	1
9. SLEEPWEAR		2
White goods	Hot wash	
Colored goods	Med. wash	
10. PLASTIC APPAREL (See #11)		3
Imitation leather and suede	Hand wash; no press	

Table 9-2 *(Cont'd)*

Item	Renovation Method	Rate (Years)
11. RAINWEAR		
Film and plastic coated fabrics	Hand wash; no press	2
Fabric		
Unlined	Med. wash, dryclean	3
Lined and quilted	Dryclean	
Rubber	Wipe down with damp cloth; no press	3
12. ROBES		
Silk or wool	Dryclean	3
Other:		
Unlined	Med. wash; dryclean	
Lined	Dryclean	
13. SHOES		
Can be cleaned and polished, resoled, heeled. Thread in uppers holds sections securely for normal service life without undue breakage.		
MEN'S		3
BOYS'		1
14. SHIRTS		
Dress and plain sports		2
White and partly colored	Hot wash	
Colored	Hot wash; no bleach	
Sports (Fancy)		
Cotton and blends	Med. wash; dryclean	3
Wool or Silk	Dryclean; hand wash	2
15. SHORTS (See #17)		
16. SKI JACKETS (See #11)		
17. SLACKS AND SHORTS (including matching sets)		
Wool or wool blends	Dryclean	4
Cotton	Med. wash; dryclean	2
Synthetics	Dryclean	2
18. SNEAKERS	Med. wash; bleach; Air or tumble dry.	0
19. SOCKS	Hand wash	
Wool		
Other	Med. wash	
20. SPORT COATS		
Wool and wool blends	Dryclean	4
Cotton and synthetics	Dryclean	2

Table 9-2 *(Cont'd)*

Item	Renovation Method	Rate (Years)
21. SUITS		
Summer Weight:		
Wool or wool blends	Dryclean	3
Cotton and synthetics	Dryclean	2
Winter weight	Dryclean	4
Wash suits	Med. wash; dryclean	2
22. SWEATERS		3
Wool and synthetics	Hand wash; dry flat only; dryclean; wetclean	
23. UNDERWEAR		2
White	Hot wash	
Colored	Med. wash	
24. UNIFORMS		1
Unlined and work types	Med. wash; dryclean	
Lined and dressy	Dryclean	
25. VESTS		2
Fancy and regular	Dryclean	
26. WINDBREAKERS (See #11)		
27. WORK CLOTHING		2
Customarily shows noticeable signs of wear to greater or lesser degree depending on amount of use. Color may be expected to appear rubbed off in areas. Fabric has strength to withstand strains of use and laundering at 160F. with heavy duty soap..		

WOMEN'S AND GIRLS' WEAR

Item	Renovation Method	Rate (Years)
28. APRONS		
Regular	Med. wash; bleach white only.	1
Fancy	Hand wash; dryclean	4
29. BLOUSES		
Dress and Sports		
White cotton	Hot wash; dryclean	3
White synthetics and all colored.	Med. wash; dryclean	2
30. COATS AND JACKETS (See #2)		

Table 9-2 *(Cont'd)*

Item	Renovation Method	Rate (Years)
31. DRESSES		
House and sports	Med. wash; dryclean	1
Afternoon	Dryclean	3
Street	Dryclean	2
Evening or cocktail:		
High Fashion	Dryclean; special handling of delicate and decorated styles.	3
Basic	Dryclean	5
32. GLOVES		
Fabric	Med. wash separate; dryclean.	1
Leather	Leather Clean	2
33. HATS		
Felt	Clean by special hat renovation methods.	1
Straw	Same unless trim detail precludes cleaning.	2
Fur	Fur Clean	5
34. HOUSECOATS AND ROBES		
Lightweight cottons and synthetics	Mild wash; dryclean	1
Quilted and heavy	Dryclean	3
35. JACKETS (See #2 or #11)		
36. NEGLIGEE		
Cotton and nylon types	Med. wash	2
37. SLEEPWEAR		2
White goods	Hot wash	
Colored goods	Med. wash	
38. RAINWEAR (See #11)		
39. ROBES (See #34)		
40. SCARVES		2
Wool	Dryclean	
Other	Mild wash; dryclean	
Fur	Fur clean	5
41. SHOES		
Dress and walking	(See #13)	2
Work		1
Evening, formal		5
42. SHORTS (See #44)		

Table 9-2 *(Cont'd)*

Item	Renovation Method	Rate (Years)
43. SKIRTS		2
Winter and fall	Dryclean-wetclean	
Resort and summer	Med. wash; dryclean	
44. SLACKS AND SHORTS		
Lounging and tailored	Dryclean	2
Active Sport	Hand wash; dryclean	2
Dress	Dryclean	3
45. SNEAKERS (See #18)		
46. SOCKS (See #19)		
47. SPORT COATS (See #2)		
48. SUITS		
Basic	Dryclean	4
High Fashion	Dryclean. Special handling on delicate and decorated styles.	3
49. SWEATERS (See #22)		
50. SWIM WEAR	Hand wash	2
51. UNDERWEAR		
Slips	Mild wash; bleach white cottons	2
Foundation garments	Med. wash	1
Panties	Med. wash; bleach white cottons	1
52. UNIFORMS		1
Unlined and work types	Med. wash; dryclean	
Lined and dressy	Dryclean	
53. WEDDING GOWNS	Dryclean	*
54. WINDBREAKERS (See #11)		
55. WORK CLOTHING (See #27)		
CHILDREN'S WEAR		
56. COATS	Dryclean	2
57. COAT SETS	Dryclean	2
58. DRESSES	Med. wash; dryclean	2
59. HATS, BONNETS	Dryclean	1
60. PLAYCLOTHES	Med. wash	1
61. SNOW SUITS		2
Wool and wool blends	Dryclean	
Cotton and synthetics	Med. wash; dryclean	

Table 9-2 *(Cont'd)*

Item	Renovation Method	Rate (Years)
62. SUITS	Dryclean	2
63. UNDERGARMENTS		1
White goods	Hot wash	
Colored	Med. wash	
HOUSEHOLD FURNISHINGS		
64. BEDSPREADS		3
Cotton, synthetics	Med. wash; dryclean	
65. BLANKETS		
Heavy wool and synthetic fabrics	Mild wash; dryclean	10
Lightweight	Mild wash; dryclean	5
Electric	Mild wash	5
66. CURTAINS		
Sheer	Med. wash; dryclean	3
Glass fiber	Hand wash; wetclean	
67. DRAPERIES		
Lined	Dryclean	5
Unlined	Med. wash; dryclean	4
Sheer	Med. wash; dryclean	3
Glass fiber	Hand wash; wetclean	4
Linings (Attached)	Same as drapery	4
Linings (Separate)	Med. Wash; dryclean	4
68. SHEETS AND PILLOW CASES		2
White and colored	Hot wash	
69. SLIPCOVERS	Med. wash; dryclean	3
70. TABLE LINEN		
Fancy	Mild wash	5
Service		
(white)	Hot wash	2
(partly colored)	Hot wash	
(colored)	Med. wash	
71. TOWELS		
All types	Hot wash	2
72. UPHOLSTERY FABRICS		5
Hand cleanable with dry-cleaning solvent or foam cleaners. Color and finish resistant to water.		

*Indefinite life expectancy.
(Courtesy: International Fabricare Institute.)

to how long each garment may be expected to be worn. Normal wear, care, and change in fashion influences life expectancy of clothing. Table 9-3 indicates that the value for an adjustment is based on a percentage of replacement cost, depending on the degree to which the "life expectancy" of the item has been used up and the condition of the garment at the time claim is made. This method is used for figuring a reasonable estimate of the amount of loss.

LABELING

Consumers have a right to be informed about the clothing and household fabrics they buy. The most popular way a manufacturer has of informing the consumer is through the use of hangtags and labels.

The four basic reasons for labeling textile merchandise are designed to (1) identify the product; (2) aid the businessman in selling his product; (3) aid the consumer in making an intelligent selection; and (4) aid the consumer, the professional dry-cleaner, and the laundryman to properly care for the item.

Manufacturers may label fabrics and clothing by having: printed identification on the bolt or roller, spool, or wrapper; woven or printed identification on the selvage; a printed label pasted onto the item; a hangtag attached to the item; and a woven or printed label permanently attached.

Garments are usually labeled by one or both of the following methods. (1) Attaching a cardboard hangtag to the garment by a string. This label may carry factual and promotional material. It is easily removed. (2) Attaching by means of machine stitching a ribbon or cloth label in a seam or on a facing of the garment.

Other permanent labeling may be accomplished by stamping information on the garment such as the size on the neckline of a blouse and the brand and size on gloves.

TYPES OF LABELS

The information given on either a printed or woven label may be classified as follows.

Informative

An informative label attempts to help the consumer make a wise choice and care for the item by supplying pertinent information. It may state fiber content, fabric construction, and special

Table 9-3   Calculation of Claims Adjustment Values

Life Expectancy rating of article (from Table 9-2)						% of Replacement Cost — Adjustment Values		
1	2	3	4	5	10	Excellent	Average	Poor
Age of article in months					Age of article in years	100%	100%	100%
0 to 4	0 to 4	0 to 4	0 to 4	0 to 4	Less than 1 year	100%	100%	100%
4 to 7	4 to 7	4 to 10	4 to 13	4 to 16	2 to 4 years	75%	75%	60%
* 7 to 9	7 to 13	10 to 19	13 to 25	16 to 31	4 to 6 years	70%	60%	45%
* 9 to 11	13 to 19	19 to 28	25 to 37	31 to 46	6 to 8 years	50%	40%	30%
* 11 to 13	19 to 25	28 to 37	37 to 49	46 to 61	8 to 11 years	30%	20%	15%
13 mos. and older	25 mos. and older	37 mos. and older	49 mos. and older	61 mos. and older	11 years and older	20%	15%	10%

*Use only with "Average" column in figuring Adjustment Value.
Note: Ages are given to, but not including the 1st day of the month or year shown.

STEP BY STEP USE OF TABLES

1) Determine the cost of replacing the article. This is called Replacement Cost.
2) Determine the Actual Age of the article in months (in years for "ten year" items).
3) Determine the condition of the article as Excellent, Average, or Poor.
4) Select from Table 9-2 the Life Expectancy rating of the article. (See pages 337 to 342.)
5) Refer to the column in Table 9-3 at the top of which is shown the Life Expectancy rating selected in Step 4. Read down in this column to the box showing the Actual Age and across to the Adjustment Value.
6) In Table 9-3 select the box under "Adjustment Values" which applies according to condition of the article.
7) Multiply the percent figure given in Table 9-3 by the Replacement Cost figure determined in Step 1. This will be the Adjustment Value.

Example 1 — High fashion cocktail dress. Replacement cost — $200. Life Expectancy — 3 years (Table 9-2) Actual age — 30 months (Table 9-3). Condition — Excellent. Adjustment Value — 30% or $60. (Table 9-3.)

Example 2 — Man's leather coat. Replacement cost — $80. Life Expectancy — 5 years. Actual Age — 5 months. Condition — Excellent. Adjustment Value — 75% or $60.

Example 3 — Man's wool slacks. Replacement Cost — $18. Life Expectancy — 3 years. Actual Age — 60 months. Condition — Poor. Adjustment Value — 10% or $1.80.

Example 4 — Custom-made, lined draperies. Replacement Cost — $250. Life Expectancy — 5 years. Actual Age — 48 months. Condition — Average. Adjustment Value — 20% or $50.

(Courtesy of International Fabricare Institute.)

finishes that give specific appearance, serviceability, and performance properties. It may also give special instructions or precautions on care. The factual information may be based on laboratory tests and may include the size of the item as well as the manufacturer's name.

Informative labeling may also include information required by federal legislation such as the Fiber Products Identification Act or a statement that the article has met standards similar to those of L-22, Performance Requirements for Textile Fabrics, formerly of the American National Standards Institute.

Brand

This type of label is a distinctive mark, design, or symbol. One or a combination of these words can be used to identify the goods of a particular seller or manufacturer. Trademark names fall in this type of labeling.

Certification

The label indicates that the item has been tested by a laboratory, usually one independent of the manufacturer of the product. Each laboratory may establish its own fixed standards of quality. These labels are often referred to as "seals of approval" labels. Examples are The Good Housekeeping Seal of Approval, Parent's Magazine, and the International Fabricare Institutes' Seal for Washability and Drycleanability. Usually no information is given on the label except that the article has been approved or guaranteed by a particular laboratory or agency.

Union

In addition to an informative brand or certification label, there may also be a union label. This assures the consumer that the garment was made under fair working conditions. Unions operating in the clothing area are The Amalgamated Clothing Workers of America, International Ladies Garment Workers' Union, and United Garment Workers of America.

RN System

The sewn-in label RN 6821, or any other number found in a garment, means that manufacturers of wearing apparel obtain a registration number from the Bureau of Consumer Protection, Federal Trade Commission. This number is used to identify the source of the item instead of using the manufacturer's name. In 1974 FTC abolished the confidentiality of the registered number identification system in the best interests of both the apparel manufacturer and the consumer.

WOOL PRODUCTS LABELING ACT

The Wool Products Labeling Act of 1939 became law in October 1940 and was amended in 1965.

This federal law requires that all articles containing wool must be so labeled. If the wool fiber is mixed with other fibers, the percentage of wool must be stated on the label. The kind of wool must also be stated, but there is no provision in the law requiring a statement as to the quality of the wool fiber used.

The Federal Trade Commission has issued 36 rules and regulations for industry guidance under the Act.

Definitions

The following definitions are included in the Wool Products Labeling Act.

Wool means the fiber from the fleece of the sheep or lamb or hair of the Angora or Cashmere goat (and may include the so-called specialty fibers from the hair of the camel, alpaca, llama, and vicuña) which has never been reclaimed from any woven or felted wool product.

Reprocessed wool means the resulting fiber when wool has been woven or felted into a wool fabric which, without ever having been utilized in any way by the ultimate consumer, subsequently has been made into a fibrous state.

Reused wool means the resulting fiber when wool or reprocessed wool has been spun, woven, knitted, or felted into a wool product which, after having been used in any way by the ultimate consumer, subsequently has been made into a fibrous state.

Wool product means any product or any portion of a product which contains, purports to contain, or in any way is represented as containing wool, reprocessed wool, or reused wool.

FUR PRODUCTS LABELING ACT

The Fur Products Labeling Act requires that purchasers be informed on labels, invoices, and in advertising of the true English name of the animal from which the fur came, its country of origin, and whether the fur product is composed of used, damaged, or scrap fur, or fur that has been dyed or bleached. The Act further requires that the terminology in the Fur Products Name Guide, amended in 1967 and issued by the Federal Trade Commission, be used in setting forth the animal name. A 1969 amendment to the Act added further provisions in the regulation of furs that are pointed, dyed, bleached, or otherwise artificially colored. The FTC rules prohibit the use of fictitious prices in labeling and advertising.

Definitions

The following definitions are included in the Fur Products Labeling Act.

Fur means any animal skin or part thereof with hair, fleece, or fur fibers attached thereto, either in its raw or processed state, but shall not include such skins as are to be converted into leather or which in processing shall have the hair, fleece, or fur fiber completely removed.

Used fur means fur in any form which has been worn or used by an ultimate consumer.

Fur product means any article of wearing apparel made in whole or in part of fur or used fur; except that such term shall not include such articles as the Commission shall exempt by reason of the relatively small quantity or value of the fur or used fur contained therein.

Waste fur means the ears, throats, or scrap pieces which have been severed from the animal pelt, and shall include mats and plates made therefrom.

TEXTILE FIBER PRODUCTS IDENTIFICATION ACT

The Textile Fiber Products Identification Act became law and went into effect on March 3, 1960.

The purpose of the law is "to protect producers and consumers against misbranding and false advertising of fiber content of textile fiber products. . . ." This law is in addition to the existing law, The Wool Products Labeling Act.

HOW ARE ITEMS IDENTIFIED?

Manufacturers are required to stamp, tag, label, or use some other means of identification giving the following information.

1. The fiber or combination of fibers used in the item. Fibers must be designated with equal prominence whether natural

or manufactured fibers. Fibers must be identified by their generic name (see definition below) in order of predominance by weight if the weight is 5 percent or more of the total fiber weight.

2. The percent of each fiber present, by weight, in the total fiber content must be given. This is exclusive of ornamentation not exceeding 5 percent by weight of the total fiber content. If the ornamentation is 5 percent or less, it may be designated as "other fiber" or "other fibers."

3. Manufacturers must state on upholstered products, such as a mattress, cushion, and the like, if the stuffing has been used as stuffing in another upholstered product, mattress, or cushion.

4. The tag, label, or stamp must carry the name or other identification of the manufacturer of the product or one or more persons subject to the Act.

5. If the item is imported, the name of the country where the product was made or processed must appear on the label.

Additional information that the manufacturer may wish to place on the tag or label is permissable as long as it does not violate the Act.

WHAT ITEMS ARE COVERED BY THE ACT?

The Federal Trade Commission has ruled that the Act applies to the following textile products: wearing apparel; accessories such as scarfs, handkerchiefs, umbrellas, and parasols; household linens, including tablecloths, napkins, doilies, dresser and furniture scarfs, towels, washcloths, dishcloths and ironing board covers; home furnishings, including curtains, draperies, slipcovers and coverlets for furniture, afgans and throws, floor coverings, stuffings in upholstered products, mattresses and cushions; miscellaneous items including sleeping bags, hammocks, and flags; and narrow fabrics except packaged ribbons.

The Act Defines Generic Names

A generic name may be defined as a family name. The family name designates one or more fibers in a group that basically has the same chemical composition. At the present time, the Federal Trade Commission has defined 21 generic names (see Chapter 2).

Other generic names may be added to the list as new fibers appear.

How is the Act Enforced?

The Act is enforced by the Federal Trade Commission, which can obtain an injunction to restrain a person from unlawful acts and can prohibit imports when the law is broken. To aid in enforcement, manufacturers must keep records of fiber content, and persons substituting a label must keep records for at least 3 years. Manufacturers, distributors, and retailers have had problems in complying with the provisions of the Act. Criminal penalties include a fine of not more than $5000, imprisonment for not over 1 year, or both.

PERMANENT CARE LABELING RULE

The Federal Trade Commission's Trade Regulation Rule on permanent care labeling went into effect on July 3, 1972. It is important to know what articles should have permanent care labels.

WHAT DOES THE RULE REQUIRE?

The Commission has tried to produce a regulation that is workable for both the producer and consumer. The rule requires that most articles of wearing apparel bear permanent labels; permanent care labels be supplied with over-the-counter fabrics to be used for clothing (see exceptions below); and imported garments and fabrics bear permanent care labels.

SPECIFICATIONS FOR LABELS

Labels must disclose fully, clearly, and thoroughly the regular care of the garment or fabric; inform how to wash, iron, dry, bleach, dry-clean, and use any other procedures that are considered regular care; carry a warning if a usual care method appears to apply, but does not; stay attached and be readable for the reasonable life of a garment; be easy to locate; be in words, not symbols; and apply to all the findings (thread, buttons, zipper, and trim) on the garment.

Articles in sealed packaging require that the permanent care label be visible through the wrap or a duplicate of the instructions must be made discernible on the surface of the package by means of a tag or be printed directly on the package.

The Rule Specifies What Should Not Be on Labels

Labels must not use promotional language, such as "never needs ironing." The label must state at what temperature to iron in case you want to iron.

Labels must not omit warning against dry cleaning, if the garment cannot be dry-cleaned. The FTC takes the position that the consumer assumes that if a garment is washable, it is also dry-cleanable.

Labels must not be negative (such as "No bleach"). The label must be positive — tell you what to do; for example:

Machine Wash, Warm
Line Dry
Do Not Use Chlorine Bleach

CARE PRACTICES

The FTC takes the position that certain care practices are assumed to be common knowledge to consumers and, therefore, need not be stated on the label. These practices are: all fabrics are ironable under normal ironing conditions and all washable fabrics may also be dry-cleaned, unless the label specifies otherwise.

The Consumer Affairs Committee of the American Apparel Manufacturers Association (AAMA) published an edited version of the Industry Guide (see Table 9-4). The AAMA, the National Retail Merchants Association, and the American Retail Federation used this glossary of terms to create 14 basic care labels that are appropriate for most merchandise subject to the rule. All three associations are encouraging apparel manufacturers to use these labels.

CONSUMER RESPONSIBILITY

The mechanics of meeting the permanent care labeling regulation are the responsibility of the textile industry. The burden of compliance, however, is not the sole responsibility of the manufacturer. Consumers also have a role to play in meeting the goals of the FTC Rule on Permanent Care Labeling.

It is very important that home sewers buy thread, lining, zippers, trim, and other accessories that have compatible care instructions with those for the fabric used for a garment. If con-

Table 9-4 Consumer Care Guide for Apparel

	WHEN LABEL READS:	IT MEANS:
MACHINE WASHABLE	Washable / Machine washable / Machine wash	Wash, bleach, dry and press by any customary method including commercial laundering
	Home launder only	Same as above but do not use commercial laundering
	No bleach	Do not use bleach
	No starch	Do not use starch
	Cold wash / Cold setting / Cold rinse	Use cold water from tap or cold washing machine setting
	Warm wash / Warm setting / Warm rinse	Use warm water 90° to 110° Fahrenheit
	Hot wash / Hot setting	Use hot water (hot washing machine setting) 130° Fahrenheit or hotter
	No spin	Remove wash load before final machine spin cycle
	Delicate cycle / Gentle cycle	Use appropriate machine setting; otherwise wash by hand
	Durable press cycle / Permanent press cycle	Use appropriate machine setting; otherwise use medium wash, cold rinse and short spin cycle
	Wash separately	Wash alone or with like colors

	WHEN LABEL READS:	IT MEANS:
NON-MACHINE WASHING	Hand washable / Hand wash	Launder only by hand in luke warm (hand comfortable) water. May be bleached. May be drycleaned
	Hand wash only	Same as above, but **do not** dryclean
	Hand wash separately	Hand wash alone or with like colors
	No bleach	Do not use bleach
HOME DRYING	Tumble dry / Machine dry	Dry in tumble dryer at specified setting — high, medium, low or no heat
	Tumble dry / Remove promptly	Same as above, but in absence of cool-down cycle remove at once when tumbling stops
	Drip dry / Hang dry / Line dry	Hang wet and allow to dry with hand shaping only
	No squeeze / No wring / No twist	Hang dry, drip dry or dry flat only
	Dry flat	Lay garment on flat surface
	Block to dry	Maintain original size and shape while drying
IRONING OR PRESSING	Cool iron	Set iron at lowest setting
	Warm iron	Set iron at medium setting
	Hot iron	Set iron at hot setting
	No iron / No press	Do not iron or press with heat
	Steam iron / Steam press	Iron or press with steam
	Iron damp	Dampen garment before ironing
MISCELLANEOUS	Dryclean / Dryclean only	Garment should be drycleaned only, including self-service
	Professionally clean only / Commercially clean only	**Do not** use self-service drycleaning
	No dryclean	Use recommended care instructions. No drycleaning materials to be used.

This Care Guide was produced by the Consumer Affairs Committee, American Apparel Manufacturers Association and is based on the Voluntary Guide of the Textile Advisory Committee for Consumer Interests.

352

sumers fail to do this they may be disappointed when a garment fails to give good service in laundering or dry cleaning. For example, if a fabric is selected that is dry-cleanable, but the lining and trim is not, the consumer will be disappointed in the appearance of the garment when it is dry-cleaned. There is no way the manufacturer of component parts can control what the consumer puts together at the fabric counter. This is the consumer's responsibility. In summary, (1) consumers should double-check to be sure that the code number on the bolt end of the fabric corresponds with the number on the label received from the salesperson, and (2) consumers should be careful in selecting fabrics and trimmings that have compatible care instructions.

VOLUNTARY SYMBOL LABELING

Some countries have adopted a voluntary system of symbols to convey care information to the consumer and the professional launderer and dry cleaner.

Many imported garments from Canada, Great Britain, and Europe now contain labels bearing care instructions in the form of symbols. These are intended to overcome lanugage problems.

The leading symbol system of care labeling are Canadian, Dutch, and British. All systems use symbols of the same basic shape, but they vary somewhat in content. There are five basic symbols in general use. They are shown in Figure 9-1.

FLAMMABLE FABRIC ACT

Flammability in textiles, plastics, foams, and coatings is leading to a growing public concern and regulation by government and industry.

In October 1973, the 92nd Congress passed, and the President signed into law, Public Law 92-573, which created an independ-

Figure 9-1 In the Canadian and Dutch systems, red, amber, and green colors are used.

Red means stop — don't carry out the action represented by the symbol. For added emphasis a red symbol is usually cancelled out with an X.

Amber means that some caution is necessary.

Green means that no special precautions are needed.

The British use a one-color system. All symbols are printed in black ink.

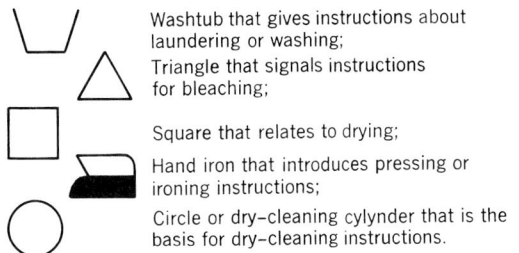

Washtub that gives instructions about laundering or washing;

Triangle that signals instructions for bleaching;

Square that relates to drying;

Hand iron that introduces pressing or ironing instructions;

Circle or dry–cleaning cylynder that is the basis for dry–cleaning instructions.

ent five-member regulatory agency to set and enforce safety standards ". . . designed to eliminate unreasonable risk of injury or death" from use of household consumer products. Such products kill an estimated 30,000 Americans and injure another 20 million each year.

The $178 million, 3-year measure authorizes the Presidentially appointed commission to issue mandatory safety standards governing the use, design, labeling, and performance of products not already subject to federal regulation.

The Federal Consumer Product Safety Commission now has the authority for administering the Flammable Fabric Act, which was passed in 1953 and amended in 1954 and again in 1957. All functions formerly carried out by the Secretary of Commerce, the National Bureau of Standards, and the Secretary of Health, Education and Welfare are now centered in the new agency. It is the agency's responsibility to collect all burn data, develop standards and test methods, and enforce violations of the Act.

Prior to Public Law 92-573, there was an Office of Flammable Fabrics, located at the National Bureau of Standards, which was responsible for research and development of fabric flammability test methods. NBS is responsible to the Department of Commerce. Since the Federal Consumer Product Safety Commission was established, it places contracts with NBS to carry out specific projects related to flammability research and test methods. The group at NBS calls itself the Programmatic Center for Fire Research; it is composed of approximately 10 sections.

Presently, fabric flammability standards cover the following.

Carpets and Rugs

All large carpets and rugs had to meet standards by April 1971. Those not complying were banned from the market. Small carpets and rugs including bath mats less than 6 feet long and covering an area no greater than 24 square feet had to be clearly, permanently, and prominently labeled with a warning of possible hazards if they did not meet the standard.

Mattresses and Mattress Pads

A final standard became effective on December 22, 1973.

Children's Clothes

A standard for children's sleepwear in sizes 0 to 6X, published in 1970, went into effect on July 29, 1972. After July 29, 1973, compliance became mandatory. Flammability of children's sleepware sizes 7 to 14 was issued by the Consumer Product Safety Commission on May 1, 1974 under the Flammable Fabrics Act; it became effective on May 1, 1975.

The Consumer Product Safety Commission published a possible need for amendment to the standard in the Federal Register on May 1, 1974. The Commission published in the Federal Register on January 20, 1975 the proposed labeling and record-keeping requirements, policy statement, and solicitation of comments for children's sleepwear, sizes 7 to 14.

In the notice, the Commission withdrew a proposed amendment to define the terms "manufacture" and "in inventory or with the trade" and instead issued a policy statement clarifying the definitions of the two terms.

According to the policy statement, the manufacturing process ends when an item has been completely assembled, all permanently affixed labels have been attached, and all functional materials have been affixed. Until these actions have been completed, an item of children's sleepwear will not be considered to have been "manufactured."

It added that all items of children's "sleepwear, sizes 7 to 14, including apparel and fabric intended for use in children's sleepwear, that are in inventory or with the trade on the effective date of the standard (May 1, 1975) are exempt from the requirements.

For domestic sleepwear to be considered "in inventory" or "with the trade" on the effective standard date, the manufacturing process must have ended prior to May 1, 1975.

For foreign-made sleepwear, the manufacturing process must have ended and the goods must have been entered into the United States before May 1, 1975.

The Commission also withdrew a proposed amendment granting oven-dry testing exceptions. The test requires that children's sleepwear be conditioned before testing by placing it in a drying oven at 105°C for 30 minutes.

After referring to a study conducted by the National Bureau of Standards, the Commission said it believes that oven-dry conditioning is representative of real-life conditions and, therefore, exceptions should not be allowed.

According to the NBS study, 75 percent of the homes surveyed have 30 percent relative humidity or less for six months of the year. It added that actual measurements in homes indicated relative humidities below 20 percent are not uncommon, especially during winter.

A second part of the study measured the surface-moisture

content of fabrics while being worn as compared with the relative humidity of the room. It revealed that the moisture content of close-fitting portions of natural fiber apparel differ significantly from room conditions.

Loose-fitting clothes, however, reflect room conditions and, in the case of synthetic apparel, both close- and loose-fitting clothes reflect surface humidities close to room humidities.

The study also found that exposure to a commercial space heater for as little as 5 minutes can effectively "oven-dry" an article of apparel and, in fact, remove more moisture from flame-retardant clothing than the oven-dry conditioning procedure.

Proposed rules and regulations for labeling, record keeping, and other requirements under the standard also were listed in the Federal Register.

1. If any agent or treatment is known to cause deterioration of the flame resistance of the item of apparel, such item shall be prominently labeled with precautionary care and treatment instructions to protect it from such harmful agent or treatment.
2. Complying and noncomplying sleepwear must be segregated by the retailer so the two are not mixed.
3. Every manufacturer, importer, or other person initially introducing such sleepwear into commerce must maintain written and physical records. The records must establish a line of continuity through the process of manufacture of each production unit, or fabrics or related materials intended or promoted for use in children's sleepwear, to the sale and delivery of the finished items and from the specific item to the manufacturing records.
4. Any person not subject to the above-mentioned requirement but who markets or handles children's sleepwear shall keep and maintain for three years records to show the source, date of receipt and identity of items marketed or handled; the identity of purchasers other than ultimate retail purchasers, and the date of sale.
5. Tests for guarantee purposes shall be those tests performed after any sampling plan devised to the requirement of the standard.

There is a definite procedural route the Consumer Products Safety Commission uses for developing such standards. The Commission must:

1. Issue a notice that there may be a need for a new standard. All interested parties then have a chance to present their views.

2. Issue a second notice establishing a proposed standard for flammability levels for the end product(s) under consideration. Interested parties may respond.
3. Publish a final notice setting forth the details of the standard and test method which becomes effective one year later or a suitable time following publication. After a one-year period, it becomes unlawful to produce and sell products which do not meet the established standards.

However, a proposal to reduce the notice of need for a flammability standard from a three-step procedure to a two-step procedure was published in the Federal Register March 17, 1975. The Consumer Product Safety Commission approved the proposal that would combine the first two steps with a notice to give finding of a possible need for a standard and a proposal for a flammability standard or amendment, and then the standard would be published in the Federal Register. The comment period is 30 days after publication in the Register.

One firm has produced the first full-fledged flame-retardant dress collections in girls sizes 1 to 12. Its dresses, meeting Federal Standards FF5, are selling in chains.

It is predicted that proposed flammability regulations will cover about half of the apparel industry in the United States and it is estimated that it could eventually cost the consumer $3 billion a year.

WHY IS THERE CONCERN?

One hundred fifty thousand Americans are seriously burned each year, and as many as 3000 of them die. Those who do survive undergo physical suffering and long and costly medical treatment. Some are disfigured for life; others suffer emotionally.

The Public Health Service, Department of Health, Education and Welfare reports that in the case of 300 items that met flammability standards, it was found that 70 percent of all burn cases involving males resulted from ignition of shirts (45 percent) and trousers (26 percent). Over 80 percent of the cases involving females resulted from ignition of their nightwear (41 percent), sweaters (17 percent), blouses (15 percent), and bathrobes (11 percent).

In the case of children under 10 years of age, the most common types of clothing that burned were nightclothes (40 percent) and shirts or blouses (35 percent).

Types of fiber in the clothing that ignited, with burns resulting, were: cotton, 87 percent; nylon, 7 percent; "synthetic" not otherwise classified, 3 percent; wool, 2 percent; and cotton-polyester blends, 2 percent.

There is a great need to develop flammability test methods that have a better correlation with actual occurrences of flaming, burning, charring, and melting.

INDUSTRY RESPONDS

Flame retardation is given first priority by the textile industry, since the Federal Consumer Product Safety Commission is considering proposing legislation to require fabric manufacturers and importers to certify that their products meet United States flammability standards. The textile industry is ardently trying to solve the complex problems of flammability. Some manufacturers are modifying their fibers and putting flame resistant chemicals into the solution before it is made into a fiber. Others are blending fibers to achieve a fire-resistant fabric. Still others are developing new finishes to apply to the surface of the fabric.

For discussion of the new flame-retardant fibers, see Chapter 2. For discussion of the flame-retardant finishes and consumer acceptance, see Chapter 5.

The burden of testing is on the manufacturer. Testing is costly. There are many groups working on flammability standards. As each group decides to set a particular standard, it often results in a new test method with different requirements from existing methods. Sometimes the same type of product undergoes two different types of testing to meet two different standards of flammability. For example, 19 different domestic tests have been established by different groups for flammability. Laws differ from one city, county, and state to another, as do the federal laws. There are cases where some tests are contradictory. There is an obvious need for standardization, and no doubt the Consumer Product Safety Commission will see that this is done.

The textile industry recognizes that the development of flame-retardant fabrics in the sleepwear industry is only the first step toward a wider range of fabrics for all fashion applications, not only infants and children, but the elderly, the infirm, and the ordinary consumer. Certainly curtains and draperies will be considered along with other household fabrics.

The textile industry is also anticipating an extension of the rules for dresses and sportswear. The textile industry also recognizes that there is some potential in the women's market, notably in career apparel. Now that they have the commitment and the technology, they have invested in research and testing equipment. It makes good sense to go after new markets.

LABELING FOR FLAMMABILITY

It is now required that garment manufacturers and fabric producers who supply over-the-counter fabrics tell the consumer what flammability protection may be expected and permanently attach care instructions, as required by the Care Labeling Rule.

Guidelines for labeling children's sleepwear are given in sleepwear standards 7 to 14 in the Federal Register, January 20, 1975. The guidelines for labeling requirements were changed by the Consumer Protective Agency as published in the Federal Register on July 2, 1975.

One portion of the proposed amendments requires sleepwear complying with the flammability standard to have an affirmative label so that prospective customers can distinguish between complying and noncomplying sleepwear.

The Commission believes 3 years is enough time to clear the market of noncomplying sleepwear and has proposed that time limit for the affirmative labels.

The labels, which would read: "flame resistant U.S. standard FF5-74," do not have to be permanently attached and may appear on a hangtag on the item itself or on the package enclosing the item, as long as the statement is readily seen at point of sale. The Commission also proposed that the labeling requirement preempt any similar state labeling requirement.

The Act implies that manufacturers must put a clear and conspicuous label on their apparel warning consumers of any danger from flammability that might result if the products are laundered at home or by the commercial laundry.

It is the responsibility of the manufacturers to test their products to ascertain how many washings the flame-retardant finish will actually take.

The retailer is also obligated to test and warrant the products he sells, or he can be forced to remove goods from sale and from store catalogs.

It is also recommended that labels be at least 3×5 inches in size, permanently affixed and durable for all the washings specified, and that consumers be informed through advertising as well as labels.

Consumers who purchase the new flame-retardant garments will find complicated washing instructions on the labels. Unless those instructions are followed, the flame-retardant properties of the clothes can be washed out (see pages 253, 254).

TRADE PRACTICE RULES AND REGULATIONS

The Federal Trade Commission has, from time to time, set up certain trade practice rules with regard to textile fibers. Many of these rules were eliminated after the Fiber Products Identification Act became effective, since the new Act covers the provisions of the trade practice rules, with the exception of the provision relating to silk weighting.

The Federal Trade Commission still requires the disclosure of any metallic weighting, loading, or adulterating materials in silk other than the dyeing and finishing materials necessary to produce the desired color or finish.

The Federal Trade Commission has also regulated the use of terms to describe shrinkage of cotton fabrics only. It specifies that fabrics must be labeled in such a way as to not lead consumers to believe that goods have been preshrunk to a greater degree than is actually true. For example, if a label states that shrinkage is less than 2.0 percent and a fabric shrinks to a greater degree, the fabric is mislabeled.

General notice of any proposed rule making is published in the Federal Register. If an oral hearing is held in connection with the proposed rule making, interested persons may appear and express their views and may suggest amendments, revisions, and additions. Written statements may also be accepted.

After consideration of all relevant matters of fact, law, policy, and discretion, including all relevant matters presented by interested persons in the proceeding, the Commission then adopts and publishes in the Federal Register a rule or order to become effective not less than 30 days after the date of publication.

The Federal Trade Commission issues administrative interpretations of the textile and fur laws for the guidance of industry in order that they may comply with the legal requirements. The industry guides provide the basis for voluntary and simultaneous abandonment of unlawful practices by industry.

The industry guides may be promulgated by the Commission either on its own initiative or by any interested person or group, when the industry guide would be in the public interest and would serve to bring about more widespread and equitable observance of laws administered by the Commission.

As with the trade regulation rules, the Commission may conduct investigations, make studies, and hold conferences or hearings.

In cases arising under the textile and fur laws and rules where it appears to the Commission to be in the public interest to do so, the Commission will apply to the courts for injunctive relief against the unlawful sale of products under question.

LEARNING EXPERIENCES

1. You may wish to do a class project, each student taking a selected test method and reporting to the class its purpose and scope, the basic principles involved, the equipment needed, how test specimens are prepared, and the methods of measuring and evaluating test results. If possible, determine the reliability of test results and how the findings are applied to consumer goods. Make a search of the literature.
2. Take a personal experience you have had with your dry cleaner when an item failed in dry cleaning. If you have never had a complaint, take a hypothetical case. Use the formula given in the International Fair Claims Guide for Consumer Textile Products and calculate your fair adjustment claim. Discuss the examples in class to determine if you have figured your claim accurately.
3. Survey the stores in your area to determine the extent to which fiber content labels are used. In your opinion, what are the loopholes in the Textile Fibers Product Identification Act?
4. Assemble permanent care labels that are examples of poor, fair, and good care procedures. Also assemble examples of confusing care labels, inaccurate care labels and false care labels.
5. Survey the stores in your area to determine the extent of merchandise available that is made of fire-resistant fibers. What price differential did you discover for identical items made of regular and fire-resistant fibers.
6. Assemble flame-retardant labels or hangtags that inform the consumer adequately on what he may expect in regard to safety. Also study the recommended care procedures. Determine if the information is adequate or inadequate.

APPENDIX A
FIBER TRADEMARKS
LISTED BY GENERIC
FIBER NAME

ACETATE

Acele	Filament yarn	E. I. du Pont de Nemours and Co., Inc.
Ariloft	Filament yarn	Eastman Kodak Co., Tennessee Eastman Co. Div.
Avicolor	Solution-dyed filament	FMC Corp., Fiber Division
Celacloud	Crimped staple fiberfill	Celanese Fibers Marketing Co., Celanese Corp.
Celanese	Staple filament, cigarette filter, and fiberfill	Celanese Fibers Marketing Co., Celanese Corp.
Chromspun	Solution-dyed filament yarn	Eastman Kodak Co., Tennessee Eastman Co. Div.
Estron	Filament yarn and cigarette filter tow	Eastman Kodak Co., Tennessee Eastman Co. Div.
Estron SLR	Filament yarn	Eastman Kodak Co., Tennessee Eastman Co. Div.
FMC	Filament yarn	FMC Corp., Fiber Division
Loftura	Slub voluminized Filament yarn	Eastman Kodak Co., Tennessee Eastman Co. Div.
SayFR	Fire resistant Filament acetate	FMC Corp., Fiber Division

ACRYLIC

A-Acrilan	Staple and tow	Monsanto Textiles Co.
Acrilan	Staple and tow	Monsanto Textiles Co.

Bi-Loft	Fibers, filaments	Monsanto Textiles Co.
Creslan	Staple and tow	American Cyanamid Co.
Orlon	Staple and tow	E. I. du Pont de Nemours and Co. Inc.
Zefran	Acrylic, dyeable, and producer colored	Dow Badische Co.

ARAMID

| Kevlar | Filament | E. I. du Pont de Nemours and Co., Inc. |
| Nomex | Filament and staple | E. I. du Pont de Nemours and Co., Inc. |

BICONSTITUENT FIBER

| Source | Biconstituent nylon-polyester | Allied Chemical Corp., Fibers Division |
| Monvelle | Biconstituent nylon-spandex | Monsanto Textiles Co. |

FLUOROCARBON

| Teflon | Fluorocarbon | E. I. du Pont de Nemours and Co., Inc. |

METALLIC

| Lurex | Yarn of slit film | Dow Badische Co. |

MODACRYLIC

A-Acrilan	Staple and tow	Monsanto Textiles Co.
Acrilan	Staple and tow	Monsanto Textiles Co.
Elura	Modacrylic	Monsanto Textiles Co.
Orlon	Staple and tow	E. I. du Pont de Nemours & Co., Inc.
Sef	Modacrylic	Monsanto Textiles Co.
Verel	Modacrylic	Eastman Kodak Co., Tennessee Eastman Co. Div.

NYLON

Actionwear	Nylon	Monsanto Textiles Co.
Anso	Nylon filament and staple soil-resistant carpet yarn	Allied Chemical Corp., Fibers Division
Antron	Nylon	E. I. du Pont de Nemours & Co., Inc.
Astroturf	Nylon	Monsanto Textiles Co.
Ayrlyn	Continuous filament	Rohm and Haas Co., Fibers Div.
Beaunit Nylon	Nylon filament, staple, and tow, plied and heat set 2500 denier and white and space dyed	Beaunit Corp.
Blue "C"	Nylon	Monsanto Textiles Co.
Bodyfree	Static-resistant filament apparel yarn	Allied Chemical Corp., Fibers Division
Cadon	Filament yarn and multilobal monofilament	Monsanto Textiles Co.
Cantrece	Nylon	E. I. du Pont de Nemours & Co., Inc.
Caprolan	Yarns, monofilaments, and textured yarns	Allied Chemical Corp., Fibers Division
Captiva	Textured filament hosiery yarn	Allied Chemical Corp., Fibers Division
Cedilla	Textured nylon filament yarn	Fiber Industries, Inc., Marketed by Celanese Fibers Marketing Co., Celanese Corp.
Celanese	Nylon	Fiber Industries, Inc., Marketed by Celanese Fibers Marketing Co., Celanese Corp.
Cordura	Nylon	E. I. du Pont de Nemours & Co., Inc.
Courtaulds Nylon	Nylon producer Crimped nylon yarn	Courtaulds North America, Inc.

Crepeset	Patented continuous monofilament that develops a regular crimp, also available in anticling yarn	American Enka Co.
Cumuloft	Textured filament carpet yarn	Monsanto Textiles Co.
Enka	Nylon filament, staple	American Enka Co.
Enkaloft	Textured multilobal continuous filament carpet yarn and staple	American Enka Co.
Enkalure	Multilobal continuous filament apparel yarn and textured delayed soiling carpet yarn	American Enka Co.
Enkalure II	Textured multilobal soil-hiding continuous filament carpet yarn and staple.	American Enka Co.
Enkalure III	Anticling fine denier nylon	American Enka Co.
Enkasheer	Continuous monofilament torque yarn for ladies' stretch hosiery (patented process)	American Enka Co.
Guaranteeth	Apparel and home furnishings nylon and polyester yarn	Allied Chemical Corp., Fibers Division
Monvelle	Biconstituent nylon-spandex	Monsanto Textiles Co.
Multisheer	Multifilament producer-textured stretch yarn for panty hose	American Enka Co.
Phillips 66 Nylon	Multifilament nylon yarn	Phillips Fibers Corp.

Phillips 66 Nylon BCF	Bulk continuous filament yarn	Phillips Fibers Corp.
Qiana	Nylon	E. I. du Pont de Nemours & Co., Inc.
Random-Set	Heat set BCF nylon	Rohm and Haas Co.
Random-Tone	Fashion and styling yarns of BCF nylon fiber	Rohm and Haas Co.
Shareen	Nylon mono-filament textured yarn	Courtaulds North America Inc.
Source	Biconstituent nylon-polyester	Allied Chemical Corp., Fibers Division
Stria	Bulked nylon carpet yarn, modified twist	American Enka Co.
Stryton	Variable denier continuous fila-ment nylon yarn	Phillips Fibers Corp.
Super Bulk	Heat-set, high-bulk continuous filament nylon carpet yarn; lux-urious thick look of spun nylon	American Enka Co.
Tango	Fine denier nylon	Allied Chemical Corp., Fibers Division
Twix	Bulk nylon carpet yarn, modified twist	American Enka Co.
Ultron	Nylon	Monsanto Textiles Co.
Variline	Variable denier continuous fila-ment yarn (pat-ented process)	American Enka Co.
Zefran	Nylon	Dow Badische Co.

OLEFIN

Herculon	Continuous multifilament, bulked continuous multifilament staple and tow	Hercules Inc., Fibers Div.

Marvess	Staple, tow, and filament yarn	Phillips Fibers Corp.
Marvess III BCF	Bulk continuous filament yarn	Phillips Fibers Corp.

POLYESTER

Avlin	Filament yarn and staple	FMC Corp., Fiber Div.
Blue "C"	Polyester	Monsanto Textiles Co.
Dacron	Filament yarn, staple, tow, and fiberfill	E. I. du Pont de Nemours & Co., Inc.
Encron	Continuous filament yarn, staple, fiberfill	American Enka Co.
Encron MCS	Staple with modified cross section	American Enka Co.
Encron 8	Octalobal polyester that reduces glitter	American Enka Co.
Enka	Filament and staple	American Enka Co.
Esterweld	Polyester	American Cyanamid Co.
Fiber 200	Polyester	FMC Corp., Fiber Div.
Fortrel	Filament yarn, staple, tow, and fiberfill	Marketed by Celanese Fibers Marketing Co., Celanese Corp.
Fortrel 7	Continuous filament fiberfill	Fiber Industries, Inc., Marketed by Celanese Fibers Marketing Co., Celanese Corp.
Golden Touch	High-denier per filament Encron polyester for luxurious hand	American Enka Co.
Guaranteeth	Apparel and home furnishings nylon and polyester yarn	Allied Chemical Corp., Fibers Division
Kodel	Filament yarn, staple, tow, and fiberfill	Eastman Kodak Co., Tennessee Eastman Co. Div.
Quintess	Polyester multifilament yarns	Phillips Fibers Corp.

Source	Biconstituent nylon-polyester	Allied Chemical Corp.
Spectran	Polyester	Monsanto Textiles Co.
Strialine	Slub-effect, variable dyeing Encron polyester	American Enka Co.
Textura	Producer textured polyester yarn	Rohm and Haas Co., Fibers Div.
Trevira	Polyester	Hoechst Fibers Inc.
Vycron	Filament, staple, tow, and fiberfill	Beaunit Corp.
Zefran	Polyester	Dow Badische Co.

RAYON

Avicolor	Solution-dyed filament and staple	FMC Corp., Fiber Division
Aviloc	Adhesive-treated high-strength rayon yarn	FMC Corp., Fiber Division
Avril	High wet modulus staple	FMC Corp., Fiber Division
Avril FR	Fire-resistant, high wet modulus rayon	FMC Corp., Fiber Division
Beau-Grip	Specially treated viscose high-tenacity yarn	Beaunit Corp.
Briglo	Bright luster continuous filament yarn	American Enka Co.
Coloray	Solution-dyed staple	Courtaulds North America Inc.
Encel	High wet modulus staple	American Enka Co.
Englo	Dull luster continuous filament yarn	American Enka Co.
Enka	Rayon	American Enka Co.
Enkrome	Patented acid-dyeable staple and continuous filament yarn	American Enka Co.
Fiber 40	High wet modulus staple	FMC Corp., Fiber Division

Fiber 700	High wet modulus staple	American Enka Co.
Fibro	Staple	Courtaulds North America Inc.
Fibro DD	Deep-dyed rayon staple fiber	Courtaulds North America Inc.
Fibro FR	Flame-retardant rayon staple fiber	Courtaulds North America Inc.
FMC	Rayon	FMC Corp., Fiber Division
I.T.	Improved tenacity staple	American Enka Co.
Jetspun	Solution-dyed continuous filament yarn	American Enka Co.
Kolorbon	Solution-dyed staple	American Enka Co.
SayFR	Fire-resistant filament rayon	FMR Corp., Fiber Division
Skyloft	Bulked continuous filament yarn	American Enka Co.
Softglo	Semidull luster continuous filament yarn	American Enka Co.
Super White	Optically brightened rayon	American Enka Co.
Suprenka	Extra high-tenacity continuous filament industrial yarn	American Enka Co.
Suprenka Hi Mod	Extra high-tenacity high-modulus continuous filament	American Enka Co.
Xena	High wet modulus staple	Beaunit Corp.
Zantrel	High wet modulus staple	American Enka Co.
Zantrell 700	High wet modulus staple	American Enka Co.

SPANDEX

Lycra	Spandex	E. I. du Pont de Nemours & Co. Inc.

| Monvelle | Biconstituent nylon-spandex | Monsanto Textiles Co. |

TRIACETATE

| Arnel | Filament yarn and staple | Celanese Fibers Marketing Co., Celanese Corp. |

TRADEMARKS OF MEMBER COMPANIES NOT CLASSIFIED AS "FIBER TRADEMARKS"

This list of trademarks indicates trademarks used by members that do not come within the Federal Trade Commission definition of "fiber trademark" but that may be used, from time to time, to identify the source of certain manmade fibers or other products of the company.

Trademark	*Member Company*
ACT	Allied Chemical Corporation, Marketed by Specialty Chemicals Division
ADORATION	E. I. du Pont de Nemours & Co., Inc.
ANGELREST	Fiber Industries, Inc., Marketed by Celanese Fibers Marketing Company, A Division of Celanese Corporation
ANTELETTE	Fiber Industries, Inc., Marketed by Celanese Fibers Marketing Company, A division of Celanese Corporation
ASTROTURF	Monsanto Textiles Company
AVISCO	FMC Corporation, Fiber Division
BEAUNIT	Beaunit Corporation
BYTRECE	E. I. du Pont de Nemours & Co., Inc.
CELABOND	Celanese Fibers Marketing Co., Celanese Corp.
CELAIRE	Celanese Fibers Marketing Co., Celanese Corp.
CELANESE	Celanese Fibers Marketing Co., Celanese Corp.
CELANNA	Celanese Fibers Marketing Co., Celanese Corp.
CELASPUN	Celanese Fibers Marketing Co., Celanese Corp.

Trademark	*Member Company*
CHEMSTRAND	Monsanto Textiles Company
COURTAULDS	Courtaulds North America Inc.
CUPROFINO	Beaunit Corporation
DU PONT	E. I. du Pont De Nemours & Co., Inc.
DYE I	Monsanto Textiles Company
EASTMAN	Eastman Kodak Company, Tennessee Eastman Company Division
EKTAFILL	Eastman Kodak Company, Tennessee Eastman Company Division
ELURA	Monsanto Textiles Company
ENKA	American Enka Company
FMC	FMC Corporation, Fiber Division
HERCULES	Hercules Incorporated
HYTEN	E. I. du Pont de Nemours & Co., Inc.
LEKTROSET	IRC Fibers Company, Subsidiary of American Cyanamid Company
LOKTUFT	Phillips Fibers Corporation, Subsidiary of Phillips Petroleum Company
LOWLAND	American Enka Company
LYRIC	Eastman Kodak Company, Tennessee Eastman Company Division
REEMAY	E. I. du Pont de Nemours & Co., Inc.
SERENE	Fiber Industries, Inc., Marketed by Celanese Fibers Marketing Co., A Division of Celanese Corporation
SPUNIZE	Allied Chemical Corp., Fibers Division
SUPERBA	Fiber Industries, Inc., Marketed by Celanese Fibers Marketing Company, A Division of Celanese Corporation
TASLAN	E. I. du Pont de Nemours & Co., Inc.
TYPAR	E. I. du Pont de Nemours & Co., Inc.
TYVEK	E. I. du Pont de Nemours & Co., Inc.
WEAR-DATED	Monsanto Textiles Company
ZEFSTAT	Dow Badische Company
ZEFWEAR	Dow Badische Company

APPENDIX B
FIBER PRODUCERS
AND ASSOCIATIONS;
PUBLICATIONS

FIBER PRODUCERS AND ASSOCIATIONS

NATURAL FIBERS

Cotton   Cotton, Inc.
1370 Avenue of the Americas
New York, N.Y. 10019

National Cotton Council of America
Box 12285, Memphis, Tenn. 38112

Supima Association of America
350 Fifth Avenue, New York, N.Y. 10001

Linen   Belgian Linen Association
280 Madison Avenue, New York, N.Y. 10016

Irish Linen Guild
1271 Avenue of the Americas,
New York, N.Y. 10020

Wool   American Sheep Producers Council
200 Clayton St., Denver, Col. 80206

American Wool Council
1460 Broadway, New York, N.Y. 10038

Mohair Council of America
151 W. 40th St., New York, N.Y. 10018

Wool Bureau
360 Lexington Ave., New York, N.Y. 10017

Silk   International Silk Association
299 Madison Ave., New York, N.Y. 10017

MEMBERS, MAN-MADE FIBER PRODUCERS ASSOCIATION, INC.

Allied Chemical Corp., Fibers Div.,
One Times Square, New York, N.Y. 10036

American Cyanamid Co., Fibers Div.,
Berdan Ave., Wayne, N.J. 07470

American Enka Company, A Part of Akzona, Inc.
Enka, N.C. 28728

Beaunit Corporation
261 Madison Ave., New York, N.Y. 10016

Celanese Corp., Celanese Fibers Marketing Co.
1211 Ave. of the Americas, New York, N.Y. 10018

Dow Badische Company
Williamburg, Va 23185

E. I. du Pont de Nemours & Co., Inc.
Textile Fibers Dept., Wilmington, Del. 19898

Eastman Kodak Co., Tenn. Eastman Co. Div.,
Marketed by Eastman Chemical Products Inc.
Kingsport, Tenn. 37662

Hercules Inc., Fibers Div.,
910 Market St., Wilmington, Del. 19899

Hoechst Fibers Incorporated
1515 Broadway at Astor Plaza, New York, N.Y. 10036

Monsanto Textiles Company
800 N. Lindbergh Blvd., St. Louis, Mo. 63166

Phillips Fiber Corporation
Subsidiary of Phillips Petroleum Co.
P.O. Box 66, Greenville, S.C. 29602

Rohm & Haas Co., Fibers Div.,
Independence Mall West, Philadelphia, Pa. 19105

TRADE ASSOCIATIONS

American Apparel Manufacturers Association,
1611 North Kent Street, Arlington, Va. 22209

American Carpet Institute,
350 Fifth Avenue, New York, N.Y. 10001

American Dye Manufacturers Institute, Inc.,
74 Trinity Place, New York, N.Y. 10006

American Institute of Men's and Boys' Wear,
1290 Avenue of the Americas, New York, N.Y. 10019

American Printed Fabric Council,
1440 Broadway, New York, N.Y. 10018

American Silk Council, Inc.,
185 Madison Avenue, New York, N.Y. 10016

American Textile Manufacturers' Institute, Inc.,
1501 Johnston Building, Charlotte, N.C. 28201

Association of Home Appliance Manufacturers,
20 North Wacker Drive, Chicago, Ill. 60606

Association of Interior Decor Specialists, Inc.,
4420 North Fairfax Drive, Arlington, Va. 22203

Association of Knitted Fabrics Manufacturers,
1450 Broadway, New York, N.Y. 10018

Belgian Linen Association,
280 Madison Avenue, New York, N.Y. 10016

The Bonded Fabric Council,
350 Fifth Avenue, Room 5623, New York, N.Y. 10001

Corduroy Council of America,
15 East 53rd Street, New York, N.Y. 10022

Denim Council,
155 East 44th Street, New York, N.Y. 10017

Durene Association of America,
350 Fifth Avenue, New York, N.Y. 10001

Fabric Laminators Association,
110 West 40th Street, New York, N.Y. 10018

Foam Fashion Forum,
40 East 49th St., New York, N.Y. 10010

International Fabricare Institute
Headquarters: Joilet, Ill. 60434
Research Center: 12251 Tech Drive, Silver Spring, Md. 20910

International Color Authority,
24 East 38th St., New York, N.Y. 10016

International Nonwovens & Disposables Association,
10 East 40th Street, New York, N.Y. 10017

Knitted Fabrics Institute, Inc.,
1450 Broadway, New York, N.Y. 10018

Lace and Embroidery Association of Amerca, Inc.,
111 Fifth Avenue, New York, N.Y. 10008

Leavers Lace Manufacturers of America,
87 Weybosset St., Providence, R.I. 02903

Man-Mad Fiber Producers Association,
1150 Seventeenth St., NW, Washington, D.C. 20036

National Knitted Outerwear Association,
51 Madison Avenue, New York, N.Y. 10010

National Retail Manufacturers Association,
100 W. 31st St., New York, N.Y. 10001

National Safety Council,
425 North Michigan Avenue, Chicago, Ill. 60611

American Print Fabric Council,
1440 Broadway, New York, N.Y. 10018

Supina Association of America,
603 First National Building, El Paso, Texas 79901

Textile Distributors Association,
1040 Avenue of the Americas, New York, 10018

Vinyl Fabrics Institute,
60 E. 42nd St., New York, N.Y. 10017

Yarn Spinners Association, Inc.,
Box 99, Gastonia, N.C. 28052

SCIENTIFIC, CIVIC, PROFESSIONAL ORGANIZATIONS

American Association of Textile Chemists and Colorists,
P.O. Box 12215, Research Triangle, Durham, N.C. 27709

American Association for Textile Technology, Inc.
11 West 42nd St., New York, N.Y. 10036

American National Standards Institute, Inc.,
1403 Broadway, New York, N.Y. 10018

American Society for Testing and Materials,
1916 Race St., Philadelphia, Pa. 19103

Institute of Textile Technology,
Charlottesville, Va. 17160

Textile Research Institute,
P.O. Box 625, Princeton, N.J. 08540

PUBLICATIONS

American Dyestuff Reporter, SAF International, Inc.,
44 East 23rd St., New York, N.Y. 10010

American Fabrics Magazine, Doric Publishing Co., Inc.,
24 East 38th St., New York, N.Y. 10016

America's Textiles Reporter/Bulletin, Clark Publishing Co.,
106 East Stone Ave., P.O. Box 88, Greenville, S.C. 29602

The Clemson University Marketing Letter,
College of Industrial Management and Textile Science,
Serrine Hall, Clemson University, Clemson, S.C. 29631

Daily News Record, Fairchild Publications, Inc.,
7 East 12th St., New York, N.Y. 10003

Fabrics, Fashions/Fact, Fiction, International Fabricate Institute, Box 940, Joliet, Ill. 60434

Journal of Home Economics, The American Home Economics Assn.,
2010 Massachusetts Ave., NW, Washington, D.C. 20036.

Knitting Times,
51 Madison Avenue, New York, N.Y. 10010

Modern Textiles, Rayon Publishing Corp., 303 Fifth Avenue,
New York, N.Y. 10016

Modern Knitting Management, Rayon Publishing Corporation,
303 Fifth Avenue, New York, N.Y. 10016

Texas Tech, Tips and Topics in Home Economics,
College of Home Economics,
P.O. Box 4170, Texas Tech University, Lubbock, Texas 79409

Textile Chemist and Colorist,
Journal of the American Association of Textile Chemists and Colorists,
P.O. Box 12215, Research Triangle Park, N.C. 27709

Textile Industries, W.R.C. Smith Publishing Company,
1760 Peachtree Road, N.W., Atlanta, Ga. 30309

Textile Organon, Textile Economics Bureau, Inc.,
489 Fifth Avenue, New York, N.Y. 10017

Textile Technology Digest,
Institute of Textile Technology, Charlottesville, Va. 22904

Textile World, McGraw-Hill Publications,
1175 Peachtree St. NE, Atlanta, Ga. 30309

APPENDIX C
REACTION OF TEXTILE FIBERS TO HEAT AND FLAME

REACTION OF TEXTILE FIBERS TO HEAT AND FLAME

Test Procedure: A specimen of the fiber is moved slowly toward a small flame, and the reaction of the fiber to heat is observed. One end of the specimen is then pushed directly into the flame to determine the burning characteristics of the fiber. After removal from the flame, the fiber's burning characteristics are again observed and the burning odor is noted. (The burning odor can be compared with that of known fibers.) The specimen is then allowed to cool, and the characteristics of the ash are checked.

Groups of fibers, short lengths of yarn or small pieces of fabric can be used as test specimens unless the product to be tested contains a combination of yarns or a blend of fibers. In such cases, individual fibers selected from the textile material with the aid of a magnifying glass may be used.

Caution: This test should be made with care to prevent burning of the fingers and to avoid inhaling excessive amounts of smoke from the burning sample. Hold the yarns or fabric with a pair of tweezers. Do not allow molten material to drop on your skin. It can cause a severe burn.

TYPICAL BEHAVIOR OF FIBER SPECIMEN

Fibers	When Approaching Flame	When in Flame	After Removal of Flame	Odor	Typical Ash Characteristics
Cellulose Fibers					
Cotton	Does not fuse or shrink away from flame.	Burns quickly without melting.	Continues to burn without melting afterglow.	Burning paper.	Small, fluffy gray ash.
Linen	Does not fuse or shrink away from flame.	Burns quickly without melting.	Continues to burn without melting afterglow.	Burning paper.	Small, fluffy gray ash.
Protein Fibers					
Natural Silk	Fuses and curls away from flame.	Burns slowly with some melting.	Burns very slowly; sometimes self-extinguishing.	Burning feathers.	Round black bead, brittle, pulverizes easily.
Weighted Silk	Fuses and curls away from flame.	Burns slowly with some melting.	Burns very slowly; sometimes self-extinguishing.	Burning feathers.	Leaves ash the form or shape of fiber or fabric. Glows like a red-hot wire.
Wool	Fuses and curls away from flame.	Burns slowly with some melting.	Burns very slowly; sometimes self-extinguishing.	Burning hair.	Lumpy, blistered ash, brittle, breaks easily.
Man-Made					
Azlon	Fuses and curls away from flame.	Burns slowly.	Sometimes self-extinguishing.	Burning hair.	Brittle black bead.
Mineral Fibers					
Natural Asbestos	Does not ignite.	Does not melt. Glows in high heat.	No change.	No odor.	Remains unchanged. May blacken.
Man-Made Mineral					
Glass	Does not burn.	Softens and glows.	Hardens.	None.	Changes shape. Hard bead.

Fibers	When Approaching Flame	When in Flame	After Removal of Flame	Odor	Typical Ash Characteristics
Metallic.					
Pure Metal	Does not burn.	Glows red.	Hardens	None.	Original shape.
Coated Metal	Fuses and shrinks.	Melts.	Depends on coating used.	None.	Hard bead.
Man-Made Fibers (Cellulose)					
Rayon	Does not shrink away from flame.	Burns very rapidly.	Leaves a creeping ember.	Burning wood.	Small or no ash.
Man-Made Modified (Cellulose)					
Acetate	Fuses away from flame	Burns with melting.	Continues to burn with melting.	Acedic acid or vinegar.	Leaves brittle, black, irregular-shaped bead.
Tri-Acetate	Fuses away from flame.	Burns with melting.	Continues to burn with melting	Burning paper.	Brittle, black irregular shaped bead.
Man-Made Fibers					
Acrylic	Fuses away from flame.	Burns rapidly with melting.	Continues to burn with melting. Shreds material.	Acrid.	Leaves hard, brittle, black, irregular-shaped bead.
Anidex	Fuses away from flame.	Burns with melting.	Continues to burn with melting.	Chemical.	Leaves black charred ash.
Aramid	Fuses and shrinks away from flame.	Burns slowly with melting.	Self-extinguishing.	Sweet.	Leaves a hard brown ash.
Mod-acrylic	Fuses away from flame.	Burns very slowly with melting.	Self-extinguishing.	Acrid.	Leaves hard, black irregular shaped bead.
Novoloid	Fuses and shrinks from flame.	Burns slowly with a glow.	Self-extinguishing.	Phenolic.	Retain shape but turns black.
Nylon	Fuses and shrinks away from flame.	Burns slowly with melting.	Usually self-extinguishing.	Boiling string beans.	Leaves hard, tough, gray, round bead.
Nytril	Fuses away from flame.	Burns slowly with melting.	Continues to burn with melting.	None.	Leaves hard, black irregular shaped bead.
Olefin	Fuses, shrinks and curls away from flame.	Burns with melting.	Continues to burn with melting.	Chemical.	Leaves hard, tough tan, round bead.
Polyester	Fuses and shrinks away from flame.	Burns slowly with melting.	Usually self-extinguishing.	Chemical.	Leaves hard, tough black, round bead.
Rubber	Fuses away from flame	Burns rapidly with melting.	Continues to burn with melting	Sulphur.	Soft, tacky, irregular mass.
Saran	Fuses and shrinks away from flame.	Burns very slowly with melting.	Self-extinguishing.	Sharp, acrid.	Leaves hard, black, irregular bead.
Spandex	Fuses but does not shrink away from flame.	Burns with melting.	Continues to burn with melting.	Chemical.	Leaves soft, fluffy, black ash.
Vinal	Fuses and shrinks away from flame.	Burns with melting.	Continues to burn with melting.	Chemical.	Leaves hard, tough, tan bead.
Vinyon	Fuses and shrinks away from flame.	Burns slowly with melting.	Self-extinguishing.	Acrid.	Leaves hard, black, irregular bead.

APPENDIX D
MICROSCOPIC
TESTS AND
APPEARANCE

MICROSCOPIC TEST

Test Procedure (Longitudinal)
1. Pull a yarn from the warp or lengthwise direction of the sample. 2. Tease the yarn apart into fibers. 3. Mount the fibers on a slide with a drop of distilled water. Place a cover glass over the mount. 4. Examine at low magnification (50 to 60x). 5. Examine under high magnification (250 to 500x) (see page 32.) 6. Compare with a known sample or photomicrograph. 7. Repeat with a yarn pulled from the filling or crosswise direction of the fabric.
Test Procedure (Cross-section)
Considerable technique is required to make cross-sections of textile fibers. See the Technical Manual of the American Association of Textile Chemists and Color-ists, Method 20-1973, or the method of the American Society of Testing Materials, Test Method D-276-60T.

MICROSCOPIC APPEARANCE*

Fiber	Longitudinal	Cross-Section
Cellulosic Fibers		
Cotton (Merceri-zed and not mer-cerized)	Ribbon-like. Convolutions sometimes change direction. No significant lengthwise striations.	Tubular shape with tubes usually collapsed and irregular in size.
Linen	Bamboo-like. Pronounced cross-markings nodes and fissures. No significant lengthwise striations.	Tubular shape with tubes often col-lapsed and very irregular in size as well as shape.
Ramie	Similar to linen but much larger. Very heavy cell walls and well defined lumen or broad and flat wall with indistinct lumen.	Thick, irregular convolutions.
Jute	Long cell elements with frequent joints. Uneven in diameter. Broken tissue usually evident. Broad lumen.	Irregular-shaped with central lumen.
Protein Fibers Natural		
Silk (Weighted silk)	Smooth surface like a glass rod. No significant lengthwise striations.	Triangular. Points of triangle are rounded. Irregular in size and shape.
Wool	Serrated surface and cross-markings due to surface scales.	Round or nearly round.
Man-Made		
Azlon (Chinon)	Smooth surface like a glass rod.	Similar to silk. Irregular shape with 6 rounded lobes that are ir-regular in size and shape.

* Tradenames are used only when longitudinal or cross-sections differ from generic names.

Fiber	Longitudinal	Cross-Section
Mineral Fibers		
Natural		
Asbestos	Straight surface like a finely polished metal rod.	Irregular striated shapes.
Man-Made		
Glass	Rod-like with smooth surface.	Round cross-sections.
Metallic		
Pure metal	Long, smooth, rod-like.	Round, smooth.
Coated metal	Irregular widths, pigmented. Varies with method of construction.	Rounded lobes that vary according to construction.
Man-Made Fibers (Cellulose)		
Rayon		
Viscose	Very distinct lengthwise striations. No cross-markings.	Irregular shape. Serrated outline.
High tenacity	Smooth, rod-like. No irregular striations.	Irregular in shape with few serrations.
High wet modules	Smooth, rod-like.	Oval or round shape.
Cuprammonium	Smooth glass-like rod.	Round.
Man-Made (Modified Cellulose)		
Acetate Triacetate	Glass-like rod with distinct lengthwise striations. No cross-markings.	Irreular shape. Serrated outline.
Man-Made Fibers		
Acrylic		
Acrilan, Creslan, Zefran	Rod-like. Smooth surface and outline.	Round or nearly round. May include bean shape.
Orlon	Broad. Indistinct lengthwise striations. No cross-markings.	Dog-bone.
Bicomponent Orlon	Lengthwise striations. No cross-markings.	Irregular - mushroom or acorn.
Anidex		
Anim/8	Wide translucent with lighter central canal.	Round.
Aramid	Smooth surface like a glass rod.	Round.
Modacrylic		
Dynel	Lengthwise striations. No cross-markings.	Ribbon-like; irregular.
Verel	Broad and often indistinct lengthwise striations.	Dog-bone.
Nylon	Glass-rod. Smooth surface.	Round or nearly round.
Antron	Broad rod-shape, indefinite lengthwise striations.	Trilobal (3 lobes).
Novaloid	Amorphus (shapeless). No micro structure.	Amorphus (shapeless).
Nytril	Distinct lengthwise striations.	Irregular shape. Serrated outline.
Olefin	Rod-like with a smooth surface and outline.	Round or nearly round.
Polyester	Rod-like with a smooth surface and outline.	Round or nearly round.
Trevira	Broad rod shape, indefinite lengthwise striations.	Pentalobal (5 lobes).
Dacron (T68)	Broad, sometimes indistinct lengthwise striations. No cross markings.	Trilobal (3 lobes).
Dacron 8	Broad rod shape, indefinite lengthwise striations.	Octolobal (8 lobes).
Rubber		
Extruded	Opaque, pigmented ribbon-like.	Round, oval with crystal particals on wall.
Cut	Opaque, pigmented ribbon-like.	Square, rectangular.
Saran	Rod-like with a smooth surface and outline	Round or nearly round.

Fiber	Longitudinal	Cross-Section
Spandex	Broad. Indistinct lengthwise striations. No cross-markings.	Dog-bone.
Globe DC100	Vary in size. Flat ribbon-like with striations.	Irregular, round.
Vinal		
Vinyon	Resembles mercerized cotton; lumen-like channel running through the middle of filament with an occasional twist.	Dog-bone.
Photomicrographs on following pages courtesy of E. I. DuPont de Nemours and Company, Inc.		

PHOTOMICROGRAPHS OF MAN-MADE TEXTILE
FIBERS *(All photomicrographs reproduced full size)*

Longitudinal View at 250X   Cross-Sectional View at 500X

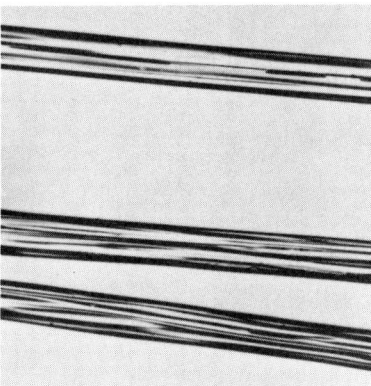

ACETATE FIBERS

Acele* (secondary acetate)
3.8 denier per filament
bright luster

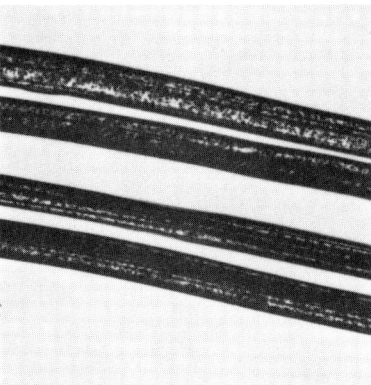

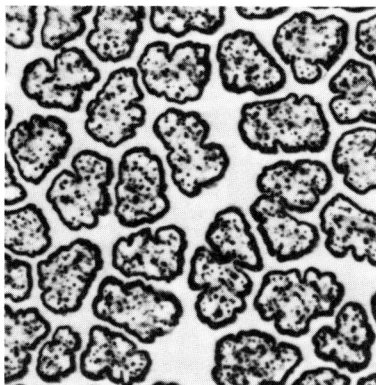

"Arnel" (triacetate)
2.5 denier per filament
dull luster

*Du Pont's registered trademark
for its acetate fiber

Longitudinal View at 250X   Cross-Sectional View at 500X

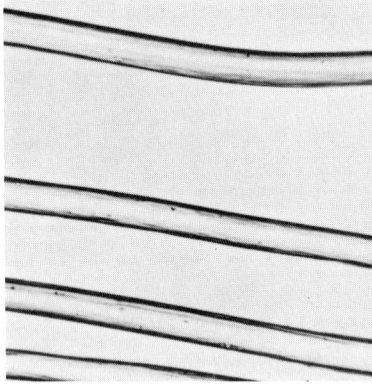

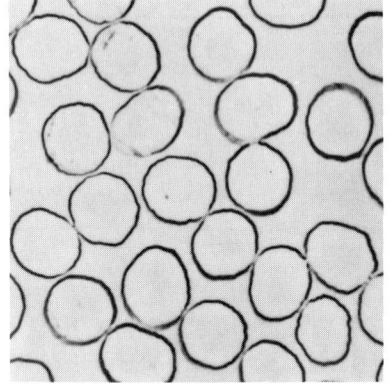

ACRYLIC FIBERS

"Acrilan" regular
3.0 denier per filament
bright luster

"Creslan"
3.0 denier per filament
semidull luster

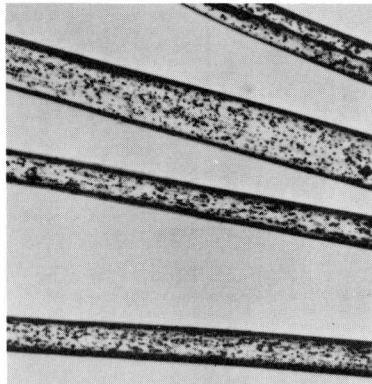

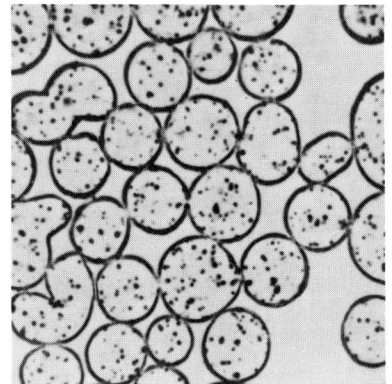

Orlon* regular
3.0 denier per filament
semidull luster

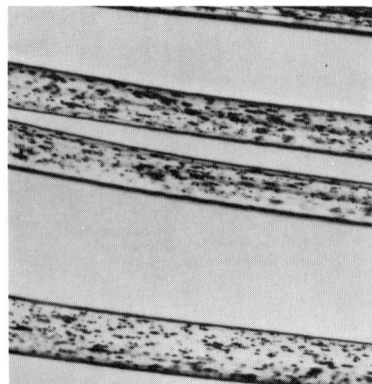

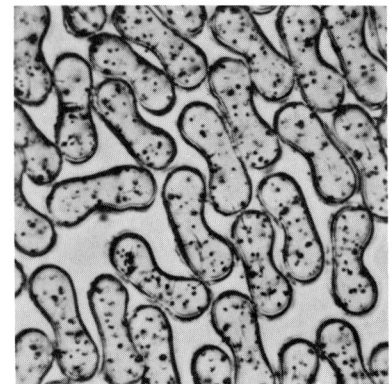

*Du Pont's registered
trademark for its acrylic
fiber

Longitudinal View at 250X   Cross-Sectional View at 500X

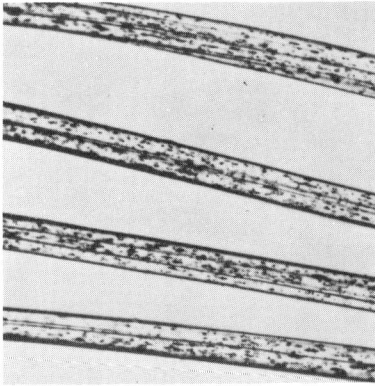

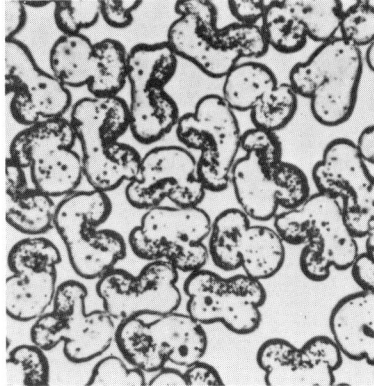

Orlon Sayelle*
3.0 denier per filament
semidull luster

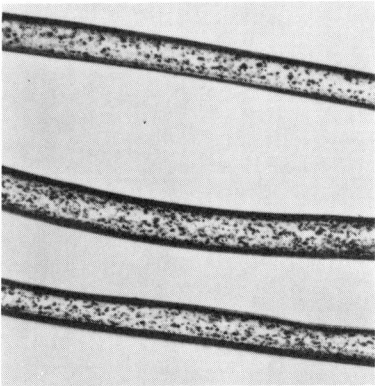

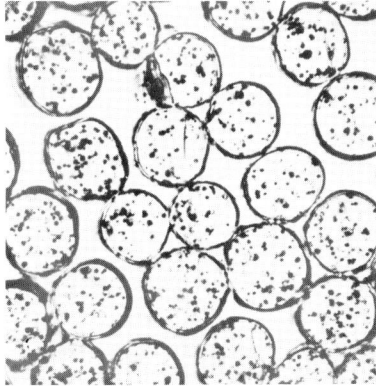

"Zefran"
3.0 denier per filament
semidull luster

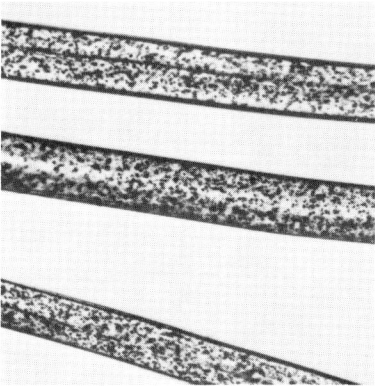

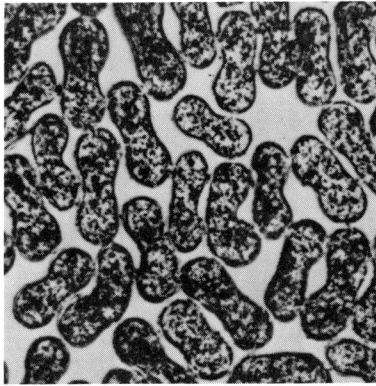

MODACRYLIC FIBERS

"Verel" regular
3.0 denier per filament
dull luster

*Du Pont's registered
trademark for its
bi-component acrylic fiber

NYLON FIBERS

Longitudinal View at 250X

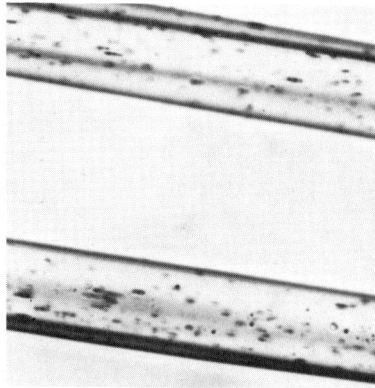

Cross-Sectional View at 500X

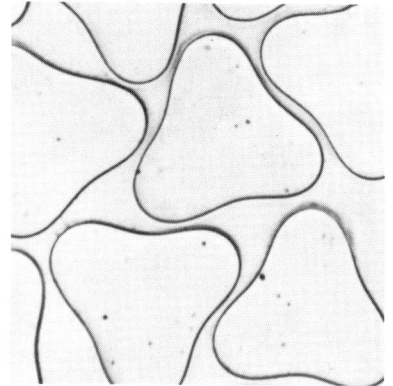

Antron*
15 denier per filament
bright luster

Nylon 6
3.1 denier per filament
semidull luster

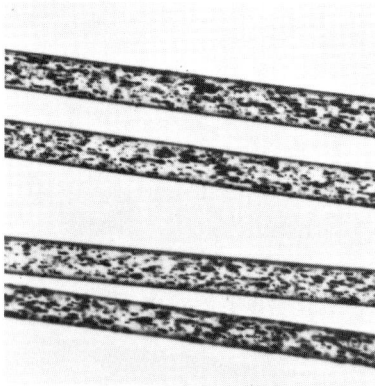

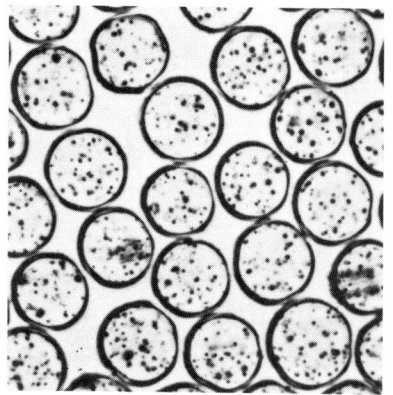

Nylon 6-6 regular
3.1 denier per filament
semidull luster

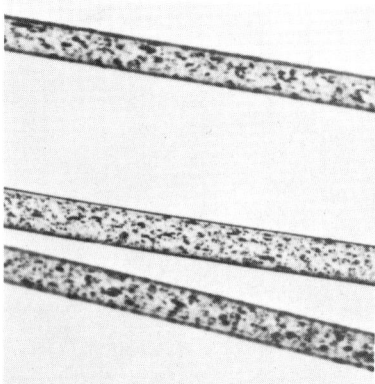

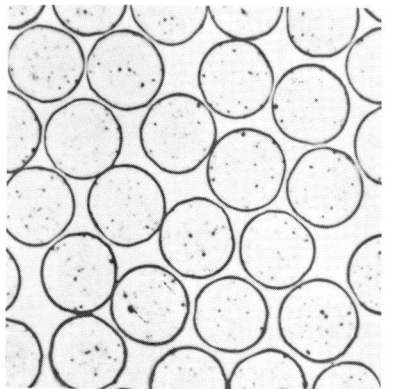

*Du Pont's registered trademark
for its trilobal multifilament nylon
6-6 yarn

Longitudinal View at 250X   Cross-Sectional View at 500X

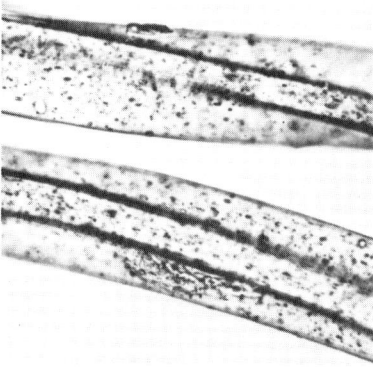

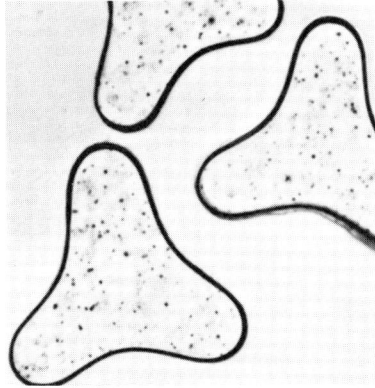

Nylon 6-6 Du Pont Type 501
18 denier per filament
semidull luster

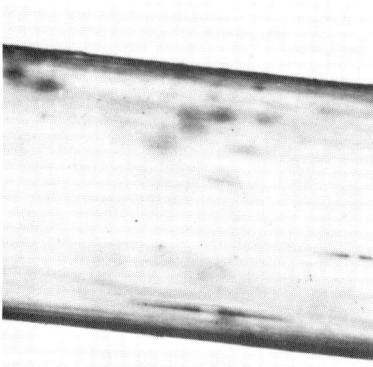

OLEFIN FIBERS

Polyethylene
90* denier per filament
natural luster

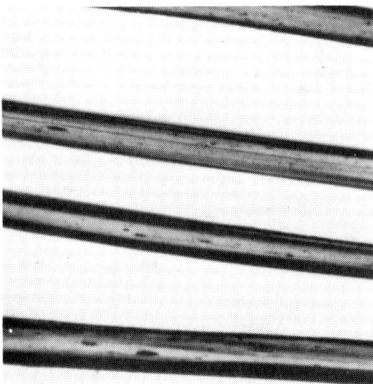

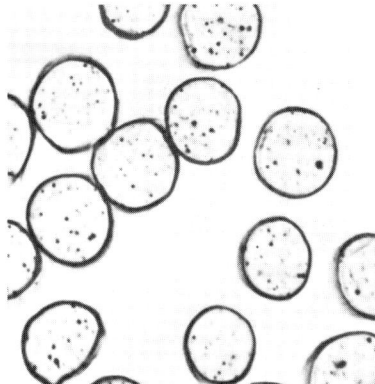

Polypropylene
3.0 denier per filament
natural luster

*4 to 5 mil (diameter) monofila-
ment yarn

Longitudinal View at 250X   Cross-Sectional View at 500X

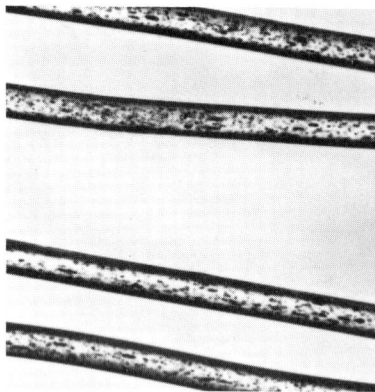

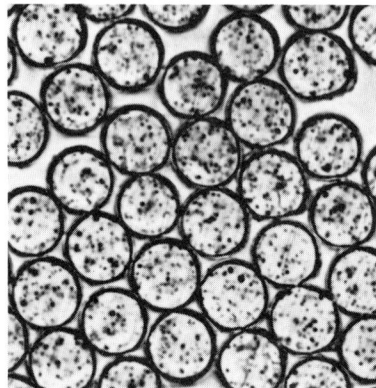

POLYESTER FIBERS

Dacron* regular
3.0 denier per filament
semidull luster

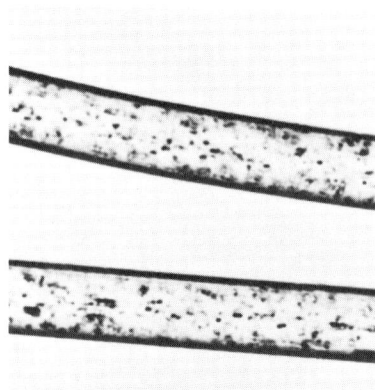

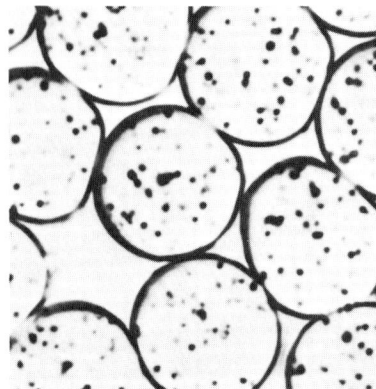

Dacron Type 62
1.4 denier per filament
semidull luster

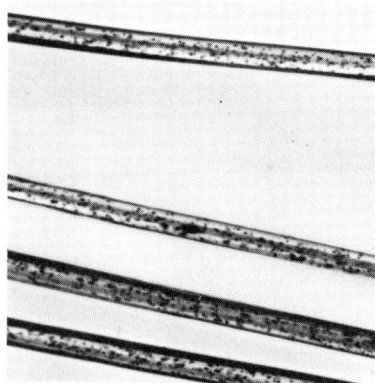

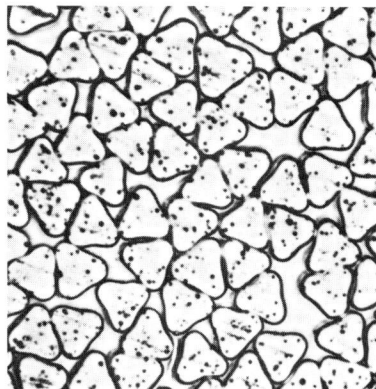

Dacron Type 64
3.0 denier per filament
semidull luster

*Du Pont's registered trademark
for its polyester fiber

Longitudinal View at 250X   Cross-Sectional View at 500X

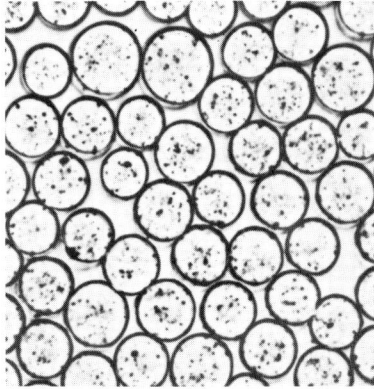

"Kodel"
2.3 denier per filament
semidull luster

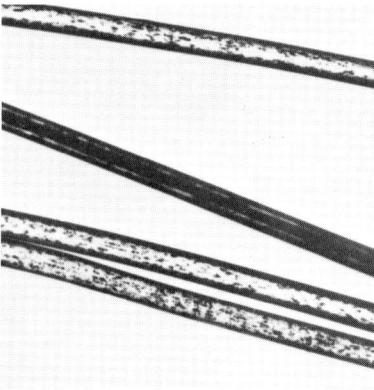

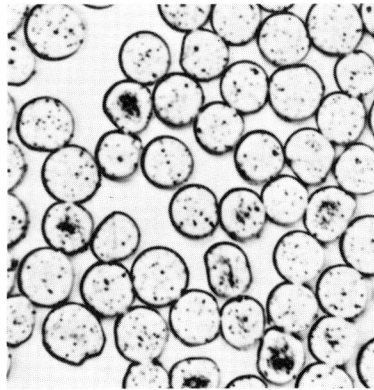

"Vycron"
1.5 denier per filament
semidull luster

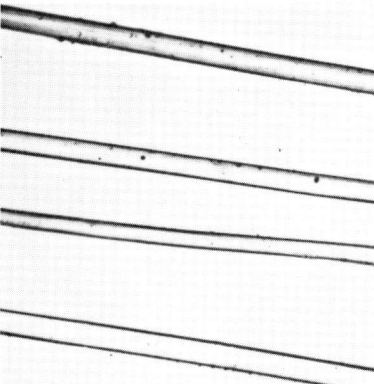

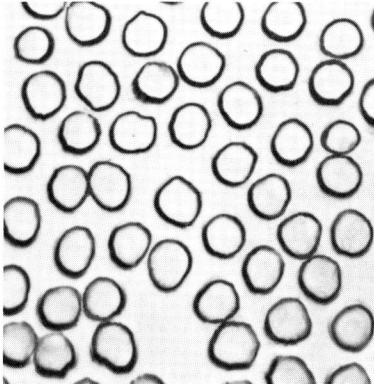

RAYON FIBERS

Cuprammonium
1.3 denier per filament
bright luster

Longitudinal View at 250X   Cross-Sectional View at 500X

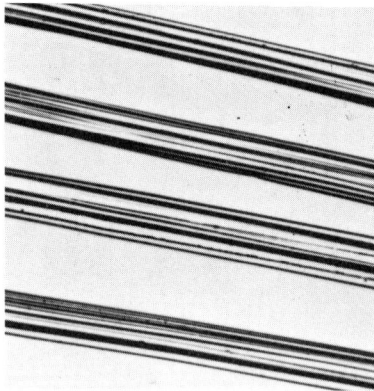

Viscose regular
3.8 denier per filament
bright luster

SARAN FIBER

Saran
16 denier per filament
natural luster

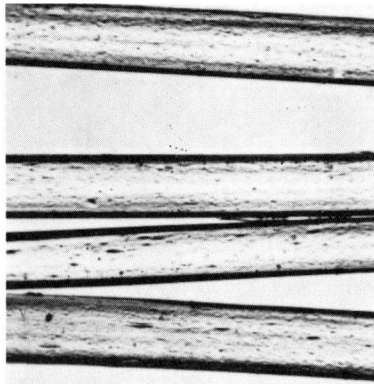

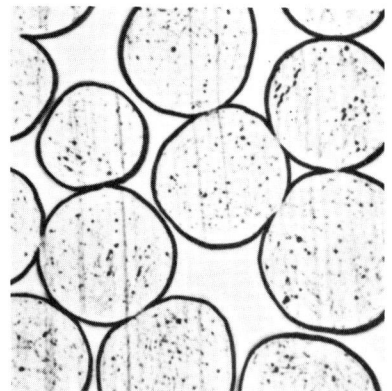

SPANDEX FIBERS

Lycra*
12 denier per filament
dull luster

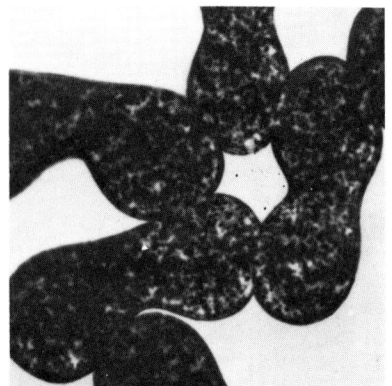

*Du Pont's registered trademark
for its spandex fiber

Longitudinal View at 250X   Cross-Sectional View at 500X

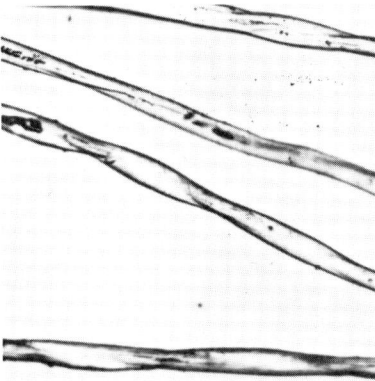

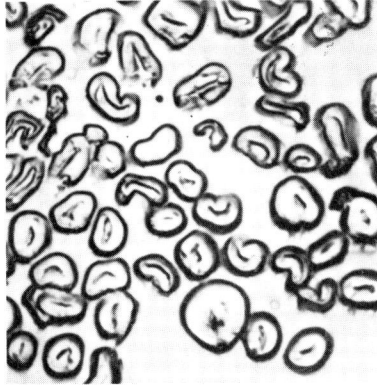

COTTON FIBERS

Cotton, mercerized
1.5* denier per filament
natural luster

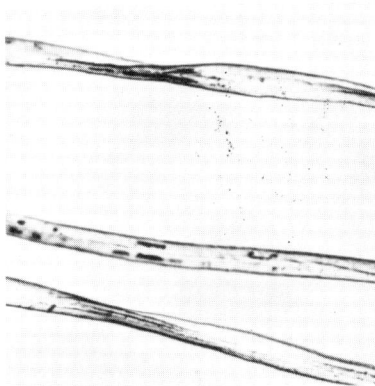

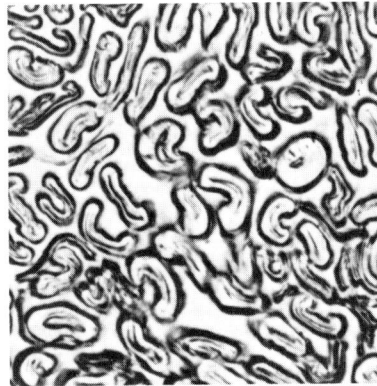

Cotton, not mercerized
1.5* denier per filament
natural luster

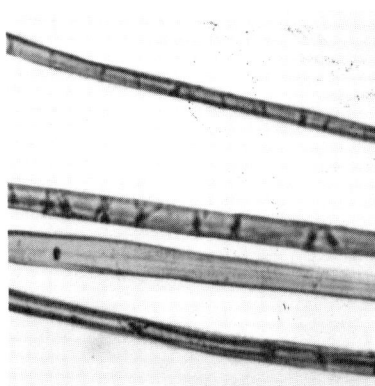

FLAX FIBER

Flax, bleached
3.0* denier per filament
natural luster

* Approximate average denier per filament

Longitudinal View at 250X   Cross-Sectional View at 500X

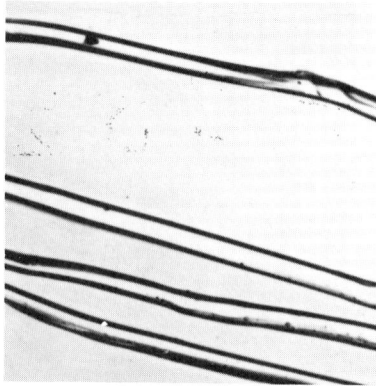

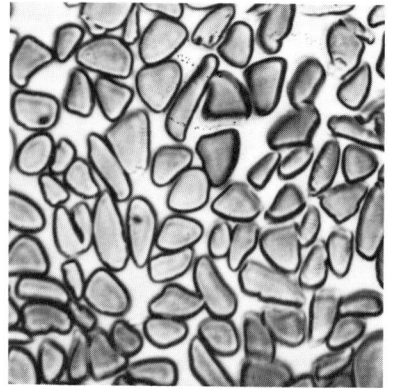

SILK FIBER

Silk, boiled-off
1.2* denier per filament
natural luster

WOOL FIBERS

Cashmere
3.0* denier per filament
natural luster

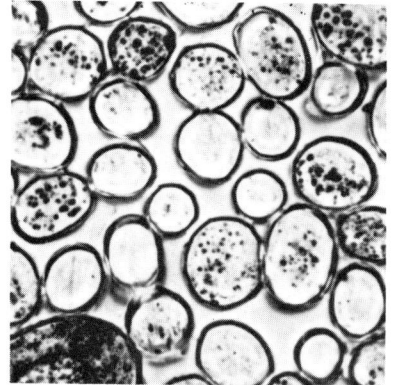

Mohair
6.5* denier per filament
natural luster

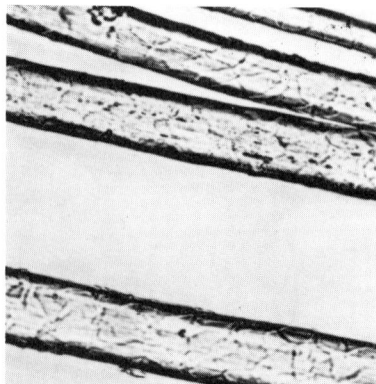

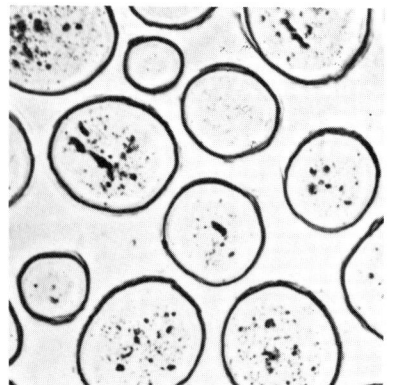

*Approximate average denier per filament

Longitudinal View at 250X

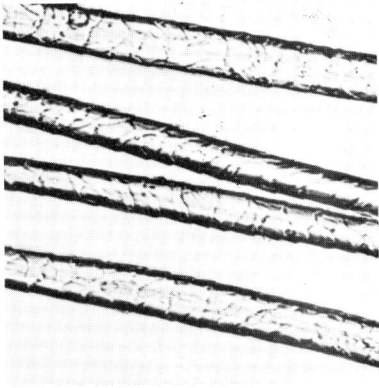

Cross-Sectional View at 500X

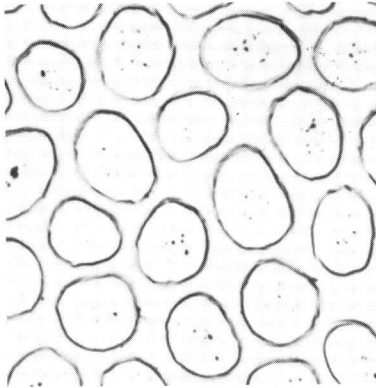

Regular (Merino)
4.0* denier per filament
natural luster

*Approximate average denier per filament.

APPENDIX E
SOLUBILITY
OF FIBERS;
STAIN TESTS

For tests at room temperature (20°C.) place a small sample of the fibers in a watch crystal, test tube or 50 ml beaker and cover with the test solvent. Use about 1 ml of solvent per 10 mg of fiber.

If the test is conducted at the boiling point of the solvent, first bring the solvent to a boil (use boiling chips) in a beaker on an electric hot plate in a ventilated hood. Adjust the hot plate temperature to maintain slow boiling and keep watch so that the solvent does not boil dry. Drop fiber sample into the boiling solvent.

If the test is conducted at some intermediate temperature, heat a beaker of water on a hot plate and adjust the temperature with a thermometer. Place the fiber sample in the test solvent in a test tube and immerse in the heated water bath.

Note if the fiber dissolves completely, softens to a plastic mass or remains insoluble. Compare with data on fiber solubility in Table E-1.

TEST PROCEDURE

If the composition of the textile material is not known or indicated, a representative sample of the textile material or fibers selected from the sample should be immersed in the liquids prescribed in Table E-2 in the numerical sequence shown. The concentration and temperature of each liquid should be as specified.

When small clumps of fibers or individual fibers are used in the test, they should be selected carefully to insure that each of the different classes of fibers in the textile material are tested in every liquid. Good illumination is required for observing the

395

Table E-1 Solubility of Fibers †

	Acetic Acid	Acetone	Sodium Hypochlorite	Hydrochloric Acid	Formic Acid	1,4 Dioxane	M-Xylene	Cyclohexanone	Dimethyl Formamide	Sulfuric Acid	Sulfuric Acid	M-Cresol	Hydrofluoric Acid
Concentration (%)	100	100	5	20	85	100	100	100	100	59.5	70	100	50
Temperature (C)	20	20	20	20	20	101	139	156	90	20	38	139	20
Time (minutes)	5	5	20	10	5	5	5	5	10	20	20	5	20
Acetate	S	S	I	I	S	S	I	S	S	S	S	S	
Acrylic	I	I	I	I	I	I	I	I	S	I	I	P	I
Anidex	I	I	I	I	I	I	I	I	I	I	I	I	
Azlon	I	I	S										
Cotton and Flax	I	I	I	I	I	I	I	I	I	I	S	I	I
Glass	I	I	I	I	I	I	I	I	I	I	I	I	S
Modacrylic	I	SE	I	I	I	SP	I	S	SP*	I	I	P	
Nylon	I	I	I	S	S	I	I	I	N	S	S	S	
Nytril	I	I	I	I	I	I	I	S	S	I	I	SP	
Olefin	I	I	I	I	I	I	S	S	I	I	I	I	
Polyester	I	I	I	I	I	I	I	I	I	I	I	S	I
Rayon	I	I	I	I	I	I	I	I	I	S	S	I	I
Saran	I	I	I	I	I	S	S	S	S	I	I	I	
Silk	I	I	S	I	I	I	I	I	I	S	S	I	
Spandex	I	I	I	I	I	I	I	I	S	SP	SP	SP	
Teflon	I	I	I	I		I	I	I	I	I	I	I	I
Vinal				S	S	I	I	I	I	S	S	I	
Vinyon	I	S	I	I	I	S	S	S	S	I	I	S	
Wool	I	I	S	I	I	I	I	I	I	I	I	I	

S = Soluble	SE = Soluble except for one modacrylic fiber characterized by low
I = Insoluble	flammability and liquid inclusions visible in cross-section.
P = Forms plastic mass	N = Nylon 6 is soluble, nylon 6/6 is insoluble.
SP = Soluble or forms plastic mass	* = Soluble at 20 C without plastic mass.

† Solubility of Fibers. Reprinted with the permission of the American Association of Textile Chemists and Colorists.

effect of the liquids on single-fiber specimens. The liquids must be used in the numerical sequence specified if each class of fibers is to be systematically removed. The order of removal of the fiber classes by the series of liquids is also shown in the table below. If certain fibers are known to be absent from the textile material, the solvents for these fibers can be omitted from the tests.

Table E-2 Schematic Solubility Method for Identification of Fibers Procedure

1. Take a sample of the fabric to be analyzed. The sample should remain in the solvent for five minutes before proceeding to next step. Observe the sample to determine removal of fiber(s) after each test.
2. Proceed in numerical order given in the table. Always rinse the residue thoroughly after each step.
3. For verification, examine the residue for microscopic identification.

Solvent	Removes
1. Acetic acid (glacial) 75°F	Acetate, triacetate
2. Hydrochloric acid (20 percent concentration) 75°F	Nylon 6, nylon 6.6
3. Sodium hypochlorite (5 percent available chlorine) 75°F	Silk, wool
4. Dioxane (212°F)	Saran
5. Xylene (meta) at boil	Olefins
6. Ammonium thiocyanate (70 percent by weight) at boil	Acrylics
7. Butyrolactone (70°F)	Modacrylics, nytrils
8. Dimethyl formamide (200°F)	Spandex — verify
9. Sulfuric acid (75 percent by weight) 75°F	Cotton, flax, rayon, nylon, acetate
10. Cresol (meta) (200°F)	Polyester, nylon acetate

FIBER IDENTIFICATION USING STAIN NO. 4*

TEST PROCEDURE

Wet out material thoroughly in hot water before dyeing. Enter the fabric or yarn into a boiling 1.0 percent solution of Du Pont Fiber Identification Stain No. 4, using a 20:1 bath to fiber ratio. Run bath at the boil for one minute, remove material, rinse lightly, and dry. Should there be any difficulty in distinguishing "Dacron" polyester fiber from "Orlon" acrylic fiber Type 42, return the material to the bath, add 5.0 percent of sulfuric acid and boil for five minutes. The "Dacron" will yield a gold shade and the "Orlon" will appear as a dull orange.

*Available from the Dyes and Chemicals Division, Organic Chemicals Department, E. I. du Pont de Nemours and Company, Inc.

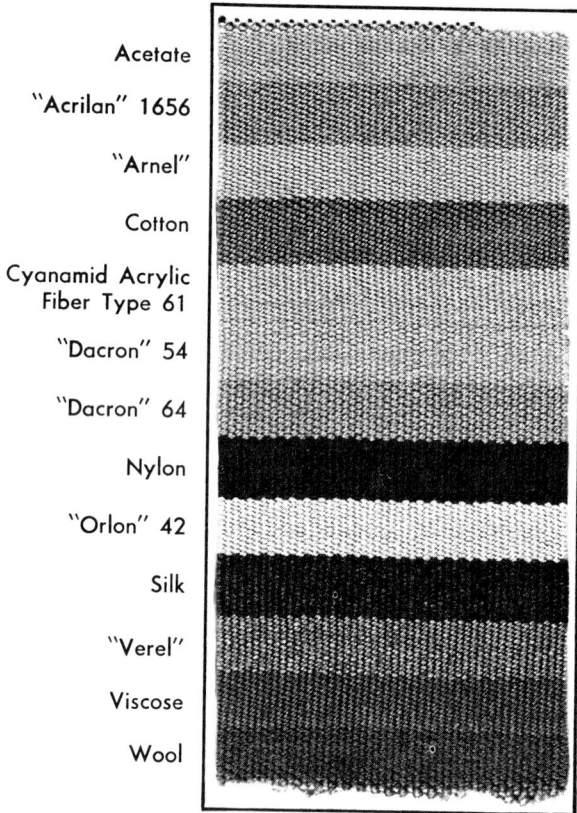

Acetate
"Acrilan" 1656
"Arnel"
Cotton
Cyanamid Acrylic
Fiber Type 61
"Dacron" 54
"Dacron" 64
Nylon
"Orlon" 42
Silk
"Verel"
Viscose
Wool

DuPont Fiber Identification Stain No. 4 provides a simple means for identifying individual fibers quickly, whether alone or used in a blended fabric. The stainings shown are representative of the results normally obtained on some of the fibers encountered in textile use. Variations in quality, preparation, or processing may cause differences from the stainings shown, and further analysis is recommended.

APPENDIX F
SPECIFIC GRAVITY OF TEXTILE FIBERS; PHYSICAL PROPERTIES—MAN-MADE FIBERS

TEST PROCEDURE

A single filament or single fiber specimen is placed in a series of specially prepared liquids of known specific gravity. If the specific gravity of the fiber is greater than that of the liquid, the specimen will sink in the liquid; conversely, if the specific gravity of the fiber is lower, the specimen will float. (The fiber's surface must be free of air bubbles since they can affect the results of the test.)

A suitable series of liquids for this test may be prepared by mixing, in various proportions, carbon tetrachloride (specific gravity of 1.60 at room temperature) with xylene (specific gravity of 0.87 at room temperature). Before using any of the liquids for fiber identification, their specific gravity should be checked with a calibrated hydrometer (Tables F-1 and F-2).

Table F-1

	Fibers	Specific Gravity§
	Man-Made	
Acetate	Secondary (Acele)* and triacetate ("Arnel")	1.32
Acrylic	All (including Orlon* and Orlon Sayelle†)	1.14 to 1.19

Table F-1 (Cont'd)

Fibers		Specific Gravity§
Modacrylic	"Dynel"	1.30
	"Verel"	1.36
Nylon		
	Nylon 6 and nylon 6-6 (including Antron‡ and Du Pont Type 501)	1.14
Nytril	"Darvan"	1.18
Olefin	Polyethylene and polypropylene	0.92
Polyester	Dacron,* "Fortrel," "Terylene," "Toray-Tetoron"	1.38
	"Kodel"	1.22
	"Vycron"	1.37
Rayon	All	1.52
Saran	All	1.70
Spandex	Lycra*	1.21
	"Vyrene"	1.35
	Natural	
Cotton	All (including mercerized and not mercerized)	1.52
Flax	Bleached	1.52
Silk	Boiled-off	1.25
Wool	Cashmere, mohair, and regular (Merino)	1.32

Courtesy E. I. Du Pont de Nemours & Co., Inc.

*Du Pont registered trademark
†Du Pont's registered trademark for its bi-component acrylic fiber
‡Du Pont's registered trademark for its trilobal multifilament nylon yarn.
§These are average values; hence, individual determinations on the same fiber specimen may produce values that vary by as much as 0.02.

Table F-2 Some Physical Properties of Man-Made Fibers
(Standard Laboratory Conditions for Fiber Tests: 70°F and 65 percent relative humidity)

Fiber	Breaking Tenacity* (Grams per Denier)		Standard Moisture Regain† (Percent)
	(Standard)	(Wet)	
Cellulosic Fibers Acetate (filament and staple)	1.2 to 1.5	0.8 to 1.2	6.0

Table F-2 (Cont'd)

Fiber	Breaking Tenacity* (Grams per Denier)		Standard Moisture Regain† (Percent)
	(Standard)	(Wet)	
Rayon (filament and staple)			
Regular tenacity	0.73 to 2.6	0.7 to 1.8	13
Medium tenacity	2.4 to 3.2	1.2 to 1.9	13
High tenacity	3.0 to 6.0	1.9 to 4.6	13
High wet modulus	2.5 to 5.5	1.8 to 4.0	13
Triacetate (filament and staple)	1.2 to 1.4	0.8 to 1.0	3.2
Noncellulosic fibers Acrylic (filament and staple)	2.0 to 3.5	1.8 to 3.3	1.3 to 2.5
Modacrylic (filament and staple)	2.0 to 3.5	2.0 to 3.5	.4 to 4
Nylon			
Nylon 66 (regular tenacity filament)	3.0 to 6.0	2.6 to 5.4	4.0 to 4.5
Nylon 66 (high tenacity filament)	6.0 to 9.5	5.0 to 8.0	4.0 to 4.5
Nylon 66 (staple)	3.5 to 7.2	3.2 to 6.5	4.0 to 4.5
Nylon 6 (filament)	6.0 to 9.5	5.0 to 8.0	4.5
Nylon 6 (staple)	2.5	2.0	4.5
Olefin (polypropylene) (filament and staple)	4.8 to 7.0	4.8 to 7.0	—
Polyester			
Regular-tenacity filament	4.0 to 5.0	4.0 to 5.0	0.4 or 0.8‡
High-tenacity filament	6.3 to 9.5	6.2 to 9.4	0.4 or 0.8‡
Regular-tenacity staple	2.5 to 5.0	2.5 to 5.0	0.4 or 0.8‡
High-tenacity staple	5.0 to 6.5	5.0 to 6.4	0.4 or 0.8‡
Saran (filament)	Up to 1.5	Up to 1.5	—
Spandex (filament)	0.6 to 0.9	0.6 to 0.9	.75 to 1.3
Vinyon (staple)	0.7 to 1.0	0.7 to 1.0	Up to 0.5

*Breaking Tenacity. The stress at which a fiber breaks, expressed in terms of grams per denier.

†Standard Moisture Regain. The moisture regain of a fiber (expressed as a percentage of the moisture-free weight) at 70°F and 65 percent relative humidity.

‡Depending on type.

Note. Data given in ranges may fluctuate according to introduction of fiber modifications or additions and deletions of fiber types.

APPENDIX G
METRIC AND
TEMPERATURE
CONVERSION
CHARTS

Table G-1   Metric Conversion Chart*

Approximate Conversions TO Metric Measures			Approximate Conversions FROM Metric Measures		
When You Know	Multiply by	To Find	When You Know	Multiply by	To Find
LENGTH			LENGTH		
inches	2.5	centimeters	millimeters	0.04	inches
feet	30	centimeters	centimeters	0.4	inches
yards	0.9	meters	meters	3.3	feet
miles	1.6	kilometers	meters	1.1	yards
			kilometers	0.6	miles
AREA			AREA		
sq inches	6.5	sq centimeters	sq centimeters	0.16	sq inches
sq feet	0.09	sq meters	sq meters	1.2	sq yards
sq yards	0.08	sq meters	sq kilometers	0.4	sq miles
sq miles	2.6	sq kilometers	hectares (10,000 m²)	2.5	acres
acres	0.4	hectares			
MASS (weight)			MASS (weight)		
ounces	28	grams	grams	0.035	ounces
pounds	0.45	kilograms	kilograms	2.2	pounds
short tons (2000 lb)	0.9	tonnes	tonnes (1000 kg)	1.1	short tons

403

Table G-1 Metric Conversion Chart *(Cont'd)*

Approximate Conversions TO Metric Measures			Approximate Conversions FROM Metric Measures		
When You Know	Multiply by	To Find	When You Know	Multiply by	To Find
VOLUME			**VOLUME**		
teaspoons	5	milliliters	milliliters	0.03	fluid ounces
tablespoons	15	milliliters	liters	2.1	pints
fluid ounces	30	milliliters	liters	1.06	quarts
cups	0.24	liters	liters	0.26	gallons
pints	0.47	liters	cubic meters	35	cubic feet
quarts	0.95	liters	cubic meters	1.3	cubic yards
gallons	3.8	liters			
cubic feet	0.03	cubic meters			
cubic yards	0.76	cubic meters			
TEMPERATURE (exact)			**TEMPERATURE** (exact)		
Fahrenheit temperature	5/9 (after subtracting 32)	Celsius temperature	Celsius temperature	9/5 (then add 32)	Fahrenheit temperature

*The National Bureau of Standards has prepared a plastic wallet card that contains these data needed for converting from customary to metric units and vice versa. The price is 10 cents each, $6.25 per hundred. Order prepaid from the Superintendent of Documents, U.S. Government Printing Office, Washington, D.C. 20402 or from local U.S. Department of Commerce Field Offices as SD Catalog No. C13.10:365.

Table G-2   Temperature Conversion Chart

°C	°F	°C	°F	°C	°F	°C	°F	°C	°F
0	32.0	45	113.0	90	194.0	135	275.0	180	356.0
1	33.8	46	114.8	91	195.8	136	276.8	181	357.8
2	35.6	47	116.6	92	197.6	137	278.6	182	359.6
3	37.4	48	118.4	93	199.4	138	280.4	183	361.4
4	39.2	49	120.2	94	201.2	139	282.2	184	363.2
5	41.0	50	122.0	95	203.0	140	284.0	185	365.0
6	42.8	51	123.8	96	204.8	141	285.8	186	366.8
7	44.6	52	125.6	97	206.6	142	287.6	187	368.6
8	46.4	53	127.4	98	208.4	143	289.4	188	370.4
9	48.2	54	129.2	99	210.2	144	291.2	189	372.2
10	50.0	55	131.0	100	212.0	145	293.0	190	374.0
11	51.8	56	132.8	101	213.8	146	294.8	191	375.8
12	53.6	57	134.6	102	215.6	147	296.6	192	377.6
13	55.4	58	136.4	103	217.4	148	298.4	193	379.4
14	57.2	59	138.2	104	219.2	149	300.2	194	381.2
15	59.0	60	140.0	105	221.0	150	302.0	195	383.0
16	60.8	61	141.8	106	222.8	151	303.8	196	384.8
17	62.6	62	143.6	107	224.6	152	305.6	197	386.6
18	64.4	63	145.4	108	226.4	153	307.4	198	388.4
19	66.2	64	147.2	109	228.2	154	309.2	199	390.2
20	68.0	65	149.0	110	230.0	155	311.0	200	392.0
21	69.8	66	150.8	111	231.8	156	312.8	202	395.6
22	71.6	67	152.6	112	233.6	157	314.6	204	399.2
23	73.4	68	154.4	113	235.4	158	316.4	206	402.8
24	75.2	69	156.2	114	237.2	159	318.2	208	406.4
25	77.0	70	158.0	115	239.0	160	320.0	210	410.0
26	78.8	71	159.8	116	240.8	161	321.8	212	413.6
27	80.6	72	161.6	117	242.6	162	323.6	214	417.2
28	82.4	73	163.4	118	244.4	163	325.4	216	420.8
29	84.2	74	165.2	119	246.2	164	327.2	218	424.4
30	86.0	75	167.0	120	248.0	165	329.0	220	428.0
31	87.8	76	168.8	121	249.8	166	330.8	222	431.6
32	89.6	77	170.6	122	251.6	167	332.6	224	435.2
33	91.4	78	172.4	123	253.4	168	334.4	226	438.8
34	93.2	79	174.2	124	255.2	169	336.2	228	442.4
35	95.0	80	176.0	125	257.0	170	338.0	230	446.0
36	96.8	81	177.8	126	258.8	171	339.8	232	449.6
37	98.6	82	179.6	127	260.6	172	341.6	234	453.2
38	100.4	83	181.4	128	262.4	173	343.4	236	456.8
39	102.2	84	183.2	129	264.2	174	345.2	238	460.4
40	104.0	85	185.0	130	266.0	175	347.0	240	464.0
41	105.8	86	186.8	131	267.8	176	348.8		
42	107.6	87	188.6	132	269.6	177	350.6		
43	109.4	88	190.4	133	271.4	178	352.4		
44	111.2	89	192.2	134	273.2	179	354.2		

GLOSSARY OF FABRIC TERMS

Airplane Cloth: A plain weave cotton or linen fabric used for men's shirtings, sportswear, and boys' suits.

Albatross: A fine lightweight open plain weave fabric with a pebbly surface created by a crepe yarn. Used for negligees, infants' wear, and nuns' habits.

Alpaca: Alpaca is a specialty hair fiber classed in the camel family. It is used to make soft, lustrous, pile weave coating fabrics. The alpaca fiber may be blended with wool or synthetic fibers. Usually it has a cotton knitted or woven back.

Art Linen: A heavyweight plain weave linen fabric. Used for tablecloths, and the basis of many types of embroidered household items.

Awning or Duck: A heavy cotton or linen plain weave fabric. It may be plain colored or striped. It is used for awnings, beach and lawn umbrellas, and summer furniture covers.

Balbriggan: A fine, closely knit plain cotton fabric. It is used for underwear, sweaters, and gloves.

Balloon Fabric: A very finely, yet strongly woven plain weave fabric of cotton, silk, nylon, or high-strength rayon. It is used for shirts and dresses.

Barathea: Barathea is a broken ribbed weave fabric that gives a granular textured effect because of the short broken ribs in the filling direction. It is a rich, soft-looking, fine fabric. It may be made of silk, rayon, or acetate. A worsted filling may sometimes be used.

Bedford Cord: This is the name of a weave as well as a fabric. The lengthwise rib is made by interweaving the filling in a plain or twill weave. Stuffing yarns are introduced to make a raised cord. It is used for coats, suits, slacks, and uniforms. Heavier qualities are used in draperies and slip covers.

Bengaline: Bengaline is a firmly woven ribbed weave fabric made of single yarns in the warp and heavy ply yarns in the filling. The warp yarns may be of rayon, acetate, nylon, or silk; the filling yarns may be of cotton, rayon, acetate, wool alone, or wool in combinations. The ribs are slightly heavier and rounder than in poplin and more distinct than in faille. The fabric is usually stiffer than poplin or faille.

Bird's Eye: It is a figure weave fabric. The figure forms a diamond with a dot in the center. It is used in dresses and household items.

Bouclé: Bouclé is a term used to describe a variety of knitted and woven fabric constructions, from lightweight dress fabrics to heavy coat fabrics. Regardless of weight or construction, they may be distinguished by small spaced loops on the surface of the fabric. These fabrics may be made from either natural or man-made fibers or mixtures of both.

Boulivia: Boulivia is a fabric with a silky, thick, long pile that is woven and then cut to give a pebbled, cord, or ridge effect. In some fabrics the ridges go up and down; in others the ridges may go diagonally across the fabric. It is usually made of wool. It may contain alpaca or mohair.

Brilliantine: There are several constructions made of either a plain or twill weave. The most widely used fabric has a cotton warp and a worsted or mohair filling. It may be given a soft or stiff finish. It is used for dresses, suits, and linings.

Brocade: Brocade is derived from the Spanish word, "to figure." Brocade is a rich-appearing fabric made with a jacquard weave. It may be recognized by its prominent and raised design. It is not reversible as damask is. It may be made of natural or man-made fibers. In some fabrics a gold or silver yarn may be introduced to form the figure or design.

Brocatelle: A tightly woven, stiff, elaborate fabric made of a jacquard figure weave. The design stands in relief to the background. The design is formed by the warp yarns. The area that is not raised is backed by extra yarns. It is used chiefly as a slipcover and upholstery fabric.

Broadcloth: Broadcloth is a term used to describe several dissimilar fabrics, made with different fibers, weaves, and finishes. Broadcloth made from wool or wool mixed with man-made fibers are fine, open, twill weave fabrics that are "fulled," napped, sheared, dampened, and the nap permanently laid down in one direction. The weave cannot be seen on the right side of the fabric. This gives the fabric its characteristic smooth, lustrous, fine velvetlike texture. "Chiffon" broadcloth is a lightweight dress fabric with a high luster. Coating and suiting broadcloths are heavier. Broadcloth made from spun man-made yarns fabrics are usually made by a warp rib weave. The rib is formed by weaving a number of filling yarns as one to form the ribs. It has the finest rib of all ribbed weave fabrics. Broadcloth made from silk or filament-type synthetic yarns is woven in a plain weave with a fine crosswise rib obtained by using a heavier filling than warp yarn. The fabric is soft, pliable, drapable. It is cool and comfortable to wear. It wears and dry-cleans well with care. Broadcloth may also be made from cotton yarns. These fabrics are made the same way as the broadcloths made from spun synthetic yarns.

Buckram: Buckram is a term used to describe three types of fabrics: (1) A heavily sized and stiffened fabric made by gluing two fabrics together. One is a low count, open, plain weave fabric; the other a much finer plain weave fabric. (2) A plain weave single strong linen fabric stiffened with flour, paste, china clay, and glue. (3) A plain weave cotton scrim given a stiff finish with a nondurable sizing or a durable finish to dry cleaning and wet cleaning.

Bunting: A loosely woven plain weave fabric made of cotton or wool. It is used for flags and banners.

Byrd Cloth: A very closely and firmly woven plain weave cotton fabric made of fine carded, mercerized yarns. Its weave makes it wind-resistant. It is frequently treated with a water-repellent finish. It is used for rainwear, sports jackets, ski suits, and snowsuits.

Calico: A lightweight coarse cotton fabric made of carded yarns. It may be solid colored or printed. It is heavily sized with starch. True calico is not available today. Muslin, cambric, and other plain weave fabrics are printed with calico print designs.

Cambric: A fine, firm, close weave fabric made of either cotton or linen. It may be given a soft finish with little luster or it may be heavily starched and calendered to produce a lustrous stiff fabric. It is used for dresses, shirts, and household items such as bedspreads and draperies.

Camel's Hair: Genuine camel's hair fabrics are very expensive and not too common. The term "camel's hair" is used to describe a class of fabrics that includes soft, silky, heavy woolen fabrics, usually tan or brown in color with little or no camel's hair mixed with it.

Canvas: A heavy, closely woven firm fabric that is rather stiff, made of cotton or linen. There are many kinds and weights of canvas, from sails and awnings to slipcovers and lining fabrics.

Casement Cloth: This term is applied to a class of lightweight, closely woven opaque fabrics used for curtains.

Cashmere: Cashmere is a term used to describe many fabrics, knit and woven, that contain cashmere blended with wool and other fibers.

Cassimere: A closely woven 2 × 2 inch twill fabric made of wool. It is fulled and sheared to make a smooth, somewhat lustrous surface texture. Its chief use is for men's suits.

Cavalry Twill: Cavalry twill is usually made of wool or cotton. It may be made of man-made fibers. It is a very firmly woven, hard-surfaced fabric. It may be recognized by its very pronounced double twill. The diagonal lines go from left to right. They are spaced widely and can be seen on the back of the fabric.

Challis: An extremely soft, lightweight plain or twill weave fabric made of wool, cotton, or synthetic fibers. It usually is printed with a small floral design. It is used for dresses, blouses, negligees, men's ties and shirts, draperies, and linings.

Chambray: Chambray is a plain weave fabric distinguished by a white frosted appearance. This is achieved by using a white yarn in the warp and a colored yarn in the filling. It is used for dresses, blouses, shirts, and linings.

Cheesecloth or Tobacco Cloth: A very loosely woven plain weave cotton fabric. The yard width is called "tobacco cloth." It may be used for curtains, costumes, and cleaning cloths.

Chenille: This is a term applied to a type of yarn or a fabric woven with a chenille yarn. The yarn is covered with short, cut fibers or pile. Chenille yarns are used in knit fabrics and woven fabrics. It is used chiefly in making lounging garments, bedspreads, and rugs.

Cheviot: Cheviot was originally a fabric made of the coarse wool of sheep raised in the Cheviot hills of North England. Today it is a term used to describe medium to heavyweight fabrics made of wool, wool and cotton or spun synthetic yarns, or entirely of cotton. The weave may be plain, twill, or herringbone. Its distinguishing characteristic is the surface texture. The fabric is "fulled" to make a compact fabric, then napped to produce a ruff, shaggy surface texture.

Chiffon: Chiffon is a term used to describe many light, gossamer, sheer, plain weave fabrics. Chiffon may be made of silk, wool, or a synthetic fiber. It is woven in an open weave with tightly twisted yarns. The word is used before names of fabrics to indicate a lightness of weight, as "chiffon" taffeta, "chiffon" satin, "chiffon" velvet. Silk chiffon is made of raw silk in both the lengthwise and crosswise direction. The yarns are highly creped and twisted, ranging from 40 to 50 turns an inch to 70 to 80 turns an inch. Some chiffon constructions made of fibers other than silk are sized with a water-soluble sizing to give them the hand and feel of silk.

Chinchilla: Chinchilla is a term used to describe a variety of wool and cotton fabrics made of a twill, double cloth, or knitted construction. The fabrics are characterized by the thick, full, soft, dull, irregular surface texture resulting from the curled tufts or nubs. The long, floating yarns are teaseled by a chinchilla machine to raise a long nap to the surface of the fabric. The nap is then rubbed into small, rounded, curled tufts.

Chintz: Chintz is the term applied to a large group of gaily printed or solid colored, highly glazed plain weave fabrics. The better qualities are made of a firmly woven cotton fabric having a hard twisted warp yarn and a coarser, slacky twisted filling yarn. Some of the fabrics are "fully" glazed; some are "semiglazed." There are two methods of producing a glazed finish on this group of fabrics: (1) nondurable — the fabric is given a wax and starch finish and then pressed between hot rollers to produce a high luster; and (2) durable — the fabric is treated with a resin (urea or melamine) under patented methods of applying and curing to produce a high luster.

Corduroy: Corduroy may be identified by the raised cut pile that runs the lengthwise direction of the fabric. Extra filling yarns float over a number of warp yarns that form either a plain or twill-weave ground. After weaving, the floating yarns are cut, and the pile brushed and singed to produce a clear cord effect. The back of corduroy is slightly napped. Corduroy was originally a cotton fabric but today cotton is blended with man-made fibers.

Covert: Covert is usually made of wool or cotton. It may be made of the synthetic fibers. It is a medium to heavyweight twill weave fabric. Its distinguishing characteristic is its mottled or flecked appearance. This is achieved by using a white or colored twisted or spun warp yarn and a solid colored filling yarn.

Crash: A rather loosely woven fabric of irregular yarns of cotton, linen, rayon, or jute. It is made in various weights. It may be dyed or printed. The fabric is finished to have a soft, lustrous appearance. It is used for upholstery, draperies, and slipcovers. Lightweight crash may be used for sportswear dresses.

Crepes: Crepe is the term used to describe a large class of fabrics made of a plain weave. The yarns are highly twisted in either the warp or filling direction, or both. Different effects may be achieved by the way the yarns are twisted. In some cases, crepes are made with a satin, twill, or jacquard weave.

Crepe fabrics range from the very fine, almost smooth surfaces to a very pronounced, definite, heavy, crepe-textured surface.

Canton Crepe: This fabric was originally made in China, from where it has derived its name. It is a soft, lustrous crepe, similar to but heavier and more textured than crepe de chine. It has a predominant heavy-crepe filling yarn that forms a crosswise rib. This is achieved by having six or more filling yarns with a regular twist, and then reversing the twist in the next six or more filling yarns.

Chiffon Crepe: A sheer fabric similar to georgette but softer. This fabric has a soft hand as the result of a special finish.

Crepe de Chine: A soft, thin, but opaque, lightweight fabric with a crepe surface. Silk crepe de chine is woven with the natural gum. The crepe effect is achieved during the de-gumming process.

Crepon: This was originally a wool fabric; however, today it may be made of silk or rayon. It is a heavy crepe fabric with a wavy lengthwise rib formed by a thicker, alternately twisted warp yarn.

Flat Crepe: A smooth, soft fabric that has a less crinkled surface than most crepes.

Morocian Crepe: A heavy crepe fabric with a slightly wavy and rather heavy filling rib.

Plissé or Crinkle Crepes: There are many crepes that fall into this class. They may be made by alternately weaving plain and crepe yarns, or they may be produced by chemical treatment of the fabric.

Romaine Crepe: A heavy crepe fabric woven with alternate right- and left-hand twist filling yarns.

Cretonne: It is plain twill or satin weave fabric made of cotton, linen, or rayon. The fabric is firmly woven and printed with very large designs. Its chief use is for draperies and slipcovers.

Crinoline: Crinoline originally was a linen and horsehair fabric used for linings and interlinings. The horsehair provided the stiffness required for this type of fabric. Today, crinoline describes a dull, low-count, coarse, medium-weight, plain weave fabric that is sized to give it stiffness. The sizing may be of two types: (1) nondurable — the cotton fabric is starched; and (2) durable — a resin is applied to give the fabric stiffness.

Damask: Damask may be made of cotton, linen, silk, wool, rayon, or any of the newer synthetic fibers. It is made with a jacquard woven pattern. The design is flat, differing from a brocade. The background is always a satin weave. The design looks the same on the reverse side as it does on the right side, but in reverse. There are three types of damask fabrics: (1) the lightweight type used for table linens; (2) the mediumweight type used for wearing apparel; and (3) the heavyweight type used for drapery and upholstery fabrics.

Denim or Dungaree: Denim originally was considered a cotton twill weave fabric made of coarse, hard, twisted ply yarns. Its warp yarns colored, its filling yarns white. Today, we also have denims made of cotton blended with man-made fibers. Denim was synonymous with blue. Today it may be brown, black, rust, or washed out pastel colors. It may be smooth, brushed, faded or worn.

Dimity: A sheer, crisp, plain weave fabric with lengthwise rib or cord. It is mercerized to give it smoothness and luster. It may be used for dresses, blouses, curtains, and bedspreads.

Doeskin: A very fine fabric, napped and then finished to give it high luster. It looks like soft-finished leather. It is used for suits, sportswear, and coats.

Double-Cloth, Double-Faced Fabrics: Double-cloths, adaptations of double-cloths, and double-faced fabrics are American made, others are European imports.

A true double-cloth is a fabric made of a double-cloth weave. This weave uses more than one set of warp or filling yarns. It may produce a fabric with two distinct faces or colors, or it may produce two distinct fabrics held together by an extra set of yarns. For example, a satin or an ottoman may be black on the face and gold, rose, or any other color on the reverse or under side of the fabric. The fabric is reversible. One or both sides may be used in designing a garment.

Double-faced fabrics are made by taking two face fabrics and binding them together with an adhesive. It is possible to create a large range of fabrics by this method of construction.

There is a very simple way you can identify a double-cloth from a double-faced fabric. Examine a seam in an unexposed part of a garment. Pull the seam apart. If you see an extra set of yarns that holds the two fabrics together, you will know that you can dry-clean the fabric satisfactorily. You can see the adhesive that holds two fabrics together in a double-faced construction.

Dotted Swiss: An open weave, sheer, crisp, plain weave cotton fabric with woven or flocked dots. It is used for dresses, blouses, and curtains.

Drill: A heavy, firm, cotton twill weave fabric. It is sized and pressed to make a compact fabric. Khaki cloth is a drill in khaki color. Middy twill or jeans are drill. It is used in sportswear, curtains, and slipcovers.

Duvetyn: Duvetyn comes from the French term "duvet," meaning "down." It is a soft, silky, velvetlike fabric. It may be made of wool, silk, cotton, the synthetic fibers, or a mixture of two of these fibers. The fibers are raised to the surface of the fabric by emery rollers, then sheared, singed, and brushed to create a smooth, lustrous surface.

End-and-End Cloth: A closely woven, plain weave cotton fabric with a fine colored stripe or pin check, made by alternating a white and colored yarn in the warp or in both the warp and filling. Used widely for men's shirts.

Eponge: A loosely woven plain weave fabric made with a bouclé yarn. Eponge is derived from a French word meaning "sponge." It is used in dresses, suits, and draperies.

Faille: Faille is a soft yet firm ribbed weave fabric made of cotton, silk, rayon, acetate, or other synthetic fibers alone or in combination. Compared with grosgrain, faille is softer and contains larger, more flattened ribs, almost inconspicuous. It resembles taffeta in its degree of stiffness.

Flannel: Flannel is a term used to describe a large group of napped plain or twill weave fabrics made of cotton, wool, or synthetic fibers. The fabrics vary in closeness or firmness of weave and degree of napping. For example, a French flannel is a very fine twill weave fabric, slightly napped on the right side only, whereas a suede flannel is napped on both sides, sheared, and the fibers pressed into the fabric, giving the appearance of a close felted fabric. Viyella flannel is a trade name for a slightly napped twill weave flannel made of part wool and part cotton. It is treated so that it is guaranteed not to shrink.

Flannelette: A soft, plain or twill weave cotton fabric lightly napped on one side. It may be dyed solid colors or printed. It is used for lounging and sleeping garments.

Foulard: Foulard is a lightweight silk, rayon, cotton, or wool fabric characterized by its twill weave. It has a high luster on the right side and is dull on the under or reverse side. It is usually printed, with designs ranging from simple polkadots to elaborate designs. It is also made in plain or solid colors. It has a characteristic feel that may be described as light, firm, and supple.

Frisé: A heavy, coarse, napped, twill weave fabric. The nap is rough-textured, producing a hard feel. It is used for coats and sport jackets.

Gabardine: Gabardine is a hard-finished, clear-surfaced twill weave made of either natural or man-made fibers. The diagonal lines are fine, close, and steep from left to right. They are more pronounced than serge. The lines cannot be seen on the wrong side of the fabric.

Georgette: Georgette is a very thin, transparent or semitransparent, loosely woven fabric. It is woven in the gum, then the gum is removed to give it is crepe finish. It has a harder finish, is less lustrous, and more crepy than crepe de chine. This fabric is usually made of silk. Today it may be made of the man-made fibers. There is also a wool georgette.

Gingham: A light to medium-weight, closely woven, plain weave cotton fabric. It is usually yarn-dyed and woven to create stripes, checks, and plaids. The fabric is mercerized to have a soft, lustrous appearance. It is sized and calendered to a firm and lustrous finish. It is used for dresses, shirts, robes, curtains, drapes, and bedspreads.

Grenadine: A yarn-dyed leno weave fabric with a loose open weave. It may have woven or flocked design. It is used for dresses and curtains.

Gros-de-Londres: Gros-de-Londres is a closely woven yet lightweight ribbed weave fabric of silk or synthetic fibers. It is distinguished by its alternate heavy and fine ribs. A heavy flat rib may be followed by one more fine ribs and then another heavy rib. It has a stiffness comparable to taffeta.

Grosgrain: Grosgrain is a hard-finished, closely woven, uniformly ribbed weave fabric made of cotton, silk, or synthetic fibers in combination. The ribs are heavier than in poplin and more rounded than in faille.

Homespun: A coarse, plain weave fabric, loosely woven with irregular, tightly twisted, unevenly spun yarns. It has a hand-woven appearance. It is used for coats, suits, sportswear, draperies and slipcovers.

Honey Comb or Waffle Cloth: This is the name of a weave and a fabric. It is a rough-textured fabric with a raised square or diamond-shaped pattern made by floating warp and filling yarns that form the ridges along the lines of the floats. It is used in dresses and bedspreads.

Hopsacking: An open basket weave fabric made of coarse yarns. It is used for sportswear and draperies.

Huckaback: This is the name of a weave as well as a fabric. It is a simple figure weave; the warp yarn floats on the surface and the filling yarn on the back. It is lightweight, made of cotton or linen. It is used for draperies, quilt covers, and may be used for shirts.

Japse Cloth: A plain weave fabric made from different colored warp yarns and a single-color filling yarn. This creates faint blended multicolored stripes. It may be made of hard, twisted cotton or rayon yarns, making a firm fabric. It is used for draperies and slipcovers.

Jean: A cotton twill or chevron twill fabric with a firm, clear surfaced texture. Sometimes it is called "Middy twill." It is used for sportsclothes and linings.

Kersey: A heavy, highly lustered, finely napped twill weave wool fabric. It is heavier and more lustrous than melton. It is used in overcoats and uniforms.

Lamé: Lamé is derived from the Frenck work "laminer," "to flatten." A true lamé is a silk brocade made with a fine metallic yarn to create a decorative design. Today the term is used generally to describe a variety of fabrics made with metallic yarns.

Lawn: A lightweight, sheer, fine cotton or linen fabric. It may be given a soft or crisp finish. It is sized and calendered to give it a soft, lustrous appearance. It is used for dresses, blouses, curtains and bedspreads.

Leno: This is the name of a weave and a fabric. It may be made of cotton, rayon, silk, wool, nylon, or any other synthetic fiber. It is made of a leno weave, or the leno weave may be used only as a decoration. It is used for dresses, blouses, curtains, and draperies.

Longcloth: A plain weave cotton fabric. It is closely woven of fine, slightly twisted yarns. It is sized lightly and calendered. It is used for shirts and children's wear.

Makinaw Cloth: A thick, heavy-felted and napped wool fabric made with either a twill weave or double-cloth construction. It is recognized by its bold plaid designs. It may have cotton and rayon warp in lower-priced fabrics. It is used for jackets and ski clothes.

Madras: A finely woven, soft, plain or jacquard weave fabric. A stripe runs in the lengthwise direction, and jacquard or dobby patterns are woven in the background. Some madras is made with woven checks and cords. It may be used for blouses, dresses, and shirts.

Matelassé: Matelassé is derived from the French term "matelas," meaning mattress pad. A true matelassé is an adaptation of a double-cloth construction, made of natural or synthetic yarns. It may be described as two distinct fabrics united in weaving to produce the surface quilted effect when the fabric is relaxed after weaving. Other methods are used to make fabrics that are sometimes called "matelassé." For example, a fabric may be made by interlacing crepe yarns with a straight yarn in both the warp and filling directions, or in some cases only the filling direction. Some fabrics called "matelassé" may be woven with small dobby designs on a box loom. Still other fabrics may be embossed to look like a true matelasse.

Melton: Melton is a thick, heavily felted or fulled wool fabric (twill or satin weave) with a smooth, lustrous, napped surface. In the less expensive fabrics, the warp or lengthwise yarn may be cotton instead of wool.

Milanese: A sheer fabric knitted on a Milanese machine. The stitch makes a fine twill rib, running diagonally on the fabric. It may be used in blouses and evening wear fabrics.

Mohair: Mohair is a fiber derived from the Angora goat. It is also a term used to describe two entirely different types of fabric constructions: (1) Mohair may be blended with wool or wool and synthetic fibers in a pile fabric construction for coating, drapery, and upholstery fabrics. (2) Mohair may be used with cotton, wool, or rayon and woven into a shiny, stiff, wiry dress and suiting fabric.

Momie Cloth or Mummy Cloth: Originally this fabric was made with a silk warp and wool filling. It has low luster because of the crepe yarns. Today's fabric is made of cotton, wool, silk, rayon, or linen. It has a fine warp and heavy filling yarn in a crepe weave. It is used for dresses and shirts.

Monk's Cloth: A heavy, loosely woven basket-weave cotton fabric. It may be plain colored or have woven-in stripes or plaids. It is used chiefly for draperies and slipcovers.

Mousseline de Soie: Mousseline de Soie is a French term for silk muslin. It is a plain weave, crisp, sheer fabric, more closely woven and stiffer than chiffon. It is not as soft as voile. The yarns are highly twisted and sized before weaving. This sizing is not removed by any subsequent finishing operation when the fabric is made in Europe. In domestic-made fabrics the sizing may be applied to the fabric after the weaving operation.

Mull: A soft, sheer, lustrous, plain weave fabric made of cotton, rayon, or silk. Originally this fabric had a cotton warp and silk filling. It is used in blouses, shirts, and children's wear.

Muslin: This includes a large group of plain weave cotton fabrics ranging from light to heavyweight. The sizing may range from light to heavy. It may be solid colored or printed. It is used for dresses, shirts, and household items.

Nainsook: A very fine, lightweight, plain weave cotton fabric. It is mercerized and has a soft luster. One side may be calendered to give it a high gloss. It is used for blouses and dresses.

Ninon: A very thin, smooth, crisp, plain weave fabric made of silk or synthetic fibers. It is used for evening dresses or curtains.

Nun's Veiling: A very sheer, thin, soft, plain weave wool fabric. It is made with finely twisted yarns, which give it a firm feel. It is used for dresses and nun's veiling.

Organdy: Organdy is a term used to describe a crisp, sheer, transparent, lightweight cotton fabric, woven with tightly twisted fine yarns. The crispness may be achieved by two methods: (1) nondurable — the fabric is starched and calendered; and (2) durable — the fabric is given a chemical finish by application of thermosetting resins that change the fiber itself, producing a transparency, a silkiness, and a crispness that is durable. Other fabrics that fall within this class are:
Organza: This fabric is similar to organdy, but it is made of rayon yarns. The yarns are highly twisted, ranging from 10 to 20 turns an inch.
Silk Organdy: This is a lightweight silk fabric given a crisp finish either by natural gums or applied resin finishes. When this fabric is printed, it resembles mousseline de soie.

Osnaburg: A rough, strong, plain weave cotton fabric of low thread count. The yarns are uneven, producing a rough texture. It may vary in weight from light to heavy. It is used for sportswear, curtains, slipcovers, and draperies.

Oxford Cloth: A 2×2 inch basket-weave fabric made of cotton. It may range from light- to heavyweight. Better grades are mercerized to give the fabric a soft luster. It is used for dresses, shirts, sportswear, draperies, and bedspreads.

Ottoman: Ottoman is the heaviest of the ribbed weave fabrics. It has large, heavy, more rounded and pronounced rib because of the heavy three- to six-ply filling yarn. The single ply warp yarn may be of silk, rayon, or acetate. The filling yarn may be of cotton, cotton and wool, or wool and man-made fibers.

Peau de Soie — Peau D'Ange: "Peau de soie" is a French term meaning "silk skin." Originally it was a silk fabric made with an eight-shaft satin weave. It looks the same on both sides, thus differing from most other satin fabrics. It has a very smooth, silky, semidull appearance. It is much heavier than most satin constructions. Today this fabric may be made of silk and acetate, Orlon and silk, or 100 percent acetate. Peau d'ange is similar but different from peau de soie. Peau d'ange has a dull satin face and back. It feels like "angle skin," which the name implies.

Percale: A firm, smooth, plain weave cotton fabric. It has a little luster. It is starched and calendered. Some are given a crinkled or crepe finish. It is used for curtains, bedspreads, dresses, and shirts.

Percaline: A plain weave cotton fabric that is glazed or moiréed. It is sized and calendered to give it a high sheen. It is used for linings and costumes.

Piqué: Piqué is a term used to describe a class of ribbed weave fabrics with varied surface textures formed by a raised rib or wale in the lengthwise direction of the fabric. These wales may vary in width and thickness. Piqué may be made by embossing a fabric to make it appear like a woven piqué fabric. The fabrics in this group may be described as follows: *Pinwale Piqué:* Very fine cords running the lengthwise direction of the fabric.
Birdseye Piqué: This is a woven simple figure weave, or embossed with a small diamond shaped design with a small dot in the center.
Waffle Piqué: This fabric is woven with a raised cord, or embossed to resemble a honeycomb or a waffle.

Pongee: A plain weave silk fabric woven with irregular tussah or wild silk yarns in both warp and filling. The uneven yarns give it a broken crossbar effect characteristic of pongee. It is ecru in color. It is used for blouses, dresses, shirts, and curtains.

Poult de Soie: "Poult de soie" is a fine silk grosgrain fabric having the rustle of a taffeta. The yarns are so woven that the surface of the fabric has a grainy appearance, yet close observation discloses a fine rib running in the filling or crosswise direction. It is stiffer than peau de soie.

Radium: A firm, closely woven plain weave fabric made of silk or rayon. It has a characteristic smoothness, softness, and high luster. It is used for dresses and linings.

Ratiné: Ratiné is a type of nubby yarn used to make plain or twill weave fabric. It also may be used in knitted constructions. The surface texture of all these fabrics is due to the knotlike irregularities of the ratiné yarn. It is used for dresses, blouses, coats, suits, and curtains.

Rep or Repp: Rep or repp is a firmly woven ribbed weave fabric with a prominent rounded rib. It may be made of cotton, silk, or the synthetic fibers. The rib may run either in the lengthwise or crosswise direction of the fabric.

Sailcloth: A very heavy, strong, plain weave fabric made of cotton, linen, or jute. There are many qualities and weights. It may be used for sportswear and slipcovers.

Satin: Satin is the name of a weave as well as the name of the fabric woven in this weave. Satin fabrics may be made of any fiber or combination of fibers and in different weights and qualities. If the warp yarns are visible on the surface, the fabric is a warp-faced satin; if the filling yarns are on the surface, it is a filling-faced satin. Many fabrics are made of satin weave, but are not called satin. There are many types of satins, and manufacturers use different tradenames to describe their particular satin fabric. The following are some of the most common ones.

Antique Satin: A heavy, dull lustrous fabric woven with uneven yarns.

Baronet Satin: Most lustrous of all satins. It has a rayon face and a cotton back. Usually it is dyed in brilliant shades.

Canton Satin: This is a soft, slightly heavy fabric with a satin face and a crepe back that has a ribbed effect because it has a heavy filling yarn. These ribs give the crepe side of the fabric a pebbly texture.

Charmeuse: A medium-weight satin fabric with a very high luster on the surface and a very dull back. It has a soft, draping, clinging quality.

Ciré Satin: A satin fabric is given a finish by applying wax under heat and pressure to give a very high luster and a degree of stiffness to the fabric.

Crepe-back Satin: This may be called "satin-back crepe." It is a reversible fabric. On one side the satin weave is visible; on the other side the crepe weave is visible.

Duchess Satin: A very heavy, stiff satin.

Hammered Satin: This is a satin fabric embossed to give the surface a textured appearance.

Messaline: A lightweight five-shaft satin fabric made of very fine yarns and woven very loosely.

Panné Satin: A highly lustrous satin with a stiff finish.

Peau D'Ange: A 12-shaft satin weave that gives a smooth, lustrous finish that is supposed to resemble the "skin of an angel."

Ribbed Satin: Some ribbed fabrics may be woven with a satin weave, producing alternating rib and satin stripes. These are sometimes given a moiré finish.

Slipper Satin: Heavy, lustrous face, cotton back.

Sateen: Sateen may be either a warp or filling satin weave. In the filling sateen, a filling yarn passes under one warp yarn and then floats over a number of warp yarns to again weave under one warp yarn, etc. The sheen is crosswise in the fabric. In a warp sateen, the warp passes under one filling yarn and then over a number of filling yarns, and again under one filling. A warp sateen is sometimes called "satine." Some of these fabrics are mercerized and calendered to produce a high luster. It is used for sportswear, dresses, draperies, comforter covers, bedspreads, slipcovers, and linings.

Scrim: An open, plain weave cotton or linen fabric. It is made of coarse yarns. It may be mercerized. It is used for curtains.

Seersucker: A true seersucker is a plain weave fabric with permanently woven-in, crinkled stripes running lengthwise in the fabric. This distinguishes it from a plissé crepe produced by plissé printing. It is used for sportswear, dresses, blouses, housecoats, bedspreads, curtains, and slipcovers.

Serge: Serge is a twill weave fabric with a pronounced diagonal rib on both the right and wrong sides. The lines run from lower left to upper right on the face of the cloth and from left to right on the underside of the fabric. There are many different weights of serge fabrics. For example, a "storm serge" is a coarse, wiry fabric, whereas a "French serge" is made of a very fine, soft yarn producing a fine twill.

Shantung: Originally shantung was a name for a hand-loomed plain weave fabric made in China. The fabric, made of wild silk, had an irregular surface. Today shantung is a term that may be applied to a plain weave fabric with heavier, rougher yarns running the crosswise direction of the fabric. The fabric may be made of cotton, silk, or any synthetic fiber. There are certain terms used to describe various types of shantung.

Douppioni Shantung: This is the heaviest and the most expensive of the shantung fabrics.

Spun Silk Shantung: This fabric is made of short lengths of silk fibers twisted together to form irregular slubs. It is less expensive than Douppioni shantung.

Shantung Taffeta: This is a silk shantung from which the natural gum is not removed after weaving. It has the crispness of a taffeta.

Rayon Shantung: Usually made with a filament acetate yarn in the warp and a spun rayon yarn in the filling.

Nylon Shantung: Usually made with a nylon filament warp and a spun nylon yarn in the filling. This fabric has a peculiar type of stiffness that differs from other shantung fabrics.

Changeable Shantung: Sometimes called "antique shantung." The warp yarns are dyed one color, the filling yarns another. Sometimes the slub filling yarn is dyed several colors. This creates a changeable color on the surface of the fabric that are caused by light reflection.

Shantung with Figure Weaves: A design may be woven into the fabric to produce a figure on a shantung background.

Sharkskin: There are two distinct types of sharkskin. (1) Sharkskin made of acetate, rayon, triacetate, or other man-made fibers: These may be described as sleek, hard-finished, crisp, yet pebbly surfaced fabrics with a chalky luster. Filament yarns are twisted and woven tightly in either a plain or basket weave construction, depending on the effect desired. (2) Wool sharkskin; which is characterized by its twill weave. The yarns in both the warp and filling are alternated, white with a color such as black, brown, or blue. The diagonal lines of the twill weave run from left to right; the colored yarns or lines run from right to left.

Silk and Wool Combinations: There are many men's and women's dress and suiting fabrics made of silk and wool, both imported and American-made. The majority of these fabrics are made with a silk yarn in the warp or lengthwise direction of the fabric (approximately 15 percent by weight), and a yarn-dyed wool yarn in the filling or crosswise direction. The fine silk yarns are invisible. There are variations in color, weave, and proportion of silk to wool yarns in this class of fabrics. Alaskine, Solange, and Startime are some of the trade names used to describe these fabrics.

Sueded Cotton: A closely woven plain or twill cotton sheeting is napped on one side to resemble genuine suede. Cotton suede fabrics have a luxurious appearance. Lightweight fabrics are used for dresses and suits; heavyweight fabrics are used for coats and jackets. The suede fabrics are available in any color, and most colors possess good colorfastness properties. Cotton suede fabrics can be treated with crease-resistant finishes and water-repellent finishes.

Surah (Sometimes Called "Silk Serge"): Surah is a semidull, soft, lightweight fabric. It may be made of silk or rayon. It may be identified by the fancy twill weave. It has very definite diagonal lines. It may be yarn-dyed to create plaids and checks or solid colors. Surah may also be printed. The fabric is loom-finished.

Taffeta: Taffeta is the term used to describe a group of fabrics of different fiber content — silk, rayon, acetate, and nylon, alone or in combination. It is a plain weave fabric, but the filling yarn is heavier than the warp yarn, giving a fine ribbed appearance. Actually, taffeta has approximately the same number of yarns in each direction, forming a firm, close weave with a characteristic dull luster and a stiffness that produces a rustle. Terms used to describe definite types of taffeta are as follows.

Loom-Finished Taffetas: Most taffeta fabrics are loom-finished. The warp yarns are sized to give them the strength necessary to withstand the strains of weaving. Sizings are also used to impart the "hand" and "rustle" desired in the finished fabric. Sizings may be of two types: (1) nondurable — these may include the gelatins and gums that are water-soluble. They may be affected by perspiration and moisture in wear and in cleaning; and (2) durable — these sizings are made up of different resin finishes. They are not removed by dry-cleaning solvents.

Piece-Dyed Taffetas: Some taffetas are piece-dyed. They are soft, not stiff like the loom-finished taffetas, because the sizing used in weaving the fabric is removed in a subsequent finishing operation.

Paper Taffeta: A taffeta fabric is given a lacquer finish to give it a high degree of stiffness and rustle.

Tapestry: A jacquard weave fabric woven with multicolored yarns. It is made with two warp yarns and two or more filling yarns. It has a rough texture. It is characterized by its distinctive tapestry pattern, which is large and pictorial. Used for draperies, wall hangings, and upholstery.

Tarlatan: A lightweight, open, plain weave fabric of cotton. It is transparent, stiffened, and sometimes glazed. It is used for costumes, curtains, linings, and stiffenings.

Terry cloth: This is an uncut pile weave fabric made of cotton or linen. The loops may be on one or both sides of the fabric. Designs may be woven in by the dobby or jacquard weave method. It may be used for draperies, bedspreads, and slip-covers.

Ticking: This term covers a large group of cotton and linen fabrics made of a twill, herringbone twill, satin, or jacquard weave. It may be used as upholstery and pillow covers.

Tricot: A fine, closely knitted warp knit made on a tricot machine. The loops run lengthwise on one side and crosswise on the opposite side. It is used in dresses, blouses, and shirts.

Tricotine: A clear-finished, hard-textured twill weave fabric made of wool or synthetic fibers. It is used in slacks, sportswear, suits, and uniforms.

Tweed: The term "tweed" is derived from the river Tweed in Scotland, where these fabrics were first woven. The term is now used to describe a wide range of lightweight to heavy-weight, rough-textured, sturdy fabrics. They are characterized by their mixed colored effect. Tweeds may be made of a plain, twill, or herringbone weave of practically any fiber or mixture of fibers. They may be monocolored (different shades of the same color), checked, plaid, striped, or patterned. There are certain names famous among tweeds.

Harris Tweed: This fabric is made by hand in the outer Hebrides off the coast of Scotland. The dyes in the yarns are cooked over peat. The smell of peat often remains in the fabric and may become noticeable when the fabric becomes damp.

Donegal Tweed: This is a thick fabric made of colorful slubs like the original homespun tweeds. They are hand-woven in Donegal County, Ireland.

Velvet: There are many different types of velvet. All are made of a pile construction. The pile may be cut, uncut, or cut and uncut. Velvets may be made of silk, wool, mohair, rayon, and acetate nylon. The background may be a plain, twill, or satin weave. Velvets are classed as V-type and W-type. In the V-type, the pile goes under only one warp yarn; in the W-type, the pile goes under and over two warp yarns. The terms used to describe certain definite types are:

Brocade Velvet: This sometimes is called faconné velvet. The fabric is woven like other velvets, then chemicals are applied in the desired pattern to the back of the fabric. This carbonizes the pile when heated and leaves the untreated pile to form the pattern. The background weave that is unaffected by the chemical treatment is readily visible on the right side of the fabric.

"Chiffon" Velvet: A lightweight soft velvet with a short, thick pile. On close examination, it can be seen that the pile forms narrow stripes. This type of velvet may be made from silk or the synthetic fibers, such as nylon.

Cotton-Backed Velvet: Cotton background weave, silk, or synthetic fibers are used in the pile.

Crushed Velvet: This fabric is placed between rollers and heat; moisture and pressure are applied. The pile is not pressed in one direction, like panné velvet; therefore there is a variation of reflection of the pile, creating a mixed effect, dull with bright.

Embossed Velvet: This may also be called "sculptured velvet." In making this fabric, the areas of the pattern that are to stand higher (the longer pile) are first laid flat. Then the fabric is sheared to a lower height (the short pile). The fabric is then steamed to raise the pile that has been flattened so that it stands higher than the sheared part of the design.

Lyons Velvet: A heavy, crisp, closely woven, stiff fabric with an erect, short, thick pile. It may have a cotton or silk back with a silk or synthetic fiber pile.

Moireéd Velvet: The fabric is passed through rollers that are engraved with a design. In the presence of heat, pressure, and moisture, the design is transferred to the fabric. Some of these fabrics are given a water-repellent finish.

Panné Velvet: This fabric has a rich-looking, satiny appearance because the pile is pressed down in one direction by passing the fabric over rollers in the presence of steam and pressure.

Silk Velvet: Silk background weave, silk pile.

Transparent Velvet: A very lightweight, soft velvet, with fairly short pile. When you hold it to the light, you can see through it; therefore the name "transparent."

Velveteen: Velveteen is sometimes called "cotton velvet." It is classed as a filling pile construction because two sets of filling yarns are used to one warp yarn. One filling yarn weaves with the warp yarn to form the ground weave (plain or twill). The other filling yarn weaves into the warp at intervals and then floats over a number of warp yarns. After weaving, the floating yarns are cut and brushed to form the short, closely set pile. The pile is not as erect as velvet. It slopes slightly, thus making the fabric surface lustrous.

Velour: Velour is a French term meaning "velvet." The terms velour and plush are used interchangeably for a pile velour construction. But velour also includes a variety of woolen fabrics characterized by a short, soft, thick pile, with either a twill or satin background, and given a velour finish. Velour fabrics may be made of cotton, wool, silk, mohair, or synthetic fibers. These fabrics may be distinguished from duvetyn because they have a thicker and longer nap and the base weave is not concealed, as in duvetyn fabrics.

Venetian Cloth: A smooth, strong, lustrous fabric made with a warp-faced satin weave. It may be napped and pressed. It is used for suits, coats, dresses, draperies, and slipcovers.

Voile: A sheer, transparent, soft, lightweight, plain weave fabric made of highly twisted yarns. It may be made of wool, cotton, silk, or a synthetic fiber. It is used for blouses, dresses, curtains, and bedspreads.

Whipcord: Whipcord is a twill weave fabric made of wool, cotton, synthetic fibers, or a blend of synthetic fiber with a natural fiber. The diagonal lines of the weave are very steep and usually run from left to right. In some fabrics the back or underside of the fabric is napped slightly. The fabric may be a solid color, or colored fibers may be mixed with white fibers, resulting in a salt-and-pepper effect.

BIBLIOGRAPHY*

INTRODUCTION

Things To Come 1974 to 2001. American Fabrics and Fashions, No. 100. Spring 1974. p. 86.

Young Adults Attitudes Toward Clothing Selection and Care. Survey, International Fabricare Institute 1972.

CHAPTER 1
AN ANALYTICAL APPROACH TO TEXTILE PERFORMANCE

Hoffman, R. M. "Measuring the Aesthetic Appeal of Textiles." *Textile Research Journal*, Vol. 35, No. 5, May 1965.

Is Color Planning Important In Your Work? International Color Authority.

"3M's "Color-in-Color" System Brightens the Textile Industry." *Women's Wear Daily*, March 5, 1973. p. 41.

"Some Psychological Connotations of Color." *American Fabrics*, No. 96, Winter 1972, pp. 63-65, 66, 73.

CHAPTER 2
TEXTILE FIBERS

Acetate. Selling Sense Bulletin SS-7. National Institute of Drycleaning, 1972.

Acrylics — Handle With Care. Selling Sense Bulletin SS-10. International Fabricare Institute, 1972.

American Fabrics Encyclopedia of Textiles. Doric Publications, New York, 1960.

"Aramid." *Federal Register*, Vol. 38, No. 327. Tuesday, December 11, 1973.

A New Sunlight-Resistant Dull Acetate Yarn. Fabrics Fashions Bulletin FF-115. National Institute of Drycleaning, 1964.

Anidex. Fabrics Fashions Bulletin FF-224. International Fabricare Institute, 1973.

Anidex. Selling Sense Bulletin SS-10. International Fabricare Institute, 1972.

*The books and bulletins published by the National Institute of Drycleaning are now the property of the International Fabricare Institute, Joliet, Illinois.

Porczynski, C. Z. *Manual of Man-Made Fibers*. Chemical Publishing Company, Inc., New York, 1961.

Chinon — A New Silk-like Fiber. Fabrics Fashions Bulletin FF-223. International Fabricare Institute, 1974.

Cotton. Selling Sense Bulletin SS-1. National Institute of Drycleaning, 1971.

Drycleaning Orlon Sayelle Knits. Fabrics Fashions Bulletin FF-100. National Institute of Drycleaning, 1962.

Dryclean or Wetclean Spandex. Selling Sense Bulletin SS-15. International Fabricare Institute, 1972.

Easy Care Polyesters. Selling Sense Bulletin SS-12. International Fabricare Institute, 1972.

Fabrics Made of a New Glass Yarn — Fiberglas Beta. Fabrics Fashions Bulletin FF-124. National Institute of Drycleaning, 1965.

Fibers and Fabrics Designed to Meet Requirements of the Flammable Fabrics Act. Fabrics Fashions Bulletin FF-214. International Fabricare Institute, 1972.

Fiber Identification. Fabrics Fashions Bulletin FF-236. International Fabricare Institute, 1974.

Fiberglas Yarns for the Textile Industry. Owens-Corning Fiberglas Corporation, Toledo, Ohio, 1951.

Fiber Resistant to Heat and Flame — Nomex, Aramid, Kynol, Novoloid. Fabrics Fashions Bulletin FF-237. International Fabricare Institute, 1974.

Guide to Man-Made Fibers. Man-Made Fiber Producers Association, Washington, D.C., 1973.

Hall, A. J. *The Standard Handbook of Textiles*. Chemical Publishing Company, Inc., New York, 1965.

Handling Fabrics Containing Rovana. Fabrics Fashions Bulletin FF-94. National Institute of Drycleaning, 1962.

Handling Saranspun Draperies. Fabrics Fashions Bulletin FF-57. National Institute of Drycleaning, 1959.

Harris, Milton, ed. *Handbook of Textile Fibers*. Textile Book Publishers, Inc., New York, 1954.

Heat Sensitive Fibers. Selling Sense Bulletin SS-13. International Fabricare Institute, 1972.

Heat-Sensitive Fibers and Fabrics. Fabrics Fashions Bulletin FF-147. National Institute of Drycleaning, 1967.

Hollen, M., and J. Saddler. *Textiles*, 3rd ed. The Macmillan Company, New York, 1968.

Identification of Fibers In Textile Materials, Bulletin X-156, the Du Pont Company, December 1961.

Joseph, Marjory L. *Textile Science*, 2nd ed. Holt, Rinehart and Winston, Inc., New York, 1972.

LaBarthe, Jules. *Textile: Origins to Usage*. The Macmillan Company, 1964.

Linen. Selling Sense Bulletin SS-2. National Institute of Drycleaning, 1971.

Linton, G. E. *Applied Textiles*, 6th ed. Duell, Sloane and Pearce. Meredith Press, New York, 1961.

Mancrioff, R. W. *Man-Made Fibers*, 5th ed. John Wiley & Sons, Inc., New York, 1970.

Man-Made Fiber Fact Book. Man-Made Fibers Producers Association, Inc., Washington, D.C., 1973.

Mark, H. F., N. G. Gaylord, and Bikales (ed.) Encyclopedia of Polymer Science and Technology. 15 Vols. Wiley — Interscience, New York, 1964-1971.

Matthews, J. M., and H. R. Mauersberger. *Textile Fibers*, 6th ed. John Wiley & Sons, Inc., New York, 1954.

Metallic Fibers. Selling Sense Bulletin SS-14. International Fabricare Institute, 1972.

Modacrylic Fabrics Dryclean Beautifully. Selling Sense Bulletin SS-11. International Fabricare Institute, 1972.

Natural and Man-Made Textile Fibers. Duell, Sloane & Pearce. Meredith Press, New York, 1963.

"Novoloid." *Federal Register*, Vol. 37, No. 10, Tuesday, January 15, 1974.

Nylon. Selling Sense Bulletin SS-8. International Fabricare Institute, 1972.

Polypropylene — An Olefin Fiber. Fabrics Fashions Bulletin FF-134. International Fabricare Institute, 1962.

Polyvinyl Chloride Fiber Causes Complaints. Fabrics Fashions Bulletin FF-93. National Institute of Drycleaning, 1962.

Preston, J. M. *Fibre Science*. Manchester, the Textile Institute, 1953.

Rayon. Selling Sense Bulletin SS-6. National Institute of Drycleaning, 1972.

Silk. Selling Sense Bulletin SS-3. National Institute of Drycleaning, 1971.

Specialty Fibers. Selling Sense Bulletin SS-5. National Institute of Drycleaning, 1972.

Stout, Evelyn E. *Introduction to Textiles*, 3rd ed. John Wiley & Sons, Inc., New York, 1970.

Stoves, J. L. *Fibre Microscopy*. D. Van Nostrand Company, Inc., Princeton, New Jersey, 1958.

Technical Manual of the American Association of Textile Chemists and Colorists. Vol. 49, 1973.

Textile Handbook, 4th ed. American Home Economics Association, Washington, D.C., 1970.

The Hidden Part of the Energy Crisis. The Petro Chemical Energy Group, Man-Made Fibers Producers Association, Washington, D.C., 1973.

The Musk Ox Project. American Fabrics, No. 95, Fall 1972.

Verel. Fabrics Fashions Bulletin FF-50. National Institute of Drycleaning, 1958.

Wetcleaning Best For Glass Fabrics. Selling Sense Bulletin SS-9. International Fabricare Institute, 1972.

Wilkinson, Paul F. "The Domestication of the Musk-Ox." *The Palor Record*, Vol. 15, No. 98, 1971, pp. 168-169.

Wingate, Isabel. *Dictionary of Textiles*. Fairchild Publications, Inc., New York, 1967.

Wool. Selling Sense Bulletin SS-4. National Institute of Drycleaning, 1971.

CHAPTER 3
YARN CONSTRUCTION

An American Fabrics Marketing Report, Stretch Fabrics. E. I. Du Pont de Nemours Co., Inc., Wilmington, Del.

Chiffon. Fabrics Fashions Bulletin FF-35. National Institute of Drycleaning, 1957.

Core and Effect Yarns. Selling Sense Bulletin SS-29. International Fabricare Institute, 1974.

Correspondence on file from Du Pont, Chemstrand, Eastman Chemical Company, Joseph Bancroft and Sons, America Enka Corporation, Universal Winding Company, Spunize Marionette Mills, Herberlein Patent Company, Textured Yarn Company, Deering Milliken Research Corporation, National Spinning Co., Inc.

Damage To Summer Fabrics. Fabric Fashions Bulletin FF-23. National Institute of Drycleaning, 1956.

Dembeck, Adeline A. *Guidebook to Man-Made Textile Fibers and Textured Yarns of the World*, 3rd ed. United Piece Dye Works, New York, 1969.

Elastic Yarns. Selling Sense Bulletin SS-26. International Fabricare Institute, 1973.

Georgette. Fabrics Fashions Bulletin FF-224. International Fabricare Institute, 1973.

Handling Metallic Yarns. Fabrics Fashions Bulletin FF-36. National Institute of Drycleaning, 1973.

Hathorne, Berkeley L. *Woven, Stretch and Textured Fabrics*. John Wiley & Sons, Inc., New York, 1964.

Heat Stains on Dacron Blends. Fabrics Fashions Bulletin FF-52 National Institute of Drycleaning, 1958.

Kirk, William Jr., and J. M. Ibrakin. *Fundamental Relationships of Fabric Extensibility to Anthropometric Requirements and Garment Performance*. E. I. Du Pont de Nemours & Co., Inc., Wilmington, Del.

Loss of Elasticity in Waistbands. Fabrics Fashions Bulletin FF-5. National Institute of Drycleaning, 1955.

Man-Made Fiber Fact Book. Man-Made Fiber Producer Association, Inc., Washington, D.C. 1974.

Puffed Fabrics Made With Elastic Yarns. Fabrics Fashions Bulletin FF-155. National Institute of Drycleaning, 1967.

Staple, Filament Yarns. Selling Sense Bulletin SS-27. International Fabricare Institute, 1973.

Stretch Fabrics. Fabrics Fashions Bulletins FF-105 and FF-106. National Institute of Drycleaning, 1963.

Stretch Yarns. Selling Sense Bulletins SS-30 and SS-31. International Fabricare Institute, 1974.

Stretching In Knits. Fabrics Fashions Bulletin FF-153. National Institute of Drycleaning, 1967.

Shrinkage Complaints — Soft Woolens. Fabrics Fashions Bulletin FF-148. National Institute of Drycleaning, 1967.

Shrinkage in Polyester Double Knits. Fabrics Fashions Bulletin FF-221. International Fabricare Institute, 1973.

The National Spinning Story and Reports. The National Spinning Company, New York, New York, 1975.

Wool and Silk Combinations. Fabrics Fashions Bulletin FF-148. National Institute of Drycleaning, 1968.

Yarn Structure. Selling Sense Bulletin SS-28. International Fabricare Institute, 1974.

CHAPTER 4
CONSTRUCTION

A.F.F. Appriases the Non-Wovens. American Fabrics and Fashions, No. 101. Summer 1974. pp. 39-44.

A New Type of Felt-Reenforced Felt. Fabrics Fashions Bulletin FF-38. National Institute of Drycleaning, 1957.

Bendure, Z., and G. Pfeiffer. *American Fabrics.* The Macmillan Company, New York, 1947.

Chemically Quilted Velvet. Fabrics Fashions Bulletin FF-160. National Institute of Drycleaning, 1968.

Crepe. Fabrics Fashions Bulletin FF-188. National Institute of Drycleaning, 1970.

Double Cloth, Double-Faced Fabrics. Fabrics Fashions Bulletin FF-157. National Institute of Drycleaning, 1967.

Fabrics Quilted Chemically. Fabrics Fashions Bulletins FF-132 and FF-126. National Institute of Drycleaning, 1965.

Felt Fashions. Fabrics Fashions Bulletin FF-159. National Institute of Drycleaning, 1968.

Flattening and Loss of Pile. Fabrics Fashions Bulletin FF-212. International Fabricare Institute, 1972.

Fiberwoven Blankets. Fabrics Fashions Bulletin FF-203. National Institute of Drycleaning, 1971.

Gabardine. Fabrics Fashions Bulletin FF-227. International Fabricare Institute, 1973.

Hess, Katherine P. *Textile Fibers and Their Uses,* 6th ed. J. P. Lippincott Co., Philadelphia, 1950.

Klapper, Marvin. *Fabric Almanac.* Fairchild Publications, Inc., 1966.

Knits. Fabrics Fashions Bulletins FF-197, FF-198, FF-199, and FF-200. National Institute of Drycleaning, 1971.

Knitting Dictionary. National Knitted Outerwear Association, New York, 1966.

Knitted Stretch Technology. National Knitted Outerwear Association, New York, 1965.

Rosatto, Vittoria, Edward L. Gallee, and George G. Armstrong, Jr. *Leavers Lace.* American Lace Manufacturers Association, Inc., 1949.

Lyle, Dorothy S. *Focus On Fabrics.* National Institute of Drycleaning, Silver Spring, Md, 1967.

Mali — A Different Fabric Construction. Fabrics Fashions Bulletin FF-176. National Institute of Drycleaning, 1969.

Malimo Drapery Fabrics. Fabrics Fashions Bulletin FF-215. International Fabricare Institute, 1972.

Malipol Constructions. Fabrics Fashions Bulletins FF-209 and FF-210. International Fabricare Institute, 1972.

Man-Made Textile Encyclopedia. Textile Book Publishers, Inc., New York, 1959.

Matte Jersey. Fabrics Fashions Bulletin FF-230. International Fabricare Institute, 1973.

Modern Textile Dictionary, 2d ed. Duell, Sloan & Pearce. Meredith Press, 1963.

Non-Woven Blankets. Fabrics Fashions Bulletin FF-186. National Institute of Drycleaning, 1970.

Non-Woven and Knitted Paper Fabrics. Fabrics Fashions Bulletin FF-143. National Institute of Drycleaning, 1966.

Non-Woven Stitch-Bonded Fabrics. Fabrics Fashions Bulletin FF-195. National Institute of Drycleaning, 1971.

Performance of Fabrics Bonded to Fabric. Fabrics Fashions Bulletins FF-139 and FF-140. National Institute of Drycleaning, 1966.

Pizzuto, J. J. *101 Weaves in 101 Fabrics.* Textile Press, New York, 1961.

Pizzuto, J. J., and P. L. D'Alessandro. *101 Fabrics.* Textile Press, New York, 1952.

Pop Corn Stitch Raschal Crochet Knit. Fabrics Fashions Bulletin FF-190. National Institute of Drycleaning, 1970.

Price, Arthur, and Allen C. Cohen. *Fabric Science.* Review of Joseph J. Pizutto. Fairchild Publications, Inc., 1974.

Puff Fabrics Made With Elastic Yarns. Fabrics Fashions Bulletin FF-155. National Institute of Drycleaning, 1967.

Raschal Knits in Home Furnishings. Fabrics Fashions Bulletin FF-226. International Fabricare Institute, 1973.

Reichman, Charles, J. B. Lancashire, and R. P. Darlington, *Knitted Fabric Primer.* National Knitted Outerwear Association, New York, 1967.

Reichman, Charles. *Double Knit Fabric Manual.* National Knitted Outerwear Association, New York, 1961.

Simulated Cuir Sauvage and Antique Leathers. Fabrics Fashions Bulletin FF-172. National Institute of Drycleaning, 1969.

Simulated Leather and Film Bonded Fabrics. Fabrics Fashions Bulletin FF-217. International Fabricare Institute, 1972.

Textured Acetate Knits Cause Complaints. Fabrics Fashions Bulletin FF-121. National Institute of Drycleaning, 1964.

Thermal Blankets. Fabrics Fashions Bulletin FF-158. National Institute of Drycleaning, 1967.

Ultrasuede. Fabrics Fashions Bulletin FF-218. International Fabricare Institute, 1972.

Velour. Fabrics Fashions Bulletin FF-194. National Institute of Drycleaning, 1970.

Velvets. Fabrics Fashions Bulletin FF-111. National Institute of Drycleaning, 1963.

Warp Knits With Weft Insertion. Fabrics Fashions Bulletin FF-229. International Fabricare Institute, 1973.

Wool and Silk Combinations. Fabrics Fashions Bulletin FF-173. National Institute of Drycleaning, 1969.

CHAPTER 5
FABRIC FINISHES

Banville, Robert, and Ethel McNeil. *Applied Microbiology, Vol. 14,* No. 1, January 1966, pp. 1-7.

Dickinson, J. C., and R. E. Wagg. *J. Applied Bact.,* Vol. 30, No. 340, 1967.

Hartshorn, L., and W. B. Ward. "Static Electricity in Drycleaning Processes". *J. Soc. Chem. Ind.,* Vol. 57, pp. 178-133, 1938.

Hess, R. *Krankenhaus,* Vol. 52, pp. 90-98, 1960.

Jackson, Lloyd E. *American J. of Public Health,* Vol. 12, No. 6, June 1922, pp. 507-509.

LeBlanc, R. Bruce. *What's Available for Flame Retardant Textiles.* Textile Industries. February 1974, pp. 115-120.

Marsh, J. T. *An Introduction to Textile Finishing.* John Wiley and Sons, Inc., 1951, p. 243.

Martin, Albert R. *Flame Retardant Finishing — Not a Simple Technology.* Technical Bulletin T-485, 1972.

Martin, Albert R. *Should Drycleaners Use Bactericides?* Technical Bulletin T-463. National Institute of Drycleaning, 1970.

McNeil, Ethel, et al. *American Dyestuff Reporter,* December 9, 1963, pp. 87-90.

New Chemistry May Improve Flame Retardant Cotton. Vol. 1, No. 11, Textile Industry Product Safety, Washington, D.C., 1973.

Rhodes, W. K. *Der Fachverband,* Vol. 8, No. 55, 1968.

Serba, P. J., and R. F. Feldman. "Electrostatic Charging of Fabrics at Various Humidities." *J. of the Text. Inst.,* Vol. 55, T-288-298, 1964.

Sidwell, R. W., G. J. Dixon, and Ethel McNeil. *Applied Microbiology,* Vol. 15, 1967, pp. 921-927.

Static Electricity. NFPA Publication 77M. National Fire Protection Association, 60 Batterymarch Street, Boston, Mass., 1961.

Stuart, L. S. *Soap and Chemical Specialties,* Vol. 33, No. 95, 1957.

Textile Finishing, 3d ed. Chemical Publishing Company, Inc., New York, 1966.

Textile Finishing Terms prepared by the Research and Development for Finishing Division, Cone Mills Corporation.

U.S.D.A. Circular No. 466, March 1938 and Patents (Public) 1,961,108; 1,990,292; 2,012,686, and 2,017,805.

U.S.D.A. Report to Consumers, No. 115. August-September 1973.

Wagg, R. E. *Chemistry and Industry,* October 20, 1965, pp. 1830-1834.

Wentz, Manfred, Ivan J. Andrasik, and William F. Fisher. *Knit Shrinkage in Drycleaning, Statistics and Causes.* Unpublished Paper.

CHAPTER 6
APPLIED SURFACE DESIGN

Another Non-Permanent Pique. Technical Bulletin No. T-217. National Institute of Drycleaning, 1949.

Brocade, Woven and Embossed. Fabrics Fashions Bulletin FF-81. National Institute of Drycleaning, 1961.

Embossed Rib-Weave Fabrics. Fabrics Fashions Bulletin FF-9. National Institute of Drycleaning, 1955.

Glued Glitter. Technical Bulletin No. T-223. National Institute of Drycleaning, 1950.

Lacquer Stencil Prints. Fabrics Fashions Bulletin FF-231. International Fabricare Institute, 1974.

Linen Fabrics. Fabrics Fashions Bulletin FF-24. National Institute of Drycleaning, 1956.

Metallic Prints. Technical Bulletin No. T-247. National Institute of Drycleaning, 1950.

Moiré. Fabrics Fashions Bulletin FF-175. National Institute of Drycleaning, 1969.

Plastic Decorative Trim. Fabrics Fashions Bulletin FF-166. National Institute of Drycleaning, 1968.

Polyester Applique Prints. Fabrics Fashions Bulletin FF-164. International Fabricare Institute, 1968.

Screen-Printed Drapery Fabric. Fabrics Fashions Bulletin FF-179. National Institute of Drycleaning, 1969.

Sculptured Velvet. Fabrics Fashions Bulletin FF-65. National Institute of Drycleaning, 1960.

Staining From Bead Trim. Fabrics Fashions Bulletin FF-165. National Institute of Drycleaning, 1968.

Unserviceable Moirés Again. Technical Bulletin No. T-187. National Institute of Drycleaning, 1947.

CHAPTER 7
COLOR

"Color — Basic Methods of Dyeing; the Printing of Textiles," *American Fabrics*, No. 96, Winter 1972.

Color Change in Red Dyes. Fabrics Fashions Bulletin FF-66. National Institute of Drycleaning, 1960.

Color Changes In Red Dyes. Fabrics Fashions Bulletin FF-183. National Institute of Drycleaning, 1970.

Color Damage From Cold Wave Solution. Technical Bulletin No. T-254. National Institute of Drycleaning, 1951.

Delusterizing and Dye Loss on Acetate Fabrics. Fabric Fashions Bulletin FF-145. National Institute of Drycleaning, 1966.

Dyes Bleeding In Drycleaning. Technical Bulletin No. T-295. National Institute of Drycleaning, 1952.

Fabric Damage from Perspiration, Deodorants and Antiperspirants. Fabrics Fashions Bulletins FF-117 and FF-118. National Institute of Drycleaning, 1964.

Fabric Damage – To Yellow Prints. Fabrics Fashions Bulletin FF-1. National Institute of Drycleaning, 1954.

Fabrics That Change Color. Fabrics Fashions Bulletin FF-142. National Institute of Drycleaning, 1966.

Fluorescent Dyed Fabrics. Technical Bulletin No. T-267. National Institute of Drycleaning, 1951.

Fume Fading. Fabrics Fashions Bulletin FF-141. National Institute of Drycleaning, 1966.

Household Fabrics May Cause Problems. Fabric Fashions Bulletin FF-216. International Fabricare Institute, 1972.

Loss of Brightness in Fluorescent-Dyed Fabrics. Fabrics Fashions Bulletin FF-60. National Institute of Drycleaning, 1959.

Loss of Color in Blue Cottons. Fabrics Fashions Bulletin FF-11. National Institute of Drycleaning, 1955.

Loss of Printed Designs on Sweaters. Fabrics Fashions Bulletin FF-90. National Institute of Drycleaning, 1962.

Madras. Fabrics Fashions Bulletin FF-223. International Fabricare Institute, 1973.

Multi-Colored Dacron Dresses Cause Problems. Fabrics Fashions Bulletin FF-85. National Institute of Drycleaning, 1961.

Pigment Color Failures on the Increase. Fabrics Fashions Bulletin FF-206. National Institute of Drycleaning, 1971.

Problems With Knits. Fabrics Fashions Bulletin FF-208. International Fabricare Institute, 1972.

Screen Prints in Menswear Fashions. Fabrics Fashions Bulletin FF-184. National Institute of Drycleaning, 1970.

Silk Prints Causing Problems. Fabrics Fashions Bulletin FF-72. National Institute of Drycleaning, 1960.

Solvent-Soluble, Resin-Bonded Pigment Colors. Fabric Fashions Bulletin FF-46. National Institute of Drycleaning, 1958.

Sublistatic® Fabric Printing. Fabrics Fashions Bulletin FF-177. National Institute of Drycleaning, 1969.

CHAPTER 8
COMPONENT PARTS

Andersen, Gerald. "Fusible Maker Urges Caution on Product Use," *Daily News Record*, October 14, 1968, pp. 1 and 16.

Beads. Fabrics Fashions Bulletin FF-165. National Institute of Drycleaning, 1968.

Belts. Fabrics Fashions Bulletin FF-75. National Institute of Drycleaning, 1960.

Buttons. Technical Bulletins No. T-175 and T-189; Fabrics Fashions Bulletin FF-40. National Institute of Drycleaning, 1947 and 1957.

Closures. Technical Bulletin No. T-379. National Institute of Drycleaning, 1959.

Giesy, Don. "Fused Coats Leave US Makers Nervous." *Daily News Record*, October 21, 1969, p. 13.

Graves, Patsy H. *The Performance of an Iron-On Adhesive Web When Used for Hem and Interfacing Application.* University of Alabama, May 19, 1969.

Innerlinings. Technical Bulletin T-180. National Institute of Drycleaning, 1969.

Interfacings. Fabrics Fashions Bulletin FF-117. National Institute of Drycleaning, 1964.

Lippa, S. "Stitchless Sewing Makes Big Strides," *Women's Wear Daily,* January 22, 1968, pp. 23-30.

Linings. Technical Bulletin No. T-271; Fabric Fashions Bulletin FF-17. National Institute of Drycleaning, 1956.

Plastic Beads. Fabrics Fashions Bulletin FF-166. National Institute of Drycleaning, 1968.

Plastic Trim. Fabrics Fashions Bulletin FF-144. National Institute of Drycleaning, 1966.

Petti-Pleats. Fabrics Fashions Bulletin FF-44. National Institute of Drycleaning, 1958.

Press-On Bindings. Fabrics Fashions Bulletin FF-154. National Institute of Drycleaning, 1967.

Press-On Linings. Fabrics Fashions Bulletin FF-138. National Institute of Drycleaning, 1966.

Saviola, Kevin M. "Fusible Fronts on Coats Seen Aiding Suits Retain Shape." *Daily News Record*, September 5, 1968, p. 12.

Sequins. Technical Bulletin No. T-205; Fabrics Fashions Bulletin FF-99. National Institute of Drycleaning, 1948, 1962.

Shoulder Pads. Technical Bulletins Nos. T-190 and T-258. National Institute of Drycleaning, 1948, 1951.

Sonic Sewing. Fabrics Fashions Bulletin FF-232. International Fabricare Institute, 1974.

Stitchless Sewing. Fabrics Fashions Bulletin FF-187. International Fabricare Institute, 1970.

Thread. Fabrics Fashions Bulletin FF-193. National Institute of Drycleaning, 1970.

Zippers. Fabrics Fashions Bulletins FF-107 and FF-108. National Institute of Drycleaning, 1963.

CHAPTER 9
PERFORMANCE IN END USE

A Yardstick of Fabric Performance — Color Problems. Fabrics Fashions Bulletin FF-123. National Institute of Drycleaning, 1964.

Consumer Use Problems. Fabrics Fashions Bulletin FF-129. National Institute of Drycleaning, 1965.

Complaints on Leather and Simulated Leather Trim. Fabrics Fashions Bulletin FF-116. National Institute of Drycleaning, 1964.

Damage to Window Curtains. Fabrics Fashions Bulletin FF-234. International Fabricare Institute, 1974.

Drapery Problems. Fabrics Fashions Bulletin FF-235. International Fabricare Institute, 1974.

Drycleaning Durable Press Garments. Fabrics Fashions Bulletin FF-168. National Institute of Drycleaning, 1968.

Household Fabrics May Cause Problems. Fabrics Fashions Bulletin FF-216. International Fabricare Institute, 1972.

Imitation Persian May Cause Complaints. Fabrics Fashions Bulletin FF-128. National Institute of Drycleaning, 1965.

Imported Coats Cause Problems. Fabrics Fashions Bulletin FF-205. National Institute of Drycleaning, 1971.

International Fair Claims Guide For Consumer Textile Products. International Fabricare Institute, 1973.

New Problems With Urethane Foam Laminates. Fabrics Fashions Bulletin FF-112. National Institute of Drycleaning, 1964.

Performance of Fabrics Bonded to Fabric. Fabrics Fashions Bulletin, Part 1, FF-139; Part 2, FF-140. National Institute of Drycleaning, 1971.

Problems With Knits. Fabrics Fashions Bulletins FF-207 and FF-208. National Institute of Drycleaning, 1972.

Qiana Nylon. Fabrics Fashions Bulletin FF-182. National Institute of Drycleaning, 1969.

Shrinkage in Cotton Knit Dresses. Fabrics Fashions Bulletin FF-109. National Institute of Drycleaning, 1963.

Shrinkage of Mohair Looped Knit Fabrics. Fabrics Fashions Bulletin FF-99. National Institute of Drycleaning, 1962.

Stretching in Knits. Fabrics Fashions Bulletin FF-153. National Institute of Drycleaning, 1967.

Textile Damage Analysis Statistics for 1973. Technical Bulletin. International Fabricare Institute, 1973.

Textured Acetate Knits Cause Complaints. Fabrics Fashions Bulletin FF-121. National Institute of Drycleaning, 1964.

Yarn and Seam Slippage. Fabrics Fashions Bulletin FF-163. National Institute of Drycleaning, 1968.

A Voluntary Industry Guide for Improved and Permanent Care Labeling of Consumer Textile Products. National Retail Merchants Association, 1967.

Abbott, Richard L. "Taking the Mystery Out of Fabrics." *The New Coin Launderer and Cleaner,* November-December 1971, p. 28.

British Textile Care Labeling Scheme — Conditions of Use. The Home Laundering Consultative Council, 1972.

Care Labels Can Save You Money and Trouble. Federal Trade Commission Buyers Guide No. 10, 1972.

Conner, Gail. *Care Label Mini-Survey.* University of North Carolina, June 1973. (unpublished).

Care Labeling Guide. National Retail Merchants Association, 1972.

Care Labeling for Textiles. Bureau of Consumer Affairs, 1971.

Confusing Labels (on file). Fabrics Fashions/Fact Fiction Bulletins FFFF-5 and FFFF-6. International Fabricare Institute, 1972.

Consumer Care Guide for Apparel. American Apparel Manufacturers Association, 1972.

Fire Retardants. Skeet Laboratories, Inc., Vol. I, Textiles, March 1972.

FTC Calls for Ending R.N. Coding System. Fabrics Fashions/Fact Fiction Bulletins FFFF-5 and FFFF-7. International Fabricare Institute, 1972, 1973.

FTC Realignment (correspondence on file). *Look For That Label.* Consumer Bulletin No. 6, Federal Trade Commission, 1972.

"FTC Says: Garments Labeled Wash Can Also be Drycleaned." *Coin Launderer and Cleaner,* September 1972, p. 32.

"It's What the Customer Thinks That Counts." *IFI Special Reporter,* May 1973.

Klapper, Marvin. "The Label Business — Easy Street It's Not." *Women's Wear Daily,* July 3, 1973.

"New Standards to Insure Sleepwear," *Consumer Alert, FTC,* Vol. II, No. 7, July-August 1972.

Permanent Care Labeling, Parts I and II. Fabrics Fashions Bulletins FF-219 and FF-220. National Institute of Drycleaning, 1973.

"Purdue Consumer Survey Shows FTC Labeling Inadequate." *Coin Launderer and Cleaner,* June 1973, p. 21.

Powderly, Daniel W. "Permanent Care Labeling — Potential Effects on Manufacturer and Converter Costs and Impact Upon Voluntary Standards." *AATT Technical Review and Register,* p. 63.

Rules and Regulations Under the Flammable Fabrics Act. Federal Trade Commission, 1953 amended.

Rules and Regulations Under the Fur Products Labeling Act. Federal Trade Commission, 1951 amended.

Rules and Regulations Under the Textile Fiber Product Identification Act. Federal Trade Commission, 1960 amended.

Rules and Regulations Under the Wool Products Labeling Rule. Federal Trade Commission, 1939.

Standard Definitions of Terms Relating to Care of Consumer Textile Products and Recommended Practices for Use of These Terms on Permanently Attached Labels. D 3136-72. American Society for Testing Materials, 1972.

Symbols On Care Labels. Bulletin P-109. National Institute of Drycleaning, 1972.

"Textile and Apparel Identification Number — FTC Terminates Confidential States — Effective 10-17-74," *Federal Register,* Friday, July 17, 1974. Vol. 39, No. 140, p. 26398.

Trade Practice Rules and Federal Register. Federal Trade Commission.

Triangle System of Labeling for Over-the-Counter Fabrics. Textile Distributors Association, 1972.

Trade Regulation Rule Including a Statement of Its Basis and Purpose Care Labeling of Textile Wearing Apparel. Federal Trade Commission, 1972.

INDEX